WOODWORKER DICTIONARY

DICTIONARY

VIC TAYLOR

Argus Books

Argus Books Limited
1 Golden Square
London W1R

ISBN 0 85242 877 4

Phototypesetting by En to En, Tunbridge Wells
Printed and bound by R. J. Acford, Chichester

Introduction

This book is largely based on the *WOODWORKER'S DICTIONARY* which was a monthly series in *Woodworker* magazine from 1962 to 1970. There were some entries in the original which related to such extraneous subjects as concreting, decorating, metalwork, etc., and these have been replaced by a wider coverage of antique furniture, furniture decoration, and the updating of materials and techniques.

We have included woodworking terms used in the USA, together with many examples of purely American furniture designs, and we are confident that the Dictionary will be equally useful to readers on both sides of the Atlantic. While some French terms are necessarily included because of the enormous influence of French designers and craftsmen, the book is primarily devoted to British and American furniture and woodwork.

Metrication had not come fully into effect when the series finished in the magazine and consequently only Imperial measurements were used; we have given metric equivalents wherever possible. As a result there is one item which needs explanation and that is the expression of the weights of various timbers. In the series this was shown as pounds per cubic foot, but since metrication timber has been measured in cubic metres and the weight is therefore quoted in kilogrammes per cubic metre.

Readers will find that historic designers and craftsmen are listed in a separate section at the end of the book, and furniture styles and periods are dealt with in the same way. It was felt that this would allow a fuller treatment than if they were included in the main text where the demands of space could be a limitation. We have also included lists of the sovereigns of England, and the kings and presidents of France.

The pages of the original series were intended to be cut out and made up into a book by the reader, and the response at the time was very gratifying. We are sure, therefore, that this book will prove to be indispensable to anyone who is interested in woodwork and wishes to learn more of its scope and history.

A

abacus The top member of a capital, taking the form of a moulded or square-edged cushion or seating.

Abbotsford chair Popular in the middle of the 19th century, this design was called 'Elizabethan' although it is equally reminiscent of the Charles II era. It derives its name from the house of Sir Walter Scott, who was responsible for encouraging a romantic view of the medieval way of life.

ABBOTSFORD CHAIR

abrasive materials These are used to coat what are loosely called 'glasspaper' or 'sandpaper' — both are misnomers, as glass or sand particles are no longer used; the correct term is 'abrasive paper'. There are three types of material, namely aluminium oxide, garnet, and silicon-carbide, *(q.q.v.).*

abura *(mitragyna ciliata)* Equatorial African hardwood, 35 lb (561 kg). Used for furniture, fitments, etc. Resists acids and is so used for battery boxes, laboratory tables, etc. Light brown colour.

acanthus The stylised carved leaf ornament found on the capitals of Corinthian columns; it derives from the foliage of acanthus spinosa (bear's breeches). Widely employed in the 17th and 18th centuries. Generally identified by the overlapping of the lower lobes over those above, the corners taking the form of recessed eyes. (See *eyes.*)

accelerator A hardener added to polyester lacquers for cold curing.

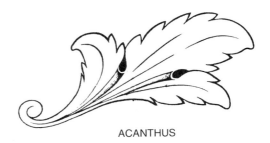

ACANTHUS

acetic acid Used in some furniture revivers, and for removing ink stains. Poisonous.

acid finish One of the methods of finishing a french-polished surface after fadding and bodying. One part of sulphuric acid is added to seven of water. Used with Vienna chalk.

acorn hinge A butt hinge having decorative acorn-shaped terminals. Often used in clock cases.

ACORN HINGE

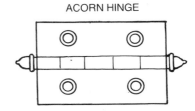

acorn turning A turned ornament resembling an acorn, mainly used in the Jacobean period, particularly on chair backs.

acroterium A pedestal mounted on a pediment, intended to support a statue or small carved figure.

Act of Parliament clock A drop-dial mural clock (also called a 'tavern clock' or 'stage coach clock'. They had large dials which could be from 21 inches to 30 inches (533 to 762 mm) in width, and were circular, shield-shaped, square with canted corners or square with a curved top; usually they were painted in dark colours. The Act referred to was that passed in 1797 by William Pitt imposing a tax on clocks and watches; however, many clocks of the type were made long before that date, and in any case, the Act was repealed within a year.

adhesives (see under *casein, fish, polyvinyl, rubber based, scotch, synthetic resin.*)

adze A tool of the axe type, but with a curved blade fixed at right angles to the handle. Used in the preliminary rough-dressing of wood; also in ship building and in wheelwrights' shops. Sharpened similarly to an axe but on one side only.

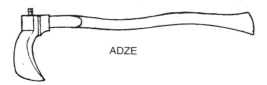

ADZE

afara *(terminalia superba)* Nigerian hardwood, 35 lb (561 kg). Light oak colour. General utility work.

afina *(strombosia pustulata)* West African hardwood, 58 lb (929 kg). Seldom seen in Great Britain. Used locally for telegraph poles, turnery, etc.

African cherry Alternative name for makoré. *(q.v.)*

African mahogany *(khaya ivorensis, etc.)* (see under: *axim, benin, grand bassam, lagos, okoumé, sapele, sekondi*)

afrormosia *(afrormosia* species) African hardwood, 44 lb (705 kg). Brownish yellow colour. Used for furniture, joinery, etc.

afzelia *(afzelia africana)* West tropical African hardwood, 45-50 lb (721-801 kg). Reddish brown colour. Used in general joinery, etc.

agba *(gossweilerodendron balsamiferum)* Hardwood from S. Nigeria and Congo. Weight 30 lb (481 kg). Yellowish pink wood which works easily. Stains well to mahogany. Furniture, fittings, etc.

aieli Alternative name for canarium *(q.v.)*

air-seasoned Timber that has been allowed to dry naturally in the open (under protection from rain).

akamatsu A softwood from Japan.

albizzia *(albizzia* species) Hardwood from Uganda, Nigeria, Ghana; 42 lb (673 kg). Light to medium brown colour. Used for cabinet work, fittings, flooring, etc.

alburnum Sapwood.

alder *(alnus glutinosa)* Europe, Asia and W. Africa. A durable minor hardwood used in the preparation of charcoal and for the cores of blockboards etc. 30-40 lb (481-641 kg).

alerce *(fitzroya cupressoides)* Softwood from Chile. 30 lb (481 kg). Reddish brown colour, straight-grained and even. All normal softwood purposes.

aligna Alternative name for afzelia *(q.v.)*.

alkanet root Used in making red oil. The root is bruised and steeped in linseed oil for about three days. It enriches the colour of the wood.

alligatoring A term used to describe the wrinkling of a surface (resembling the cracked hide of an alligator) which is caused by (1) painting unseasoned wood, (2) the too-rapid evaporation of thinners from a paint film, (3) applying a thick surface film over a coating which is still relatively soft.

almery Also called an 'aumbry' *(q.v.)*. A recess in the chancel wall of a church for storing altar vessels, linen, holy oils, etc.

alstonia *(alstonia congensis)* Hardwood from Ghana, Nigeria, Uganda. 27 lb (432 kg). Pale yellow colour. Used chiefly for core stock and interior work.

Alternax The name for a patented swinging chisel mortiser. The special chisel is connected to an eccentric which causes it to swing in a pendulum-like motion throughout the complete length of the mortise (unlike the Maka *(q.v.)*; the length of the swing can, of course, be controlled. The resulting mortise has a slightly curved bottom and square ends. The chisel has three components, namely, two stabbing chisels which operate alternately and a swing chisel mounted between them. The stabbing chisels have serrated inside edges to remove chips; their outside edges cut the ends of the mortise.

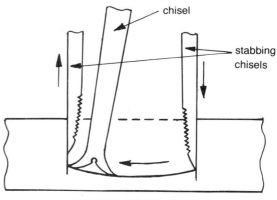

chisel

stabbing chisels

ALTERNAX SWING CHISEL

alto-relievo A term applied to carved relief work where the projection of the carving is more than half the real proportions. (See also *bas-relief* and *mezzo-relievo*.)

aluminium oxide This is an abrasive material which is completely man-made. The base is a soft, white rock called 'bauxite' and the powder from it is fused in an electric furnace with silica and some ferrite (iron). The top surface in contact with the air forms an oxide and when cool and hard, it is pulverised. It is grey-brown in colour and harder than garnet *(q.v.)* and this hardness means that, if used by hand or on slow-running machines, it tends to leave scratches. It is therefore mostly used on powered sanders where its effect can be controlled.

alva A dried seaweed from the Baltic used as a first stuffing in upholstery. Seldom used today.

amaranth Alternative name for purpleheart *(q.v.)*.

amboyna *(pterocarpus indicus)* This is the richly figured burr of Padauk *(q.v.)*.

American oak (see *oak, American*).

American whitewood (see *whitewood, American*).

ammonia A colourless, pungent chemical, used for fuming oak and, in some cases, mahogany. If applied direct it darkens oak slightly. Sometimes used in making stains to increase their penetrating properties. It is painful to the fingers and causes the eyes to water. It should be stored in a glass-stoppered bottle. Usual strength is .880 (ask for 'point eight eighty'). (See also *fuming*).

amorini Winged cupids, often used in late 17th and early 18th century woodwork. See *crowns* and *boys and putti*.

amyris *(amyris balsamifera)* Central and South American hardwood. 64 lb (1025 kg). Sometimes used in turnery, carving and cabinet work.

anan *(fagraea fragrans)* Strong, durable hardwood, light yellow colour, from Burma. Weight 60 lb (961 kg).

angel bed A bed, sometimes called a 'half-tester', in which the canopy (or tester) covered a quarter to a third of the bed area and was suspended on chains from the ceiling. Circa 1700.

angelin *(andira inermis)* Hardwood from West Indies and Central and South America. 50 lb (801 kg). Colour from reddish-brown to nearly black. Straight-grained but rather coarse. Used for billiard cues, turnery, structural work, etc.

angle brace A diagonal tie fitted to strengthen the angles of square or rectangular framings.

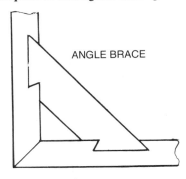

ANGLE BRACE

angle bracket (see *corner bracket*).

aniline dyes Available in powder form in a wide range of colours, such as Vandyke brown, Bismarck brown, black, yellow, blue, violet, green, mauve, etc. They are obtainable soluble in water, oil, or methylated spirit and should be ordered in accordance with the medium to be used. The stains are made by dissolving sufficient powder in spirit, oil (turps), or water to produce the shade desired, then straining through muslin to remove sediment. A binder for spirit stain is a small quantity of clear shellac polish; a binder for water stain is thin glue size and, consequently, this stain should be applied warm. For oil stain add a little gold size.

animal glue (see *scotch glue*).

annual rings The circular rings, alternating soft and hard, seen on the end section of a log. In the spring the cells are thin walled, with relatively large cavities, but in the summer (autumn) are thicker walled with correspondingly smaller cavities. If softwood timber is examined, this can usually be seen quite clearly. There will be alternating bands, one fairly wide and relatively colourless, followed by a narrow, darkish band of denser wood elements. These two bands together make up a growth ring (or annual ring, as it is less correctly called), the wider band being the 'spring-wood' (or 'early-wood') and the denser band the 'summer-wood', (or 'late-wood').

annulet A small moulding, either square or round in section, around the lower part of a Doric capital.

anobium punctatum The furniture beetle. (See *wood-boring insects*.)

antefix In furniture design, the term refers to ornamental corners which are hipped above the cornice as on a tester.

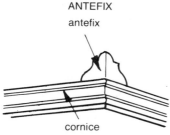

ANTEFIX

antefix

cornice

anthemion Greek ornament based on the foliage of the chamomile plant. A favoured decoration in 18th and 19th century furniture.

ANTHEMION

antiaris (*antiaris africana*) Ghana, Nigeria. 26 lb (416 kg). Yellow-grey, woolly, does not turn well. Interior fittings, core stock, etc.

antique finish Although an antique finish is often given to reproduction period furniture, it is also sometimes used for new furniture. It consists of a rubbed effect in which the highlights are made slightly light by rubbing the stain before it dries, or by rubbing with pumice powder afterwards. The effect is also heightened by polishing with antique or black wax which leaves a dark deposit in corners and recessed parts.

antique nail A dome-headed pin used to fix upholstery covers. Usually with a brass-plated finish; also called a 'chair nail' (*q.v.*).

ANTIQUE NAIL

apitong (*dipterocarpus* species) Hardwood from the Philippines, used mostly locally.

apple (*malus pumila*) Europe and America. 45 lb (721 kg). Hard and dense; used for tool handles, turnery, mallet heads, etc.

apron In furniture 'apron piece' refers (generally) to the shaped part often fitted under the middle drawer of a knee-hole writing- or dressing-table. Other applications of the word are: (*a*) 'apron board', the wide front board beneath the top of a bench; (*b*) 'apron lining', the vertical lining covering the joists in the well of a staircase; (*c*) 'apron rail', the central rail of a door having a raised moulded or other piece planted or worked on its surface. The term 'apron piece' is also used to designate the false trimmer at the top of a flight of stairs which carries the landing joists.

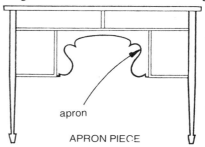

apron

APRON PIECE

Archimedean drill Primarily a small drill for thin wood or metal. By means of a spiral stem up and down which a finger-barrel is moved, the fine steel bit rotates rapidly, the cutting being continuous when the tool is fitted with balance weights and ratchet. Drill points range from $\frac{1}{32}$ in 1 mm. diam. upwards.

ARCHIMEDEAN DRILL

architrave In architecture this applies to the lower division of the entablature which rests on the top of a column. In joinery it is the name for the moulded surround of a door or window. Architrave moulding is a standard milled commodity.

ARCHITRAVE

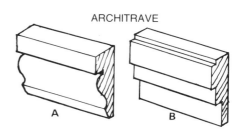

A   B

ark Medieval term for a chest used to store flour, meal and bread. (See *boarded chest*).

Arkansas oilstone A natural stone, similar to the washita stone, but much finer and considerably more expensive. It is very hard, dense, and ideal for hard steel tools. Chiefly used by wood carvers who require a superfine edge on tools.

armadio Italian term for a large cupboard similar to an armoire which was originally used for the storage of ecclesiastical vestments and later became the equivalent of a clothes press.

arming chair A term to describe the armchair circa 1670, and particularly referring to those of the early Restoration period.

arming chest Chest specially designed with compartments to house armour and weapons.

armoire A large cupboard which later developed into the wardrobe. It was usually monumental in character and was mostly used in France and the Netherlands. (See *wardrobes, development of.*)

armour-plate glass A type of shatter-proof glass which withstands heavy blows. It is used for glass shelves, and for covering dressing table tops, etc.

arris The sharp edge on squared wood, stone, or metal. In the case of furniture the sharpness is removed with glasspaper.

arte povera Italian term meaning 'the poor man's art' and referring to decoupage *(q.v.)*.

artist's tables Popularised in the early 18th century by amateur artists and draughtsmen, some of these tables had a central section which could be raised and tilted on a quadrant; others had a double-rising top and a 'lazy tongs' framework to enable the users to stand at their work.

Art Nouveau chair Designed by Charles Rennie Mackintosh, who was a Scottish designer in the Art Nouveau style.

ash *(fraxinus excelsior)* A hardwood, light brown to greyish white in colour and close-grained. Valued for its toughness and elasticity, it is used for furniture, tool handles, billiard cues, sports goods, and bent wood furniture 46-47 lb (737-753 kg).

There is another ash from the USA, *(fraxinus nigra)*, 34 lb (545 kg); and also the white ash *(fraxinus americana)* 41 lb (657 kg).

ashlaring Short uprights, fitted between an upper floor and sloping roof to avoid an acute corner. Also fitted on top of a wall flush on the inside to meet the sloping roof rafters.

aspen *(populus tremula)* European hardwood. 23-28 lb (368-449 kg). Used for matches, casks, pulp, etc.

asphaltum Dissolved in turpentine this yields a deep brown stain. A little gold size is added as a binder, and the liquid strained to remove any sediment. If the work is to be wax polished the stained wood must be given a coat of french polish to seal it.

astragal A combined bead and fillet moulding used on the shutting joint of double doors. More decoratively it is the moulding (in narrow widths) employed for barred doors of bookcases and display cabinets. The same moulding is common on friezes, neckings, etc.

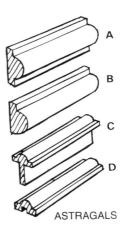

ASTRAGALS

Athenienne A candelabrum consisting of an urn supported on a classical tripod, usually in bronze or gilded wood. Invented in 1773 by J. H. Eberts.

auger A long twist, hand-boring tool used for heavy timbers. Normal length ranges from 20 in (508 mm) to 25 in (635 mm), the cutting diameter being from $\frac{1}{2}$ in (12 mm) to 2 in (51 mm). For use with a brace, the twist bit is sometimes spoken of as an auger bit. The old type of wooden pump was bored with a giant auger.

AUGER

aumbry Also 'ambry' and 'almery'. In the 14th century this was a recess in a wall which was enclosed by a door but in the Middle Ages it developed into a free-standing cupboard. (See *almery; court cupboard*.)

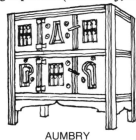

AUMBRY

auricular (see *lobate*).

Australian laurel (see *laurel, Australian*).

Australian walnut (see *Queensland walnut*).

aventurine Minute particles of gold wire sprinkled over the surface of some Japan work.

avodiré *(turroeanthus africana)* Hardwood from Ghana, West Africa. 35 lb (561 kg). Light yellow wood used for furniture, plywood, fittings, etc.

awl (see *birdcage maker's awl, bradawl, marking awl*).

axe Used chiefly for rough outdoor work, i.e., the chopping, cleaving, or splitting of wood. Common types measure 14 in (355 mm), 16 in (406 mm), and 18 in (457 mm) long. Felling axe handles are 3 ft (915 mm) long. Handles are of hickory or ash. Most axes, have a head tapering from heel to cutting edge. The side axe, however, is ground and sharpened, like a chisel, on one side only. The cutting edge is sharpened with an oilstone after grinding.

axim An African mahogany from West Africa, 30 lb (481 kg). Colour is good but quality varies.

ayan *(distemonanthus benthamianus)* Nigerian hardwood. 45 lb (721 kg). Golden-yellow wood, durable, and with interlocked grain. Furniture, fittings, flooring, etc.

baby cage Also called 'baby trotter' or (today) 'baby walker'. It was a framework resembling a cage into which the baby was placed: it was fitted with small castors or wheels so that the baby could push it about and learn to walk. They were known in the Middle Ages and have survived, in various shapes and materials, until the present day.

bachelor's chest A small chest of drawers (circa 1730) which is equipped with either a pull-out slide which is housed under the top, or a fold-over hinged top which is supported by pull-out lopers. Typical size: 29¾ in (755 mm) high by 30 in (760 mm) wide by 17½ in (455 mm) deep.

bachelor chest (USA) A tall two-section piece with two long, deep drawers in the middle; at the bottom a cupboard enclosed by two solid doors and containing shelving. The whole supported by turned ball or bun feet.

back board Thin board used for backing pictures, mirrors, etc. Today generally of plywood or hardboard.

back cutting A term used in spindle cutting in which the wood is drawn in the direction of the rotation of the cutter as a preliminary to the final cut against the oncoming cutter. It saves splitting out in some circumstances, but is dangerous in unskilled hands.

backeroni tool A wood-carving tool of limited use but preferred by some carvers for cutting acanthus leaf work.

BACKERONI
PROFILE

back-flap hinge A strong wide-winged type used in cases where the hinge is recessed into the face (as distinct from edge) of both frame and door, lid, or flap. Hinge is sunk in flush. Made in both iron and brass. Blank back-flaps for drilling as required are also obtainable.

backfoot The back leg of a chair: (trade term).

back iron The cap or covering iron fixed to a plane cutter. Its purpose is to minimise tearing out the grain. The closer it is set to the cutting edge the sooner the shaving is broken as it is raised, and the smoother the finish. (A) wood plane; (B) metal plane.

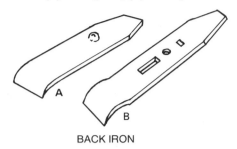

BACK IRON

backing block A rebated block of wood sometimes used in machine planing to hold down the end of the wood.

back-saw Applied to any saw having a rigid spine clamped to the back edge of blade to keep it straight. Typical examples are tenon saw (A) and dovetail saw (B) *(q.v.)*. The back may be in brass or iron.

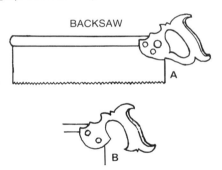

BACKSAW

backstand A term describing the portion of a chair's back leg above the seat.

backstool Early form of side chair (1600 to 1640) which was essentially a stool whose back legs continued above the level of the seat and were joined by a rail or rails. Sometimes referred to as a 'chaise lorraine'.

bacon bench Common name for a settle which has a cupboard in the back; bacon and hams were stored in it.

badam Alternative name for white Bombay *(q.v.)*.

badger plane A plane similar to a jack plane in shape, but either with the iron flush at one side, or with a rebate along one side, the cutter flush with the rebate. Intended for planing wide rebates.

badigeon (see *sawdust*).

bagasse boards (see *particle boards*).

bahut A protective covering, usually wood or leather, to keep rain from damaging coffers *(q.v.)* during travel in the 15th century.

bail A half-loop metal pull handle, usually of brass suspended from bolts which pierce the drawer front. Used in America about 1700, and in England from 1720 to 1770.

baize Material used for lining card table tops, cutlery drawers, etc.

baldachino A canopy built over an altar.

ball and claw foot A carved foot used on cabriole legs; it was probably adopted from the Chinese as it represents a dragon's claw clutching the pearl of wisdom. Widely used in England during the Queen Anne, early Georgian, and Chippendale periods. In America, the claws were those of an eagle.

BALL & CLAW
FOOT

ball castor A castor having a metal ball which revolves in a socket. It may have either flange or screw fixing.

ball catch Catch for closing edges of a cabinet door. The bullet type (also known as the Bales catch)

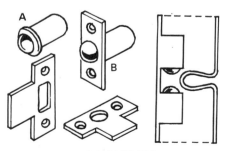

BALL CATCHES

7

requires a hole (suiting its diameter) to be bored and countersunk slightly. It is tapped in flush. The catch plate is either sunk flush or screwed on the surface of the door aperture or upright division. Its true position is found by applying marking ink to the ball and gently closing the door. Face plate types are available, including double-action types.

balloon-back chair There were two styles — the early balloon-back about 1835, followed by a more sophisticated design from 1850 onwards.

balloon-back Windsor chair In this design, the comb is deliberately made less wide than the seat and forces the sticks in the back into a curved shape.

balloon seat A seat often found in Queen Anne style chairs, particularly those made in Philadelphia, USA.

balsa (*Ochroma lagopus,* etc.) The lightest of all known timbers. Used for rafts, life-belts, model-making, etc. Its weight, lighter than cork, is only 6-12 lb (96-192 kg) per cu. ft.

Baltic pine (see *pine*).

baluster The upright supporting the handrail of a staircase or balcony. Balusters are frequently turned, and in the best way are sunk into the string and let into a groove beneath the handrail. In a simple way they are cut to a tight fit and fixed by skew nailing.

baluster leg A turned leg-pattern resembling the design of a staircase baluster.

BALUSTER

balustrade A row of balusters surmounted by a capping or rail.

bamboo A variety of giant tropical grass (*bambusa*) which has stems that are jointed along their length.

Light-weight occasional furniture made in bamboo became popular from about 1800 and right through the Victorian era; probably the main instigator of its use was the Prince Regent, who employed it extensively in his Pavilion at Brighton. Such furniture was so highly prized that imitation bamboo, which was ordinary wood turned and painted, was incorporated in some furniture.

banak *(virola koschnyi)* Timber from British Honduras resembling mahogany, but neither as strong nor as heavy. Weight 33-35 lb (529-561 kg).

banana oil (USA) Common name for amyl acetate.

band and hook A type of hinge for heavy doors and gates. The band is screwed to the door or gate, and is also bolted to it through a square hole — this prevents removal of the door by withdrawing the screws. The hook is screwed to the post and allows the door to be lifted off. (See *gate hinges*).

band cramp A flexible cramp often used by chairmakers for shaped seat frames. The cramp consists of a flexible metal strip which can be bent around the frame and then secured to apply the necessary tension. Modern ones frequently use webbing or nylon straps instead of metal with a ratchet device for securing.

bandings Strips on inlay in various patterns made up in widths from about $\frac{1}{8}$ in (3 mm) up to 2 in (51 mm) or so. Thickness is in the region of $\frac{1}{16}$ in (2 mm).

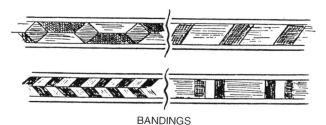

BANDINGS

band resaw A large bandsaw for sawing logs, etc., into boards. It has a mechanical roller feeding device.

bandsaw A machine for sawing external shapes only. It consists of an endless blade, about $\frac{1}{4}$ in (6 mm) or more wide, toothed at one edge and passing around two, or sometimes three, wheels. Size of the machine varies from a small bench model with 6 in to 10 in (152 to 254 mm) dia wheels up to a large pedestal type with wheels up to 48 in (1219 mm) diameter. The table is usually made to cant to enable bevels to be sawn. Some smaller machines have three wheels, the advantage being that the throat clearance is increased, but adjusting for blade-tracking is more difficult. All machines should be provided with guides and thrust wheel, and there should be a tracking device to enable the position of the saw on the wheel to be adjusted. A tensioning device is also essential.

bandsaw formulae   The linear speed of a saw in metres per minute = 3.14 × D (the wheel dia in metres) × R (rpm). Required length of a bandsaw in metres = 3.14 × D (the wheel dia in metres) + 2C (C = wheel centre distance in metres).

banister   (see *baluster*).

bank   Archaic term for a long bench-like seat.

banker   A cushion or upholstered covering for a seat. Also spelt 'bancors' or 'banquer'.

banner cupboard   A recess in a church usually about 12 ft high, 18 in wide and 12 in deep (3656 by 457 by 305 mm) with a wooden door. Banners and crosses for medieval processions were stored in them.

banner screen   A pole-screen *(q.v.)* which had a sliding screen which could be adjusted to shield the face from the heat of the fire. The screen was usually oval in shape and contained embroidery.

Bantam work   A type of incised lacquer work, called after an East Indian port of the same name through which it was exported.

barber's chair   A variation of the early Georgian corner chair *(q.v.)* about 1740 which had an extension built into the corner cresting to support the occupant's head while he was being shaved by the barber. Also called a 'shaving chair'.

bar cramp   Generally refers to a cramp made from a wood bar fitted with cramp heads. In a more general way it is sometimes applied to any long cramp whether of wood or metal.

bare   A term meaning 'slightly less than'. Thus 'one inch bare' would be $^{31}/_{32}$ in (24 mm) approximately; the converse is 'full' *(q.v.)*.

bare-faced tenon   This has only one shoulder. Its use is on cross-rails between uprights, forming a framework for match-boarding, so that the boards lie flush at the face side as shown. The same tenon may also be cut on the upright slats in bed ends, etc., and

other positions in which the tenoned piece is thinner than that with the mortises.

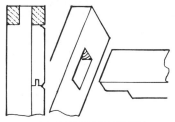

BARE-FACED TENON

barge board   The wood member set at an angle beneath a sloping roof to protect the ends of the purlins and ridge board. They are usually made decorative by moulding, carving, or piercings.

barjier, burjair   Colloquial English equivalent of the French word *bergere*, which (in France) referred to an armchair with closed sides and a loose cushion — see also *fauteuil*. The term was first used in England circa 1725; today it refers to a chair or settee with canework backs and arms and loose cushions.

bark   The outer covering of trees, the function being to protect the cambium *(q.v.)*.

barley-sugar twisting   A twisted pattern resembling barley-sugar.

barred doors   An outstanding feature in furniture of the eighteenth century was the traceried barred door. It is still popular, but its form has altered to conform with modern design. Examples of barred doors are found in bookcase doors, china cabinet doors, showcase doors, etc. The mouldings fit over bars or ribs, and in the best work are grooved. The bars are checked into the door framework, and the mouldings mitred at the intersections. The line of the mitre should always halve the over-all angle of the joining mouldings.

barred gate   A field gate consisting of horizontal rails and vertical stiles.

barrel bolt   A fitting having a cylindrical casing around the bolt.

barrel moulding   A moulding with a convex or bellied profile. Also called a 'pulvenated' moulding.

BARREL MOULDING

basil The angle to which the cutting edge of a plane iron or chisel is ground. (See also *cannel.*)

basin stand (See *washing stand*).

bas-relief A term applied to carved work where the projection of the carving is less than half the proportions. (See also *alto-relievo* and *mezzo-relievo.*)

bassinet A type of cradle, without rockers, originally made of osiers and later of wicker-work; they were fitted with hoods.

basswood *(tilia glabra)* Timber from USA and Canada, almost identical with the lime of this country. Sometimes confused with canary-whitewood. Weight 30 lb (481 kg). Used chiefly in pianoforte work and joinery.

bastard A term used for woods which are not a true species.

batten A softwood timber term referring to lengths of wood varying from 5 in (127 mm) to 8 in (204 mm) wide with a thickness of 2 in (51 mm) to 4 in (102 mm).

battenboard A manufactured board consisting of two outer layers with an inner core of solid strips having the grain running at right angles, differing from blockboard and laminboard in that the core strips are up to 3 in (76 mm) wide. The advantage of such boarding is that it can be manufactured in large sheets like plywood. Due to its wide core strips, battenboard is liable to become wavy at the surfaces and is therefore unsuitable for important veneered work. (See also *blockboard* and *laminboard*).

BATTENBOARD

baudekin A rich fabric now called brocade; originally a very rich silk woven with gold.

baulk or balk A cut-timber term referring to timber roughly squared for further conversion and exceeding 4 in (102 mm) by 4½ in (115 mm) in size. The section is usually much larger. Half-timber is a baulk which has been cut in half.

bayonet saw (USA) Corresponds to British jigsaw *(q.v.);* also a sabre saw.

baywood Sometimes wrongly applied to Honduras mahogany, owing to early consignments having been shipped from the Bay of Honduras. No connection with the bay tree of Asia.

b.B. Abbreviation for bead butt *(q.v.).*

bead A small rounded moulding (A). A quirked bead is shown at (B). If possessing two quirks, it is known as a double-quirked bead (C); if below the surface, a sunk bead (D). A cocked bead, projecting from the surface, is given at (E). (See also *quirk*).

BEADS

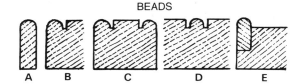

A   B   C   D   E

bead and reel Ornamental turning resembling these objects.

BEAD & REEL
TURNING

bead butt (b.b.) A panelled framework in which the panel is flush beaded at the edge *with* the grain, but butts against the rails at the end grain. (See also *bead flush*).

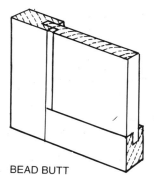

BEAD BUTT

bead flush (b.f.) Framework with flush panel with bead all round. The bead with the grain is usually stuck in the solid, but that across the grain is planted on. (See also *bead butt*).

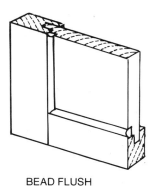

BEAD FLUSH

bead plane A small moulding plane for working beads. If for centre beads it has no fence (A); otherwise it is shaped as at (B). Made in various sizes.

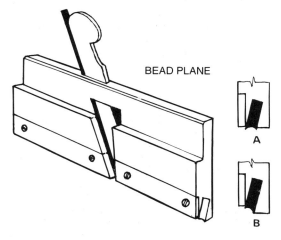

BEAD PLANE

bead saw A small back saw with turned or octagonal handle and with 16-18 points per inch (25 mm). Used mostly for mitreing mouldings and stripwood. For extra small work there is the still smaller jeweller's saw — the teeth of which are superfine, varying from 24 to 32 points per inch (25 mm). It is ideal for cutting tiny dovetails in ⅛ in (3 mm) wood, mitreing inlay banding, etc. There is no set to the teeth of this saw and it leaves a smooth surface. It is sometimes called a gent's saw.

bearer Wood rails used in the veneering process for pressing down cauls. Usually made in pairs with curved edges so that when cramps are applied at the ends the pressure is exerted in the middle first thus pressing the glue outwards towards the edges.

Also a term with wide applications, generally referring to members which support stair winders and staircase landings.

bearer rail As distinct from the top carcase rail this is the rail fitted between the carcase ends and below the top drawers of such pieces as sideboard, writing table, dressing chest, etc.

beaumontage A wax stopping used for filling small cracks, nail holes, etc. It is made up in little sticks or kept in a tin. It is made by melting a lump of beeswax in an empty shoe polish tin, adding about an equal quantity of resin, a few flakes of shallac, and some colouring pigment such as burnt sienna or Venetian red for mahogany; burnt umber for oak, or lamp black for ebony. Uncoloured beaumontage is suitable for natural oak and similar light-coloured woods. When melted the stopping is applied with a matchstick, or by holding a stick of it against a hot pointed iron. It sets almost at once, any excess being removed by paring with a chisel, followed by glasspapering.

beaufait A kind of built-in corner cupboard (*q.v.*).

bed Modern beds are almost invariably made to fit standard sizes of mattresses. The recognised length of the steel framing of spring mattresses and of boxspring mattresses is 74 in (1879 mm). Standard widths (over frame) are 30 in (762 mm), 33 in (838 mm), 36 in (914 mm), 42 in (1066 mm), 48 in (1219 mm) and 54 in (1372 mm). 'Twin' beds are usually in the 36 in (914 mm) size. A common width for double bed is 48 in (1219 mm) but 54 in (1372 mm) affords greater comfort. High ends are now rarely seen. Usually a separate head board is fitted. Height from floor at which the bed irons are fixed varies from 14 in (355 mm) to 16 in (406 mm) but here again the depth of the mattress has to be considered.

bed-chair An open-sided armchair in which an extensible frame with legs is stored under the seat, together with extra cushions. The back can be adjusted to several angles or lowered to the horizontal, when it is supported on a folding leg-frame.

bedroom table A small table with a set of shallow drawers and a top with a gallery around the sides.

bed-settee A kind of convertible bed-settee, called *leito a inglesa*, was made in Portugal during the 18th century, although few examples have survived. Today there are many styles developed by various manufacturers and, in general, they rely on the back sliding down to align itself with the seat and form a bed. (See also *day beds*.)

bedside cabinet (Known also as bedside cupboard or pedestal.) In style this matches wardrobe, chest, etc., of suite. Recognised height is 28 in (711 mm) to 30 in (762 mm); carcase width 14 in (356 mm) and depth (front to back) 13 in (330 mm) to 14 in (356 mm). One shelf is provided. If door opens *within* ends the carcase width may be slightly increased.

bed stocks Early form of bedstead used by wealthier classes in the 12th to 14th centuries, consisting of a framework of four rails joined to short posts (which also acted as legs), one at each corner. The rails were drilled with holes through which rope could be threaded to form a support for the mattress.

bed tables and trays Sizes vary according to requirements, but for general use a good average is 22 in (559 mm) by 14 in (356 mm), fixed or folding legs being provided. The structure should be light and the top fitted with a moulded surround or a low rail at sides and back. Many of these tables are also provided with adjustable reading racks. Sometimes the tray is detachable.

beech *(fagus sylvatica)* A hard, close-grained, and durable wood extensively used for chair making, general turnery, tool handles, planes, domestic woodwork, textile machinery parts, and toys. It is unsuitable for outdoor woodwork. A large quantity of Canadian beech is imported for the chair-making trade. Weight 45 lb (721 kg).

beehive chair These were made in Britain during the Roman occupation. They were made of wickerwork and were tub-shaped sometimes having a hood built on to the back. (See *wicker chair*.)

beeswax The best quality beeswax is usually honey-coloured and sold in cakes. Used chiefly for making wax polish. Bleached wax is also available and is suitable for light woods. (See *carnauba wax, paraffin wax, wax polish*).

beetle General term for insects which attack wood. (See *death-watch, furniture, longhorn, pinhole borer, powderpost, etc.*) Also the name of a heavy mallet or striking tool used in riving oak and other woods.

b.f. Abbreviation for bead flush *(q.v.)*.

belfast truss A roof truss consisting of a bowed top member and a straight lower string joined by criss-cross braces. Also termed a bow-string truss.

belian *(eusideroxylon zwageri)* Hard, durable wood, dark yellow to reddish brown, from North Borneo and Malaya. Difficult to saw. Weight 63 lb (1009 kg).

bell flower A form of decoration based on the catkins of the bush *Garrya elliptica*. It was frequently used in combination with a carved shell on the knees of cabriole legs. Sometimes called husk or wheat ear.

bell seat Another name for the balloon seat *(q.v.)*.

belt sanders These are machines for finishing flat panels, and there are three principal types: (1) a motorised portable type with two wheels and with the belts 3 or 4 in (75 or 102 mm) wide, which is passed over the work. Damage to the surface can result if the sander is allowed to stay too long in one place. (2) Small table sanders for small workshop or light industrial use. Fitted with a sliding table which is adjustable for height and can be drawn forwards to remove the work. The 6 in (152 mm) wide belt is held on to the work with a pad which is moved by hand. (3) Large industrial wide-belt machines with belts up to 36 in (914 mm) wide. They are totally enclosed and flat panels can be fed in at one end and taken off at the other.

bench 1. There are various shapes and sizes of benches, but a good size is one measuring at least 4 ft 6 in (1371 mm) long, 2 ft (610 mm) wide and 32-33 in (812 to 838 mm) high (for tall workers) or 30 in (762 mm) high (for small workers). The main top should preferably be beech or a similar hardwood, about 14 in (356 mm) wide by 2 in (51 mm) thick. A tool trough is desirable, this being 10 in (254 mm) wide, with a back strip level with the main top. A good bench vice flush with the top should be fitted. (See *vice, bench*).

bench 2. A form of seating consisting of a board or boards supported by truss-ends (early 16th century) or splay turned legs (17th century). In the truss-end design, the underframing protruded through the ends and was pegged on the outside; when splay legs were used an extra pair was often introduced at the centre and they were all joined by H-underframing.

bench dog Metal or wood sprung pegs which fit into a line of square holes, usually about 1 in × 1 in (25 × 25 mm), to form an end stop in conjunction a tail vice when cramping long pieces flat on a bench top.

bench end   The upright end of a pew or seat in church.

bench hook   A simple wooden appliance which, placed upon a bench top, prevents wood from shifting about when being cut into lengths. The bottom fence grips against the edge of the bench. The top fence may have a guiding slot for square cutting or mitre cutting.

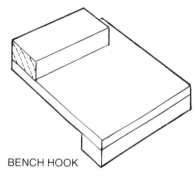

BENCH HOOK

bench pads   Used by the woodworker and polisher to prevent the bench top marking polished articles. Made in pairs and covered on one side with strips of carpet or thick felt.

bench planes   These are the planes in constant, everyday use, and generally comprise the smoothing, jack, and trying or panel planes.

bench screw   The screw fitted to the bench vice. Formerly of wood, it is now invariably steel.

bench stop   (see *stop, bench*).

bended back chair   Alternative name for the fiddle back chair or the spoon-back chair *(q.q.v.)*.

bending properties   The propensity or capability of various species of wood to bending.

benteak   *(lagerstroemia lanceolata)*   West Indian timber, reddish brown. Weight 53 lb (849 kg).

Bentwood furniture   A style of furniture, mainly chairs, which employs steam-bent wooden parts. The technique of steam-bending wood was developed by Michael Thonet, who set up a factory in Vienna in 1849; similar furniture is still being produced.

benzine   Sometimes known as benzoline. Used when varnishing to remove excess oil or grease.

benzoin glaze   Made by dissolving crushed gum benzoin in methylated spirit, using sufficient of the latter to cover the benzoin. Leave to dissolve for a couple of days and then pour out the liquid without disturbing the sediment. Benzoin glaze is used in awkward corners on work that cannot be dealt with in the normal manner with a polishing rubber. It is applied with a rubber or pencil brush.

bergere   (see *barjier*).

bergere bow   A Victorian design of Windsor chair with a high curved back with ornate scrolled arms; circa 1860 to 1890.

bergeries   Pastoral scenes of shepherds and shepherdesses; often found on upholstered chairs, tapestries, etc, particularly those associated with Robert Adam.

Berlin black   A form of black varnish which dries flat without shine. It is applied to work where gloss is undesirable.

berlinia   *(berlinia heudelotiana* and *auriculata)* Reddish brown wood sometimes well figured, from West Africa. Structural work mostly. Weight 42 lb (673 kg).

betty saw   (see *chairmaker's saw*).

bevel   An edge which is at any angle other than a right angle.

bevel-edge chisel   A chisel having the long edges of its blade bevelled to facilitate waste removal; it is not as strong as a firmer chisel *(q.v.)*. Available in all normal widths and with either tang or socket fixing.

bevel of saw teeth   The angle at which the file is held when sharpening a saw. The angle varies from 60 degrees for hardwood to 45 degrees for softwood. Cross-cut, tenon, and dovetail saws have this bevel, but ripsaw teeth are sharpened straight across at right angles.

BEVEL OF SAW TEETH

bevel, sliding   Used for marking out or testing odd angles. The blade is adjustable and is fixed by a small bolt and winged nut or a screw.

bichromate of potash Obtainable in crystals for staining mahogany and sometimes oak. They are steeped in water which assumes a clear orange colour. This, however, bears no relation to the colour produced on the wood. The action of the stain is chemical and the result depends upon the amount of tannin in the wood. Some varieties of mahogany are more affected than others. It is usual to make up a concentrated solution and dilute it as required. A slight dust deposit is left on surfaces when it dries and this should be brushed off.

billet A term with several applications. It may refer to a short log, halved or quartered log, or to one which is roughly dressed.

bill hook Tool used in rustic work, etc., for removing twigs, small branches, etc.

billiard tables Billiards is an ancient game and the first mention of a billiard table is in France in 1429. It remained popular until the 18th century, and none of the well-known designers mention it, except Sheraton in his 'Cabinet Dictionary' of 1803; it is, of course, extremely popular today.

bill of materials (USA) Corresponds to British 'cutting list' *(q.v.)*.

binding Term generally applied to hingeing in which part of the wood fits too tightly against another causing rubbing or preventing closing or opening.

bine The ridge or raised part of a twist turning *(q.v.)*; there are single, double, triple, and open bines.

binuang *(octomeles sumatra)* Pale brown or greyish yellow timber from North Borneo or Malaya. Weight 23 lb (368 kg).

birch *(betula pendula)* A hardwood used in chair and brush making; its main use, however, is for plywood. Because of its plain, undistinguished surface it is exceptionally responsive to staining. 43 lb (689 kg).

There is also the paper birch *(betula papyrifera)* from the USA and Canada, 34 lb (545 kg); and the yellow birch *(betula alleghaniensis)* from the same districts, 43 lb (689 kg). The latter is the more important commercially.

birdcage-maker's awl Used for making holes in thin wood and near the edges. The tapered blade is square in section, and does not tend to split the wood since the fibres are eased away by the sharp corners.

birdcage movement An all-wood movement fitted between the column and the top of a tripod table, which enables the top to be tilted from the horizontal to the vertical. Corresponds to USA 'crow's nest'.

wedge

BIRDCAGE MOVEMENT

bird's beak lock Used on tambour roll-top desks and piano falls; so-called because the bolt resembles a bird's beak. Now superseded by the roll-top desk lock *(q.v.)*.

bird's eye A figuring found in maple. It is due to conical formations in the grain which, when sliced through either by rotary cutting or plain sawing, produce a series of circular markings dotted at random over the surface.

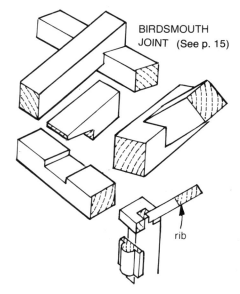

BIRDSMOUTH JOINT (See p. 15)

rib

bird's-mouth joint   Three common forms of this joint are shown on p. 14. It is used widely in roofing work and structural framings. Rafters are generally bird's-mouth jointed to the wall-plate and front side plate of lean-to sheds, or to a ridge piece and wall-plates. In cabinet work the joint is often used for the diagonal ribs of barred doors, the notched end of the rib fitting on the corner of a square or oblong frame.

biscuit jointer   (see *hand jointer*).

bishop's mitre   A variation of the mason's mitre in which one of the members is stopped level with the main intersecting moulding, but is restarted beyond and completed up to the mitre line.

Bismarck brown   An aniline dye of fiery red colour. Should be used with caution as it is powerful.

bit   (see under various headings: *centre, countersink, expanding, Forstner, Gedge, Irwin, Russell-Jennings, shell, spoon, twist, etc*).

bitumen powder   This is a mineral pitch which was used in making repeat patterns for marquetry. The pattern was pricked through with a needle, the powder dusted through, and the paper beneath heated when the powder solidified.

black bean *(castanospermum australe)*   Finely figured brown timber working to a fine finish. Stands well when properly seasoned. Used for furniture, etc. Weight 46 lb (737 kg).

blackboard coating   Ready-made preparation can be obtained. Alternatively, give coat of black priming paint. Rub down when dry and give second coat to which about two tablespoons of fine pumice powder to the pint (½ litre) has been added.

black cabbage bark *(lonchocarpus castilloi)*   A hard-wood, 57 lb (913 kg), from Central America and Honduras, brown or reddish-brown in colour. The grain is usually interlocked and the texture open. It is a strong and durable timber for general purposes.

black polish   Used in the ebonising finish. Made by dissolving ½ oz (14 grams) spirit black aniline dye in one pint (0.28 litre) white or transparent french polish. Strain through muslin or an old nylon stocking before use. For a richer colour add a small piece of Reckitt's blue (US 'laundry blue').

Blackstone   A small portable writing desk made by George Seddon (circa 1790) for Sir William Blackstone.

blackwood, African *(dalbergia melanoxylon)*   A dense, heavy timber used mainly for musical instruments, cutlery handles, etc. Takes on a natural shine when turned. Weight about 80 lb (1281 kg).

blank hinge   (see *back flap*).

bleach   Some woods can be lightened in colour slightly by the use of oxalic acid dissolved in water. The liquid is allowed to remain on the wood, and a second application made if necessary. All traces of the acid must be removed afterwards with water. Chloride of lime can also be used for oak.

The bleached effect popular nowadays, however, is produced by the use of proprietary two-solution bleaches manufactured specially for the purpose. These are effective on medium-toned woods, but are of little value for dark hard-woods such as rosewood, ebony, and the denser varieties of Spanish mahogany. They are of no value for lightening stained wood.

bleached shellac   Used in the manufacture of white french polish. It is orange-shellac bleached with chemicals and pulled out to form sticks of knots. It should be kept under water. If it is stale it becomes denatured and fails to dissolve in methylated spirit.

bleed through   The penetration of an adhesive to the outer surfaces of a piece of wood or veneer: also the effect when an undercoat is soluble in the finishing material and works through and blends with it.

blind bolt   A bolt which is let flush into the edge or back of a door.

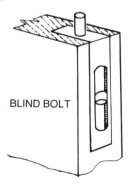

BLIND BOLT

blind stitch   A stitch used by upholsterers which does not show on the exterior.

blister in veneers   (see *bubble*).

blitz back saw   (USA) A back saw for cutting fine dovetails and similar delicate work. A hook projects from the toe end which controls vertical or angled sawcuts.

blockboard A manufactured board, consisting of a core of strips about $\frac{7}{8}$ in (22 mm) wide cemented together and covered on both sides with thin layers, the grain of which is at right angles with the core. Obtainable in large sheets. It keeps flatter than battenboard but is not so reliable as laminboard. (See *battenboard* and *laminboard*).

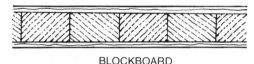

BLOCKBOARD

block cutters Small carving chisels used for carving wooden printing blocks but equally suitable for delicate work by wood carvers. The handles are dome-shaped to fit the palm of the hand.

block floor A floor consisting of wood blocks fixed with mastic to a concrete base. The edges are usually dovetail shaped to give a key to the mastic. Also called a parquet floor.

block plane A small metal plane, generally with screw adjustment for regulating the depth of cut; it can give a very fine finish. Sizes range from $3\frac{1}{2}$ in (89 mm) to 7 in (178 mm) with cutter widths of 1 in (25 mm) to $1\frac{5}{8}$ in (42 mm). Block planes are invaluable for trimming small work and end grain. There is no back iron to the cutter which is used with the bevel uppermost. Some types are double-ended, the cutter being reversed for use as a bull-nose plane when necessary. General model has pitch of 20 degrees. Special low angle block plane has 12-degrees pitch.

BLOCK PLANE

block saw A saw which was specially designed for use with the mitre block. A wooden handle is riveted to one side of the saw blade.

bloom A bluish film which appears on french polished surfaces due to dampness in the atmosphere of the room in which the polishing is carried out. The remedy is to set the work aside in a warm room until

BLOCK SAW

the bloom or mist vanishes of its own accord, and then continue the polishing.

board In softwood it may be 4 in (102 mm) or more wide and under 2 in (51 mm) thick. In hardwood it may be of any width and up to $1\frac{1}{4}$ in (32 mm) thick.

boarded bed An early type of bed (14th to 16th century) which resembled an open box with low sides, and fitted with a straw palliasse or a feather mattress.

boarded chest A development of the basic 'dug-out' chest (*q.v.*). It consisted of six planks pegged together at the ends, each plank forming either one of the sides, the bottom, or the top. On early examples, often called *arks,* the sides were raised at the back and the lid was hinged into them on wooden pegs, thus forming a pivot. By the end of the 13th century iron strap hinges were used instead and the planks were smoothed off with an adze. (See *plank chest*).

boat bed This was a French Empire style, and was reminiscent of Greek and Roman classical designs. One side of the bed was set against the wall, and the head and foot ends were shaped to resemble the curved prow and stern of a boat. Drapes were suspended from a canopy above it.

bobbin sander A sander for concave shapes. The abrasive paper is fixed to a small rotating cylinder which also moves up and down; it is usually employed in conjunction with a large 24 in (610 mm) dia disc sander.

bodger A wood turner who worked in the Buckinghamshire beech woods, turning chair legs and spindles on a pole lathe. Now defunct.

Bodleian Windsor chair A comb-back chair of crude appearance with legs not turned but only shaved, and with no underframe. Used in Bodleian Library, Oxford, from 1766.

bodying After staining, filling, fadding, and colouring, the next stage in french polishing is bodying, in which the main body of polish is built up. A rubber is dipped into the polish and used with a circular or figure-of-eight movement. When the rubber becomes dry, it is recharged and the process repeated. It can be lubricated by dipping a finger in linseed oil and applying a spot of the oil on the centre of the pad. When rubbing, take care to touch all edges and corners of the work. Continue in this way until a gloss of polish is built up. Finally use a straight movement to take out any rubber marks. No oil must be used at this stage.

bog oak Fossilised oak found embedded in bogs. The wood is excessively hard and of a glossy black colour. So rare is it now that its sole use is for trinkets and similar small ornaments.

boiled oil (see *linseed oil*).

boil-resistant plywood These are classed as BR and will survive immersion in boiling water; they are suitable for severe weather conditions. The adhesive used is UMF *(q.v.)*.

boiserie French term for wood panelling, often painted or gilt.

bole The main trunk of a tree.

bolection moulding A moulding rebated at one edge to enable it to fit over a framework. The moulding thus stands out from the face of the work.

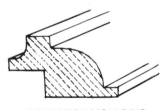

BOLECTION MOULDING

bolt (see under *carriage, handrail, etc.*).

bolt clearance circle The circular path of the fixing bolt at its greatest projection in the square cutter block of a spindle. Clearly the cutters at their minimum cutting point must project beyond this circle.

bombax *(bombax malabaricum)* Yellow-white wood from India, Ceylon and Burma. General utility wood for light purposes. Weight 22-25 lb (352-400 kg). The cotton tree of India.

bombé A form of compound curvature in furniture in which the front surface of a cabinet bellies forward and is curved in both plan and elevation. It is usually associated with French work of the Louis XV period.

bone dry Term sometimes used in connection with the moisture content of timber. It is applied to wood which has been heated in an oven until no more moisture is given up. Also known as oven dry.

bonnet guard A circular hat-like guard used over a spindle-moulder head in conjunction with a ring fence *(q.v.)*. It is, of course, a safety measure.

bonnet-top A kind of swan-neck pediment used in the USA; it should be covered from front to back and not just a fascia.

book carrier A small tray, with a gallery on three sides, for carrying books from library shelves to the reading table.

bookcases (1) These, in modern days, have to be restricted in size to the floor space available. So-termed 'dwarf' bookcases may be 54 in (1371 mm) in height, but are often 36 in (914 mm) and even lower. In planning, waste of timber may be avoided: (1) by keeping shelves to the appropriate width and (2) by fitting them to accommodate books of standard size without unnecessary clearance room. Few books exceed 7 in (178 mm) in width (few indeed exceed 6 in) (153 mm) and thus 8 in (203 mm) is usually ample for carcase depth. If, however, the case is over 4 ft (1219 mm) in height the question of balance is important and it may be desirable to add a plinth or to allow the ends to project an inch or so at floor level.

bookcases (2) As such, bookcases date back to the Restoration period (circa 1660), being preceded by bookshelves, which were used from the 16th century onwards; in fact, Samuel Pepys (the English diarist) had some bookcases made about 1668. By the middle of the next century (1750) they were found in library rooms of large houses and generally comprised a low cupboard with drawers above, surmounted by the bookshelves which were enclosed by glass doors, the whole being topped by an ornate pediment or cornice. Frequently, wing bookcases were added and these were usually not so deep as the main case so that the whole piece became a break-front bookcase. Alternative designs for accommodating smaller numbers of books were the bureau-bookcase and the secretaire-bookcase: the former was a glazed cabinet with shelves which was mounted on a sloping-front bureau, while the latter was a similar cabinet on a vertical-front secretaire. (See also *revolving bookcase*.)

bookcase-bureau   (see *bookcase (2)*).

book matching   (see *'halved pattern'*).

boot-jack chair   (USA) So-called because of the shape of the pierced banister, which resembled the appliance used to remove jack boots.

borax   An ingredient of some strippers and certain water varnishes.

boring tools   (see under various headings: *bits, brace, bradawl, drills, gimlet, etc.*).

Borneo rosewood   Alternative name for red zebra *(q.v.)*.

boss   A decorative block used over the intersection of two timbers, generally in ceilings. It is usually carved, but sometimes turned.

bosting   A term used in wood carving to describe the main modelling of the wood before carving the detail.

Boston Rocker   (USA) Also popular in Britain, this rocking chair was probably a development of the Windsor rocking chair *(q.v.)*, and dates back to the turn of the 18th/19th centuries. It is characterised by a broad top back rail which is often decorated with painted stencil designs; a tall spindle back and a planked seat: it was almost always painted. (See also *Brother's rocker; Hitchcock rocker.*)

bottle turning   Turning used in table and chair legs, etc., and staircase balustrading. So called because of the similarity to the shape of a bottle.

bottoming   The process of adzing out the saddle seat of a Windsor chair.

boule   A term used in the British timber trade to describe the butt of a tree which has been sawn through-and-through and is sold as one complete unit; the planks are, of course, waney-edged and the two outer planks are mainly bark and are called 'slabs' *(q.v.)*.

Boulle   This is the term applied to a type of marquetry developed by Andre Charles Boulle (1642 to 1732) a French *maitre-ebeniste* from Paris. Although it is doubtful if he invented the process, he was instrumental in developing and refining it. The method was to glue one or more thin sheets of tortoiseshell to a similar number of brass sheets, alternating them in a 'sandwich'; a paper pattern was glued to the top sheet and the whole thing was cut out

by a saw. When separated, a sheet of brass would be combined with one of tortoiseshell and, as the brass predominated, the combination would be called *première partie* (first part), and the converse where tortoiseshell was the main component was called *contre-partie*, or counterpart. The brass was often engraved and contrasted with other materials such as silver, pewter, mother-of-pearl, or shells.

The demand for boulle work died out towards the end of the 18th century but a similar technique called 'Buhl' was introduced to England in the early 19th century (see *Buhl*).

bow back   A hoop-shaped back bent from ash or yew, associated with the Windsor chair *(q.v.)*.

bow front   A term applied to any piece of furniture which is rounded in plan at the front. Examples are bow-front sideboard, chest, wardrobe, etc.

bow-saw   A frame-saw made from beech for taking blades which are tensioned by a cord or a threaded rod at the lugs of the frame. The ends of the blade are secured by a knob and handle by which the blade can be turned to facilitate cutting shapes in boards.

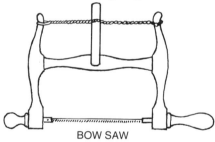

BOW SAW

box bed   A 16th century design of bed which was enclosed on two or three sides by panelling, the open side or sides being fitted with curtains. The top was covered with a flat tester. Often they were fitted with shelves under the bed to hold linen.

box corner joint   (USA) A corner joint for boxes, cases, etc. which corresponds to the British comb joint *(q.v.)*. (Illustrated on p. 19.)

box corner moulding   A double-grooved moulding by means of which boxes, clockcases, and other small items can be assembled quickly. Panels of plywood or thin wood are cut to size and glued in the grooves. (See also *corner cover moulding.*) (Illustration on p. 19.)

boxed frame   The hollow window frame in which the counter-weight of the sashes run. When there are

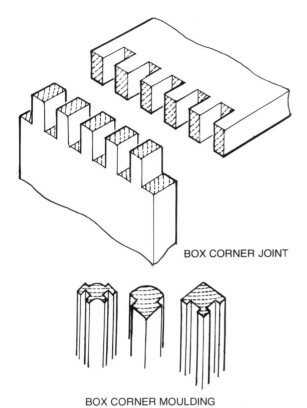

BOX CORNER JOINT

BOX CORNER MOULDING

two sliding sashes the weights are separated by a loose feather or parting strip, sometimes known as a wagtail, fixed at the top only.

boxed heart   Timber so converted that the centre pith or heart is contained within a centre square.

boxed tenon   A type of double tenon, the two parts in the form of an L. Used chiefly in corner posts.

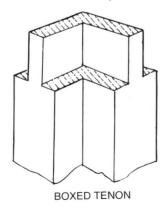

BOXED TENON

box nail   (USA) Corresponds to British french nail (*q.v.*).

box stretchers   Usually found on Windsor chairs; describes the positioning of underframe rails in the form of a box.

box-wood (*buxus sempervirens*)   A hard, heavy, and close-grained timber with remarkable resistance and a beautifully smooth surface. Its chief uses have been for engravers' blocks, lathe chucks, tool handles, scales and rules, inlaid strings, ornamental boxes, and small turnery. Weight 55-60 lb (881-961 kg).

box for inlaying   A long box open at top and bottom with either a screw or wedge fitting at one end. Used to hold tapered or turned legs whilst being inlaid. The scratch stock is worked against the side of the box, the leg being so held that the side of the box is parallel with the required path of the cutter.

boys and crowns   An old-fashioned description of the motif often found on Restoration furniture, particularly chairs and day-beds and consisting of a central crown supported on either side by *putti* which were naked small boys, similar to amorini (*q.v.*).

brace   Used for boring holes in wood. It has a chuck to hold various kinds and sizes of bits. It can be of either the simple plain type or the ratchet kind. The latter can be used in a corner, the handle being moved through part of the sweep only, the return stroke leaving the bit stationary in the wood. Size of brace is known by the amount of the sweep.

brace, door   The diagonal member fitted to a door to prevent sagging. Most braced doors are made from matchboarding held together with ledges. The brace is recessed into the ledges as shown: the brace must rise diagonally from the hinge side to the outside edge.

bracket   This may be a simple piece of wood, shaped at one end and hinged at the other to a table frame, the purpose being to support a leaf. Another form of bracket, generally built up, is used to support shelves, etc. If made flat, as shown at (A), the bracket is more suitable for hingeing to the framework of a folding flap wall table. The type at (B) is more suitable for screwing to a wall for shelves, cupboards, etc. There are also metal brackets (D), plain or with struts. Corner brackets are often fitted to chair frames, stands, etc., to strengthen the joints (C). The term bracket also refers to a decorative return for the cut string (*q.v.*) of a staircase. (illustration on p. 20.)

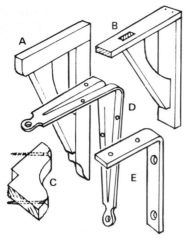

BRACKETS

bracket clocks A style of clock which probably evolved from the lantern clock, and which first appeared in Holland about 1670. The movements (clockwork) were spring-driven and controlled by short bob pendulums; many additional functions such as repeaters, calendars, chimes, automated figures, etc. were incorporated. Designs imitated the hood features of long case clocks, although (as the name implies) the clocks were intended to stand on brackets.

bracketed staircase One having a string *(q.v.)* with decorative brackets forming returns for the risers *(q.v.)*.

bracket foot A corner support for a case piece of furniture comprising two pieces butting against each other to form a corner; the pieces were shaped to one or other of the styles illustrated. This type of foot was introduced in the early 18th century and was greatly favoured by Thomas Chippendale.

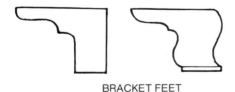

BRACKET FEET

brad A cut nail slightly tapering in width but of equal thickness. Largely used for flooring.

bradawl Used mostly for making nail or screw holes. Blade sizes range from about $\frac{1}{32}$ in (1 mm) to $\frac{1}{8}$ in (3 mm) or so in diameter. The tang of the blade fits into a hardwood handle. The cutting edge must be kept sharp by filing and honing on an oilstone. The edge of the blade should be *across* the grain, not *with* it. When screwing, the bradawl is used for making the hole for the thread of the screw. The brace and bit are used for making the larger shank hole. (See *birdcage-maker's awl* and *marking awl*.)

Braganza foot A style of foot found originally on Portuguese furniture and which became popular in England because of its association with the wife of Charles II, Catherine de Braganza, who was Portuguese.

BRAGANZA FOOT

brass, glue for Use freshly made Scotch glue, and stir in a little plaster of Paris. A little garlic or onion also increases the strength and keeps the glue fresh. Alternatively add a teaspoonful of Venice turpentine.

brass inlay (see *Boulle* and *Buhl*).

bratticing Pierced or open carved work as in church screens.

Brazilian walnut (see *imbuya*).

Brazil nut Sometimes used to take off whiteness of scratches in french polished surface. It is broken and rubbed over the scratch.

Brazil wax Alternative name for carnauba wax *(q.v.)*.

break This refers to a change in direction of a surface, moulding or other similar part.

breakfast table A small table to seat one or two persons. It had narrow hinged flaps along the long sides, and an undershelf. The framing often contained fretted panels — a favourite device used by Chippendale.

break-front The front of a piece of furniture in œœich the centre portion stands forward by 2 or 3 in (50 or 75 mm).

breaking down The preliminary sawing or opening up of a log.

breaking through The process of cutting through the false wooden fence of a spindle moulder. The false fence is attached to the metal fence and is continuous. It is placed clear of the cutters, the spindle set in motion, and slowly moved forward so that the cutters break through and project as required.

breast drill A breast drill differs from a hand drill *(q.v.)* in that a more powerful thrust is obtained by the use of a breast plate, leaving both hands free for steadying the tool and turning the handle. Although intended primarily for drilling holes in metal, it is also invaluable for woodwork. (See *electric drill* and *hand drill.*)

bressumer A beam which was a partner to the rood beam in the structure of a rood loft. The loft was situated under the rood *(q.v.)* and apart from giving access for cleaning the rood, it often served as a musicians' gallery.

Brewster chair (USA) An armchair named after William Brewster (1567 to 1644) who was an elder of the Plymouth plantation. It is characterised by the use of a great number of turned spindles, with two rows in the back and two more between the front legs; the seat was rush-covered.

briar teeth The hook-shaped teeth of some circular saws.

BRIAR TEETH

brick groundwork A built-up form of groundwork for veneered shaped work in which short grain is reduced to a minimum. Good quality softwood is used, and the layers built up brick fashion with the joints staggered. When a bandsaw is available the bricks are cut about $\frac{1}{2}$ in (12 mm) extra wide so that the whole can be sawn to shape afterwards. For handwork the bricks are to just over the finished size, and care taken to build up vertically.

Bridgwater dresser A dresser in which both the cupboard base and the upper shelves are built as integral parts of the design and cannot be separated, because the uprights supporting the shelves and upper part extend to the base and form part of the cupboard framing. Bridgwater is a West Country town in Somerset, England. (See also *dressers.*)

bridle joint Often used at the top of the centre leg of a cabinet having three legs at the front. It enables the top rail to run right through. Also often used for fixing the uprights of a firescreen to the feet.

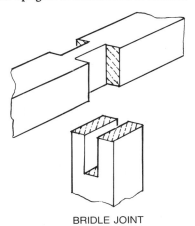

BRIDLE JOINT

brocade Furnishing fabric usually made from rayon, cotton, or synthetic materials, and having a raised figuring or pattern.

brocatelle An imitation brocade in coarse silk or cotton.

broken arch pediment (see *swan-neck pediment*).

Brother's Rocker (USA) Designed and made by the Shakers (an American religious sect) and used from the early 19th century; these chairs had a tall, slim ladder-type back, and a woven taped seat *(q.v.)*. The stumps (that is, the front supports for the arms) were extensions of the front legs and terminated in mushroom-shaped knobs above the arms. The ladder back enabled it to be hung up on a peg driven into the wall to save space.

Broughton countersink An attachment which, when fixed to a shell bit, enables the screw hole and its countersinking to be executed in one operation. It can be fixed in any position along the shank of the bit, being held by the set-screw which engages with the groove.

brown furniture British antique-dealers' term for 18th century mahogany furniture.

brown oak A variety of English oak which has suffered a form of decay known as foxiness. The strength is not affected, and the wood assumes a most attractive warm brown colour.

brown polish Generally refers to polish made from orange or garnet shellac, though it sometimes denotes shellac polish to which a spirit-soluble powdered stain has been added. (See *french polish*.)

brown umber A brown pigment which can be worked up in water or turps. Mixed with water and bound with glue size it makes a cheap water coating. Also used to tint plaster of paris when used for filling dark oak.

bruise An indentation on a wood surface caused by a blow. Can usually be raised in solid wood by applying a hot iron over a damp rag.

Brunswick black A thick black liquid drying with a shine. Often thinned out with turps. to make a floor stain. Should be fixed with french polish or varnish.

brush box (*tristania conferta*) A strong, firm wood, yellow in colour, from New South Wales, used chiefly for tool handles. Weight about 60 lb (961 kg).

bruzze A tool resembling a parting tool as used by a wood carver, but heavier and bevelled at the inside. It was used by wheelwrights for chopping mortices in the nave of the wheel. In the trade it is often known as a 'buzz'.

BRUZZE

bubble (in veneer) An area of veneer which has lifted away from the groundwork. In old work it is generally necessary to cut through with a thin knife, work in fresh glue, and cramp a block over the top with paper interposed.

bubinga (*copaifera arnoldiana*) A West African wood used in furniture making, generally in veneer form sometimes known as kevazingo. Reddish brown in colour. Weight 53 lb (849 kg).

bucket bench (USA) A small bench with a cupboard beneath to store buckets.

buckle-back Windsor chair Has a central back stay pierced to resemble a belt-buckle; the backstands (*q.v.*) have two scratched grooves.

buckram Originally a thin fabric of cotton and linen used in early 14th century for drapes and covers. From the early 15th century it refers (and does today) to canvas stiffened with glue and paste.

buck saw (USA) A wooden frame saw for rough sawing such as cutting up logs etc.

buffet In 1603, this was described by Sir Thomas Kyton as 'a thing like stayres to set plate on'. In other words, it comprised a set of shelves joined together and arranged above each other, which displayed plate; the greater the number of shelves, the more important the owner. Thus, Cardinal Wolsey had one with six shelves, and Henry VIII nine or ten. The shelves were draped when in use, often with sumptuous carpets. There were also portable designs which had no backs or canopies, which could be dismantled for travelling.

Buhl This is the name given to a method of inlaying brass similar to that used in Boulle (*q.v.*). It was brought to England by emigrés after the French Revolution, and the best-known was Louis Caigneur who started a Buhl factory in London about 1820.

built-up Refers to construction when two or more pieces of timber are glued together to give the required width or thickness. Frequently the building-up is local only to save the wastage involved in using large timber, much of which would be cut away as waste.

built-up patterns, veneer Term used for veneered panels in which different woods or varying direction of grain are used to give a decorative pattern.

bulbous Turned legs or balusters in which the centre part is swollen, often beyond the size of the squares above and below (see *cup and cover; melon bulb*). A characteristic of late Elizabethan and Jacobean woodwork.

bullace (*prunus insititia*) The wild plum tree; its wood was sometimes used in conjunction with satinwood or ebony in 16th century furniture. Also called 'bullet wood'.

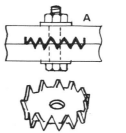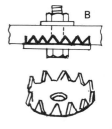

BULLDOG TIMBER CONNECTORSORS (See over)

bulldog connectors   These are steel discs with a central hole for a bolt fixing; they have pronged teeth both sides and are suitable for most forms of light timber construction where wood-to-wood fixing is needed.

bull's eye mirror   A popular description of a small circular mirror with either a concave or convex glass, surrounded by a carved and gilt frame; they were popular in the early years of the 19th century and have enjoyed a recent revival.

bull-nose plane   A small metal plane, resembling a shoulder plane but with shortened nose which enables the tool to be worked up fairly close to corners of stopped rebates, chamfers, etc. The nose, in some cases, is adjustable or detachable, enabling the plane to work right into a corner.

BULLNOSE PLANE

bullnose step   The bottom-most step of stairs, one end of which is rounded in plan to give a neat finish.

bun foot   A turned wooden foot resembling a flattened ball, used from late 17th century onwards.

bureau (1)   The term has never been clearly defined but today it refers to a cabinet of drawers surmounted by a writing compartment with a fall-front. The compartment contains pigeon-holes, drawers, etc, and the fall-front acts as a writing surface when open. The name was not used until the end of the 17th century, and what today are called bureaux would then have been called escritoires, scriptors, scrutoires, secretaires.

bureau (2)   In the USA this describes a chest of drawers, with or without a mirror, for use in the bedroom.

bureau plat   A writing table on tall legs, with a flat top with drawers beneath. Originated in France at the end of the 17th century.

bureau-toilette   A piece of bedroom furniture used by ladies for their toilet, and for writing letters.

burl   Alternative term for burr (2) *(q.v.)*. Also used in the USA.

burnished finish   Suitable only for dense hardwoods. Produced by rubbing over the surface with a bone, polished steel, or other hard instrument.

burnisher   A short length of hardened steel rod set in a handle and used to turn the edge of a cabinet scraper. Also known as a ticketter *(q.v.)*.

burnt sienna   A warm, brown pigment used in making stains, stoppings, etc.

burnt umber   Cold brown pigment used in making stains stopping etc.

burr (1)   A wire-like edge formed when sharpening a plane cutter or chisel on an oilstone. It must be removed by stropping on the hand or on a leather strop. The only tools from which the burr is not removed are the wood spokeshave, some turning tools, and cabinet scrapers — the last-named depend on burrs for their cutting action.

burr (2)   A special figuring in some woods formed from a curious wart-like excrescence which develops, usually towards the base of the tree. What happens is that a number of buds or eyes begin to grow but are unable to develop fully owing to lack of nutriment. A cut through such a burr reveals its characteristic appearance, which is like a number of small knots packed closely together in a convoluted formation. Solid wood in this form is useless owing to the difficulty of working the wild grain, but in some veneers considerable use is made of burrs. Typical woods are ash, elm, maple, walnut, and yew.

butler's tray   A tray mounted on legs, or more usually, on a folding stand; first made about 1750 and popular throughout the 18th and 19th centuries. The tray could be either rectangular, or kidney shaped.

butt   The bottom end of a tree from the ground to the point where the main branches begin.

butterfly table   So-called because of the resemblance of the gate support to a butterfly's wing; the style originated in the William and Mary period.

butt gauge   A small all-metal gauge used by carpenters and joiners for marking the recesses for butt hinges on room doors, three separate marks being required: (1) the thickness of the butt hinge, (2) the depth on the door, and (3) the depth on the jamb. The two latter markings are necessary as allowance has to be made for the thickness of the paint on both door and jamb. There are thus three markers on the gauge, and when that giving the door depth is set, the second cutter is set automatically to the jamb. Butt gauges have other uses, one of which is the marking of lines close up to the corner of a rebate.

butt hinges   These are brass or steel hinges which are sunk flush in cabinet doors, etc.

butt joint   Simple joint in which joining parts are merely cut square. That at (A) is used in rough carpentry work, box making, etc. Nails are used as well as glue. When making up widths it is usual to butt joint the edges of boards together with glue as at (B). If only glue is used, the edges of the boards must be planed straight and the excess glue rubbed out and the work set aside to dry. When narrow boards are being joined, there should be a slight hollow in the middle so that pressure from a sash cramp closes the gap and gives extra pressure at the ends.

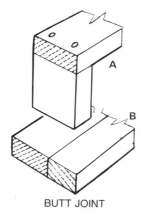

BUTT JOINT

button   A device used to fix cabinet and table tops, or the stands of cabinets. It gives a rigid fixing yet allows for shrinkage. A screw passes through the hole into the top, and the projecting tongue enters a groove cut in the rail.

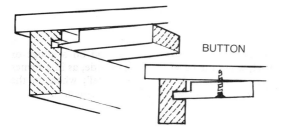

BUTTON

buttoning   In upholstery, a method of holding interior stuffing in place by means of buttons arranged in a pattern on the upholstery cover. They can be either tied in place or fixed by means of a bifurcated snape (q.v.).

button polish   A yellowish french polish which tends to be slightly opaque, but which is most durable. Made from 6 oz (17 grams) button shellac dissolved in one pint (0.56 litre) methylated spirit.

button shellac   Yellowish brown shellac used in making button polish.

C

cabin bed   Also called a 'shut' bed, this was a kind of bunk with wooden boards which fitted into an alcove in a wall. Sometimes two tiers high, it was used in Saxon times.

cabin hook   A small hook and eye originally used on cabin doors aboard ship but also used to fasten cabinet doors and flaps.

cabinet bolt   A small bolt, generally brass or chromium-plated, for screwing to the back of a cabinet door. It is not recessed into the wood.

cable moulding   Carved around a half-round moulding in imitation of rope.

cabochon   Carved detail having a raised or convex shaping.

cabriolet   A French dining chair with a small back to allow waiters to pass between.

cabriole leg   A type of leg which appeared in England during the Queen Anne period and based on the French *pied de biche* — cabriole is a French dancing term for a bound or leap. The leg is cut from a square and as a rule there is a top square into which the rails are jointed. Ear pieces are often glued on at each side and the leg terminates in a club foot, claw and ball, lion's paw, eagle's claw, or hoof, etc. In a well-shaped leg the knee is high and flat and from the knees downwards the leg should taper until the ankle is reached no matter from which angle it is viewed. Often the knee is carved with an acanthus motif, or a shell, husks, a lion's head, or a mask.

caffoy   Cut woollen velvet used for upholstery, early 18th century.

cage guard A guard used on a spindle moulder (*q.v.*).

cake stands These usually have a height of 3 ft (914 mm), with three cake platters about 9 in (229 mm) in diameter pivoted between the uprights and hinged to a back strut. To keep the platter open and held thus, a metal stay is affixed between one platter and the back strut. Platters may be circular or octagonal in shape, being either recessed in a lathe on the face side or fitted with an applied rim.

callipers Gauges for measuring inside or outside diameters of circular or tubular objects. There are two types: one for inside gauging and another for exterior diameters. The latter are in constant use in wood-turning. They are either plain, with a rigid hexagonal nut at joint, or are provided with spring and adjustment screw.

cambium The cells which lie just beneath the bark of a tree or plant; they are responsible for the transmission of the sap.

cambric An inexpensive cotton fabric resembling linen and formerly used for upholstering.

cam clamps A clamp with a deep throat; pressure is applied by cocking a cam.

came A moulded and grooved strip of lead used in making some glazed doors and windows. The glass is embedded in a composition in the grooves.

camel back A kind of serpentine-shaped top rail used by Hepplewhite (circa 1780) on chairs and settees.

camlet A furnishing fabric, being a mixture of silk, wool, and hair; used in the early 18th century for curtains and wall hangings.

campaigning chair A collapsible chair for use on military campaigns (circa 1800); the seat, back, and arms were caned. All the parts could be dismantled, leaving an underframe which also folded and which was fitted with brackets so that staves could be inserted to render it portable. Advertised by Morgan and Sanders, of London.

camphor Used in some furniture revivers.

camphorated oil Sometimes used to remove heat and water marks from furniture. Consists of 4 parts nut oil and 1 part camphor.

camphorwood (True *cinnamomum camphora.*) From China and the Far East. Difficult to obtain. About 40½ lb (650 kg). Light brown colour, strongly scented.

Borneo camphorwood *(dryabalanops aromatica)* is not botanically related to the true camphorwood, but has a similar scent when newly cut. About 48 lb (769 kg). Works well but not a good polishing timber. It is more generally known in Britain as Kapur as it is not related to the true camphor wood.

East African camphorwood *(Ocotea usambarensis)* again is not related to true camphorwood, but has similar scent. About 35 lb (561 kg). Resists fungal attack. It is not a true member of the camphorwood family.

canarium *(canarium schweinfurthii)*, also known as aieli. From East and West Africa. About 33 lb (529 kg). Rather coarse textured. Pinkish brown colour.

canary-whitewood *(liriodendron tulipifera)* or American whitewood, is the timber produced from the great tulip tree of eastern USA and Canada. Light in weight 28-29 lb (449-465 kg) it is easily worked and is used for all kinds of interior woodwork, mouldings, kitchen furniture, piano construction, and as a groundwork for veneering. For outdoor work it is unsuitable on account of its liability to decay in damp situations.

candel beam A wooden crossbeam fitted with spikes or sockets for candles on the arms and suspended from the ceiling or roof. Used in medieval times.

candle board A small shelf or ledge fitted under a table top which swings out on a pivot to support a candle-stick. A device often used by Sheraton.

candle screen A small glass or wooden screen to protect a candle flame from draughts. Some were mounted on a tripod base, while others were of the 'horse' design with the panel sliding up and down between two uprights.

cane Used for chair seats and backs, and panels generally from the mid-seventeenth century.

cannel The angle of bevel ground on a gouge or chisel; when the bevel is on the outside, as in a firmer gouge, it is described as 'out-cannel'; when on the inside as in a scribing gouge it is 'in-cannel'.

cant An inclination or angle as in a bevel.

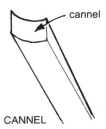

CANNEL

canteen, cutlery A container for table cutlery. It may have a hinged lid, or be fitted with drawers. In some cases it takes the form of a table. The interior is specially fitted up to hold the items, and is lined with baize or felt.

canterbury A small, low stand on castors with a single drawer with vertical divisions above to hold sheet music, rather in the style of the modern magazine rack. An alternative form held plates and cutlery, and Sheraton suggested that the name derived from the Archbishop of Canterbury, who ordered the first one.

cantilever chair A chair which dispenses with front legs, the seat and back being cantilevered on a frame which forms the feet. Normally made in metal, some have been designed to employ laminated wood bends, and are contemporary in style.

cantoon A kind of stout fustian *(q.v.)* with a corded surface on one side and a smooth surface on the other.

cant rail Fencing rail with top edge at angle to throw off moisture.

canvas Sometimes used in making tambour doors. The best, fine mesh quality should be used. It is also used in upholstery, particularly on the underside of chair seats.

capital Member at the top of a pillar or pilaster beneath the entablature. Each architectural period or style has its own designs, and there are many variations.

capping rail Usually refers to the top rail of a fence, the top edges sloping to throw off moisture.

capstan table Another name for a drum table *(q.v.)*.

captain's chair (USA) An American design of Windsor chair (c 1860 to 1865) used in the pilot houses of Mississippi river steamers.

caquetoire Also called 'caqueteuse' or 'gossip' chair. A joyned chair of the 16th century based on a French design.

carbon tetrachloride Used to degrease oily woods when gluing.

carborundum powder An abrasive powder used in the fine grade for blackboard coatings. Also used with oil to rub down worn oilstones.

carcase The term applies to the skeleton framework of an article of furniture (e.g. sideboard, bookcase, cabinet, wardrobe, etc.) before doors, drawers, plinths, cornices, and other parts are fitted. When a carcase is completed it is spoken of as being 'assembled'. During gluing it is tested repeatedly for squareness and freedom from winding, and the framed or plywood back is often fitted to keep the structure rigid.

carcass An alternative spelling (USA) for carcase *(q.v.)*.

carcassing A site term covering carpentry framework in building structures such as stud walls; refers to the un-clad components.

card-cut A term applied to fret or lattice work which is blind; i.e. not pierced.

card table A table intended specially for card playing. The height is 27-29 in (685-736 mm), and the top varies from 20 in (508 mm) up to 35 in (889 mm) square, and it may be rigid or made to fold in two. Other types have a detachable top with folding legs. When the top is intended to fold and is pivoted the pivoting point is found as in drawing. Draw in top in

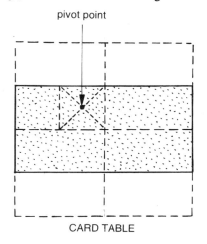

pivot point

CARD TABLE

full size in closed position and mark centre lines. Draw a square using the two centre lines and edge of top as three of the sides. Put in diagonals, intersection of which is pivoting point. Generally a rail is dovetailed to the rails to enable the pivot to be fixed. The pivot and special hinges are shown below. The hinges are of the double-throw type leaving no projection at the top.

card table fittings   Pivot for top is shown at A. B is spring clip sometimes used when table has pivoted counter and ash-tray cups. Edge double-throw hinge is at C, and surface type at D. There are no projecting knuckles on the surface. Both types are let in flush.

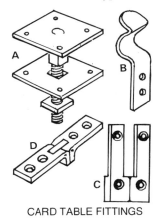

CARD TABLE FITTINGS

Cardigan stick-back chair   A crude form of Windsor chair with a bent arm forming the back, a flat U-shaped seat, and three plain legs; 18th century.

Carlton House table   A writing table on four slender legs and fitted with a drawer in the carcase; the top is D-shaped and is surrounded by a gallery enclosing small cupboards and drawers. Originally introduced about 1770 it was given its name in 1796, presumably because one was made for Prince George at Carlton House, London.

carnauba wax   A hard vegetable wax often added to beeswax when making wax polish. It has the property of making the polish harder than when beeswax alone is used. It is also used on its own for polishing turnery.

carriage bolts   These bolts are black, round-headed, square-shouldered, partly threaded, and have square nuts. They have many uses in woodwork. They are obtainable 1 in (25 mm) long by $^3/_{16}$ in (5 mm) thick up to 16 in (406 mm) long by $^1/_2$ in (12 mm) thick. The latter is a special size used under the rungs of ladders.

A special feature is that the head shouldering prevents the bolt shank from turning when tightening or removing the nuts. In softwood the shouldering makes a bed for itself, but in hardwoods a square recess should be cut with a chisel. The nut should have a washer to prevent biting into the wood.

CARRIAGE BOLT

carriage clocks   These clocks were used by their owners on journeys and were not fitted to carriages. They were spring-driven and balance-controlled; the majority had metal cases although some were made in wood.

carriage piece   A rail fixed beneath the centre of a flight of stairs to strengthen it.

carriage screws   These are a type of bolt which is tapered and threaded like an ordinary wood screw, but has a square head without a slot. It therefore has to be turned home with a spanner, and a washer should always be used beneath the head.

carriage varnish   A hard oil varnish suitable for either inside or outside work.

cartonnier   Originally a low cupboard with open shelves, sometimes surmounted by a clock built into the framework. Also, a flat topped writing table with drawers under the top, and with cabriole legs.

carton pierre   A type of French papier-mache which was improved by George Jackson & Sons Ltd, of Hammersmith, London, and was used in much the same way as gesso for mouldings and ornaments.

cartouche   Carved detail in the form of a scroll on which lettering or a crest is carved or painted.

carver chair   Term popularly used in England to differentiate the armchair from accompanying small or side chairs in the suite.

Carver chair   (USA) An American chair, usually made from ash, hickory, or maple, with a rush seat. Named after John Carver (1575 to 1621), a prominent New England leader. The chair was made during the period 1660 to 1700.

carver rack cramp   A small metal cramp having its threaded portion at right angles to the shaft.

carver's burrs These are attached to a flexible shaft driven by an electric motor, and are milled to grind away the wood rather than to cut it. Made in a variety of sizes and shapes.

carver's chisel Made in the various forms shown here. The straight chisel (A) is the most generally used form. The corner chisel (B) is similar but is ground at an angle. For cleaning out acute corners the spoon or entering chisel (C) is used. Spade chisels (D) and long pod spade chisel (E) are lighter versions of chisels used for finishing, lettering, etc. The long spade chisel (F) is the form in which larger chisels are generally made. Tools (A, B, D, E, and F) are sharpened equally on both sides. (C) has the main bevel beneath but is usually given a smaller secondary bevel at the top. Some of the lighter tools are also made unshouldered.

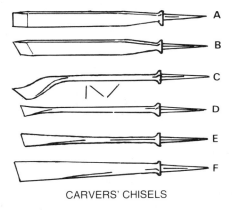

CARVERS' CHISELS

carver's gouges Chief types are shown here. A. Straight, used for bulk of work; B. Curved, for deep work where straight gouge cannot reach; C. Front

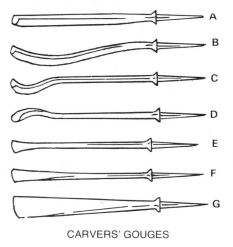

CARVERS' GOUGES

bent, for acute curves; D. Back bent, for awkward recesses; E. Fish tail, delicate finishing work; F. Long pod, similar uses to above; G. Long spade. All are obtainable in wide range of sizes and degrees of curvature.

carving planes These have a spoon-shaped handle and shave off wood, rather than plane it. Made with curved and flat soles.

carving tools (see under separate headings — *chisel, gouge, mallet, screw, strop, etc.*).

caryatid A carved figure supporting an entablature. Sometimes the figure springs from a form of pilaster.

case furniture A term describing furniture which is designed to contain things, such as cabinets, bureaux and the like; as opposed to furniture which stands, such as tables, chairs, stools etc.

case-hardening Wood which through faulty seasoning has been dried at the outside too quickly. Stress is set up so that in any subsequent conversion the wood may spring out of shape.

casein glue A cold glue which is considerably more water-resistant than animal glue. It is derived from skimmed milk, and is available in the form of a whitish powder. Most caseins are used cold, though some special hot-setting varieties are available. All joints need to be cramped because the glue is not of a tacky nature. One disadvantage is that most caseins are liable to stain woods such as oak, mahogany, and other woods having an acid content. Many of the non-staining varieties are not free from the trouble. Oxalic acid is used to remove the stain.

casement A glazed frame or sash which is either hinged or pivoted as distinct from one which slides.

casting The twisting or warping of a board out of truth. May be due to faulty seasoning or caused by the pull of veneer on one side.

castors These are made in many forms. Chief fixings are: round socket, square socket, screw, spring peg, plate. The wheel may be metal, plastic, wood, or rubber tyred. There is also the ball castor. For tea trolleys a special large size wheel is made for riding over carpets, and often a spring is incorporated to help the movement. For heavy duty a ball-bearing type is used. There are also special proprietary types of spherical form which give extremely easy movement.

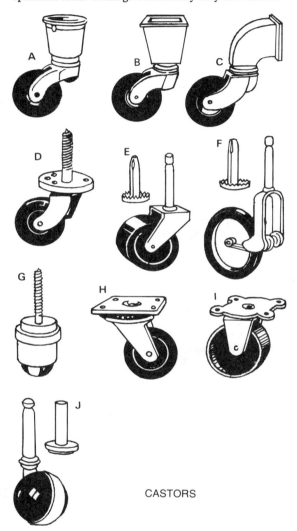

CASTORS

castor types A, round socket; B, square socket; C, tripod socket; D, screw-plate; E, peg and sleeve; F, trolley table; G, ball; H, ball-bearing; I, plate; J, easy movement.

cat A stand used in the middle of the 18th century to warm plates from which food was eaten in front of a fire; it consisted of three arms joined to three feet with slots or ridges to hold the plates.

catalyst lacquer; catalysed lacquer (see *lacquer (3)*).

caul A flat panel of wood or zinc used when veneering. It is heated and cramped down over the veneer with a sheet of newspaper between, the purpose being to press the veneer down on to the groundwork. Zinc cauls retain their heat longer but need to be backed with wood. Also used, especially in the USA, to describe blocks or pads that spread cramping pressure.

caustic potash (*potassium hydroxide*) Used to strip paint, polish, etc. In powder form to be dissolved in water. Both poisonous and harmful to touch. Open the container with care and wash well after use. Avoid splashes. Tends to darken some woods.

cavetto A hollow moulding. The curve may be circular or elliptical.

CAVETTO

cedar The red cedar (*cedrela*) of Central America is the fragrant timber familiar to all in cigar boxes. In this country, however, the wood is sometimes used for bent parts in light boats. African pencil cedar (*juniperus procera*), a softwood of the juniper family, is unrivalled in the pencil-making industry. Also Virginian pencil cedar (*juniperus virginiana*). The Western red cedar (*thuja plicata*) of British Columbia is a large tree which yields valuable timber for all classes of joinery, two of its great merits being that it is almost immune from warping and twisting, and its resistance to decay in severe climatic conditions.

cedar, Port Orford (*chamaecyparis lawsoniana*) A softwood from South Oregon and northern California; 30 lb (481 kg); light yellow to pale brown colour. It tends to be gummy and shrinks considerably during seasoning, but is durable and resists acids. Used for joinery and roof shingles.

ceiba (*ceiba* species) An African wood, about 30 lb (481 kg). Similar to bombax (*q.v.*). Light colour. Works easily but has little strength and is not resistant to decay. Does not polish well.

cellarette A tray, or a deep drawer in a sideboard, for housing bottles.

cellar fungus (*coniophora cerebella*) A form of wet rot attacking both hardwoods and softwoods. It causes rapid decay but does not usually spread. Decayed wood must be cut out and replaced, and source of dampness removed.

cellulose lacquer This is obtainable in a variety of colours for applying to metal or wood with brush or spray-gun. It is difficult to use with the brush over a large surface as it dries rapidly. Most cellulose polishes are intended to be applied with the spray though there are some varieties which can be put on with the rubber. They have the advantage of being largely heat- and damp-resistant. (See *lacquer (2)*.)

celour A backdrop of curtain material above the head of a bed. Also spelt 'celure'.

celtis (*celtis* species.) African timber of 50 lb (801 kg). Light colour, has interlocked grain, but works and finishes well.

centering A temporary timber erection to support the bricks or other components of an arch whilst being built.

centre bit This has a centre point, scriber or nicker, and cutter. It is fast-cutting in most woods and is obtainable for boring holes ¼ in (6 mm) to 2 in (51 mm) diameter. The cutter is sharpened with a file. The centre bit is not intended for boring deep holes; it is used mainly for making recesses for bolt heads, etc., or as a means of clearing away waste wood. It is not suitable for making holes in end grain, as it is liable to drift. The improved centre bit with centre screw in place of the point is easier in use, as the bit is drawn into the wood. Less pressure is necessary.

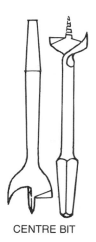
CENTRE BIT

centre hinges Straight pattern (A) used when centre is within thickness of the work, generally when there is a loose cornice (which must be screwed). Cranked pattern (B) brings centre to outer corner of door, and may be needed to clear other parts or other doors. Hinges are in pairs, that at bottom having raised collar or washer so that the two plates have clearance.

CENTRE HINGES

centre punch When drilling a hole in metal, the position should be first popped with a centre punch to prevent the drill moving out of position. It is also needed for wood when a morse drill is used.

centres Used to pivot wood at the tail stock of a lathe. Usual type is the ring centre (A). Small point gives centre, and ring resists side thrust. Flat channel between point and ring enables centre to push against work. Plain point centre (2) sometimes used in heavy work. The revolving centre (3) turns with the wood and reduces friction. Often useful when a supporting block has to be used between work in the three-jaw or cup chuck and the tail stock.

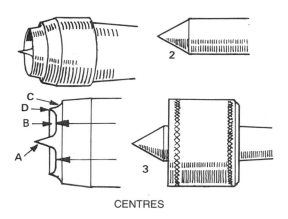
CENTRES

chain mortiser (see *chain mortising set*).

chain mortising set A set comprises a chain, a guide bar, and a driving sprocket; at the upper end of the guide bar is the driving sprocket and a tensioning device, and at the lower there is a roller which leads the chain through 180 degrees. A chip breaker is also fitted close to the upward side of the chain. The chain consists of an endless series of links with sharp hooked teeth which literally dig out the wood to form the mortise — it follows, therefore that as the lower end of the chain is following around the bottom roller it is bound to cut a mortise with a round bottom. In view of this it is normally only used to cut through mortises. The chains vary in width from about $^3/_{16}$ in. (4 mm) up to $1^1/_4$ in. (32 mm), and can be arranged side-by-side to achieve the requisite width of the mortise — three links or five links side-by-side are commonly used. The thinner chains naturally have links with a smaller pitch, and there are three pitch sizes.

chair bed An armchair (circa 1805) made specifically for use on military campaigns; it was also known as 'Butler's patent chair bed' after its designer Thomas Butler. The seat could be extended to form a bed, and poles could be inserted into sockets in the back and arms to carry a canopy and curtains.

chairmaker's brace By the nature of their work chairmakers often only need to bore holes of two or three diameters and consequently had a brace fitted with a fixed bit for each diameter.

chairmaker's saw Also known as a Betty saw. Although used mostly by chairmakers, this saw is useful for dealing with large shapes in cabinet work. It is a bow-saw, but, unlike the latter, is used vertically, the timber being cramped down on the bench and projecting over the edge sufficiently for clearance. The longer top arm is held by the right hand, and the vertical bar with the left hand.

chair nail An upholstery nail with a domed head; they can be 'close-nailed' or 'space-nailed' *(q.q.v.)*. When given an antique finish they are called 'antique' nails *(q.v.)*.

chairs The earliest designs of chairs developed from stools which have been used as seating since ancient classical times. Until about 1600, the term referred exclusively to chairs with arms, other types being called backstools; such armchairs were always reserved for the use of royalty or the nobility and there would probably have been only one in any establishment. (See under their individual headings.)

chair-table A small bench or chair which has a circular or oval back which is hinged so that it can be swung over to lie on the arms, where it is usually secured by pegs. Often (mistakenly) called a 'monks bench'; it did not appear until 30 or 40 years after the monasteries were dissolved about 1535.

chaise longue A low reclining couch, sometimes with wheels at one end for easy moving.

chaise Lorraine (see *backstool*).

chamber horse A late 18th century contrivance for exercising the occupant who sat on a leather-covered seat which had several compartments like a concertina. When sat on, the air was expelled and the seat sank down and the occupant pulled on two standards to lift himself as if riding a horse.

chamfer An angle planed at an edge. Its purpose is chiefly to lighten the appearance and, in the case of wagons and other vehicles, to reduce weight. Frequently the chamfer is stopped at one or both ends, the stop being fashioned in various decorative ways. A distinction sometimes made between bevel and chamfer is that the latter is a small flat surface worked at an edge, whereas a bevel is a sloping edge running across the entire thickness of the wood.

chamfer plane A separate adjustable sole is incorporated, the position of which controls the depth of the chamfer. The plane is seldom seen today.

chancel screen A screen dividing the chancel from the nave of a church. There were two designs made in wood, namely square-framed and arched; the former was in use prior to the end of the 14th century and was replaced by the latter style.

chariot plane Small metal plane with cutter near to front of sole. Will work up close to a stop. Almost obsolete today.

Charnley Forest oilstone A natural stone found in the Midlands. Gives fine edge but is slow cutting. Seldom used today.

chase mortise A joint used when a member has to be fixed between two pieces which are already in position. At the side of the mortise is a slot or chase which enables the stub-tenon to be pushed in sideways. The joint at the other end of the member is a normal stub-mortise and tenon.

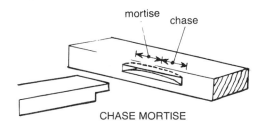

CHASE MORTISE

chatter Term applied to the digging-in action of a plane, usually caused by the cutter being ground at too low an angle, by its being at too high a pitch, or by not bedding properly on the frog. The cutting edge is bent back and downwards, flies up again, and so on, resulting in a series of unsightly marks across the wood. In a circular saw it refers to the noise set up when a piece of bent wood is being sawn hollow-side downwards.

check A term sometimes used for a rebate. Also refers to a split along the length of a board, generally across the annual rings. Often occurs during seasoning.

cheek A term applied to the sides of a tenon, or to the pieces sawn away in cutting the tenon. Sometimes also used for the sides of a mortise. It has also more general applications in various trades.

cheese coaster A boat-shaped dish on castors which contained a cheese; it was mounted on castors so that it could be pushed around the dining table.

chenchen (see *antiaris*).

cherry, African (see *makoré*).

cherry (European *prunus avium*, American *prunus serotina.*) Reddish colour, fairly hard, 33-45 lb (529-721 kg). Used in chair-making, brush backs, etc., but seldom available.

chest A receptacle for all kinds of household goods, including food when it was called an 'ark', *(q.v.)*. It differs from the coffer in that it had a flat lid and was not intended for travelling purposes. The first chests were 'dug-out' *(q.v.)* followed by the planked chest in the 15th century and the joined chest in the early part of the 16th century when framed-up (post and rail) construction was used.

Chesterfield An upholstered couch with adjustable drop-ends which are controlled by a mechanical action operated by a cord.

chestnut, sweet *(castanea sativa)* Similar in colour and grain to oak, but has no silver grain. Is easily worked and holds glue well. Weight 35 lb (561 kg).

chest of drawers By the end of the 16th century, the predecessors of chests of drawers had appeared and consisted of chests with sets of drawers underneath and it was not long before these evolved into cases containing drawers resembling the present-day pieces. By 1720 some designs appeared in which

the chests of drawers were mounted on a stand of table height, often with cabriole legs and a drawer with a shaped apron underneath.

chest on chest Also called a 'tallboy' *(q.v.)*. As its name implies, this piece comprised an upper set of drawers mounted on a lower set to form two chests, one on top of the other. The corners of the upper chest were often canted to make the design appear lighter.

cheval mirror A tall mirror giving a full-length view and supported on a frame. It occupies little floor space. An average size for mirror is 4 ft (1219 mm) by 18 in (457 mm), this being so hung that the top mirrors have now largely been superseded by frameless glasses clipped to a wood back. There are many styles for standards, these being connected by cross rails and furnished with splayed feet or with a plinth set on toes. Position for pivoting is just above the centre line of glass.

cheveret A small writing table, with a top about 18 in by 12 in (460× 305 mm) which sometimes opens out and is then supported on lopers; the characteristic feature is a portable book-trough with small drawers which stands on the table top. The table itself commonly contains drawers in the frieze beneath the top.

chevron A carved moulding of zig-zag form.

chiffonier Basically consisting of a cupboard (with interior shelves) surmounted by a set of open shelves; it originally became popular during the first half of the 19th century. It was convenient for use as a substitute for a sideboard in small dining-rooms: later designs (c 1880) became more ornate and often had a semi-circular mirror instead of the backboard. In France, the term described a tall chest of drawers.

Chiltern range A term describing the range of furniture available under the Utility Scheme during, and shortly after, the Second World War. It was superseded by the Cotswold range *(q.v.)*.

china cabinet A cabinet fitted with shelves and enclosed by two doors, with a case with glazed doors surmounting it. The case contained shelves for the display of china and porcelain. One of the earliest was made for Samuel Pepys in 1666.

china cupboard A piece of furniture resembling a sideboard in size and shape but with shelves for the display of china and porcelain; they were displayed behind an open fretwork of Chinese-Gothic design.

china stand An ornamental stand for displaying choice pieces of china.

Chinawood oil Another name for tung oil *(q.v.)*.

chintz Also spelt 'chint'. A cotton fabric printed or painted in colours or fast dyes, first imported from India in the early 17th century.

chipboard A manufactured board made usually in 12 mm and 18 mm thicknesses. They consist of small chips of wood impregnated with a synthetic adhesive and compressed under heat; the normal kind is compressed between heated rollers, but there is an extruded type which has facing veneers. These must not be grooved or otherwise cut as there is little lateral strength once the facings are cut. There is also a variety called 'stoutheart' which has a core of large chips sandwiched between layers of smaller chips. Special grades are manufactured to suit particular purposes such as flooring grades and moisture-resistant grades; and there is a wide variety of melamine-faced (plastic) boards, some displaying wood veneers and others showing patterns. Because of its composition chipboard cannot be machined satisfactorily as cut edges tend to break away, and in any case TCT *(q.v.)* cutters should be used.

chip breaker A device fitted to cutter blocks which turns and breaks the chip to give a better finish. (See *spindle moulder, surface planer,* and *china mortising set*.)

chip carving A simple means of decorating a surface with geometrical patterns. It consists of a series of recesses or pockets, the sides of which slope to the centre as shown. Special chip carving knives are available, but gouges and chisels can also be used. Vertical cuts are made along the centre lines and the wood sloped away at each side.

Chippendale bow-back Windsor chair Late eighteenth century chair with cabriole legs, pad feet, and pierced splat.

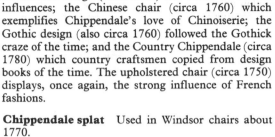

CHIPPENDALE
BOW-BACK
WINDSOR

Chippendale chairs Illustrated are four chairs: the Rococo design (circa 1750) was based on French influences; the Chinese chair (circa 1760) which exemplifies Chippendale's love of Chinoiserie; the Gothic design (also circa 1760) followed the Gothick craze of the time; and the Country Chippendale (circa 1780) which country craftsmen copied from design books of the time. The upholstered chair (circa 1750) displays, once again, the strong influence of French fashions.

Chippendale splat Used in Windsor chairs about 1770.

Chippendale Windsor chair A design which includes several of the following Chippendale characteristics: Cupid's bow shape top rail; well-shaped cabriole legs with carved husk decoration on the knee; cabriole legs at the back as well as the front; and a crinoline (cow-horn) stretcher *(q.q.v.)*.

chisels (see under separate types: *bevelled-edge, carver's, coachmaker's, cold, drawer lock, firmer, millwright's, mortise, parting, paring, registered, round-nosed turning, sash mortise, sash pocket, socket, swan neck, tang, turning.*)

chive Tool used by the cooper to cut the grooves to receive the head of a cask.

chloride of lime Used in the weathering process to impart a greyish tinge to oak.

choking Applied to a plane or machine in which the shavings or chips cannot escape freely, and cause a blockage. In a plane it is generally caused by a badly fitting back iron, or insufficient clearance at the mouth or escapement.

chuck A device to hold a cutter or boring bit in either a brace, drill, lathe, or other rotary machine. In a lathe the chuck usually serves to hold the work rather than the cutter. (See under individual types: *cup, drill, four-pronged, independent, Jacobs, prong, screw-point, scroll, self-centering, three jaw.*)

chuglum, white (see *silver-grey wood*.)

church oak varnish A hard, dark oil varnish suitable for outdoor and indoor work.

cinquefoil A Gothic design for tracery having five cusps.

circle on circle Work which has compound curvature, shaped in both plan and elevation.

circular saw This is made in a very wide range of sizes from about 4 in (102 mm) up to 60 in (1524 mm) or more, and in various gauges and types of teeth. The most useful sizes in the small workshop are from 7 to 10 in (178-254 mm). Power of motor required is generally:

saw size	h.p. of motor	saw size	h.p. of motor
7 in (178 mm)	$\frac{1}{3} - \frac{1}{2}$	14 in (356 mm)	2 — 3
8 in (203 mm)	$\frac{1}{2} - \frac{3}{4}$	16 in (407 mm)	3 — $4\frac{1}{2}$
10 in (254 mm)	$\frac{3}{4} - 1$	18 in (457 mm)	5
12 in (305 mm)	$1\frac{1}{2} - 2$	20 in (508 mm)	7

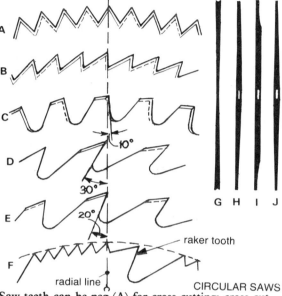

CIRCULAR SAWS

Saw teeth can be peg (A) for cross-cutting; cross-cut (B) in which front of tooth is radial to saw: cross-cut (alternative) (C); rip (D) for cutting softwood with the grain; rip (E) for ripping hardwood; combination (F) for both ripping and cross-cutting. There are also special forms of saws such as the hollow-ground or dimension saw (G), thinner at centre than at periphery and with no set to teeth, and giving a smooth cut; swage saw (H), flush on one side but tapered towards rim at other, used for cutting narrow stuff; ground-off saw (I) for still narrower stuff; and taper saw (J) similar to swage saw but tapered on both sides.

Table of saw should be provided with fence for ripping, and should be grooved to take a mitre gauge, and there should be a riving knife to prevent saw kerf from closing up and binding on the saw. Table should be made to rise and fall to enable grooving, rebating, etc., to be done, and either it or the saw should preferably tilt so that wood can be sawn at an angle. A guard should be provided. Optimum peripheral speed of saw is 9,500 ft per minute, (2,896 metres per minute), and revolutions per minute (r.p.m.) are found thus:

$$\frac{\text{peripheral speed}}{\text{diameter of saw} \times 3\frac{1}{7}}$$

Speeds thus work out at:

diameter of saw	r.p.m.
7 in (178 mm)	5,000
8 in (203 mm)	4,500
10 in (254 mm)	3,600

In practice many small circular saws run at considerably lower speeds, and, provided that the teeth are properly sharpened and other things are in order, cut quite well. The more teeth in any given diameter of saw, the finer the cut. By far the best results come from TCT *(q.v.)* blades which last far longer than ordinary high-speed steel blades.

circular saw formulae Correct speed of rotation is calculated from the formula R (r.p.m.) = 1,000 × P (required rim speed in metres per minute) divided by 3.14 × D (saw dia. in mm). The rim speed (also called periphery speed) can be obtained by transposing the factors thus: P (rim speed) = 3.14 × D × R, divided by 1,000 (to convert mm to metres).

cissing The recession of varnish from a given point. Usually caused by grease. Work should be rubbed down and wash-leathered before varnishing.

cist A casket or chest, especially for containing holy relics. Our word 'chest' *(q.v.)* is probably derived from it.

cladding The outer covering of a shed or building, usually consisting of boards or sheet material.

clamp Large dining-table tops, bureau falls, and so on, made up in width from narrow boards and tongue-jointed, are often fitted with end clamps fixed with mortise and tenon joints. The clamps help to keep the top flat. Sometimes, in order to give a thicker appearance to the top, the end clamps are made thicker, and side clamps are added and mitre-jointed at the corners. The four clamps are fitted flush at the top side of the main boards. Tenons are formed at the board ends by first cutting a long tenon from side to side, then dividing it into smaller tenons. Wood must be well seasoned, as the clamps do not allow for shrinkage.

clamp (USA) Equivalent to British 'cramp'. Also used in Britain to describe a small cramp.

clapboard The smaller pieces of riven oak used for wainscot panelling.

clash The figure obtained by quartering oak so that the medullary rays are more or less parallel to the faces of the boards. (See also *flash* and *silver grain*.)

claw and ball foot (see *ball* and *claw foot*).

claw hammer Used by carpenters. Claw enables nails to be withdrawn without changing the tool. Sizes range from head weights 13-28 oz (34-79 grams). Average weight 20 oz (68 grams).

cleaning up Term applied to the finishing of cabinet work and joinery with smoothing plane, scraper, and glasspaper.

clearance The space between a moving part and that to which it is pivoted to avoid rubbing.

clears and door stock US equivalent to British first grade joinery softwood (*q.v.*).

cleat Has many applications, but in general is a batten used to support a shelf, resist a thrust, or to act temporarily as a clamp.

cleft A term which is applied to timber which has been split with an axe, or by means of a beetle and wedge.

clinching The bending over of the point of a nail after passing through the wood so that it acts as a sort of rivet. Sometimes spelt 'clenching'.

clockcase hinge Has one flange wider than the other so that a raised and moulded door can be pivoted. Narrow flange fits projecting door, and wider one the carcase. Usually acorn ended to give neat appearance.

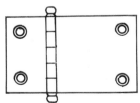

CLOCKCASE HINGE

close chair A chair, or sometimes a drum-shaped type of stool, used for sanitary purposes. Also called a 'night' chair. The term 'commode' which is sometimes used to describe it is, strictly speaking, incorrect. (See *commode*.)

close-contact adhesive Synthetic resin adhesives for wood suitable only for joints which can be cramped up so that the glue-line does not exceed 0.005 in.

close couple Span roof with the rafters tied at the foot with a beam.

close nailing Refers to the practice of antique dome-headed nails (*q.v.*) being driven in so that they touch each other; compare with 'space nailing' (*q.v.*) where they are inserted with a space between each.

closed string A staircase string into which the treads and risers are housed at both sides.

cloudiness Occurs in french polishing and appears as a milky film. Due to dampness, either in the work or the atmosphere, and may be caused by a draught. Work in a warm room and try rubbing with half-and-half linseed oil and turps, or equal quantities of linseed oil and methylated spirit.

clout nail Nail with large head used for fixing down roofing felt, canvas, webbing, etc. Made in sizes ¾-3 in (19-76 mm). Can be obtained galvanised for exposed work.

CLOUT NAILS

club foot A turned foot used at the bottom of some cabriole legs. Widely used in Queen Anne and Early Georgian furniture. The turning has to be hand finished into the shaped leg. (See also *cabriole leg*.)

CLUB FOOT

cluster columns or legs A Gothic detail which consists of columns (or cylindrical legs) grouped in clusters of three or four; it was widely used in the Chippendale period.

coach screws (see *carriage screws*.)

coachwood (*ceratopetalum apetalum*) Australian wood, 43 lb (689 kg), works and polishes well. Pale brown colour. Used in general cabinet-making.

coaster A receptacle used on a dining table for moving bottles from place to place. It can take the form of a small wagon with tiny wheels or that of a small circular tray with a low gallery around it and

covered with biaze on the bottom to avoid marking the table. (See also *cheese coaster*.)

coat Term applied to the arrangement of abrasive particles on a sanding belt or paper; thus there are 'close' coats and 'open coats'. Sanding belts consist of a backing (either paper, cloth or a combination of both) to which a 'make' coat is glued; this coat carries the abrasive particles which have a further 'size' coat added to lock them in position.

Coburg varnish A pale oil varnish.

Coccus lacca The name of an insect which feeds on the juices of various trees in India; its secretions form the basis of shellac *(q.v.)* . The word 'lacca' derives from the Sanskrit numeral for 100,000 as the insects are extremely numerous.

cocked bead A small projecting bead used generally around drawers and doors, etc. It may occupy the entire thickness of the wood or be let into a rebate. Sometimes called 'cock bead'.

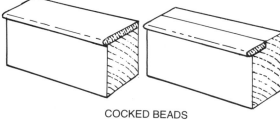

COCKED BEADS

cock's head hinge (USA) The equivalent of the British 'snake' hinge *(q.v.)*.

cockfighting chair Alternative name for a reading chair *(q.v.)*.

cocktail cabinet A cabinet which contains bottles, glasses, and other accoutrements for drinking. There is no standard design but most cabinets feature a lid which lifts to reveal a hidden compartment from which the drinks are dispensed.

cocktail cabinet stay Used for lowering the fall front of the cabinet simultaneously with raising the lid. The position of the centre pivot and the fixing plates is usually found by making a full-size drawing and plotting the movement, the pivot remaining stationary. (See *stays*.)

cocobolo *(dalbergia retusa)* Central and South American wood, 86 lb (1378 kg), of rich red colour. Used for small turnery items, cutlery handles, etc.

cocus *(byra ebenus)* Dark rich heavy wood from Jamaica and Cuba. About 70 lb (1121 kg). Used mainly for musical instruments.

coffee table A small occasional table with square, oblong, circular, or oval top. Height may vary from 12 in (305 mm) to 20 in (508 mm). Sometimes the top is loose and acts as a tray, the stand portion folding up when not in use.

coffer A kind of portable chest *(q.v.)* for use when travelling; it usually had handles, no feet, and a domed or coved lid. They were either slung over the backs of horses, pannier-style, or carried in wagons. Alternative names were: trussing coffers, sumpter chests, and standards (large coffers). Sumpter is the old word for pack-horse.

coffin stool Any kind of small joyned stool; such stools formed supports for a coffin when deceased persons were kept at home from the time of death until the funeral.

cofre Norman-French word corresponding to 'coffer'.

cogged joint Sometimes used for ceiling joists. The purpose is to prevent horizontal movement.

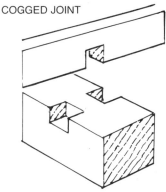

COGGED JOINT

coigue beech *(Nothofagus dombeya)* A Chilean wood, 36 lb (577 kg). Used for flooring, furniture, etc. Somewhat like European beech in colour. Sapwood often wide.

cold-setting adhesive One capable of curing at room temperature; that is, 21 degrees C or 70 degrees F.

collar-beam roof A span roof having a collar or tie beam raised above the wall-plate level. Sometimes the term *collar* is applied to the annulet of a column.

Colonial (USA) Term applied to furniture made by early colonists during 17th century.

colour polish White or transparent french polish coloured with spirit-soluble aniline dye.

colouring A stage in the french polishing process. It follows fadding and precedes coating and bodying. Its purpose is to correct the colour of local parts to make an even tone.

comb The top back rail of certain designs of Windsor chairs. It varies from about 3 in (76 mm) to about 5 in (127 mm) in width, is slightly curved, and is positioned on the ends of the backstands.

comb-back Windsor chair A bow-back Windsor chair on which the central back spindles extend upwards beyond the bow and are capped by a yoke-shaped comb.

combination oilstone Having two grades of stone, *coarse* one side, *fine* the other.

combination plane A metal plane for beading, dadoing, fillistering, rebating, tonguing, grooving, etc. It has several cutters, with spurs for cross-grain work, adjustable depth gauge, fence, beading stop, and shaving deflector.

combination planer (see *thicknesser*.)

combination saw A circular saw having its teeth arranged in sets of five or seven, of which one is a raker tooth, the purpose of which is to clear dust from the kerf. (See *circular saw*.)

comb joint A form of corner joint used for making small boxes, cases, etc. The pins and sockets are equal in size. If desired, the sharp corners may be rounded

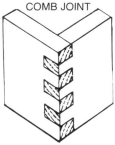

COMB JOINT

over without spoiling the neat appearance of the joints. The joint is generally confined to machine work as the stronger dovetail joint can be cut just as easily by hand. Sometimes known as the finger or box pin joint.

comforters (USA) These were extra bedclothes which were wound around a wooden roller fixed at the foot-end of the bed; they could be pulled up when extra warmth was needed.

commode Originally a French low chest with drawers; Chippendale used the term to describe almost any piece of furniture which contained drawers, and made 'commode-tables' and 'commode-clothes presses', while other makers offered 'commode chests-of-drawers'. Towards the end of the 18th century and until the present day it has been used to describe a chair or stool for sanitary use. (See *close chair*.)

compass plane The modern form is all-metal, and is intended for planing concave and convex surfaces. It has a flexible steel sole which is adjusted and locked by screws. The normal cutter with back iron is fitted but the pitch is higher. For concave surfaces, the sole should be set a trifle more acute than the curve necessary, otherwise dubbing over at the ends may occur. For convex shapes the sole is set slightly flatter. It is imperative to hold the plane straight with the work — not askew, as when making a slicing cut. After use the sole should be left straight, otherwise the sole may become permanently bent. A form of compass rebate plane is also shown.

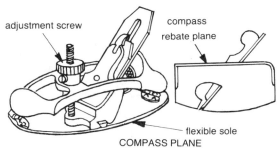

adjustment screw   compass rebate plane   flexible sole
COMPASS PLANE

compass rebate plane Rebate plane for working curved rebates.

compass saw Used for cutting flat curves or in places where a panel saw would be restricted. The blade of the saw is 12 in (305 mm) to 18 in (457 mm) long.

compo An abbreviation for the term 'composition'. It consists of a mixture of whiting, resin, and glue which sets to become a rock-hard material. Decorative mouldings and ornaments can be cast from moulds carved from wooden patterns. It is also called 'stucco'.

composite   The fifth order of Grecian architecture, being a combination of Ionic and Corinthian.

compound cut   A cut which is other than a right-angle in both the width and thickness.

compressed air press   A machine press used in veneering shaped work. There is a table on which the work with veneer in position is laid, and a large semi-cylindrical head having a rubber sheet stretched across it. The head is lowered over the work and is clamped down. Compressed air is fed into the head so that the rubber sheet is forced down on to the veneer, pressing it tightly down on to the groundwork.

compressed air tools   (see *pneumatic tools*).

concertina action   A device used on card tables in the eighteenth century so that the frame could be extended to support the open flaps. The back part of the frame comprises two hinged sections that can be folded inwards or outwards.

conifer   Cone-bearing trees such as the fir and the pine which are generally regarded as softwoods, and which do not shed their leaves in winter. (see *deciduous*.)

confidante   A form of upholstered sofa which is S-shaped in plan.

Connecticut chest   (USA)   Made chiefly in Connecticut during the seventeenth and eighteenth century, this chest often had one or two drawers beneath the upper chest. Usually ornamented with split-turning *(q.v.)* and applied decoration; they also carried low-relief carving in conventionalised floral patterns.

console   A shaped and often carved bracket. A console table is one usually supported by large brackets and intended to stand between two windows. The term console as applied to a cabinet refers to one which is wider than it is high.

Constitution mirror   (USA) A wall mirror in a general Chippendale style, having a swan-neck pediment with a central acroterium *(q.v.)* on which stands an eagle. The frame usually is either walnut or mahogany, carved with leaves and flowers, and sometimes parcel gilt.

contact adhesive   An adhesive which sticks firmly immediately on contact, and needing only slight pressure. Based on neoprene *(q.v.)*.

Continental headboard   A modern day design whereby two single divans share the same headboard, it is often padded and sometimes incorporates two bedside cabinets.

continuous hand rail   One used in a geometrical staircase in which there are no newels *(q.v.)*. The hand rail runs from top to bottom without a break, any change of direction being accomplished by means of wreaths *(q.v.)*.

contour   The profile or sectional outline of a moulding.

contour chair   A chair designed to conform to the shape of the human frame. Usually made in glass fibre, and contemporary in date.

conversation chair   A curved settee which allowed the occupants to more or less face each other. Also called a 'causeuse' or a 'tête-à-tête'.

conversion   The method by which a log is sawn up into smaller sizes for working. There are many ways of doing this depending upon the species of wood, the grain figuring required, and economics. (See under individual methods as *boxed heart, flat sawn, rift, slash*.)

coopered joint   A butt joint in which the parts meet at an angle. Cylinders or semi-circular objects are coopered. The joint halves the overall angle of the joining pieces. Thus all joints radiate. The width, thickness, and bevelling angle at edges is determined by setting out a full-size sectional drawing on paper. Edges should be planed on a shooting-board, the staves resting on blocks giving the correct tilt (planing angle). Staves should be glued together in pairs and then halves. Finally the two halves are tested together and glued. Corners are rounded over if a circular cylinder is wanted — generally it is turned.

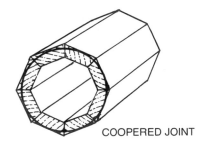

COOPERED JOINT

copal varnish A good-quality clear oil varnish, pale or medium colour, for indoor or outdoor use. It dries by oxidation, not evaporation. Made from copal, a natural resin.

coped joint (USA) Corresponds to British 'scribed joint' *(q.v.)*.

coping saw A form of fretsaw in which the blade is held in tension by a metal frame. Used for cutting shapes in thin wood. The blade is made taut by turning the handle. It can be held at an angle in the frame enabling a cut to be made parallel with the edge.

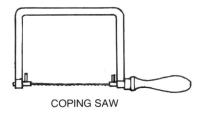

COPING SAW

copperas Three kinds are available: green (sulphate of iron), blue (copper sulphate), white (sulphate of zinc). First is most generally used for woodwork. Dissolved in water. On oak it gives a blue-grey tone. Also turns sycamore grey (harewood). Used weak on mahogany it gives appearance of walnut. Blue copperas is sometimes used but is not so effective. Both should be sealed with white polish before filling with plaster.

copper sulphate (see *copperas*).

coquillage A carved decoration with a shell motif predominating; often found around the edges of a circular table top.

coral-wood *(adenanthera pavonina)* From India and Burma, about 56 lb (897 kg). Of coral colour when exposed. Hard surface and takes polish well.

corbel An architectural term for a bracket which supports a superimposed member such as a cornice or pediment.

cord A measurement of felled timber: one cord contains 128 cu.ft (3.624 cu.metres).

cording (USA) Corresponds to British piping cord *(q.v.)*.

core The internal filling of blockboard, plywood, and other manufactured boards. Also term used in pattern making for the portion of sand used to form inner shapes and holes in castings. In staircasings refers to the inner metal strip of a wooden handrail. In sawmills the heart of a log which has been boxed is termed the core.

core box plane Used by pattern makers to plane semi-circular hollow shapes. The soles are at right angles, and in bearing against the top inner edges enable the cutter to remove wood down to a semi-circle, no more. The bulk of the waste is removed by other methods first.

Corinthian The third order of Grecian architecture.

cork rubber A cork block, usually about 4½ in (115 mm) by 2½ in (64 mm) by 1¼ in (32 mm) around which abrasive paper is wrapped when cleaning up a surface.

corner bracket Applied to any bracket fitting in a corner, but notably to those fitting at seat level in a chair to bind the rails and legs together.

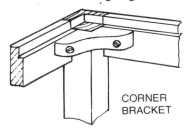

CORNER BRACKET

corner chair Introduced about 1740, these chairs had low backs about 12 in (300 mm) high on two sides of the seat and were used for reading and writing. A similar type with a higher back was sometimes used by barbers. (See *barber's chair*.)

corner chisel (see under *carver's chisels*.)

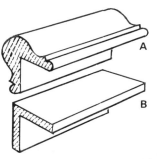

CORNER COVER MOULDINGS

corner cover moulding　Used to hide the joints of a box or similar object. (See also *box corner mouldings*.)

corner cupboard　The early designs (circa 1700) were built into a panelled wall and were called 'beaufait', and usually comprised an open unit with an upper section which was fitted with shaped shelves, the lower portion being either open with bookshelves or enclosed with doors as a cupboard. The free-standing two-tier design was made between 1745 and 1820 and is still popular; the hanging types (circa 1700 to 1820) were primarily intended as storage cupboards and not for display.

cornflour　Sometimes added to wax polish to help fill in the grain quickly.

cornice moulding　A moulding fixed at the top of a piece of woodwork, generally above eye level. It thus slopes outwards at about 45 degrees. Typical 18th century sections are shown. (See also *mouldings*.)

CORNICE MOULDINGS

cornish　Archaic term for a cornice *(q.v.)*.

coromandel ebony　(see *ebony*.)

Coromandel lacquer　A combination of lacquer, carving and painting originating from the Coromandel coast of eastern India. The technique consisted of coating the wooden base with a paste of fine white clay, overlaid with a coating of fibrous grasses and then three more coats of clay rubbed down smooth. The black lacquer was then painted on, and the design carved out intaglio to expose the white clay — these exposed areas were painted in brilliant colours or gilded.

corona　A style of drapery which is suspended from a fitting in the wall above the bed so that it resembles an open-fronted cone. Also a type of moulding. (See *drip moulding*.)

corrugated joint fasteners　These are made with points ground at both sides. They are used in cheap work across mitre or butt joints, etc. The corrugations converge so that the joint is forced together.

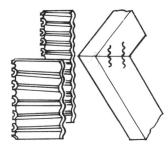

CORRUGATED JOINT FASTENERS

cosy corner　A corner fitment popular around the 1890s consisting of upholstered seats arranged in three sides of a square with shelves for books, bric-a-brac, etc. The designs were vaguely reminiscent of Art Nouveau styles.

costers　Panels of fabric hung on the walls of a room, and which matched the bed draperies.

cot　A type of cradle which is not mounted on rockers, but is designed to swing between two uprights, one at each end. Sheraton devised one which swung automatically, being worked by clockwork. What we call a 'cot' today is actually a 'crib'.

Cotswold range　A range of furniture available under the Utility Scheme during, and shortly after, the Second World War; it was a more decorative and sophisticated version of the Chiltern range *(q.v.)*.

cotton tree　(see *bombax*.)

cottonwood *(populus deltoides)*　Poplar trees from America. About 25 lb (400 kg). Greyish white colour. Similar to the European poplar.

cotton wool　Used in making the rubber for french polishing. Use the unbleached variety.

couches　A comprehensive term including day-beds and sofas, the definite characteristic being that the piece is intended for reclining on. A couch is similar to a sofa but has a roll arm at one end only.

counter　A type of worktable, often with a hatch or cupboard beneath the top; in some instances the top was used for reckoning accounts — hence the modern usage of the term.

counterboring　Method of recessing a screw head deeply into the wood. Often used when fixing a top through deep rails. A hole large enough to take the screw head is bored first, and a smaller clearance hole afterwards for the shank. It enables a much shorter screw to be used.

counter-flap hinges   A double-joint hinge usually made from heavy brass, as shown at (A). The hinges are sunk flush in the wood so the flaps act as dovetails, thereby increasing strength. (B) is a special flap hinge for work of light construction. In both cases there is no projecting knuckle at the top.

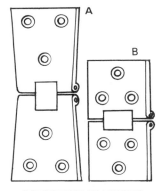

COUNTERFLAP HINGES

countersink   A bit used to recess a screw head flush with the surface. (A) is the snail type used for wood. Also made with two cutting edges and parallel shank for use in a boring machine. Rose countersink is given at (B). This is intended for brass. (C) gives the type used for iron.

The word also describes the process of recessing for the head of the screw.

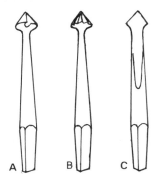

COUNTERSINK DRILLS

counter veneer   Double thickness of veneer. The lower veneer is at right angles with the grain of the groundwork, and the upper one in line with it. Both sides of the groundwork should be counter veneered.

counterwood   Alternative name for afzelia (q.v.).

couple   A pair of rafters in a span roof.

couple roof   A narrow span roof with pairs of rafters without a tie beam or collar.

courbaril (hymenaea courbaril)   From West Indies. Orange brown colour which darkens with exposure. About 50 lb (801 kg). Used for furniture, turnery, etc. Interlocked grain which tends to tear out on planing.

court cupboard   A descendant of the buffet (q.v.), popular between 1500 and 1700, and were so-called as they were short (French court), usually not exceeding 48 in (1220 mm) in height. The middle shelf often contained a drawer. The cupboard, or aumbry, sometimes held foodstuffs.

cove   A large hollow. Applied to furniture, it describes a large hollow cornice; it can also mean a niche or curved recess in a wall intended to accommodate a statue or similar ornament.

cow horn stretcher   (see crinoline stretcher.)

crabwood (carapa guianensis)   Central American wood, similar to mahogany. Inclined to tear out in planing. Used locally for furniture, sills, etc.

crackle finish   A finish produced by applying a coat of lacquer designed to shrink or crack on to a more flexible undercoat. Usually the coats are of different colours.

cradle (1)   A built-up framework used to support wood whilst being worked in some way. It may take any form to suit the form of the structure. The example shown is for assembling work of coppered construction. Also loosely applied to many other structures, usually temporary.

cradle (2)   A baby's bed mounted on rockers. Earliest mention was in the 14th century in Piers Plowman (1362).

cramps   (see under individual items band, bar, corner, cramp heads, flooring, G, sash, T-bar).

cramp heads   Separate screw and shoe for adding to wood bar of any convenient length.

crazing   A network of fine hairline cracks caused by the effect of age on a finish.

credence   A small side-table placed near the altar in a church, on which the vessels for the Eucharist stand prior to consecration. It is a form of console table, except that the top is supported by carved legs instead of brackets. It stands about 30 in (761 mm) or 36 in (914 mm) high.

credenza An Italian sideboard or buffet with cupboards; used for the display and storage of plate and similar valuables.

creosote An oily liquid derived from coal-tar used as a preservative to outdoor woodwork. It is applied with a brush, special attention being given to end grain, joints, etc. Creosote which has become too thick can be thinned with paraffin. The latter is also used for cleaning brushes, hot soapy water being used to finish off.

cresting The shaped, and often carved, top back rail of a chair: the term can also apply to a pediment.

crest rail The uppermost rail (usually of a chair).

crib (see *cot*).

cricket table Also called 'cracket table'. A three-legged table with a circular jointed top, rarely exceeding 30 in (760 mm) diameter and usually having an undershelf. The three-legged stance enabled it to stand steadily on uneven floors; it was widely used in cottages and inns.

crinoline stretcher A curved stretcher usually found on Windsor chairs; the bowed shape accommodated the crinoline skirt of the occupant. Also called a *'cow horn' stretcher*, or a *'spur' stretcher*.

crocus powder Used as a fine abrasive for dusting over a brightly polished surface to dull it. Also mixed with oil and applied to a leather strop for carving tools.

Croft A movable cabinet containing a large number of small drawers for filing purposes and with a top for writing; used in libraries. Named after its inventor.

Cromwellian chair One of the few innovations of the Inter-regnum (1649 to 1659), this type of chair was made about 1655 and built sturdily in oak. The back and seat were pieces of leather close-nailed in place; the general appearance is austere and the only decoration was on the front legs and stretcher rail, which were turned.

crossbanding Term used mainly in veneering, and refers to strips of veneer with the grain running crosswise. Often used around the edges of panels, tops, drawer fronts, etc.

cross bearers Term sometimes used in caul veneering, referring to the bearers with curved inner edges used to press the caul on to the veneers. The curved edges ensure that the glue is forced outwards from the centre.

cross-cut saw A hand saw for cutting across the grain. The blade measures 22-28 in (559-711 mm) long, with teeth five to eight points per inch (25 mm). For rougher work, as in carpentry, the blade is usually 26 in (660 mm) long, with teeth six to seven points per inch (25 mm). Although it can be used for cutting *with* the grain, it does not cut so quickly or easily as the rip-saw. Back can either be straight or skew, as shown. (See also *handsaw, panel saw, circular saw*.) The term also applies to circular saw blades.

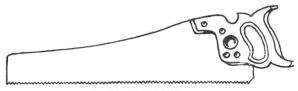

CROSSCUT SAW

cross garnet A T-hinge made from stout metal. It is used on shed doors, gates, boxes, etc. It is screwed directly to the surface without being let in.

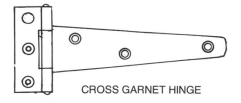

CROSS GARNET HINGE

cross-stretcher X-shaped underframe, the arms of which can be straight or sinuous. Sometimes called a saltire *(q.v.)*.

crotch (see *curl*).

crown face wheel A feature of some bandsaws which have the edge of the wheels slightly convex in section.

crow's nest movement (USA) Corresponds to British bird-cage movement *(q.v.)*.

crystal varnish A quick-drying spirit varnish, sometimes used for coating in the french polishing process.

cube A unit of measurement often adopted when selling hardwoods; softwoods are usually sold in metric measurements. In the trade a set of tables (see *Hoppus*) is used to calculate the cubic content quickly, otherwise it is a matter of multiplying the length by the width by the thickness, all in the same units.

cup-and-cover   A form of bulbous leg or pillar resembling a cup with a lid; popular on Elizabethan furniture. (See *bulbous leg; melon bulb.*)

cup chuck   Used in turning to grip work of odd, irregular shape. In some types screws are tapped through the sides to give additional grip.

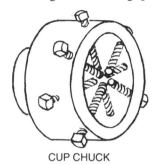

CUP CHUCK

cupid's bow   Describes the shape of the top back rail of a chair which curves up at the ends and dips slightly at the centre — it is often seen on Chippendale chair designs.

cupped center   (USA) Corresponds to British cup chuck *(q.v.).*

cup shake   A split in a log in line with the annual rings. Sometimes known as a ring shake.

CUP SHAKE

curl   Highly figured grain obtained by cutting through the junction of a trunk and large limb. Used only in veneer form. Also known as crotch or feather.

curricle chair   A tub-shaped upholstered chair popular at the beginning of the 19th century. So-called from its resemblance to the horse-drawn vehicle favoured by the young bloods of the Regency period.

curtain piece   Refers to shaped rails situated above eye level; also called 'span rails'.

curule   An X-shaped stool, usually made in metal, which was used by magistrates in Ancient Rome. It was possibly the inspiration for the many X-shaped chairs and stools which followed, although the curule itself was derived from Ancient Greek designs. There is, for instance, a good representation of an X-shaped stool on a Greek vase circa 1194 BC.

cusp   A Gothic ornament consisting of a knob or boss projecting from the intersection of two curves; it is frequently carved.

cut   (USA) Refers to the amount of shellac, measured in pounds, dissolved in a gallon of solvent (alcohol). Thus 4 lb (1.81 kg) shellac dissolved in 1 gallon (4.55 litres) is a 4-pound cut.

cutlery canteen   A container for cutlery. May be a box, nest of drawers, or cupboard. Sometimes on a stand or in table form.

cut nails   The cut clasp nail (A) is for general purpose carpentry. It has great holding power. Sizes $\frac{3}{4}$ in (19 mm) to 8 in (204 mm). Cut brads (B) also for general carpentry. Sizes $\frac{1}{2}$ in (12 mm) to 3 in (76 mm). The cut floor brad is similar but slightly heavier. Sizes $1\frac{1}{2}$ in (38 mm) to 3 in (76 mm). Cut clout nail (C) is for similar purposes to the clout nail *(q.v.)* but has sharp point easily pressed into the wood. Sizes $\frac{3}{4}$ in (19 mm) to 3 in (76 mm).

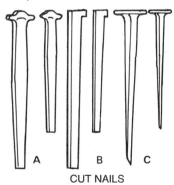

CUT NAILS

cut string   see *stepped string).*

cutter block   The rotor or block in a machine in which the cutters are fixed.

cutter projection scale   This is used to ascertain the amount of projection needed by the cutters of a slotted collar block for spindle moulders.

43

cutting gauge A tool having a steel cutter held with a wedge. It can be used for marking out, or for cutting thin wood. It is suitable for marking across the grain, for which purpose the marking gauge would scratch. The cutter should be sharpened and set so that the gauge tends to draw into the wood, not away from it. Made in beech, with boxwood setting screw. (See also *marking gauge.*)

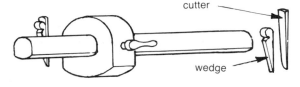

CUTTING GAUGE

cutting list A list giving the sizes to which timber has to be cut up for finishing to size. As most timber is bought ready planed the thickness should be finished size. If sawn timber is being bought, allow for planing. Thus 1 in (25 mm) stuff will finish ⅞ in (23 mm) only. Widths, however, should have from ⅛ in (3 mm) to ¼ in (6 mm) added to them, the amount depending upon the size. The smaller the piece the less allowance needed. Lengths also require working allowance. Size comes in as before, but also the purpose of the part has to be considered. Generally ½ in (12 mm) is about right, but when there are to be mortises at the ends as in door stiles, etc., extra should be allowed to avoid splitting. Parts with tenons at the ends need less. In the cabinet and building trades lengths are given first, then widths and thicknesses. The timber trade, however, puts thicknesses first. The easiest way to use a cutting list is to first make a list of the exact finished dimensions of the pieces you need to make something — information you get from your drawing, then from that make a list with all the cutting and working allowances, a preliminary list, as it were, which will give you the rough sizes you need. Add at least 10% wastage (more if the timber is notoriously awkward) and that gives you the amount to buy.

cwpwrdd Welsh term for a cupboard-dresser circa 1500 onwards. It comprises a high press cupboard about 4 ft 9 in (1450 mm) high with fielded or plain figured door panels surmounted by another small cupboard, the top of which forms a canopy with heavy turned finials at the front corners. About 1650 a third unit was added to the top, consisting of a shelf for displaying crockery and ornaments. They were called 'cwpwrdd deuddarn' and 'cwpwrdd tridarn' respectively.

cylinder lock A lock (often called a 'Yale') which is used for a wide variety of locking applications. Its distinguishing feature is that the lock contains tumblers which match teeth that are cut on the edge of the key shank; these teeth are cut to different sizes and depths so that an unlimited range of combinations is available.

cylinder-top desk A form of desk which has a curved solid wood panelled top which can be closed down and locked. (See *roll-top desk.*)

cyma recta An ogee moulding with the hollow member at the top (A). 'Cyma' is the Greek word for a wave.

cyma reversa Ogee moulding with the round member at the top (B).

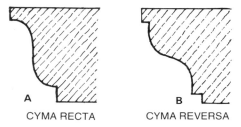

CYMA RECTA   CYMA REVERSA

cypress, bald (*taxodium distichum*) A durable wood from USA. Resists decay. Weight 33 lb (529 kg). Used for greenhouses, barrels, etc. The garden cypress has no commercial uses.

D

dado Architecturally, a 'dado' is the cube pedestal from which a column rises. In interior woodwork it is the wide panelling, usually about 39 in (990 mm) to 40 in (1016 mm) high, which is fitted around the lower part of wall in a room.

In good class work the dado is invariably of wood. In smaller houses it is often merely an applied moulding fitted at top with an embossed wallpaper below reaching to the skirting. The dado moulding, as it is termed, protects the wall from injury caused by chair backs. On staircase walls the dado mould is fixed to align with the stair rail. Mouldings vary from 2 in (51 mm) to 4 in (102 mm) wide. Pattern (A) is intended to fit over panelling, whilst (B) is the plain chair rail type.

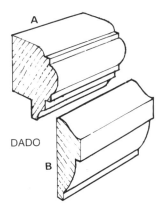

DADO

dado (USA) A groove or trench cut across the grain.

dado head An attachment fitted to a saw bench in place of the saw. Used for grooving and trenching. There are two outer saws between which are fixed one or more cutters of varying thickness, enabling any width of groove to be cut. The cutters are swage set and thus overlap slightly at the cutting edge. They must obviously be positioned at the gaps between the teeth of the saws.

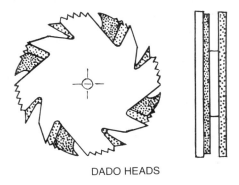

DADO HEADS

dado plane Sometimes known as the housing plane, its purpose is to cut a groove across the grain of wood, as when making a housing or groove to receive a shelf. At the front it has a second cutter shaped in the form of two spurs which cut across the sides of the groove and prevent tearing out. In use the plane is drawn back once or twice to make preliminary side cuts. It is worked against a straight-edge. Various widths available.

dahoma (*piptadenia africana*) Hardwood from Nigeria and Ghana. 40 lb (641 kg). Golden-brown colour; not easily worked and tending to split in nailing. Dust is irritant to some workers. Used for structural work, flooring, fittings, etc.

dais A raised platform to hold a chair or table and chairs to accommodate a person in authority or important guests, etc.

damask A rich silk fabric with raised figuring woven into the pattern and originally woven in Damascus (hence the name); also a linen fabric of the same style.

danta (*cistanthera papaverifera*) Hardwood from Ghana, Nigeria, and Ivory Coast. 46 lb (737 kg). Reddish-brown colour, strong and durable, tending to be greasy to touch. Turns and polishes well. Used for tool handles, boat-building, etc.

dapple figure The attractive figure consisting of light and dark patches sometimes found in mahogany and other decorative woods.

davenport A special kind of pedestal writing desk, reputedly ordered by a Captain Davenport from Gillows of Lancaster at the end of the 18th century, and intended for use on military campaigns. It comprises a bureau top with a sloping writing surface; the pedestal contains a variety of drawers and compartments, both at the front and side. The top always has a gallery at the back, returned partway down the sides. As the top overhangs the pedestal, scrolled supports or pilasters are introduced and terminate at the bottom into either sledge feet *(q.v.)* or a plinth *(q.v.)*.

day bed The day bed was basically a long stool-like structure with six legs (one at each corner and two extra in the centre) with a hinged, adjustable back-rest. Both the seat and the back-rest were carved and fitted with substantial cushions; by 1685 the hinged back-rest had given way to one which was fixed at an angle. Day beds were certainly known in the 16th century as Shakespeare makes reference to them.

dead bolt Square-type bolt fitted to dead lock *(q.v.)*. It needs to be key-operated.

dead lock A lock which can be actuated only by the key, as distinct from one with bevelled bolt which will catch as the door is closed. May be of the screw-on type with box staple, or mortise type to be let into the door as shown.

dead shore Vertical posts to carry weight as when internal walls have to be cut away. The dead shores are put at each side of the wall with needle or lintel resting on top and passed through the brickwork to take the weight.

deadwood Commercially inferior timber which comes from over-matured trees. The term, however, applies generally to withered branches which have dropped and have been left to decay, and trees which are dead before being felled.

deal In the trade a square-sawn length of softwood nominally 9 in (228 mm) to 11 in (280 mm) wide and from 2 in (51 mm) to 4 in (102 mm) thick, that is, an intermediate size between a plank and a batten. Much confusion arises through its general application to certain whitewoods, such as red or white pine.

death watch beetle *(xestobium rufuvillosum)* A boring pest which almost invariable attacks decayed wood. The eggs are laid in the decayed parts (usually hardwoods) and the larvae enter cracks or old flight holes, and remain burrowing in the wood for three to five years, when they emerge through flight holes of about ⅛ in (3 mm) dia. The use of a brush- or spray-applied insecticide in spring or early summer helps in destroying eggs or larvae, but will probably not affect larvae working well below the surface. Treatment needs to be continued for at least four years, and involves the replacement of timbers which have been seriously weakened, removal of dust, at least two applications of insecticide from April to June (the period of emergence), destruction of beetles beneath the affected parts, and continual inspection of timber.

deciduous trees These are the broad-leafed hardwood trees which in temperate zones shed their leaves in the autumn.

decoupage The technique of applying coloured prints to clocks, furniture etc. and overlaying them with many coats of clear varnish to simulate the pastoral scenes frequently painted on more expensive pieces. (See *arte povera*.)

deeping The process of re-sawing timber parallel to its wider face.

degame *(calycophyllom candidissimum)* Central and South American hardwood of about 50 lb (801 kg). Bright yellow colour, used for turnery, carving, tool handles, bows. Also known as lemonwood.

de-natured alcohol (USA) A solvent for shellac made by de-naturing grain alcohol. Corresponds to British methylated spirits *(q.v.)*.

de-nib To remove the nibs (specks of dust, hairs etc.) from a painted or varnished surface. Usually achieved by papering the surface lightly with fine grade wet-and-dry paper or proprietary de-nibbing pads.

densified laminated wood This is manufactured from individual veneers of timber which are interleaved with synthetic resin glues of the phenol-formaldehyde group, and cured by being subjected to high temperature and pressure. The predominant grain direction of the veneers can be varied to meet specific requirements. It is used for high-voltage insulators and other components of electrical equipment, and also knife handles, jigs for the woodworking industry, shuttles, and bobbins in the textile industry. Many woods can be used, but the most popular is beech, with birch, dogwood, persimmon, hickory, and some mahogany-related timbers also being utilised.

dentils An ornamental detail consisting of small rectangular blocks with spaces between them; usually incorporated in a cornice moulding. Also employed in inlaid work, the pattern being formed by contrasting woods. Also called 'mutules' *(q.v.)*.

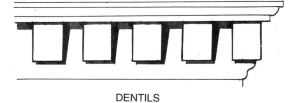

DENTILS

depth gauge A device fitted to a bit or drill to regulate the depth of the holes it will bore. Any oddment of wood can be bored to take the bit or drill and it should be such a length that, when bearing against the chuck, the amount projecting equals the

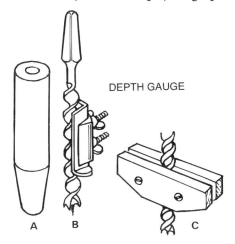

DEPTH GAUGE

A   B   C

depth of the hole required. Various proprietary devices are available which work on the same principle.

depth stop　A device fitted to any tool to prevent it from cutting below a predetermined depth. Usually applied to rebate and grooving planes. Adjustable in height.

desk　First mentioned in the Paston Letters of 1471. They were virtually boxes with sloping lids and designed to stand on a table; the size was about 30 to 36 in wide (760 to 915 mm). Frequently they were ornamented with chip carving or inlay. By about the 17th century the hinge was fitted to the bottom of the lid so that it could be lifted to reveal a fitted compartment for pens, ink, etc. From 1650 onwards desks were called 'bureaux' because of the woollen cloth (later called 'bayes', our modern baize) which covered the writing surface. In the 18th century the desk was mounted on its own stand and drawers were added so that it came to resemble the present day bureau *(q.v.)*.

desk box　Alternative term for bible box.

deuddarn　(see *cwpwrdd*).

development　A method of ascertaining the true shape of various objects. The object can be imagined as made of card and opened out flat.

Devon dresser　A dresser which has the shelving enclosed by doors.

de-waxed shellac　(USA) A superfine bleached and de-waxed form of shellac used as a basis for French polish.

dhup *(canarium euphyllum)*　Hardwood　from Andaman islands. About 25 lb (400 kg) to 30 lb (481 kg). Pale mahogany colour, used for cabinet work, floats, matches, etc.

diagonal rod　Used to test squareness of a carcase. One end has a pointed, applied piece which fits into the carcase corner, enabling the rod to clear any intervening shelves or partitions. The diagonal length is marked with pencil and the rod reversed into the opposite corners, when the same length will show if the carcase is true.

diagonal spline miter　(USA)　Corresponds　to British tongued mitre (see under *mitre, tongued*).

diaper　A regular and systematic decorative arrangement of a repeating pattern in marquetry, inlay etc. Frequently used in the decorative marquetry on Louis XVI furniture.

diffuse porous　Term used in identification of timber when end grain is examined. The pores are dispersed evenly with only slight grouping along the annual rings which thus scarcely show.

DIFFUSE POROUS

diminished stile　A house door stile narrower at the top than at the bottom so that maximum light is passed at the glazed top. (See also *gunstock stile*.)

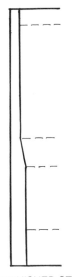

DIMINISHED STILE

dimity　A stout cotton fabric with stripes or patterns chiefly used for bed hangings.

dining table　From the late 15th century the custom of the Lord eating with the members of his manor in the great hall began to wane, and he and his family ate in a separate smaller room. This called for a smaller table than the customary trestle or joyned table, and thus the design for a dining table appeared. From this concept all the various kinds of extending and flap tables developed.

dinner wagon　Of similar form to a tea trolley, but of heavier construction and often larger. Cupboards and drawers are often fitted. The legs are generally fitted with large, rubber-tyred castors which facilitate movement over rugs, etc. (See also *tea trolley.*)

dip seat　A seat frame which is curved to match the curved seat front and back rails.

dip-up　A polishing rubber is usually charged by removing the covering and shaking polish on to it. In fadding, however, more polish is needed and the fad is dipped into the polish, hence the term.

disc sander　Two kinds: rigid disc and flexible disc. The latter is little used in woodwork except for the rough cleaning of old surfaces, removing paint, etc. The rigid disc type is used mainly for trimming rather than smoothing. Useful for trimming mitres, butt ends, short chamfers, and levelling projecting ends of joists, etc. The circular path of the abrasive makes the disc sander unsuitable for smoothing work to be polished.

dished　A surface with the centre lower than at the outside. Thus it is similar in form to a dish or plate.

display cabinet　A cabinet with glazed doors and ends. It can be either mounted on a stand or wall-hanging. The shelves can be wood but are often glass; the back of the cabinet is usually lined with velvet or baize. It is intended to display objets d'art, ornaments, or collections. (See also *vitrine.*)

distressing　The practice of subjecting furniture to treatment which simulates the effect of age. Bruising, scuffing, and staining the appropriate parts are the principal agents; sometimes dust is applied to a glued area!

divan bed　A bed in which the mattress is supported upon a low framework. There is no separate head and foot, though a loose headboard fitting in sockets is generally provided. The frame is usually dovetailed at the corners, with equidistant recessed cross rails glued and screwed beneath the side edges and finishing flush. The legs are checked for attaching to the inside corners. Frames should be made to suit the size of mattress to be used. To provide accommodation for blankets, sheets, etc., some designs of divan beds have a bottom compartment or two large drawers.

dog, bench　Metal or wood sprung pegs which fit into a line of square holes, usually about 1 in × 1 in (25 mm × 25 mm), to form an end stop in conjuction with a tail vice when cramping long pieces on a bench top.

dog, joiner's　Metal fitting with pointed ends. Used to drive into the ends of glued joints to bring the parts close together. Avoids use of cramps.

dog kennel　The open kneehole in a West Wales dresser, which has two cupboards below a row of drawers, the cupboards being arranged on either side of the kneehole.

dog-leg chisel　A carving chisel with a cranked blade. The bevel (cannel) is ground uppermost and the blade tapers back from the cutting edge. The chisel is used for finishing flat surfaces in relief carving: it is made in two widths, namely ¼ in (6 mm) and ½ in (12 mm).

dog spring　Light form of cramp for holding parts of irregular shape together whilst the glue sets.

dog teeth　Type of teeth used in some circular saws. Similar to peg tooth, but with front edge radial to saw. (See *circular saw (B)*).

dolls' houses　These enjoyed great popularity in the late eighteenth and early nineteenth centuries when they were called 'baby houses'; the Prince Regent is recorded as having one.

dolphin　A subject frequently used in conventional form as a motif for wood carving, inlay, and marquetry.

dolphin hinge　So-called because ot its supposed resemblance to a dolphin; used in conjunction with quadrant stays for secretaire (secretary) flaps. See *snake hinge.*)

domes-of-silence　Another name for gliders (*q.v.*).

donkey, marquetry cutter's　An appliance formerly widely used in marquetry cutting. The worker sat astride the seat and held the pack of veneers in a vertical position between the jaws by pressing down on the treadle. The saw was held in a frame and moved back and forth, the end of the frame supported on a rod along which it was free to slide. The rod in turn was held on pivoted rockers so that a fair amount of side movement of the saw was possible. Thus, in use, the veneer pack was turned to suit the required direction of cut.

donkey's ear shooting board A special shooting board used when trimming mitres at ends of plinths, skirting boards, and similar wide material. The ear piece or stop slopes at 45 degrees. In use, the board should be clamped in a bench vice to ensure firmness. (See also *mitre shooting-block.*)

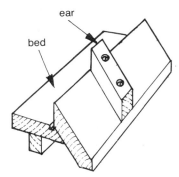

DONKEY'S EAR SHOOTING BOARD

door The common framed room door is shown here with the names of the various parts. (See also *barred, framed, flush, ledged and braced, revolving, sliding, trap, etc.*)

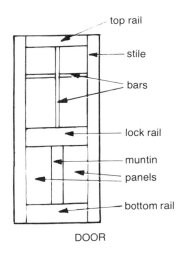

DOOR

door closers or spring Three types of door closers are shown. (A) is an oil-check type made for light, medium, and heavy doors. It closes the door firmly, but gently, without a noise even against a latch. It is fixed at the top of the door near the hinged stile, with the arm connected to the lintel; instructions are supplied with each model. (B) is a coil-spring type suitable for gates or doors. The metal ear pieces are screwed to door and post so that when the door is opened the spring tightens. A tommy bar is provided for adjustment. (C) is a helical-spring type. It is fixed to the door post so that its roller at the end of the arm runs upon the door plate.

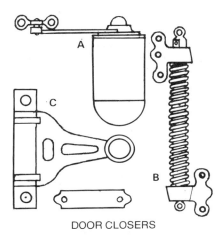

DOOR CLOSERS

door cores Flush doors consist of a framework clad with veneered panels or plastic laminate facings. In both cases the hollow interior space contains a core which not only helps to keep the two faces of the door parallel but also adds weight and reduces the reverberations if the door slams. Such cores can be solid or skeleton. Skeleton cores comprise strips of wood fixed into the interior space, leaving gaps or holes for ventilation; solid cores can be strawboard, synthetic fibre-board, or a synthetic-resin impregnated paper core in a cellular pattern.

Doric The first order of Grecian architecture; from the Dorian race in ancient Greece.

dormant table A table used in the 15th to 17th centuries in which two or more trestles (or 'horses' as they were called then) were linked together with a heavy piece of timber which acted as a longitudinal stretcher; each end of the stretcher was tusk-tenoned (*q.v.*) and pegged to give stability.

dormer An upright window in a sloping roof.

dornic Also called 'dornix'. A heavy damask linen cloth originally made at Tournai.

doty Wood which shows an early or slight stage of decay due to attack by fungi. Sometimes known as dozy or dosy.

double-bow Windsor chair A modern (1962) style, designed by Lucian Ercolani. It resembles the American 'sack-back' Windsor chair (q.v.), and has a D-shaped flat seat, an arm bow, and a back bow.

double dovetail halving A halving joint which resists stresses in both directions. Apart from the halving, each piece has two slot dovetails so that bending is resisted in both directions. It would be used only in work liable to be subjected to heavy strain.

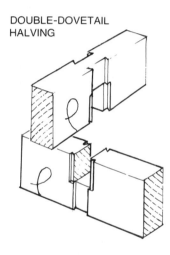

DOUBLE-DOVETAIL
HALVING

double-ended tenoner (see *tenoners*).

double-ender and profiler (see *tenoners*).

double H underframing A form of chair under-framing in which the side stretchers or rails are connected by two cross members at right angles.

double-lapped dovetail A dovetail joint in which both joining pieces have a lap. The lap in one piece is allowed to project. Thus, the only indication of the jont is the thin line of end grain. Either the piece with the dovetails or that with the pins can have the projecting lap. When the pins have the projecting lap it is necessary to cut the pins first as otherwise it is awkward to transfer the marks. The joint is often used for the tops of bureaux and cabinets. (See also *lapped dovetail* and *mitre dovetail*.)

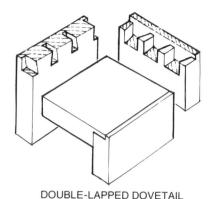

DOUBLE-LAPPED DOVETAIL

double raking shoring A form of shoring (q.v.) in which two sloping members or rakers are used to support the side of a building.

double-rebated and bead Used for external angles; needs to be secured by nailing.

double-tenon joint Used for extra wide rails. It is stronger than a single wide tenon (See A). The joint having two tenons side by side (B) is generally termed a twin tenon joint. It is used for thick stuff.

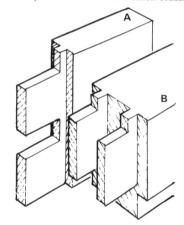

DOUBLE TENON JOINTS

double-tongued mitre joint A variation of the rebated mitre joint for external angles. It is very strong and is secured by nailing.

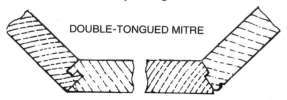

DOUBLE-TONGUED MITRE

dough table (USA) A sturdily-made planked table on which bread dough was kneaded. Also called a 'bread mixing table'.

Douglas fir *(pseudotsuga taxifolia)* The timber of one of the most noble of British Columbian trees widely used for heavy constructional work, bridges, masts, agricultural implements, interior woodwork, etc. For long it has been known under alternative names such as British Columbian pine, Oregon pine, red pine, yellow fir, and red fir. The tree is now cultivated in this country.

dovetail A joint in which one part is tapered in shape rather like a dove's tail and fits in a socket shaped to correspond. By its shape it thus resists any outward pull. The slope is not critical but should be somewhere between 1:6 and 1:8. A greater angle is inclined to cause the corners to split away. There are many variations of the joint. (See *double-lapped dovetail, dovetail halving, dovetail housing, hopper dovetail, lapped dovetail, mitre-dovetail, through dovetail.*)

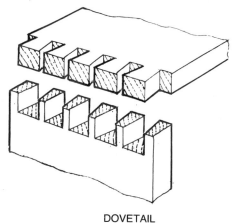

DOVETAIL

dovetail cleating A method of holding boards straight by inserting a cleat which is dovetailed in section and lengthwise so that it tightens as it is driven home.

dovetail cutter, router A rotary bit used in the electrical router or dovetailer. Cuts both dovetails and pins in one operation. Consequently, pins and tails are always of equal size.

DOVETAIL CUTTER

dovetail halving This is usually of T form, but may be at an odd angle. The halving is usually barefaced at one side and dovetailed at the other as shown.

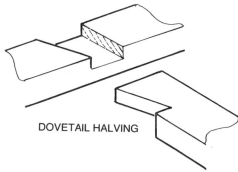

DOVETAIL HALVING

dovetail housing joint (see *p. 52.*)

dovetail key Hardwood keys which are double-dovetailed and inlaid into wide work to increase the strength of the joint; they are usually blind — that is, they do not penetrate the full thickness of the work.

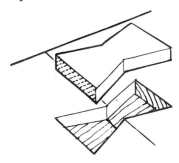

DOVETAIL KEY

dovetail marker A simple appliance enabling dovetails to be set out at the correct slope at the trimmed end of a board. The board is divided to give

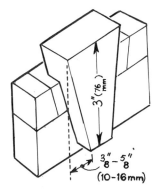

DOVETAIL MARKER

the width of the dovetails, the marker brought to each mark, and a pencil line drawn down its side. These sides slope at about ½ in (12 mm) in 3 in (76 mm). The notch on the marker enables it to engage with the board end.

dovetail saw A small backsaw with blade about 8-10 in (203-254 mm) long and with fine teeth, 18-22 points per inch (25 mm). Front of teeth are set at an angle of 75 degrees. Used for sawing dovetails and for fine bench work generally. (See also *backsaw*.)

dovetail housing joint The chief application of this is in fitting shelves in bookcases, wardrobes, etc. Its advantage over the plain housed joint is that it resists outward stress. The dovetail is a wedged fit and can be tapered on both edges or on one edge only. The latter simplifies fitting since the joint is not tight until pressed home. In good cabinet work, the joint is stopped near the front edge of the gables so the housing is not shown. Grooving is done with a tenon saw, chisel, and router. Note that the square side of the groove as distinct from the tapered side is at the bare-faced side of the joint.

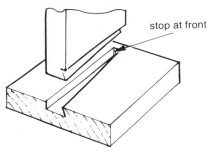

stop at front

DOVETAIL HOUSING

dowel bit A shortened version of ordinary twist bit made for boring (A). (B) is used in a brace to round off the ends of dowels. (See *dowel trimmer*.)

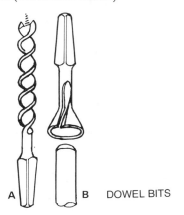

A   B   DOWEL BITS

dowel plate Used for making dowels by hand. Usually made from mild steel bar about 8 in (203 mm) by 1½ in (38 mm) by ¼ in (6 mm) with clean-cut holes ranging from ¼ in (6 mm) diameter up to ⅝ in (16 mm) diameter. The wood is planed roughly round then knocked through one of the plate holes with a mallet, the sharp rim of the plate hole removing the waste wood. The holes may be spiked at one side, the spike forming a groove on the wood as it passes through. Prepared dowels can be grooved in this way. (See also *dowels*.)

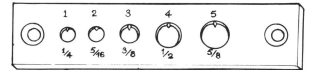

1   2   3   4   5

¼   5/16   3/8   ½   5/8

DOWEL PLATE

dowels Round wooden pegs used to join wooden parts together. They are either available in the form of rods, or cut off to length with a straight or spiral glue-escape groove and the ends trimmed. When dowels are cut off to length from the rod, a groove should be sawn along the length to allow surplus adhesive to escape.

dowel screw A double-ended screw for fixing small legs, feet, etc. to woodwork. Holes are bored in the joining parts, the screw inserted half way by gripping its shank with nippers and turning the leg or foot against it. The projecting half is then screwed to the other part by turning the foot. Dowel screws with one end threaded for a fly-nut are ideal for temporarily fixing legs, etc. to tables, stands, and so on.

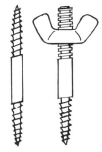

DOWEL SCREWS

dowelled joint Any form of joint in which dowels are used to hold parts together. Sometimes used in cheap work to replace the mortise and tenon. It should not be confused with the pegged joint in which a dowel is passed through mortise and tenon to hold the two together.

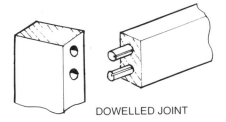

DOWELLED JOINT

dowelling jig   A tool enabling holes to be bored accurately in exact positions. Specially useful for dowelling door frames, mitres, and similar work. There are metal sleeves, varying in size, supplied with the jig enabling various bits to be used.

dowel trimmer   A bit for chamfering the ends of dowels. Shaped rather like an inverted funnel. It enables the dowel to start easily into its hole. (See *dowel bit (B)*.)

dragon's blood   Colouring agent for polish consisting of red resinous pieces. Has been largely replaced by aniline dye.

drake foot   (USA) A narrow three-toed foot often used on the Philadelphia chair (circa 1775). Also called 'Dutch foot', 'duck foot', or 'web foot'.

draw-boring   A process applied to the mortise and tenon joint. It locks the joint and forces the tenon right home into its mortise. It consists of passing a peg right through the joint, the holes being slightly staggered so that pressure on the joint is automatically exerted. The hole is bored right through the mortised piece, the tenon put in position, and the bit pressed into the hole so that it marks the tenon. The tenon is

then withdrawn and the hole bored slightly nearer the shoulder. A draw-bore pin should be knocked into the hole first, this consisting of a tapered steel rod. When this is withdrawn the wood peg can be inserted. Draw-boring can also be applied to open mortise and tenon joints.

drawer bottom slips   (A) Grooved strips to receive a drawer bottom. (B) Supporting centre muntin strip required for long drawers. The strips are usually grooved for $\frac{3}{16}$ in (5 mm) plywood. Type (C) used when slip must not project above bottom. In this case the edges of the bottom are rebated to be flush at the top.

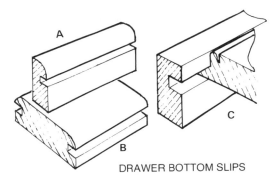

DRAWER BOTTOM SLIPS

dower chest   (USA) A chest for containing a young woman's dower (blankets, sheets, clothes, household articles) in readiness for marriage. They were often painted with folk-art decoration reminiscent of the European peasant furniture from which they derived. Christian Selzer (1749 to 1831) was a well-known maker.

drawer joints   In a well-made drawer the sides are lap-dovetailed to the front and through-dovetailed to

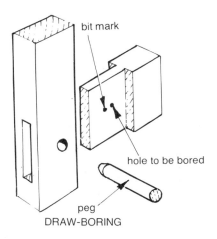

bit mark

hole to be bored

peg

DRAW-BORING

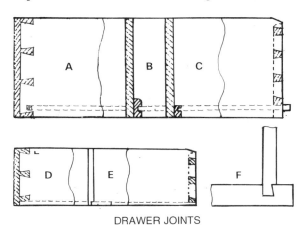

DRAWER JOINTS

the back. The pins at the front are kept small, running almost to a point. The bottom dovetail must be low enough to cover the end of the groove worked in the drawer front to hold the bottom. The back starts immediately above the bottom, the latter being screwed upwards to it. At the sides the bottom is held by grooved drawer bottom slips *(q.v.)*. In small drawers the bottom is sometimes fitted in rebates worked around sides and front. This necessitates a square part being left beneath the front bottom dovetail to fill in the end of the rebate.

drawer lock chisel A cranked chisel for cutting recesses to take cut locks in drawers. Made with cutters, the edges of which are at right angles to each other. It can be used in a confined space where it would be impossible to use an ordinary chisel. It is tapped into the wood with a hammer.

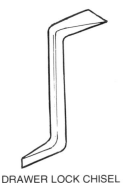

DRAWER LOCK CHISEL

drawer rail Rail fitted between cabinet ends on which the drawer runs. It is usually double-tenoned into the ends. Back edge is grooved to receive the dustboard.

drawer run (USA) Corresponds to British 'drawer runner' *(q.v.)*.

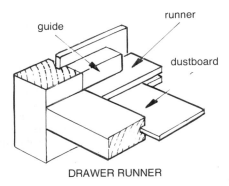

DRAWER RUNNER

drawer runner The wood rail fixed inside the cabinet behind the drawer rail. It usually fits in shallow grooves and is glued at front only. A stub-tenon at the front fits into the rail, and the rear is screwed, slots being cut to allow for the movement of solid wood.

drawer runners and rollers The most popular type is a set of paired metal strips with nylon wheels, known as 'Blum' drawer runners; they are simply screwed in place. There are several other types of metal, nylon, or plastic runners.

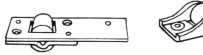

DRAWER RUNNERS & ROLLERS

draw-extension table A convenient type of dining table which, by means of two sliding leaves below the main top, may be extended in length. The leaves are operated by tapered slides which pull outwardly against stops, the main top falling into place between them. A useful average size is 36 in (914 mm) square. Thus, if the leaves are 12 in (305 mm) wide, the table will extend to either 4 ft (1,219 mm) or 5 ft (1,524 mm). Height should not exceed 29 in to 30 in (736-762 mm) the main top and leaves being built as solid framed panels.

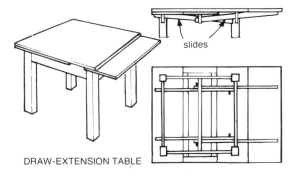

DRAW-EXTENSION TABLE

draw knife A two-handled cutting tool used for the quick shaving of wood; also for chamfering and rounding edges. In workshops it is frequently called a 'shave'.

dresser In old furniture the term refers to a free-standing wall piece in two separate parts; the lower a form of side table with fairly deep drawers, generally with turned legs, and a shallower upper carcase with shelves to receive plates, and often with tall, narrow cupboards. In later times it became a kitchen fitment, again with shelves and drawers. Today it has been largely replaced by the fitted kitchen cabinet or fitment. (See also *Welsh dresser.*)

dressing stick　A stick made up of silicon-carbide particles, and used for truing-up grinding wheels.

dressing table　This kind of table emerged as a distinct type in the 17th century, evolving from the small chest or casket used in Elizabethan and Tudor times to contain toilet articles. These chests were raised on legs and by 1730 had become tables fitted with drawers, a knee-hole, and a lift-up top with a mirror on its underside. Later in the 18th century they were swathed in drapery and separate mirrors and stands were added.

driers　A substance added to paint to make it dry more quickly. In oil polishing a little drier such as terebine is added to linseed oil to enable the latter to harden off.

drill　Although drills were originally used chiefly for metalwork, they are now also popular in woodwork, mainly because of the advantages of the morse drill (see *drill bits*). The term also refers to the tool which holds the drill and there are several kinds: hand drill; breast drill; Archimedean drill; electric drill; pillar drill; push drill; drilling machine. (See under individual headings.)

drill bits　Although used principally for drilling holes in metal, these bits have many uses in woodwork. There are both plain-shanked and square-shanked bits, the former being intended for use in a hand or breast drill, and the latter for the woodworker's brace. Drill bits for normal requirements range in size from $^3/_{64}$ in (1 mm) up to $^1/_2$ in (12 mm). Brace drills usually range from $^1/_{16}$ in (1 mm) to $^1/_2$ in (12 mm).

drill formula　The optimum drill speed is calculated from the formula S (speed of drilling in metres per minute) = 3.14 × D (drill dia in mm) × R (rpm), divided by 1,000 (to convert mm to metres).

drilling machine　Both table and drill are mounted upon a column and are adjustable in height. The table is usually adjustable anglewise and can pivot laterally. The revolving drill (often variable speed) can be lowered with pressure on to the work by an arm or group of arms. Chuck is made to take drills up to $^1/_4$ in (6 mm) or $^1/_2$ in (12 mm) according to size of machine. More popularly known as a 'pillar drill'.

drill stand　Stand into which an electric hand-drill can be mounted for accurate vertical or angled drilling.

drip moulding　Also called a 'corona' *(q.v.)*, which was a classical moulding, usually a large flat projection in a cornice moulding. Its purpose was to prevent capillary attraction by undercutting the projection so that rainwater could not soak the underside.

drop black　Berlin black *(q.v.)*.

drop-dial clocks　The term 'drop-dial' refers to the wooden case or box at the bottom of the dial on an Act of Parliament or tavern clock *(q.q.v.)*; it protects the short pendulum and bob and usually has a glass front. The bottom of the case is hinged and can be opened to give access to the regulating screw on the bob.

drop-end　Used at the end of some settees to enable the user to lie flat. There are several variations to the principle.

drop handle　Also called 'pear drop' or 'tear drop' from its shape. Popular between 1690 and 1720, the handle was usually brass (hollow or solid) and had a split pin fixing which passed through a back plate and then through the drawer front, the leaves of the pin (called a 'snape') being bent over. Modern types have a threaded shank which passes through the drawer front, secured by a nut. An alternative design was a scroll shape with a bifurcated end.

drop-in seat　A separate seat frame, usually upholstered, which fits into and rests upon a rebate worked around the framework of a chair or stool. The rebate in the rails has to be continued across the legs. In fitting the seat allowance has to be made for the thickness of the covering upholstery..

drop leaf table　(see *'flap table'.*)

drop ornament　A split turned ornament used chiefly in Jacobean furniture; also used to describe the husk or 'bell flower' *(q.q.v.)* ornament on 18th century pieces.

drum sander　The term usually refers to the heavy-production type in which the wood is carried on an endless rubber belt beneath the sanding drums which are covered with abrasive. There may be one or more drums. In the latter case the abrasive on the second and third drums becomes progressively finer. Another smaller form of drum sander has a flexible drum inflated to suitable pressure, enabling it to finish shaped surfaces of varying curvature.

drum table Also called a 'capstan', a 'loo', a 'monopodium' or (incorrectly) a 'rent' table *(q.q.v.)*. A circular table with a frieze containing drawers, mounted on a column which is supported by a base with tripod feet.

drunken saw Mounted upon the circular saw on a special arbor fitted with tapered collars. The saw is held at a slope, the angle of which can be varied by altering the position of the collars. Thus grooves of varying width can be cut. The bottom of the groove is necessarily slightly hollow, but this is so slight as not generally to matter.

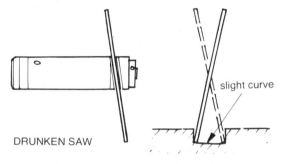

slight curve

DRUNKEN SAW

druxy A term to describe the early stages of decomposition which is characterised by white or yellowish streaks along the grain. Also spelt 'droxy'.

dry colors (USA) Coloured pigments in powder form for mixing with a solvent to form stains.

dry rot A simple term to denote one of timber's most inveterate enemies, the fungus known to scientists as *merulius lacrymans*. When a building is attacked there is no alternative but to remove and destroy every affected part. Preventive measures are briefly these. (1) Keep timber dry through adequate ventilation, avoiding leakage from roofs, water pipes, and drains. (2) Decayed wood burned and any sound wood left treated with a preservative. (3) Adjacent walls sterilised with an antiseptic. (3) New woodwork treated with a preservative prior to fitting. Creosote is one of the best known and most effective agents. In the case of the ground floor air bricks should be provided beneath on both sides to ensure a through draught. A blowlamp is effective in destroying all traces of the growth.

dry sink (USA) A piece of kitchen furniture usually made of yellow pine and comprising a cabinet with planked ends, two doors enclosing a cupboard containing shelves, the whole being surmounted by a wooden trough or sink which holds pitchers, churns, buckets etc.

dub To round off.

duchesse A kind of day bed composed of two barjier (bergere) *(q.v.)* chairs facing each other with a matching stool between them. Designs were offered by both Hepplewhite and Sheraton.

duck foot (see *drake foot*).

dug-out chest Also called a 'monoxylon' *(q.v.)*. They date back to Saxon times (circa 600 to 900), but the majority were twelfth century, squared-up tree trunks fitted with lids and with cavities for valuables. They were often fitted with several keys and there was an equal number of keyholders, none of whom could open the chest on his own. The outstanding feature was their size which often reached 10 ft (3050 mm) with a cavity of only, say, 2 ft long by 1 ft wide by 9 in deep (610 by 305 by 230 mm).

dulling A process used in french polishing to take off the extreme brightness of the shine. Tripoli powder is used, this being dusted along the surface with a fine-haired dulling brush which gives a series of fine scratches over the entire surface.

dumb waiter Corresponds to US 'lazy Susan'. There are two types: the first consists of a circular dish with a lip (often a piecrust edge) which is mounted on a base, a revolving movement being interposed between them. The second has two, or more usually, three circular trays mounted on a shaft which is fixed to a tripod base. The trays revolve, and in some cases have flaps which fold down when not in use.

duplex nail A double-headed nail used in temporary work such as scaffolding where the structure is eventually to be dismantled. The second head enables it to be withdrawn easily.

dustboard A horizontal division between drawers which was introduced to prevent the contents of one drawer piling up and jamming against the drawer above. It is most unlikely that its purpose was to keep out dust as any good cabinet maker is proud to make drawers fit snugly so that dust cannot enter; in fact, one of the tests of a well-fitted drawer is that it should expel air when it is closed.

dust extractor A suction system which draws dust and chips away from the machine, keeping the working surfaces, floor, etc., clear. It is specially necessary for sanding machines in which the abrasive dust could be harmful. In large shops a manifold system is usually installed for the withdrawal of waste.

dusting (USA) The antiquing of a finish by rubbing away a wax finish with rottenstone powder.

Dutch elm disease This is caused by a fungus *(ceratostomella ulmi)* which spreads through the pores of the Dutch elm tree and blocks them in the sapwood so that water and dissolved mineral salts cannot enter. The leaves wilt and the tree dies back. The disease is spread by the bark beetle *(Scolytus scolytus)* which carries the spores from tree to tree.

Dutch foot (USA) Corresponds to British 'club foot' *(q.v.)*.

dwarf bookcase A low bookcase about 3 ft 6 in (1066 mm) or less in height. The term dwarf is applied to any low cabinet or cupboard.

dye Used largely in wood finishing in both stain and in colouring polish. Chief kinds are aniline and spirit *(q.v.)*.

EAR PIECES

eagle, American (USA) An emblem of the USA, adopted in 1786; it represents the American bald eagle with outspread wings, and replaces the earlier emblem of a phoenix.

ear pieces The projecting pieces at the top of cabriole legs. To save waste they are invariably applied. (See Illustration opposite.)

easy chair An upholstered chair, with padded arms and backs; designed for reclining or sitting.

eaves The lower edge of a sloping roof where it overhangs the wall.

eaves fascla A board fixed vertically to the lower ends of roof rafters. Its top edge sometimes projects upwards and acts as a tilting fillet for the bottom row of tiles. The gutter is generally screwed to it.

eaves plate When the lower edge of a roof is supported on posts or piers, there being no continuous wall to take a wall plate, an eaves plate is fitted, the rafters being notched over it.

eaves soffit A board fitted beneath the bottom ends of rafters behind the fascia. It is carried on brackets nailed to the side of the rafters.

ebeniste French term for a cabinet maker from about 1743; such craftsmen were concerned with making veneered furniture, as distinct from *menuisiers (q.v.)*.

ebonising The process of finishing woodwork black in imitation of ebony. A fine-grained wood is essential. The wood is stained with black stain, either proprietary or made with black aniline dye, and the grain filled in with a black paste filler. It is then polished with black or ebony polish made with 1 pint (0.57 litre) white French polish to which $\frac{1}{2}$ oz (14 grams) black spirit aniline dye is added. To make the polish a still more intense black a piece of Reckitt's washing blue wrapped in muslin is dipped into it and squeezed until a little of the blue is dissolved. Stir thoroughly, then strain the whole through muslin. The entire polishing process is carried out with this black polish. Finally the polish is dulled by dipping a fine-haired brush into the finest pumice powder and drawing it along the surface, or using the finest grade steel wool lubricated with wax polish and rubbed in the direction of the grain.

ebony, coromandel Sometimes known as calamander, a richly striped ebony found in some of the finest trees from Ceylon.

ebony *(diospyros mespiliformis)* A very heavy and dense timber of dark colour used for piano keys, chessmen, walking sticks, small boxes, and general ornamental work. Owing to its limited supply now rarely used for furniture. The wood (unstained) is seldom quite black, but is heavily streaked with shades of deep grey, brown, and purple. East African blackwood (one of the heaviest known woods) is more uniformly black. Mascassar ebony *(q.v.)*, chiefly used in veneer form, belongs to a different timber family.

ebony polish A black polish made from 1 pint (0.57 litre) white or transparent French polish with ½ oz (14 grams) black spirit aniline dye added. After thoroughly stirring the polish is strained through muslin. Sometimes Reckitt's blue is added to give a more intense black. (See *ebonising*.)

ebony stain A black stain made with black water-soluble aniline dye dissolved in water. For a spirit stain use spirit soluble dye in methylated spirit, or for an oil stain use oil-soluble dye in turps. There are many proprietary stains also.

echinus The convex member beneath the abacus in the Greek and Roman Doric orders. It varies considerably in shape. Also sometimes applied to egg and tongue moulding *(q.v.)*.

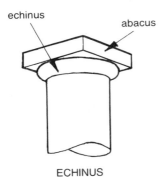

ECHINUS

edge mark A V-shaped mark made on the face edge of timber denoting that it is straight and is square with the face side which has been previously trued. All subsequent marking or testing is from either the face side or face edge.

edge plane A metal plane, sometimes called a chisel plane, having its cutter placed at the extreme front to enable it to work into corners. Used chiefly by piano case makers.

edge trimmer This trims a plastic laminate back flush with the edge of the substrate or baseboard to

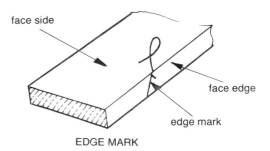

EDGE MARK

which it has been applied; the edge finish can be right-angled or bevelled according to the shape of the cutter used, or the position of the cutter relative to the work-piece. The cutters are tungsten-carbide-tipped and some have two square edges, some two bevelled edges, and some one square/one bevelled edge. The square edge is longer than the bevelled edge, and for square trimming, the cutter is set with the square edge into the cut; for bevels the cutter is lowered until the requisite amount of bevel is achieved. The machine has a standard electric motor and an ordinary drill or router chuck. A flat work guide (which can be adjusted to govern the depth of trimming) is set at right angles to the cutter axis and is held in contact with the face of the work-piece. There is also a small roller opposite to, and lined up with, the lower end of the cutter; this runs along the edge of the work-piece and controls the amount of material taken off.

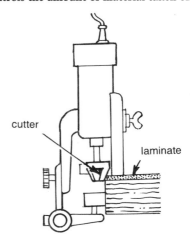

EDGE TRIMMER

edge trimming plane The sole of this metal plane is in the form of a rebate, the cutter operating on the side. In use, the upper face bears on the wood surface, the cutter removing shavings from the edge which is trimmed square, without needing to be tested with a try-square. The plane is handy for light trimming work, but has been superseded by the edge trimmer (*q.v.*).

edger Planing machine used for edges and narrow stuff. It usually has a tilting fence which can be fitted in any position across the width, and sometimes a rebating table. The machine will plane timber of any width up to the limit of the table width. Rebate depth is limited by the clearance above the main cutter block bearing.

edging Length of solid wood fixed to the edges of plywood, blockboard, or chipboard, partly to conceal the layers, but chiefly to provide a suitable fixing for the screws used for hinges and other fittings. It is usually held with a loose tongue.

The term also refers to the process of truing the edges of timber, either on the machine planer or with the hand plane.

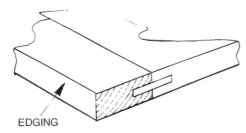

EDGING

Edict of Nantes This was granted by Henri IV of France in 1598 and authorised freedom of worship to Calvinists (Protestants). It was revoked in 1685 by Louis XIV and led to the expatriation of many Huguenot craftsmen, a large number of whom came to England.

egg and tongue ornament Carved detail often found on Renaissance and Georgian joinery and furniture, particularly on cornices. Consists of a series of egg-shapes which follow the main contour of the moulding with straps at each side. Between each egg with its pair of straps is a tongue shape. Sometimes known as 'egg and dart' moulding.

EGG & TONGUE MOULDING

eggcup chuck A chuck having a threaded ring with bevelled inner surface. Its purpose is to grip wood of a suitable size for turning an egg cup. The wood is first turned between centres, the main part being small enough to allow the ring to pass over it, but with a bevelled projecting part which the ring grips. Any small items of roughly egg-cup size can be turned in it.

EGGCUP CHUCK

ekki (*lophira alata*) A hardwood from West Africa, varying from dark red to deep brown. Coarse and interlocked in the grain. Difficult to work, and nails require pre-boring. Strongly resistant to all wood destroying agents. Weight 65 lb (1041 kg). Used chiefly for heavy structural work.

elbow chair An armchair on which the arms do not extend the full depth of the seat but only partway.

electric drill In woodwork it is used chiefly for drilling screw holes. It is fitted with trigger starting switch which can also be set for continuous running. A three-jaw chuck operated by key is an indication of the capacity, and is known by the largest size drill it will hold. Some models have two speeds and a hammer action. Many of the smaller drills have attachments such as circular saw, sander (rotary and orbital), jigsaw, grinder, polisher, etc. Also called a 'power tool' (*q.v.*).

elevation The usual method of representing a piece of woodwork in a working drawing. It shows the item seen from the front or side without perspective. It may be in full size or to scale. It is technically known as orthographic projection (*q.v.*). Main sizes are usually added, and parts are frequently shown in section to make construction and detail obvious.

ellipse The cross section of a cone at any angle other than at right angles with the axis.

elliptical arch An arch the shape of which is half an ellipse, the springing being along the line of the major axis.

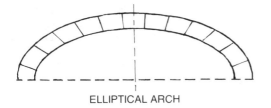

ELLIPTICAL ARCH

elm *(ulmus procera)* Principal uses are for constructional work, underwater piles and piers, ship work, coffins, and packing cases. Elm was the timber always used by the old school of carpenters for wooden pumps. Owing to interlocked grain it resists splitting, and can thus be nailed close up to the edge. Under water it appears to be almost imperishable. It can be obtained in extremely wide boards so that jointing is seldom necessary. Liable to twist and warp unless carefully seasoned. Generally needs kilning under experienced supervision.

embossed moulding A moulding in which the effect of carving is produced by embossing with a heated metal wheel on which is a reverse of the pattern. Supplied in many varieties. Made chiefly in oak, and the sapwood of the American gum — in this country often termed hazel walnut.

embula *(phoebe porosa)* Hardwood from Southern Brazil. A timber of the walnut type but is not a member of the true walnut family. Alternative titles are Imbuya or Imbula, and sometimes Brazillian walnut. Whitish when first cut but darkening to deep brown on exposure. Care needed in planing to avoid tearing out. Sawdust frequently has an irritant effect on the nasal passages. Stains and polishes well. Weight 45 lb (721 kg).

emery grinding wheel (see *grinding wheel*).

emery powder An abrasive powder made in various grades. In woodwork sometimes used on oilstones which have become hard in use, for cleaning steel tools, and sometimes in making blackboard coating.

emufohai Alternative name for odoko *(q.v.)*.

enamel A high-gloss finish made chiefly of varnish to which finely-ground pigment has been added. It is relatively slow-drying, and the brush marks flow out. Unless skilfully handled runs are liable to develop on vertical surfaces. Dust, dirt, grease, and a humid atmosphere are fatal to good enamelling.

encoignure A dwaft corner cupboard, sometimes with a super structure of shelves, popular in France circa 1750.

end check A split occurring at the end of a board during the seasoning process.

end grain The grain exposed by a cross cut made at, or approximately at, right angles with the grain direction. In drawings it is frequently shown shaded.

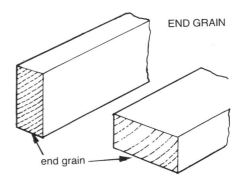

END GRAIN

end grain

endive scroll An ornamental motif used in carving (particularly on Louis XIV and XV furniture), and in marquetry. Based on the foliage of the endive plant.

ends A term used in cabinet making for the sides of a carcase. Sometimes known in the trade as the 'gables'.

enfilades French word to describe rooms opening to each other to create a vista.

eng *(dipterocarpus tuberculatus)* Pale, brownish-red timber from Burma. Used locally for boat and general building construction. Weight 40-55 lb (641-881 kg). 881 kg).

en grisaille A French term describing the fashion of painting in buff, green, and grey tones on furniture and walls.

entablature Term which embraces the architrave, frieze, and cornice surmounting the columns in classical architecture or at the head of a doorway or window.

entasis The slight swelling of a column in its length to counter the optical illusion of its being hollow.

entering chisel An alternative name for a spoon bit. (See (C) under *carver's chisel.*)

eosin powder   A red powder which can be dissolved in water and used to give warmth to water stains which are too cold in tone. It is in fact a red aniline dye.

epoxy resin   An adhesive based on thermo-setting synthetic resins which contain the epoxy groups in the uncured state: the resin and hardener must be mixed together for curing to start. They will cure at room temperature, but heat will hasten the process; can be used for bonding wood, glass, metal, and a wide range of other materials. Once cured, the bond is unaffected by most chemicals and the shrinkage is negligible. Can be bulked up with extenders *(q.v.)* and powder colour pigments can be added to tint them.

equilateral arch   A pointed arch struck with radii equal to the span. The centres are necessarily on the same horizontal line as the springing.

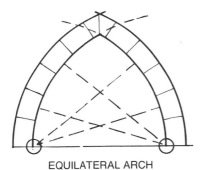

EQUILATERAL ARCH

equilateral triangle   A triangle having all three sides equal and all three angles (60 deg) equal. It is usually constructed with a 60 deg square, but can be set out with compasses.

escallop   A shell motif used in wood carving. Popular in the Queen Anne and Georgian periods. There are many variations of it, mostly conventionalised.

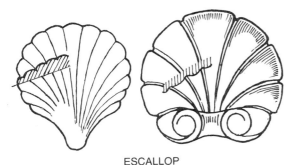

ESCALLOP

escapement   The recess in the top of a plane through which the shavings emerge. In an iron plane it can scarcely be said to exist since the plane is entirely open at the top, but in a wood plane it shows as a wide gap. In a wood spokeshave the escapement is at the rear immediately above the cutter.

escritoire   A writing desk or bureau *(q.v.)* with a vertical joint.

escutcheon   A metal protection for a keyhole. The flush type, sometimes known as the thread escutcheon, is shown at (A). The size should be a reasonably generous fit over the key. An antique pattern is given at (B). Plate escutcheons screwed or pinned to the face are given at (C), (D), and (E). That at (D) is for narrow stiles, and (E) has a cover, suitable for a room door. Some escutcheons are cut in ivory or a contrasting hardwood, and are inlaid flush into the surface. (See also *keyplate.*)

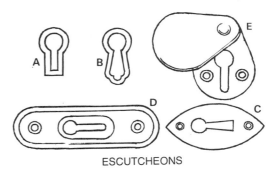

ESCUTCHEONS

espagnolette   A decorative feature sometimes employed as a mount on 18th century furniture; it depicts a woman's head with a collar ruff similar to those worn in Spain in the 17th century.

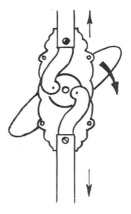

ESPAGNOLETTE BOLT

espagnolette bolt Used in french windows to secure both top and bottom (and sometimes the middle) in one operation. The bolts or rods must obviously be in alignment, and when these are held in separate guides the last-named need to be carefully placed. When there is no convenient place for boring holes to receive the bolts, special keepers are provided, these being screwed on.

etagère A set of shelves, one above the other, supported by columns. Derives from the French *table à ouvrage*, an earlier form of worktable. Popular in the Victorian era.

eucalyptus The botanical name given to a range of timbers from Australia. They include a variety of gums, ironbark, karri, stringy-bark, tallow-wood, Tasmanian oak, tuart, wandoo, etc. (See under separate entries.)

expanding bit A bit which can be adjusted to bore holes of varying sizes. For the larger holes a brace with a wide sweep is essential to increase the power. To reduce resistance, the bit has an inner nicker and cutter which work ahead of the larger outer cutter. There are two types of expanding bits, the Clark and the Steer patterns, the latter having a side screw giving accurate adjustment to the cutter.

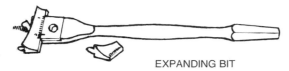

EXPANDING BIT

extenders Substances (in powder form) which can be added to resin adhesives to bulk them up and increase the rate of spreading. Ones in common use are: china clay, kaolin, and rye flour.

extending table A dining or board-room table, the length of which can be increased by the insertion of extra leaves. Various systems can be used, such as the draw-extension *(q.v.)*, screw extension, and that in which the leaves are held by metal fittings which engage in slots.

extension bit holder A holder fitted with a chuck which can be held in the brace similarly to an ordinary bit. It enables holes to be bored in a confined space where an ordinary bit would not reach, or where

EXTENSION BIT HOLDER

surrounding woodwork, etc., would interfere with the turning of the brace.

extrados The outside curve of an arch.

eye A staple for engaging a hook, a stair rod, or a padlock, etc. The term is also used generally to denote the centre point of any object such as the 'eye' of a volute on an Ionic capital, and the recess at the fold of the acanthus leaf *(q.v.)*.

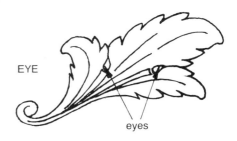

EYE

eyes

eyebrow window A window at the eaves in which the roof immediately above curves upwards in a flat curve.

F

face edge The edge of a piece of wood. It is planed straight and square with the face side. All subsequent marking and testing are from this or the face side. A pencil mark is put on the wood as shown. (See also *face mark* and *face side*.)

face mark The pencil mark put on the face side or edge of a piece of wood. (See *face side* and *face edge*.)

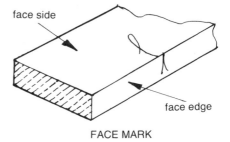

face side

face edge

FACE MARK

face measure The area in square metres or square feet of the surface of a board.

face mould A templet used in double-shaped work to mark the outline to which the material has to be cut. It is used in combination with a falling mould.

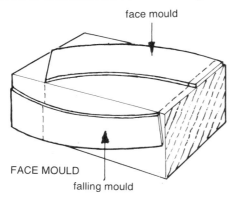

face mould

FACE MOULD

falling mould

face-plate A metal plate to be attached to a lathe mandrel in place of the usual chuck, and having a series of screw holes in it to enable the wood to be fixed to it. It is needed for turning flat items such as platters, small circular table tops, bowls, etc.

FACE-PLATE

face side The better wide surface of wood. All subsequent marking and testing is done from either it or the face edge (*q.v.*). It is denoted by the pencil mark. (See *face mark.*)

facing A thin strip of hardwood glued to a softwood shelf or some part of a carcase.

fad Used in the preliminary fadding process in french polishing. Made from unbleached cotton wool with the skin peeled away. It is folded to a convenient pear shape, soaked in polish, and left to dry. It is soaked afresh in polish and used as it is without a cloth cover.

fadding Early stage in french polishing. It follows the filling-in stage after the application of linseed oil. The latter should dry out, after which the polish is applied. It is followed by the colouring stage, or, if this is not needed, by bodying. The purpose is to provide a foundation for the bodying. The fadding is done with a special wadding rubber called a fad (*q.v.*) — medicated cotton wool is useless for the purpose. The fad is charged with french polish, pressed on to the back of an old piece of glasspaper to flatten it and distribute the polish evenly. Straight, even strokes, worked with the grain, are used, gradually covering the entire surface. On larger surfaces, the fad requires to be re-charged several times. A reasonable period for drying must be allowed between each application otherwise the fad will tend to stick. No oil must be used. If traces of wadding are left on the surface, such may be removed with the wet finger tip; if this is unsuccessful, the work is allowed to dry, then smoothed with glasspaper.

fald stool A folding stool, originally used by a bishop when officiating away from his own church.

fall The hinged writing top of a bureau or desk.

falling mould A templet for marking the edge or elevation shape in double-shaped work. (See *face mould.*)

false fence A wood fence attached to the metal fence of a spindle moulder, router, or other machine. The purpose is to support the wood being worked as close as possible to the cutter, and thus avoid splintering out. It is made continuous in length and is screwed or bolted to the metal fence. It is placed clear of the cutter, the latter set in motion, and the fence slowly shifted so that the cutter bites its way through

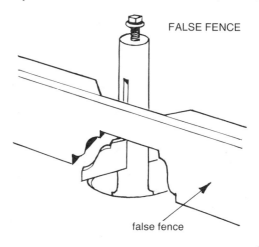

FALSE FENCE

false fence

the false fence. The only exposed part of the cutter is that which is actually cutting. The cutter has to be made correspondingly longer to reach through the false fence.

false tenon   A separate tenon inserted in the wood, notably in curved work in which the grain of a solid-cut tenon would run at an angle and be weak. Sometimes known as an 'inserted tenon'.

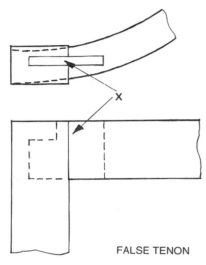

FALSE TENON

fan-back Windsor chair   In this style, the comb is slightly wider than the overall width of the seat and this has the result of fanning out the sticks in the back. Often combined with cabriole front legs.

farmhouse Windsor chair   Distinguished by having laths in the back instead of sticks.

farthingale chair   A chair (more properly called a 'back stool' as the back legs were vertical from the seat downwards) which had a low padded back and a wide, high seat with stuff-over upholstery. The purpose was to accommodate the voluminous skirts of the period (circa 1620) which were called 'farthingales'. The name appears to have been given during the Victorian era. Also called an imbrauderer's or upholsterer's chair.

fascia   A horizontal board fixed at the eaves. The gutter is frequently fixed to it. It also refers to any long horizontal board contained between mouldings, as for instance in a shop front.

fastenings   Refers to items used in fixing — nails, screws, bolts, plugs, etc.

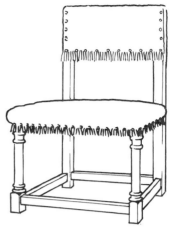

FARTHINGALE CHAIR

fat edge   A term describing the build-up of paint or varnish at the edge of the article being dealt with: it is caused by incorrect brushwork.

fauteuil   French term for an armchair with open arms and no cushion for the seat.

faux   French word meaning (in this context) 'imitation.' One can thus have 'faux bamboo', 'faux marbre' (marble), or 'faux tortoiseshell', etc. The effects are obtained by the skilful manipulation of paint.

favas   A diaper motif resembling the cells in a honeycomb used particularly in Louis XVI marquetry.

feather   A term sometimes applied to the loose tongue (*q.v.*) used in a tongued and grooved joint.

feather edge   The end of a piece of wood cut to a long, thin taper. It is not generally regarded as sound practice in a joint as the extreme end is fragile and shows a wide glue line.

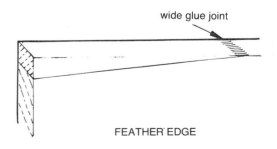

wide glue joint

FEATHER EDGE

feather-edged weather boards These are boards tapered in section with edges which overlap, or fit in a rebate. The boards are used extensively for covering sheds, poultry-houses, etc., attached horizontally, commencing from the bottom of the framework, with the thicker edge downwards. The boards are best fixed with nails, driven through. Above the rebate or overlap, which should not be more than ⅝in (15mm). This is to avoid splitting the board edges beneath, and allow for expansion and contraction. Boards cut from red cedar are the most reliable. There is a special weather board, introduced from Canada, which provides a flat outside and inside surface, due to one rebated edge fitting over another rebated edge. (See also *weather boards.*)

feed tables The tables on a machine (e.g. a planer) which carry the work while it is being introduced to the machine or when it has been machined. They are often called the 'infeed' and 'outfeed' tables; the terms are self-explanatory.

felt (1) A kind of cloth made of wool and cotton compacted together with size.

felt (2) (see *clash*).

fence A straight guiding rail of either metal or wood (or both) attached to a machine or hand tool to enable the cutter to be kept parallel with an edge. Thus there is a fence for a circular saw, planer, and sometimes bandsaw; also on a rebate fillister plane, plough, and many moulding planes. The term is also applied to a straight strip fixed to the wood to provide a bearing against which a plane can work.

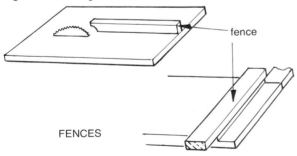

fence

FENCES

ferrule A metal collar fitted around a tool handle to prevent splitting. Also used for the metal fitting fixed to some peg legs.

festoon A carved or inlaid ornament of looped form, usually suspended from ribbon knots. Known also as a swag.

fibre Several kinds of fibre are used in upholstery. Coco or ginger fibre (taken from coconut husks) is as good as any. The best is long and is cut curled like hair. It tends to become brittle and break up in time. Wood fibre or wood wool is sometimes used but needs to be worked firmly. Algerian fibre is also widely used. It is black and green in colour. Sisal fibres are also used. Lastly there are the synthetic fibres made from the nylon group.

fibres, wood These are the thick-walled vertically-aligned cells responsible for the mechanical characteristics of a timber, and make the main contribution to its strength.

fibre board General term used for many building and wall boards made from wood pulp, cane, straw, and so on. (See under individual headings.)

fiddle-back chair Also called a 'bended back' chair. Its splat was often shaped like a fiddle (hence the name). It was made in walnut and had double curvature in the back and (usually) cabriole legs. Circa 1700.

fibre pads Ready-made pads obtainable by the yard and consisting of fibre, hair, or sisal woven on to hessian. They are cut to size and used in upholstery for pads and fillings.

fiddle-back figure Attractive ripple grain with light and dark streaks running across the grain. Found in some varieties of mahogany, sycamore, and maple. Often used on the backs of violins, hence the term.

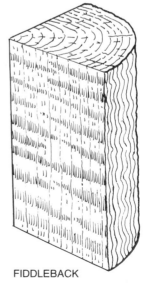

FIDDLEBACK

fiddle-back splat Describes the shape of the splat used in the Windsor chair of the same name; circa 1730. Also called the 'Hogarth' splat.

fielded panel A decorative panel used in a framework or door. It consists of a panel with a wide chamfered rebate worked around the edges. In working it a flat rebate is cut all round the wood about $\frac{1}{8}$in (3mm) deep first, then the rebate surface chamfered. Often a small moulding is worked at the inner side of the rebate. The cross grain should be worked first.

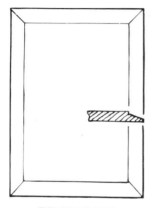

FIELDED PANEL

figure General and somewhat loosely applied term describing the decorative appearance of timber. It includes such items as curl, mottle, quilted, ripple, stripy, etc., and in particular refers to the silver grain or medullary rays in oak, beech, and silky oak.

file For woodwork the type generally used is the half-round cabinet file (A). It can be used on both concave and convex surfaces. It follows the rasp *(q.v.)*, giving a cleaner surface. For more acute concave shapes, holes, etc., the rat-tail file (B) is used. A handle should be fitted as the hand may otherwise be injured.

Metal-cutting files are required for sharpening saws, scrapers, and bits. A small flat file with safe edge is needed for the last-named. For saws either the single (D) or double ender (E) is used. The mill file is used to deepen the gullets in circular saws and certain cross-cut saws. It is similar to (C) but has rounded edges.

Ordinary chalk, rubbed into the teeth of files, reduces the tendency of filings to stick therein and acts as a lubricant. Files cut on the forward thrust only, and it is unwise to use heavy pressure when drawing the blade backwards over the metal, as it has

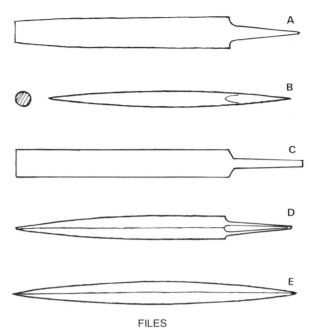

FILES

no cutting action and wears the file unnecessarily, quite apart from tending to pull off the handle. File teeth clogged with oil and dirt can be cleaned with an old suede-leather shoe brush or wire brush, or if paint is present, by immersion in strong caustic soda. Wood files, clogged with glue and dust, are cleaned by dipping into hot water, then rubbing with a scrubbing brush. Worn files, often discarded as useless, can be converted into useful scraping tools for wood turning.

filler, grain This is used early in the french polishing process on the more open-grained woods. Close-grained woods do not need filling. For fairly fine-grained woods the polish alone can be used, but it takes a lot of both time and polish, hence the use of a separate filler. One of the commonest is plaster of paris tinted with a dry pigment powder — red ochre for mahogany, brown umber for walnut and stained oak. Before being applied the work should be given two coats of french polish, partly to seal any stain that may have been applied, but chiefly to prevent the filler from turning white in the grain at a later stage. The filler is applied with a damp rag rubbed across the grain, and left for a minute or two for the glint to go off, when the surplus is rubbed off. Allow 24 hours to harden, then wipe over with linseed oil. This will kill any remaining whiteness and allow any remaining surface filler to be rubbed off. It should not be used on certain table top polishes since oil is incompatible with them.

There are many proprietary fillers, including those

which are cellulose based, and they must be used in strict accordance with the type of overall finish to be used, as the chemical base of the filler may not be compatible with that of the finish.

fillet A small square member used in conjunction with a moulding. Also applied to a rectangular strip of small section.

filling piece Piece of wood planted on to produce a flat surface, or to prevent sinking of a thin panel applied over a framework.

fillister plane A rebate plane fitted with a fence. If the fence is a fixture it is known as a 'standing' fillister; if adjustable the plane is called a 'moving' fillister. It may also have a depth gauge and tooth, the latter enabling the plane to be used across grain without previously sawing down to the depth. The tooth works ahead of the main cutter and the plane should be moved backwards a few times over the wood to scribe the line of cut. Wooden fillister planes, like most other wooden types, are becoming obsolete.

An adjustable metal rebating and fillister plane is shown. It has two positions for the cutter — one for ordinary work, and the other for bull-nose work. The plane is fitted with a $1\frac{1}{2}$ in (38 mm) wide cutter, spur, depth gauge, and adjustable fence. It is imperative that fillister plane cutters are ground and sharpened square so that the cutter edge is level with the side of the plane and does not scrape against the wood.

finger joint Used chiefly on the supporting bracket for a dropleaf table. It is similar to the knuckle joint (q.v.), but is simpler to cut in that there are no curved surfaces. Except for the centre pivoting hole, the entire thing can be cut with the saw and chisel. Note that the cuts at 45 deg enable the corners to clear each other as the bracket is moved. The pivot is usually a $\frac{1}{8}$ in (3 mm) rod of iron

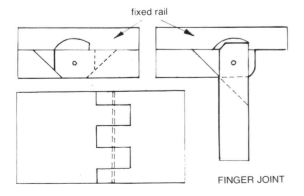

fixed rail

FINGER JOINT

finger joint (for panels). A mechanically-made joint used where flush doors are made; it enables small oddments to be glued up. It should not be used where tensile and bending strength is required.

finger planes Tiny planes used for trimming or hollowing work in cabinet and musical instrument making. Both the sole and the cutting edge of the iron are convex. Typical lengths are $1\frac{3}{8}$ in, $1\frac{3}{4}$ in, and $2\frac{1}{8}$ in (35, 45, and 54 mm). (See also *palm planes*.)

FINGER PLANE

finial Originally applied to the foliated knob at the extremity of a Gothic pinnacle, this term now describes a projecting ornament forming the termination of a newel post, or similar.

finish nail (USA) Corresponds to British 'oval nail' (*q.v.*).

finishing pins Similar to veneer pins (*q.v.*) but finer. Sizes normally range from $\frac{1}{4}$ in (6 mm) to $\frac{3}{4}$ in (19 mm).

fir See *Douglas fir*. There is also the noble fir (*abies nobilis*), the grand fir (*abies grandis*), and silver fir (*abies alba.*)

fire gilding (see *mercury gilding*).

firehouse Windsor chair (USA) A low-back chair, produced between 1850 and 1870 and used extensively by the volunteer fire brigades of the times.

fire retardants Although timber cannot be made wholly incombustible, there are two types of material which will retard the spread of fire; one type is applied to the timber by pressure impregnation, and the other is applied to the surface by brush, spray, or dipping.

The first type is normally used where there is a high risk of fire and its spreading to adjoining buildings, etc., and the second is for decorative woodwork or light wooden structures where the risk is less.

There are four ways in which a fire retardant can work, namely: the coating may swell to form an insulating layer; the fire retardant may change the thermal breakdown of the wood so that it smoulders instead of blazing; the coating may liquefy when heated to produce a glassy substance which coats the timber and cuts off the supply of oxygen; or the coating may be inert, thick, and heavy enough to keep out oxygen and absorb or dissipate the heat.

The chemicals used in the formulation of both types include: ammonium chloride, ammonium sulphate, boric acid, monoammonium dihydrogen, and zinc chloride.

Plywood panels have good fire-retardant properties because of the adhesives used in manufacture, particularly in the case of phenolic-bonded plywood. Specially-made highly fire-retardant panels are available; some have cores with incombustible materials such as asbestos, while others have been impregnated by one or other of the fire retardants already mentioned. Timber which has been treated and is to be used out-of-doors should be protected with a suitable preservative (*q.v.*); treated timber can also be glued but the manufacturer's approval should be sought in both cases.

fire screens   These were designed to give protection from the heat of open fires. They comprised three types: (1) the pole screen which had a small screen mounted on a pole supported on a tripod base. The screens often contained embroidered panels and were, at first, square but later became oval, circular, or shield-shaped; they could be moved up or down the pole to protect the face. Also called 'screen sticks'. (2) Banner screens, as the name implies, had the screen hanging from a cross-piece on the vertical pole, the latter being supported on a solid base. This type was popular in Regency times. (3) Horse or cheval screen: the screen was supported by a frame which had two legs at each end.

firmer chisel   This is the standard bench chisel. It is stronger than the bevelled chisel and is used largely for chopping. Both tang and socket types are available. Normal chisels range from about 4 in (102 mm) to 5 in (127 mm) in blade length, but extra long paring chiselscan also be obtained in the larger sizes. Firmer chisels are made from $\frac{1}{16}$ in (2 mm) full up to 2 in (51 mm) wide, with ash, beech, or box handles. (See also *bevelled-edge chisel.*)

FIRMER CHISEL

firmer gouge   This has an outside bevel for general bench work, such as cutting fluted recesses, removing waste, counter-sinking screw holes, etc. When

sharpened it is held at right angles to the oilstone and is half revolved as it is moved up and down so the entire edge is sharpened. The burr is turned back with an oilstone slip agreeing with the inside curvature of the blade. Obtainable in sizes from $\frac{1}{8}$ in (3 mm) up to $1\frac{1}{2}$ in (38 mm).

FIRMER GOUGE

firring pieces   Strips used to level up joists, etc., to enable boarding to be fixed down level.

firsts   Term describing best quality prime timber; an alternative modern term is FAS (firsts and seconds).

fish glue   Made from isinglass which is extracted from the bladder of the sturgeon. In lower grades the heads, skins, and cartilage are used. It is handy for small woodworking jobs, and is in fact used widely in the piano trade for repair work. Useful also for fixing leather, cloth, etc., to wood. Put up in tubes and cans.

fish plates   Plates of metal or wood used to join wood beams, etc., in length. They are bolted or screwed at each side, and are either plain (A) or have keyed (C) or notched joints (B).

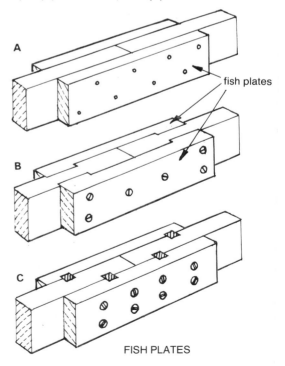

fish plates

FISH PLATES

fish skin A material prepared from fish skin, dressed and dyed to a delicate green colour, used for covering caskets, clock-cases, etc., and frequently embellished with silver mounts and fittings (circa eighteenth century).

fishtail gouge A carver's gouge, fan-shaped in length. (See *carver's gouges (E)*).

fissile Applied generally to the property that permits timber to be readily cleft or split.

fitch brushes These are made round or flat, and are of white hog hair fixed in metal ferrules with long, plain, whitewood handles. They are ideal for applying paint, polish, etc., to small mouldings, fittings, and so forth.

fitments A somewhat elastic term which includes built-in furniture generally.

fitting up The final process of finishing a piece of furniture after it has been polished, consisting of fixing handles, glass, etc.

five cutter Large industrial machine with five cutting heads which carry out five cutting operations — moulding, planning, grooving, etc. — at one pass.

fixing A process in polishing carried out with french polish to fix the previous work. Thus it follows oil staining before wax polish is used to prevent the latter from lifting the stain. It is also used after the colouring stage in french polishing to fix the colour. The rubber is applied lightly and quickly so as not to disturb the colouring coat.

flag seat Colloquial name for a 'rushed' seat.

flake white A powdered pigment sometimes added to glue to whiten it when used for light-coloured woods. It is also occasionally added to white french polish to lighten the tone of the wood.

flaking Applied to paint or varnish which has peeled away from the wood or from a previous coat owing to poor adhesion. May be caused by grease, moisture, or poor vehicles.

flap In furniture the fall-front of a bureau, secretaire, or desk; also the fall-leaf of a table. In joinery often seen in counter tops, in this case a rising flap.

flap sander This is a narrow drum which can either be mounted with its own motor, or fixed into a power drill. The drum, which is normally about 1 in (25 mm) thick and 5½ in (140 mm) dia has eight slots cut across its thickness. Strips of abrasive paper are contained inside the drum and a small amount of strip is fed through each slot; as the drum rotates its momentum forces the strips into the irregular or contoured faces of the work-piece. Behind each abrasive strip is a band of flexible bristles which support the abrasive and follow it into all the irregularities. There is also a similar design in which the abrasive strips are fixed direct to a small central drum which has an arbor allowing it to be used with a power drill or its own electric motor.

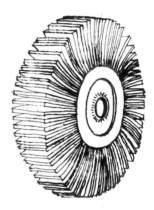

FLAP SANDER

flash A timber term describing large patches or 'flashes' of brightly shaded figure, usually in oak.

flat sawn Timber which has been cut tangentially to the annual rings. In a long cut through-and-through in parallel cuts the one or two centre boards are tangential at the pith only (this latter is not used in any case). Consequently these centre boards are largely quarter-cut, that is, radial to the annual rings. However, the term is usually taken as applying to the whole process of converting in this way. Other terms are slash sawn, plain sawn, bastard sawn.

flatting (1) Some veneers are liable to cockle as they dry out, and need to be flatted. Most veneers can be dampened and cramped between heated cauls. Difficult woods require a less drastic action. They should be dampened with glue size, and when pliable placed between flat boards with a heavy weight on top. More than one flatting process may be needed.

flatting (2) The process of re-sawing timber parallel to its edge or narrower face.

69

flatting (3) When polishing or lacquering woodwork it may be necessary to rub down the surface with the finest grade of glasspaper, although wet-and-dry paper is to be preferred. This should be 300 grade, and used wet in conjunction with soap, which acts as a lubricant.

flaxboard (see *particle boards*).

fleam teeth The acutely pointed teeth of some cross-cut saws. The included angle is in the region of 40 deg.

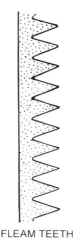

FLEAM TEETH

Flemish scroll A curved, reversed, double scroll used on William and Mary style furniture, circa 1690.

fleur-de-lis The national emblem of France: it is a stylised iris and was adopted by the Emperor Charlemagne from the country of Aquitaine after he had conquered it.

flier The parallel tread of a straight flight of stairs.

flight A term for stairs from one landing to another.

flight hole Small round holes in timber attacked by the furniture beetle. They are the holes from which the beetle emerges, not that of entry.

flitch A squared log ready for conversion for board or veneers. In softwood it is not less than 12 in (305 mm) by 4 in (102 mm) section, and 8 in (203 mm) by 4 in (102 mm) in hardwood.

float A coarse, rasp-like tool, having teeth which run right across the blade which is straight and flat. It is used chiefly in carpentry and joinery for levelling or enlarging big mortises, particularly through mortises, being used like a file.

flock An upholstery filling material made by shredding up rags. Alternatively, shredded wool fibres which are sprayed on to a surface which has been coated with an appropriate adhesive; the result is a smooth, baize-like appearence. The flock must conform to a minimum chlorine content when used for upholstery.

flooring awls These are heavier than the normal bradawl. Blades are 2¼ in (58 mm) to 2½ in (63 mm) long, in assorted widths, fitted with ash handles.

flooring board Nominal thickness of 1 in (25 mm) by 6 in (152 mm) or less. The general thickness of boards since metrication has become less and can be as little as 20 mm. The boards are finished with a plain joining edge, or grooved and tongued, sometimes (but rarely) grooved for loose tongues, or rebated. Flooring grade chipboards are available, 19 mm thick, and these are tongued on two sides and grooved on two sides, one long and one short in each case.

flooring chisel A special all-metal spade chisel, extra thin and flat to give a good cutting edge. Useful when repairing floor boards, i.e., when fitting new, short lengths, the ends being joined half-way over the thickness of joists. Also useful to plumbers, and sometimes known as the gas fitter's or electrician's chisel.

flooring cramp A special device, of which there are many varieties. All work on much the same principle, the purpose of which is to enable floor boards to be pressed tightly together when being nailed down. The pressure is produced by virtue of a strong grip obtained on the joists.

flooring saw The saw (A) having a curved edge is used when it is necessary to remove floor boards. In the usual way, the boards are cut by boring a hole

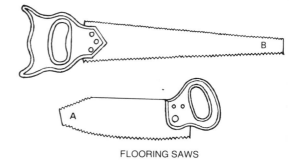

FLOORING SAWS

through them and cutting with a keyhole saw. Owing to the curvature of the flooring saw, one can make cuts across the boards until the teeth penetrate the wood, following which the end of the blade is inserted and the cutting completed. The saw (B) is a double-sided type, one side fine, the other coarse, used mainly by plumbers for cutting floor boards, but also handy for general purposes.

flour glasspaper   The finest grade of glasspaper, also known as No. 00. Used for high grade work, wood which has no definite grain direction, and in the polishing process.

flour, rye   Sometimes used to extend resin glue when used for veneering to cheapen the cost. (See *extenders*.)

flower   A term sometimes applied to the silver grain (*q.v.*) or figuring of oak.

flush   Term denoting that two surfaces are level.

flush bolt   Door bolt which is let into the wood so that it does not project from the surface. It may by fixed at the edge or back of the door.

flush doors   These consist of a framework clad with veneered panels or plastic laminate facings: the hollow interior space is filled with a core (see *door cores*).

flush panel   One which is level with the framework, at least at the front. It refers mainly to a door panel, but may be used for a framed table top. A bead is usually worked round to disguise the joint and to

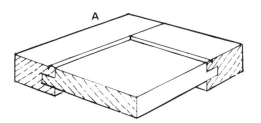

FLUSH PANELS

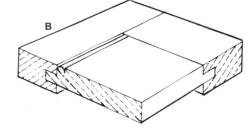

make any opening due to shrinkage less noticeable. If the bead is worked on the framework (A) it can be taken right through and the corners mitred. If worked on the panel the beads must be stopped and finished by hand, unless the end grain is left plain without a bead (B). This joint will not open because wood does not shrink in its length.

fluter   Carving gouge which is slightly deeper than a half-round gouge but not quite so deep as a veiner which is of U section (*q.v.*).

FLUTER GOUGE

fluteroni   Carving tool of section shown here. Properly sharpened it is invaluable for acanthus leaf carving in that by using different parts of the cutting edge an elliptical section can be cut, one tool only being used.

FLUTERONI GOUGE

flutes   Semi-circular sinkings spaced in rows on a column or pilaster, or (in shorter lengths) on a frieze.

fly-leaf   Applied to a hinged leaf such as that of a gate-leg table.

fly-rail   The rail or bracket that swings outwards to support the fall-flap of a table. It is usually pivoted with either the knuckle or the finger joint.

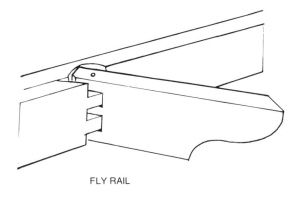

FLY RAIL

flys Odd pieces of lining, hessian, casement cloth, etc., sewn to a cover where it is not seen. Seats are often flyed on three sides; also backs inside arms where they disappear at the seat.

foil Denotes the point formed by the intersection of two circular arcs; a Gothic detail used in the 'trefoil', 'quatrefoil', and 'cinquefoil' designs. (See *quatrefoil*.)

folding leg bracket A KD fitting (*q.v.*) for fitting folding legs to tables.

folding wedges These are made in pairs, either to apply pressure or to raise the level of a structure. They are often used beneath temporary posts to support a floor or wall when an opening is being pierced. Another effective use is in cramping items together, especially large frames for which sufficiently long cramps are not available.

foliated Pertaining to the use of foils; decorated ornaments enriched with leaves.

fore plane The name given to a metal adjustable bench plane, 18 in (458 mm) long with $2\frac{3}{8}$ in (60 mm) cutter. It is a popular size, not so long as to be cumbersome, yet long enough to enable quite long joints to be planed.

fork The junction of branch to tree stem. The figure of wood at this part is referred to as curl or crotch.

fork chuck Used for the general run of between-centres turning. May have either screw or morse taper fixing in the mandrel. Known also as the prong chuck.

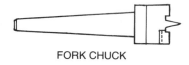

FORK CHUCK

forked tenon Term sometimes applied to the tenon portion of the bridle joint (*q.v.*).

forked turnscrew bit One having the end divided enabling it to engage a round nut with slot rather than having square or hexagonal shape.

FORKED TURNSCREW BIT

formaldehyde Used in the manufacture of resin adhesives for wood: urea-formaldehyde (UF),

melamine-formaldehyde (MF), phenol-formaldehyde (PF), and resorcinol-formaldehyde (RF). Of these the UF is the cheapest and most widely used. (See *synthetic resin*.)

former A temporary foundation or core around which the actual job is built. In particular it is used when thin wood, ply, or veneers have to be bent to shape. Thus when bending and laminating thin wood to form a circular or oval frame a former is used, the laminae being bent around the edges.

formwork The temporary woodwork used as a mould when casting concrete *in situ*. It needs to be so designed that not only does it give the shape required, but is also capable of being dismantled when the concrete has set. Also known as shuttering.

forstner bit A special bit which is guided by its circular rim rather than its centre point. The advantage of this tool is that it bores a neat, cleanly-cut hole with a flat bottom, its point serving only to ensure accuracy for the starting cuts. Because the bit point is small, a hole can be made deeply in a board without the point penetrating the opposite side.

FORSTNER BIT

four-centred arch One which is struck from four centres. The arcs at the sides necessarily have centres on the line of the springing.

fourposter bed A term loosely describing a bed with a post at each corner. More properly called a 'sealed' bed.

four-pronged chuck Used often in the trade for turning chair legs between centres.

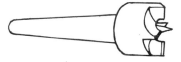

FOUR-PRONGED CHUCK

four-sided planer and moulder This machine planes and moulds sections on all surfaces of a work-piece at one pass and this is accomplished by means of cutters. The cutters may be solid, or mounted in a cutter block which is fixed to a shaft in the machine and called a 'head'. In a four-head machine, the first head works the bottom of the work-piece, the second works the inside edge, the third the opposite edge, and the fourth works the top. Five head and six head machines are also available.

foxiness An early stage of decay in wood, notably oak, which discolours it to a brownish colour. Trees grown in a certain district appear to suffer from this defect.

fox-wedged tenon joint A blind mortise and tenon joint strengthened with wedges of wood in the tenon, thereby locking it in its mortise. The mortise ends are cut to splay sufficiently at the inside. Saw cuts are made in the tenon and the wedges slipped in. When the tenon is forced into its mortise, the wedges are automatically driven deep into the saw cuts, causing the edge to splay and thus become locked in the mortise. Once this has been done, it is impossible to remove the tenon.

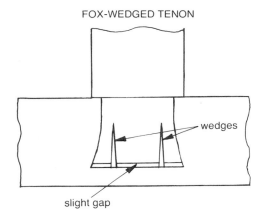

FOX-WEDGED TENON

frame A general term for any construction which involves rails and stiles. Also includes moulded and mitred picture and mirror frames.

framed, ledged, and braced door Door with top rail and stiles of equal thickness, and thinner lower ledges. Matchboarding is either tongued into the stiles and top rail or fits in a rebate, and passes over the face of the ledges. The braces are notched in and are behind the matchboarding. A framed and ledged door is the same except that the braces are omitted.

Framed door A door consisting of stiles or uprights and rails (horizontals) with one or more panels held in either grooves or rebates. The idea is that the framing members provide strength in height and width, the panel being a filling and free to shrink or swell (if in solid wood) without affecting either the appearance or the structural soundness.

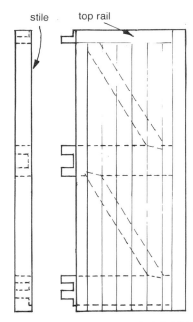

FRAMED, LEDGED, & BRACED DOOR

frameless mirror clips The common clip (A) is for edge fixing along the sides. For corners the clips (B) are used. There are similar clips available made from transparent plastic material. For face fixing, such as inside mirrors to wardrobe doors, etc., the clips (C) and (D) are used. The cast brass, chromium corner clip (E) slips over corner of glass and backing, being fixed to back with screws.

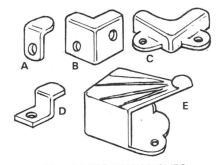

FRAMELESS MIRROR CLIPS

frame saw Refers generally to the large trade machine having several blades secured in a frame and working with a reciprocating action. Cuts several boards in one operation. It is also applied to a saw with blade about 20in (508mm) by 1½ in (38mm) wide held in tension in a frame similar to that of a bow saw.

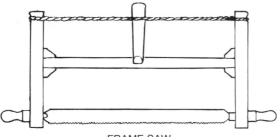

FRAME SAW

framing anchors Galvanised metal plates drilled for nail fixing. There are three types available (all handed left or right) which can take shear, compression, and tension stresses. Principal uses are for floor and ceiling framing; roof framing; and wall framing.

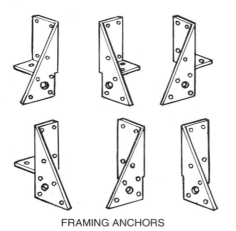

FRAMING ANCHORS

franking A detail of the mortise and tenon joint as used in making a casement window. Instead of the tenoned piece having a haunch it is recessed to fit over

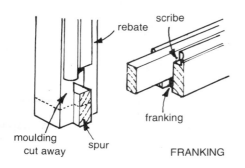

FRANKING

the spur or projecting end of the square left when the moulding is cut away on the piece with the mortise.

frass The dust resulting from the boring of the furniture beetle *(q.v.)*.

free moisture The water in the cells of timber as distinct from that contained in the actual cell walls.

freijo *(cordia goeldiana)* South American timber of 37 lb (593 kg) somewhat like cigar box cedar. Glues and stains well, but is rather soft and open in the grain. Used locally for furniture.

French chalk Sometimes used as a half-filler for oak. About a handful of chalk is added to a pint of polish, stirred frequently, and applied with a brush.

French head (see *spindle moulder*).

French spindle Machine for moulding, grooving, or grooving. (See under *spindle moulder.)*

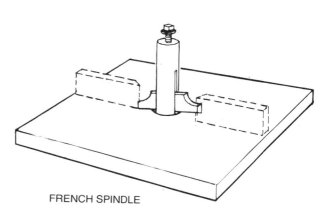

FRENCH SPINDLE

French or wire nail A flat head nail made from ½ in (12 mm) to 6 in (153 mm) used in general carpentry work, making packing cases, boxes, etc., being easier to drive than cut brads or oval nails. The heads are invariably milled to prevent the hammer

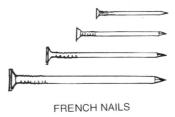

FRENCH NAILS

face or punch from slipping. Not suitable for fine work, the heads being too coarse and difficult to punch in cleanly. (See *box nail (USA)*.)

French polish   A finish used chiefly for furniture and made from shellac and industrial methylated spirits. The chief types are:
transparent, water clear and made from bleached dewaxed lac.
white, milky white colour, made from bleached shellac.
button, deep yellowish colour, slightly opaque.
orange, golden yellow colour.
garnet, deep brown shade.
All shellacs are made from the same basic seed lac, and it is a variation in the process of manufacture that produces the different kinds. Industrial methylated spirit is not available to the public, but ordinary methylated spirit can be used.

French polisher's mop   The better-quality mops have camel hair, double-wire-bound, in a quill. They enable polish to be applied evenly without streaks. Used for applying the first coat of polish over a grain-filled surface for rough polishing without a fad or rubber or for colouring and local touching up. The cheaper mops are smaller, wire-bound on a wooden handle.

French polishing   The various stages in succession are *staining, sealing, filling, fadding, colouring, bodying, finishing*. Finishing may be spiriting off, stiffing, or the acid finish. (See under separate entries.)

fret   Ornament in wood or metal from which the entire background has been cut away with a very fine saw. Chippendale frets were frequently cut from thin wood and planted on a frieze, rail, or other part. Sometimes they were laminated and left open.

fretcutting tables   These are in hardwood, fixed to the edge of a table by means of a cramp. The general size is about 8 in (203 mm) by 4 in (102 mm). The groove enables the cramp to fit in flush.

fret machine   A machine used widely when fretwood was popular. It still is useful for cutting shapes in thin wood. It is operated by an electric motor, thus leaving both hands free to manipulate the wood.

fretsaw blades   Obtainable for fine, medium, and coarse cutting, the standard length being 5 in

(127 mm). There are two kinds of fretsaw blades available, one for cutting wood and the other for metal and plastic materials.

fretsaw handframe   One popular type has a lever at the top to slacken or tighten the saw blade, the action being instantaneous. A long screw in the handle enables the tension of the blade to be regulated, and makes it possible to use shortened (broken) blades. The handframe is made in four sizes: 12 in (305 mm) 14 in (356 mm) 16 in (407 mm) and 18 in (457 mm), this being the distance from the saw blade to the back of the frame.

frieze   In furniture (such as bookcases or wardrobes, etc.) the flat band lying between the cornice or moulded top and the narrow frieze moulding. In interior decoration the top part of a wall between cornice and picture rail.

frith stool   A stool placed near the alter in a cathedral or church for the use of those claiming sanctuary.

froe   A wedge fitted with a handle; used for splitting or cleaning timber. Also called a 'fromard'.

frog   The sloping bed or back against which a plane cutter rests. In a metal plane it is usually adjustable, so enabling the mouth size to be varied.

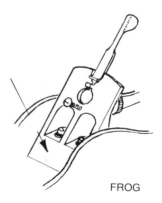

FROG

fromard   An alternative name for froe (*q.v.*).

front-bent gouge   A carver's gouge bent in its length to an acute curve. (See *carver's gouges (C)*.)

frosting punch   Tool used to give a textured background in flat pattern carving. Made in various patterns: dots, circles, crosses, etc.

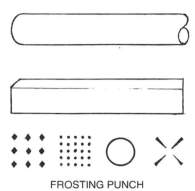

FROSTING PUNCH

frowy Wood which is brittle or short grained. The defect may occur in oak, ash, beech, and structural timbers generally, but such wood should never be used for work liable to be subjected to any strain.

fruit wood Refers to such woods as apple, pear, cherry, plum. Often used in old furniture for inlay.

frustum The lower part of a conical shaped solid left by cutting off the top part in a plane parallel with the base.

full A term meaning 'slightly more than'. Thus 'one inch full' would be $1\frac{1}{32}$in (27 mm) approximately; the converse is 'bare' (*q.v.*).

fuming A process in which small items made from oak are set in an air-tight box with lid, and surrounded with dishes of strong liquid ammonia (.880). The fumes, by chemical action, turn the wood light brown or rich brown, according to the length of exposure. Some varieties of oak darken more readily than others. Sapwood, incidentally, does not fume. Mahogany may be fumed slightly. One advantage of the process is that it does not raise the grain. It is essential that all grease, dirt, glue, etc., are removed from the surface. If an inspection glass can be arranged it is an advantage. Do not stand over the container when it is opened as the fumes are powerful. Avoid getting the ammonia on the hands. Imitation fuming is obtained by wiping the wood directly with liquid ammonia, but the effect is not the same as genuine fuming. After the wood is fumed, it may be waxed or french polished.

fungicide A substance used to destroy fungi.

fungus So far as woodwork is concerned, a parasitic growth which feeds on the wood and affects either its strength or appearance or both. Some fungi cause staining but have no other adverse effects. Others

such as dry rot and cellar fungus (*q.v.*) are extremely dangerous and call for immediate treatment.

furniture beetle *(Anobium punctatum)* Affected wood may be half eaten away or it may show nothing more than one or two holes about $\frac{1}{16}$in (2 mm) in diameter. The holes are the points from which the beetles emerge, not the points of entry. The beetles may be introduced in other furniture or they may enter through an open window, since they live in a natural state in the dead branches of trees. The female beetle lays her eggs in crevices, then dies. Small white grubs hatch out and begin to burrow into the wood. They work on in this way for perhaps a year or two years leaving behind them in the tunnel a light, fine powder. Finally the grub drives a tunnel towards the surface of the wood where it bores a chamber in which it lies up and turns into a chrysalis. After a few weeks it develops into a beetle with wings, legs, and so on, and bites its way through to the surface and emerges. Male and female beetles mate and the whole thing starts again. It is during June, July, and August that this exodus takes place, though it may be as early as May.

The most usual treatment is the application of a proprietary insecticide. The powder should be removed from the holes as far as possible to enable the liquid to penetrate. The liquid is fed into the holes with a small brush. If the area is large the liquid will have to be scrubbed in. One treatment may not effect a cure, since individual beetles may escape. A good plan is to lightly ring treated holes so that fresh ones may be recognised. Rub the insecticide into all crevices whether near the holes or not. It will sterilise any eggs which may be there and any grub which may hatch out will be unable to burrow into the treated wood. Another method of treatment, which, however, involves sending the infected furniture to a firm with the necessary equipment, is that of fumigation. When examining old furniture in which the beetle is suspected, look out for a light fine powder, (fras) which may lie on the surface or have dropped on to the floor. Look, too, to see whether the holes look clean and new. Old blackened holes are the work of an old colony which may no longer be active.

fustian A coarse twilled cotton, or cotton linen, cloth, with a short velvety pile; used for bed-hangings in ancient times and said to have been first imported from Flanders circa 1370.

fustic *(chlorophora tinctoria)* A timber imported from Central America in the 17th and 18th centuries and used by inlayers for its yellow colour but it was discontinued as the colour gradually turned a flat brownish hue.

G

gable In architecture the triangular part of the end of a building from eaves to ridge. In woodwork the end parts (solid or framed) of such a carcase as a wardrobe, bookcase, cabinet, or sideboard (see also *end*). In building construction the term 'gable roof' is applied to a roof which finishes against a gable and is open to the rafters.

gable board (see *barge board*).

gaboon *(aucoumea klaineana)* Timber from French Equatorial Africa and Spanish Guinea, weighing 28 lb (449 kg) per cubic foot. Used chiefly for plywood manufacture and inner parts of furniture. Similar in colour to mahogany. Also known as okoumé.

gadroon A form of repetitive reed decoration more generally known as nulling (*q.v.*).

gallery A wooden or metal ledge, usually pierced and/or decorated, around a table top or other case furniture.

gallows bracket A support to hold a load from a wall, usuall consisting of an upright, horizontal, and a brace. Often used to hold a shelf. (See *potence*.)

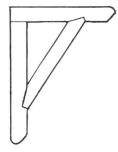

GALLOWS BRACKET

gamari *(gmelina arborea)* Light yellow wood of 38 lb (609 kg) from India and Burma. Easily worked and used in furniture making.

gamboge Bright yellow colouring material sometimes used for tinting polish, etc.

gaming tables Particularly favoured in Tudor times, these tables could be used for backgammon (then called 'tables'), chess, and dice — the playing surfaces were often inlaid with parquetry designs (*q.v.*) to suit the game being played. (See also *card tables.*)

gang mill Machine incorporating a series of reciprocating saw blades held in a frame, and used to cut several boards in one operation. Also known as a frame saw.

gang mortiser Machine which cuts several mortises in one operation.

gap-filling adhesive An adhesive suitable for bonding surfaces which cannot be brought closer than 0.05 in (0.5 mm).

gardenia *(gardenia latifolia)* Indian timber sometimes known as Indian boxwood which it closely resembles in colour and grain.

garnet paper Used for both hand and machine sanding. The grit is made from garnet stones which are found as large crystals in certain rocks, and these are heat-processed and crushed to create the grit which is bonded to the backing paper. Garnet grit is reddish-brown in colour and is very tough; the initial sharp edges are quickly lost and the surface is reduced to one which can remove wood rapidly to a fine finish. Because of this initial rate of wear, garnet abrasives are not suitable for high speed work, but are best for slower machine work or hand methods. Grades are: 36, 40, and 50 screen (coarse); 60, 80 (medium); 100, 120, 150, and 180 (fine); and 220, 240, 280 and 320 (extra fine).

garnet polish French polish made from garnet shellac, dark brown in colour. It is used chiefly in the colouring stage to darken the colour of the wood.

gate hinges A typical hinge is shown at (A) being a reversible type, with cast-iron ears and heavy pins. The square hole is for a carriage bolt, if required; made 8 in (203 mm) to 36 in (914 mm) long. (B) is a lift-off hinge, made from wrought iron 12 in (305 mm) to 30 in (762 mm). Also called 'band and hook' (*q.v.*).

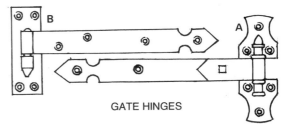

GATE HINGES

gate-leg table These tables take many shapes and forms, with tops oval or circular, but all possess the swinging legs which support the hinged flaps, hence the name. The normal height for dining is 29 in

(736mm) to 30in (762mm). It is usual to have the flaps rule-jointed, a special hinge being used. (See *rule joint*.)

gauge Tool generally used to mark lines parallel with a surface or edge. (See under individual names *butt, cutting, depth, grasshopper, marking, mortise, panel, roller*.)

G cramp Powerful cramp used for relatively small work, laminated joints, and for holding wood stationary whilst being worked. Sometimes the shoe at the end of the screw is pivoted on a ball to enable it to hold over tapered work. Made in three grades, heavy duty, general duty, and light duty.

gedge bit Twist bit having curved wings rather than separate nickers and cutters. It bores a clean hole and has a particular advantage when boring at an angle in that the screw centre sinks into its full depth before any actual cutting takes place, and thus obtains a good grip and is not so liable to be drawn out of centre as might happen in the case of nickers. Can be used for all general boring purposes. (See also *Irwin, Russell-Jennings, Scotch nose,* and *solid nose bits*.)

GEDGE BIT

gedu nohor (*entandrophragma angolense*) East and West African timber of 32lb (513kg) weight, light pink in colour, but tending to darken to mahogany brown. Can be kiln seasoned successfully, but is somewhat difficult to work owing to its interlocked grain. Is not a good turnery wood.

gent's saw (see *bead saw*).

genus The main group to which wood belongs. It is the first part of the scientific Latin name given to wood. The second part of the name is the particular species. Thus *Quercus alba* and *Quercus mongolia* are both true oaks, but the former is American white oak and the latter Japanese oak.

geometrical stairs One having a continuous handrail around a semi-circular or semi-elliptical well.

gesso Used in gilding to provide a smooth and suitable surface for the gold leaf. To make it, parchment cuttings are soaked overnight in water, placed in a double kettle, covered with water, and

GEOMETRICAL STAIRS

simmered for 3-4 hours. After straining through muslin it is left to cool. Strength should be such that when the vessel is struck against the palm of the hand it shatters. After warming up afresh (it should never be boiled) gilder's whiting is added to about the consistency of paint. Two drops of linseed oil are added and when warmed up and stirred is ready for use. An alternative to parchment cuttings is rabbit skin glue obtainable in sheets. Applied with a brush in 6 or 7 coats with drying intervals, but all coats must be laid in one day. Modern acrylic gesso is available from art shops.

ghost A french-polishing term applied to an ordinary pad or rubber that has been charged lightly with methylated spirit only and thus has no body in it — merely the 'spirit'! It is a pad used during the process of spiriting-off.

gilding There are two types: oil gilding and water gilding. The former is the simpler, but water gilding has the advantage that it can be burnished to an extremely brilliant lustre. Sometimes both are used in the same item.

In water gilding the wood is given a foundation of gesso (*q.v.*) followed by a coat of Armenian bole, a red earth. Looseleaf gold is then applied with a gilder's tip the surface being dampened with weak parchment size. When dry the work can be brought to a brilliant gloss with a burnisher (*q.v.*).

For oil gilding the wood can either have the gesso foundation or be painted with a yellow cellulose lacquer. When dry this is painted over with gold size, allowed to become tacky, and transfer gold leaf used, being ordinary gold leaf (*q.v.*) with a backing of thin paper. When pressed on the gold leaf adheres.

gimlet Chief types are: shell (A) which is similar to the shell bit but with screw point. The least liable to split the grain: twist (B) with spiral escapement; half-twist (C) fast cutting with variable spiral escapement; auger (D) for larger holes, similar to twist bit but without nickers; and bell hanger's (E), similar to shell but longer. Gimlets are not used much nowadays, and some may be difficult to obtain.

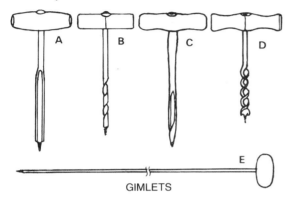

GIMLETS

gimp Narrow strip of leather or material in decorative pattern used at the edges of upholstery to conceal raw edges and fixing tacks.

gimp pin Made in two forms, wire (A), and cut (B). The former has the advantage of being sharper and therefore staying in position with pressure from the fingers before the hammer is used.

GIMP PINS

girandole A wall fixture comprising a candelabra placed in front of a mirror to reflect the light. They were particularly favoured in the middle and end of the eighteenth century, and were frequently richly ornamented and gilt.

girth The measurement around the circumference of a log. In a tapering log it is generally taken at the central position to obtain the average.

girthes Bands of webbing used on beds from the 16th century onwards to support mattresses.

give A member or part of one which will accommodate itself to stress without breaking is said to have 'give'. Thus, sometimes in assembling, a member may have to be bent to enable it to be sprung into position, and thus 'gives' sufficiently for the purpose.

Glamorgan dresser Alternative name for a South Wales dresser (*q.v.*).

glass Until the (historically) recent introduction of plate and float glass, sheet glass was hand-blown. Basically a lump of molten glass was blown to form a cylinder; the end was then burst off and the cylinder opened out flat by cutting first with a red-hot piece of iron along a marked line followed by a piece of cold iron along the same line. It was not possible to make large sheets by this method and a dimension of about 3 feet (915 mm) either way was the maximum; in addition the glass always contained flaws which distorted any image seen through it. Modern float glass is made by pouring the molten glass on to a large trough of molten tin when a perfectly clear sheet of even thickness is obtained, 2 mm being the most used thickness.

glasspaper (see *abrasive materials*).

glass plate A fixing plate for holding an object against a wall (such as a mirror). A hole is pre-drilled in the shaped top and a screw can be driven through this into the wall, or the screw can be inserted in the wall first and the hole hooked on to it so that the object can be taken down if required. There are two holes drilled in the bottom flange and they are countersunk on the reverse side; screws are driven through these into the object. (See *mirror plate*.)

Glastonbury chair A term for a type of folding chair with X-shaped ends and elbowed arms, which is reputed to have originated with one made for the last Abbot of Glastonbury, who died in 1539. Similar chairs of the same style have been made at various times ever since.

glaze A quick means of finishing french polish. Made by crushing gum benzoin and dissolving in methylated spirit. Takes about three days for it to be completely absorbed, and the container should be shaken repeatedly. Strain before use. Diluted with methylated spirit and applied with a rubber. Useful for finishing awkward edges and corners which could not be spirited-out properly. It is also a material used in graining (*q.v.*).

glazed door Any door having a glass panel or series of panes. It may vary from the simplest of doors with a single pane fitting in a rebate to an elaborate design with moulded bars. (See also *barred door*.)

glazed wheel A grinding wheel which has lost its cut owing to the pores having become clogged. It should be corrected with a dresser which has a group of alternate ring and star wheels which are free to revolve. It is brought into close contact with the revolving grinding wheel, when the star wheels dig out the pores between the granules. (See *wheel dresser.*)

glazier's points   US equivalent of British sprig (*q.v.*). They are small pieces of thin sheet metal in the shape of an equilateral triangle and are used to hold glass in place prior to puttying.

glazing bar   Bar with two rebates to hold glass at each side, and usually but not invariably moulded. Used widely in greenhouses, glazed doors, and roofs, windows, etc.

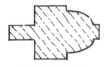

GLAZING BAR

glazing bead   Small wood bead used to hold a glass pane in its rebate. In small cabinet doors it is usually about $\frac{1}{8}$ in (3 mm) bare in thickness, but larger in room doors. In the latter case it is advisable to bed the glass into a thin putty or mastic layer before adding the bead at the back as it prevents rattle and keeps out draught. In the case of curved bars on small doors the beads can often be bedded in mastic in flexible brown.

GLAZING BEAD

gliders   Polished steel fittings of domed shape with projecting spikes. They are knocked into the bottoms of furniture legs, enabling the item to be drawn easily over the floor. (See also *domes of silence.*)

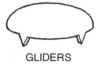

GLIDERS

glue   Chief types in general workshop use are: casein, fish, polyvinyl, rubber based (contact), Scotch (animal), synthetic resin. (See under individual titles.) Other special-purpose glues are blood albumen glue used in plywood manufacture and requiring heat pressing; vegetable glue, a cheap glue based on starch. None of these is normally available as they are made specially for factory use.

glue blocks   Small blocks of wood planed square and with a fairly broad chamfer at the outer corner. The inner sharp corner is also taken off to ensure that the surfaces bed right down. The blocks are glued and rubbed back and forth once or twice. They serve to strengthen the joint. When added to joints in which the grain runs crosswise several short glue blocks should be used with a slight gap rather than one long one as in this way shrinkage is not impeded and danger of splitting is avoided.

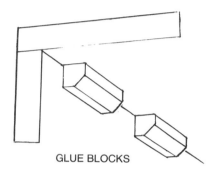

GLUE BLOCKS

glue brush   Avoid using a brush with a metal ferrule when applying synthetic resin adhesives as the metal may cause staining. A piece of dowel makes a good applicator for mortises, or a piece of bamboo cane which has had its end split into 'hairs' by hammering.

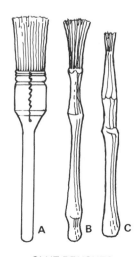

GLUE BRUSHES

glued joint   Butt joint between two pieces of wood in their width and quite plain with only glue holding the parts together. When no cramps are used the whole length should make a close joint. On no account should it be planed round so that it swivels about the middle. Joints to be cramped should be slightly hollow so that cramps put on at the middle force the ends tightly together. Other names are 'rubbed' and 'slayped' joints.

glue pot   For heating Scotch or animal glue. Made singly or in batteries of two or more pots to a single water container. The pot itself should be tinned inside or be of copper as contamination with iron may cause staining.

glue spread   The weight of the glue in a glue line per unit area surface; normally it is expressed in pounds per hundred square feet (or grams per square metre); in the USA it is in pounds per thousand square feet.

glue spreader   An appliance to enable a film of glue to be spread evenly over a wide surface. It is used in the manufacture of plywood and in veneering. The glue is in a trough from which a roller transfers it to the panel which is propelled beneath a second roller. The upper roller is adjustable in height to suit panels of varying thickness. It can be arranged for both single and double side gluing. To limit the area of spread to the panel width two divisions are fitted and can be fixed at any point along the trough. Also a small toothed plastic flat plate to facilitate spreading viscous materials.

going   Term used in staircase work, and is the horizontal distance between the faces of two consecutive risers.

gold leaf   Obtainable in books of 25 leaves, $3\frac{1}{4}$ in square, and in both 'loose leaf' and 'transfer' form. The former is free and is interleaved between tissue paper, whereas transfer gold is attached to the tissue paper with a film of wax.

gold size   For gilding, an 18-hour gold size is generally used to fix down the gold leaf, this being the time taken for it to dry. It is, however, possible to obtain a 4-hour gold size when the work has to be done quickly. For exterior work Japan gold size is generally used which goes off in about an hour; it also has other uses, as it will act as a binder for most oil-based stains, and it can also be added to glazier's putty to make a hard putty for glazed doors in cabinets, etc. A teaspoonful to a small handful of putty is about right.

Goldsmith Windsor chair   A comb-back Windsor chair with sticks and a tailed seat with arms; it belonged to Oliver Goldsmith, the playwright, who died in 1774. A modified design (1770) had a shield-shaped seat, with the bowed arm made in three parts.

goose neck   Another term describing a scroll-top pediment. (See *swan-neck*.)

gooseneck moulding   (USA) The scrolled, swan-neck moulding found on longcase clock or bureau-bookcase pediments.

Gothic mouldings   Usually deeply cut, the curves based on the circle with upright or canting fillets. Deep hollows were often filled with carved decoration.

Gothic splat   Used in Windsor chairs circa 1750.

Gothic Windsor chair   There are several designs; each contains one or other of the several Gothic features, e.g. lancet arch piercing in the splat., or an interlaced bow.

gouge   (see under individual names).

gout chair   A chair fitted with a leg-rest; Dr. Johnson had one made for him.

grading   The classification of timber to its quality. Such factors as the number, size, and type of defects present in the wood, appearance, freedom from stain or insect damage, and other characteristics decide the grade to which any individual piece of timber can be allocated.

Grading is normally done by travelling inspectors on the basis of 'grading rules'. This ensures that named grades are comparable between timbers from different sources, and that the classification is made by independent judges. The grading rules are laid down by trade organisations, but are applicable only to named timber species. These latter vary so widely in their characteristics that no rules could be framed that would cover satisfactorily and fairly the whole range of commercial woods.

There is considerable difference in nomenclature between the various grades, and it is therefore necessary to have a copy of the relevant grading rules before it is possible to estimate the likely quality of the timber on the basis of its grading.

Plywood may be graded on the appearance of the best face of the assembly and on the type of adhesive used in its manufacture. If conforming to the appropriate British Standard Specification, the plywood may be weather-resistant or boil-proof. Both are external grades in that they may be used out of doors without fear of delamination, but the boil-proof plywood can be immersed for long periods in boiling water without deterioration.

grain The arrangement and direction of the wood fibres. In straight - grained wood the fibres are parallel with the edges of the board and are free from twist. Other types of grain are wavy, spiral, or interlocked. (See also *figure*.)

grain filler (see *filler, grain*).

graining Creating a false appearance of wood grain by manipulating glazes and scumbles by means of brushes, combs, rags, etc. A glaze in this connotation is a varnish tinted with a transparent colour and applied in an even tone. Flat or gloss varnish can be used and, if necessary, reduced with turpentine. Linseed oil, turpentine, and a little driers can also be used. A scumble is similar to a glaze except that it is specially compound to remain workable for a longer period.

Grand Bassam West Africa (*khaya ivorensis*) An African mahogany of 32 lb (513 kg) it comes from the Ivory coast, and is one of the best of the African mahoganies. Some of the logs are nicely figured.

Grandfather clocks (see *longcase clocks*).

grasshopper gauge Sometimes known as the T gauge, this has a long fence enabling it to mark over obstructions. The pencil can be set with any projection to enable it to mark into recesses, grooves, etc. One side of the fence is flat, the other rounded, and the pencil can be fixed at either side. This enables the gauge to be used on shaped edges, and in particular for circle-on-circle work. It is unlikely to be available in shops, and is invariably made by the woodworker.

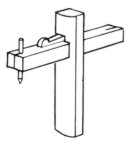

GRASSHOPPER GAUGE

Grecian key Also called 'Greek fret'. A running ornamental design used by the Ancient Greeks.

green A term used for unseasoned wood which is full of moisture.

green dye Traditionally made by dissolving aniline dye in water, spirit, or oil, according to type. A binder is needed, a little of the following being added to the above in the order given: hot glue and dash of vinegar, french polish, gold size. Many modern proprietary dyes are available.

greenheart (*ocotea rodiei*) Timber of 67 lb (1073 kg) from British Guiana, used chiefly in ship building, dock and general constructional work, and fishing rods. Resists teredo, the sea worm that attacks other woods submerged in sea water. Brown in colour, tending to green. Has remarkable elasticity, and is extremely strong.

Grenoble wood Archaic term for French walnut (*Juglans regia*).

greywood (see *harewood*).

grinder (1) Polishing rubber to which a pinch of superfine pumice powder has been added beneath the covering. Useful when bodying to get rid of stubborn rubber marks. It is slightly abrasive.

grinder (2) (see *grinding* and *grinding wheel*).

grinding Preliminary process in sharpening edge tools and cutters before the final edge is completed on the oilstone. The safest grinding is on a wet stone as the tools are kept cool with water. When a dry wheel is used the tool should be constantly dipped in water, and it is advisable to cease grinding before the actual edge is reached. (See *grindstone* and *grinding wheel*.)

grinding angle This is as distinct from the honing or sharpening angle, and is usually less than the latter. Its purpose is to reduce the labour involved in sharpening. In chisels and plane irons the grinding angle is 25 deg (A), final sharpening being at 30 deg (B). For turning gouges the grinding angle is about 45 deg, with honing at the same angle. Turning chisels are ground flat both sides to give an included angle in the region of 40-43 deg. Scraping tools for turning are ground at about 80 deg. Carving gouges are ground at

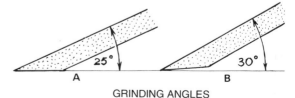

GRINDING ANGLES

a rather lower angle than chisels for general woodwork, nearer 20 deg, because a bevel is honed on the inside as well as the outside, thus increasing the included angle.

grindstone York and blue grit stones are generally used, sizes ranging from 8 in (203 mm) diam by 2 in (51 mm) width up to 24 in (610 mm) by 3½ in (89 mm) May be bench model manually driven, treadle operated, or powered. All run with water as a coolant which should be drained away when not in use so that stone does not remain partly immersed. Speeds for stones are about 95 rpm for 18 in size, and 70 rpm for 24 in diameter. The advantage of the type is that there is no risk of the temper being drawn.

grinding wheel May be manually operated bench type, a hand-held portable model, or powered with twin wheels, one coarse, the other fine. For woodworking tools aluminium oxide, a vitrified bond of 60 grain size, is a good all-round wheel. Recommended speeds are:

Diam		RPM
4 in	(102 mm)	5,000
5 in	(128 mm)	4,200
6 in	(152 mm)	3,500
7 in	(178 mm)	3,000
8 in	(203 mm)	2,500

Considerable tolerance can be allowed, but the speeds should not be seriously increased. A wheel which has become glazed should not be used as it is liable to cause over-heating. The latter is a danger in all grinding of carbon steel tools, especially small ones in which the generated heat cannot be conducted away quickly enough. It is generally advisable to cease grinding short of the edge and finish on the oilstone. Frequent dipping in water is advisable.

groin The line or rib made by, or applied to, the intersections of the panels of a vaulted roof.

groove Recessed channel, usually of rectangular section, intended to receive a panel, sliding door, or part of a joint such as a tongue.

grooved-in panel One which fits in grooves rather than rebates in the main framework.

grounder Alternative name for a spoon bit or entering chisel used by a wood carver. (See (C) under *carver's chisel*.) It is also known as a 'background tool'.

grounding in The sinking or recessing of the background in a carved pattern, leaving the design itself in relief. This is usually completed in its entirety before any modelling or detail is worked in the raised pattern itself. Fairly quick gouges are used in the early stages and nearly flat ones for finishing off.

grounds Generally refers to wood strips 2-3 in (51-77 mm) wide by ¾-1 in (19-25 mm) thick fixed to brick and similar walls with plugs. Their purpose is to provide a convenient surface to which panelling, mantelpieces, and other wood fitments can be fixed. The term may also refer to the base or groundwork on which veneers are laid.

groundwork The base to which veneer is applied. Often called a 'substrate' (*q.v.*). Today manufactured board is widely used, and of these gaboon plywood is the most reliable. Lamin board is also used and is better than blockboard in that ripples due to shrinkage in the core are less liable to show through eventually as they are narrow. In all cases the veneer should be laid at right-angles with the outer layers of the groundwork, as otherwise hair cracks may develop. Wood chipboard is also used and if of a good make is reliable. In common with all grounds both sides should be treated alike with veneers of the same thickness if the work is to remain flat. Another ideal base for veneering is medium density fibreboard or MDF (*q.v.*) which had recently been introduced.

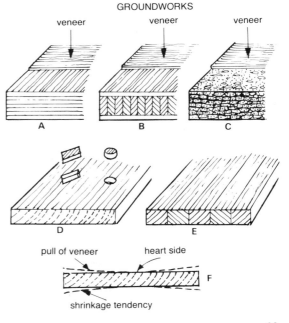

GROUNDWORKS

Solid wood is also used as a groundwork, and a straight-grained, plain, reliable wood which holds glue well is advisable. Plain mahogany is excellent, but a good quality pine is frequently used. As this is absorbent of glue it is usually sized first. Any knots (there should not be any large ones) should be chopped out and filled with a wood plug cut to shape and later levelled. Small blemishes can be bored out and the hole filled with a pellet (*q.v.*) (on no account use a dowel).

The most reliable groundwork is quarter-cut as it is not liable to twist one way or the other (*q.v.*). If this is not possible an excellent plan is to have it cut into strips of 2-3 in (51-77mm) width and glued together with the heart sides alternating back and front. In this way any tendency to twist in one direction is countered by the adjoining strip which tends the opposite way. The groundwork thus remains flat though a waviness may become apparent.

Woods with marked open grain or with pronounced figuring are unsuitable because, owing to glue contraction, the detail tends to show through to the surface, especially if the veneer is thin. Thus oak is not ideal, though it was frequently used in period furniture.

When only one side of a solid wood groundwork is veneered it is helpful to put the veneer on the heart side as the natural tendency to twist due to shrinkage opposes the pull of the veneer in the opposite direction.

growth rings Sometimes known as the annual rings (*q.v.*) visible when a log is cross cut. Growth is by a new layer or ring added at the outside beneath the bark. Each ring has an early wood zone usually of light colour and wide, and a late wood band, generally darker and narrower.

grub The larva of a wood boring insect. (See *wood borers.*)

guard A device in a machine to protect the machinist from injury. In the trade regulations regarding their use and type are strict. Essential features are that they are robustly made, not liable to collapse under strain, and be adjustable in that they can be fixed as close as possible to the wood being machined.

guarea (*guarea thompsonii*) and (*guarea edrata*) Nigerian timber of 40 lb (641 kg) weight. Reddish brown colour, sometimes with mottled figure. Often used as a substitute for mahogany. May tend to split somewhat in seasoning but holds its shape when dry.

gueridon Also called a 'giridon'. A small table, usually with a circular top enclosed with a gallery and a matching tray on the underframe. Originally employed as supports for some kind of lighting, they are now used to display objets d'art. In the 18th century, a Negro figurine holding a candelabra often stood on a gueridon, and the word derives from a well-known Moorish slave of the same name.

guides Term with wide applications and referring generally to parts which control the movement of any moving item. In particular there are drawer guides used when a carcase has pilasters or posts wider than the thickness of the ends. They prevent side racking when the drawer is moved. Also fitted to some extension tables in which the tops slide between rebated guides.

It refers also to certain appliances or jigs used in machining to guide the work over a definite course.

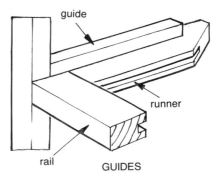

GUIDES

guilioche Ornamental device consisting of an interlacing band generally enclosing a circular space decorated with conventional carving. Used widely in the late sixteenth and early seventeenth centuries.

guillotine A knife running in guides used in trimming veneers. It may be manually worked by a lever, or power operated.

gullet The space between two teeth in a briar-toothed circular saw. It carries the sawdust and

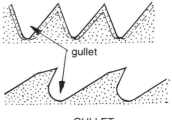

GULLET

should be rounded as shown. A jagged gullet with sharp internal corners may cause a tooth to break off. In the peg or cross-cut saw the gullet is automatically formed by the three-cornered file used in sharpening. The angles of this are at 60 deg, and the corners should be slightly rounded, not sharp, again making for a stronger tooth.

gum The American red gum (*liquidambar styraciflua*), often also known as satin walnut is a rather cold brown colour, weighing 37-38 lb (593-609 kg) per cubic foot. Seldom used in Great Britain today but widely imported before the war when it was used for furniture, railway carriages, and fitments, etc. Somewhat hard to work, close in the grain. Unless properly seasoned is liable to twist. It takes a good polish. The sapwood of the species is known as hazel pine in Great Britain, and as sap gum in the USA.

Gum also refers to a variety of Australian and Tasmanian timbers (*Eucalyptus*). These are used locally for constructional work, dock and house building, etc. Colour varies considerably with the type.

gum-arabic Used in making water varnish required chiefly for the protection of paper, card, etc.

gum benzoin Used to make glaze for finishing the french polishing process. The natural product is rather like pieces of white nuts with twigs adhering. (See *glaze*.)

gum copal A fossil resin used in the manufacture of copal varnish (*q.v.*).

gum damar A gum added to copal varnish to give elasticity.

gum sandarac A pale yellow resin used in making spirit varnish.

gummed tape Handy in veneering to prevent joints in veneer from opening as the glue dries out. To remove later it should be lightly damped and peeled off.

gun-barrel Term describing a turned column or pillar which is slightly tapered and otherwise left plain.

gun stock stile Door stile narrower at the top than at the bottom. More usually known as a diminished stile (*q.v.*).

gurjun (*dipterocarpus*, species) Dense reddish brown timber of 42-50 lb (673-801 kg) from India,

Ceylon, Burma, and China. Used for flooring and originally for railway carriage construction.

gusset plates Galvanised metal plates with pre-drilled nail holes and/or prongs. They are specifically designed for use with roof trusses.

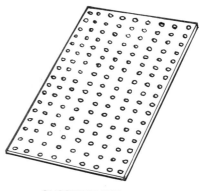

GUSSET PLATE

Hadley chest (USA) A form of dower chest made circa 1700 around Hadley, Massachusetts; it is characterised by incised carving all over the front panels, the motifs being tulips, vines, and leaves.

haffits Sometimes refers to a scribing piece (*q.v.*) or to the end of a church pew.

haft The handle of a hammer, axe, or mallet.

haircloth A cloth woven with a horsehair weft introduced circa 1750.

haldu (*adina cordifolia*) A close-textured wood, 45 lb (721 kg) from Burma, Siam, and India. Similar in colour to satinwood, and used locally for all classes of decorative work. In Great Britain it has been used for turnery and small fancy goods.

half-blind (USA) Corresponds to British 'lapped'.

half-blind dovetails (USA) Corresponds to British 'lap dovetail' (*q.v.*).

half-blind multiple spline joint (USA) Similar to a lapped comb joint, this is a machined joint in which loose splines (tongues) fit into slots.

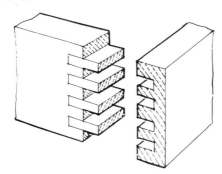

HALF-BLIND MULTIPLE SPLINES

half-blind tongue and rabbet (USA) A joint for use on drawer fronts.

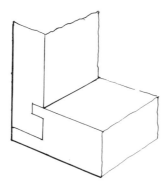

HALF-BLIND TONGUE & REBATE

half-lap joints (USA) Corresponds to British 'halved joints' (*q.v.*). The term also refers to some British joints such as 'mitred half-lap' and 'one third lap joint' (*q.q.v.*).

half-lapped joint (see *halving*).

half pitch Roof having a rise equal to half the span.

half-rotary slicing After being quartered the log is fixed as shown. In this way the knife exposes the radial sections of the log. Highly figured woods such as silky oak are cut in this way.

half-round slicing A method of slicing veneers, used particularly for cutting stumps and crotches. It is

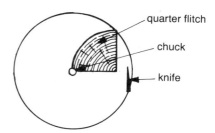

HALF-ROTARY SLICING

somewhat similar to rotary cutting (*q.v.*) but the larger sweep through which the cut passes gives a better figure for woods in which the growth rings are prominent by crossing rather than following them.

HALF-ROUND SLICING

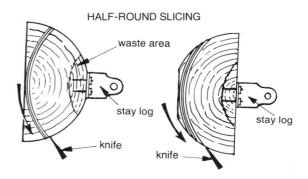

half-round step The bottom step of a staircase. It is semi-circular in plan at the end, built up of laminated blocks, with the grain alternating. The riser of the step is cut locally to about $\frac{1}{8}$ in (3 mm) thickness and is bent around the shaped blocks, being steamed to make it pliable.

half-space landing One which extends across both flights of a dog-legged staircase.

half-tester A canopy which is fixed to the bed-head and extends about halfway down the length of the bed. (See *angel bed.*)

half-timber A baulk (*q.v.*) which has been sawn in two lengthwise.

half turnings (see *split turnings*).

half-twist bit The gimlet bit, with a thread which draws the half-twisted sharp-edged stem into the wood and thus needs only a light pressure. It should not be used near the edge of the wood as it is liable to split the grain.

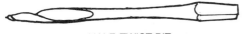

HALF-TWIST BIT

half-twist gimlet (see *gimlet*).

hall cupboard This is the correct name for what is often called a court cupboard (*q.v.*). It consists of a carcase containing shelves and enclosed by two doors, and this is surmounted by a canopy usually incorporating a small cupboard. The front corners of the canopy invariably carry drop terminals.

halve Alternative name for haft (*q.v.*).

halved pattern Device used in veneering in which two consecutive leaves are laid side by side but one turned the other way up so that the grain of the two is exactly matched and balanced. Also called 'book-matching'.

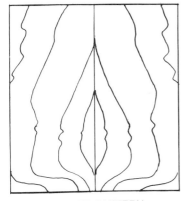

HALVED PATTERN

halving joint Sometimes known as the half-lapped joint. There are many variations according to the position and purpose, but in most cases it requires to be screwed or nailed in addition to being glued. (A) is the angle or L halving used for a light framing. At (B) is the T joint, and (C) the cross-halving. That at (D) is similar but the parts cross at other than a right-angle, and is known as the oblique halving. (E) is similar to (B) but the dovetail shape resists pull. The mitred halving (F) is used when one face must be mitred. It is useful when the face side is moulded.

hammer Chief types are shown here. (A) Warrington type used by cabinet makers and joiners with cross peen. (B) London or Exeter hammer, similar in use to (A). (C) plumber's, with straight peen. (D) ball-peen for engineers. (E) bricklayer's. (F) upholsterer's. (G) lathing, for both cutting and

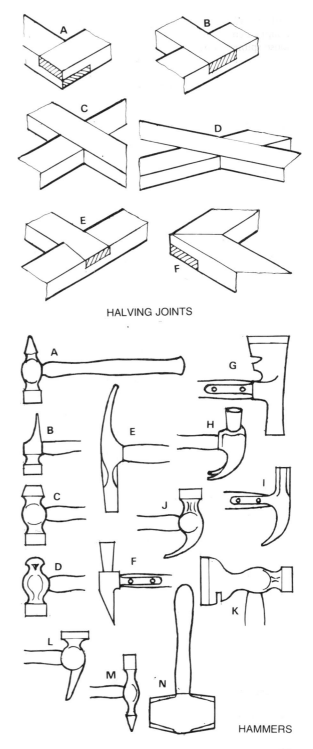

HALVING JOINTS

HAMMERS

nailing. (H) claw type used by carpenters. (I) Canterbury claw. (J) household hammer. (K) scaffolding hammer. (L) cobbler's. (M) pattern maker's similar to Warrington but lighter. (N) club, used by carpenters for plugging and by stone workers. Handles are hickory or ash. (See also *veneering hammer.*)

hammer beam   (see *hammer beam roof*).

hammer beam roof   One in which hammer beams are cantilevered out from the wall. They are supported by braces which with the wall posts rest upon corbels built into the masonry. Hammer posts are erected on the beams.

hammer-head tenon   Used when constructing a frame having a semi-circular shape at the top end, such as a door frame. It is often difficult to cramp the shape to the ends of the stiles, unless cramping 'horns' are provided. Such a tenon requires to be inserted sidewise into side mortises cut in the top piece, with allowance below the hammer-head for wedges which, driven in, draw the parts tightly together. If the semi-

circular top shape has to consist of two half pieces, these are jointed together at the centre with a double hammer-head key piece.

hammer post   (see *hammer beam roof*).

hammer veneering   Method of lying veneer by hand in which the veneer is pressed down close to the groundwork and surplus glue is squeezed out by means of a veneering hammer (*q.v.*). Scotch glue is used, and this having been applied and the veneer put in place, the surface is *lightly* dampened. A warm iron is pressed over the surface to liquefy the glue, and the veneering hammer worked with a zig-zag movement in the direction of the grain from the centre outwards.

hammock chair   One in which the back and seat form a continuous curve.

hand drills   These differ from breast drills in that there is no breast plate. A simple single-gear type is shown at (A), with a three-jaw chuck of $\frac{1}{4}$ in (6mm) capacity. (B) is an improved version, having double-gears, with ball-thrust bearing and $\frac{1}{4}$ in (6mm) capacity three-jaw chuck. It has a side grip knob, with a hollow hardwood handle for holding several drill bits. (C) is a completely enclosed hand drill, taking all sizes of drills up to $\frac{1}{4}$ in (6mm) diameter. Hand drills are often handier to use than a brace, being speedier and enabling holes to be drilled in confined quarters. (See also *breast drill, electric drill, drilling machine.*)

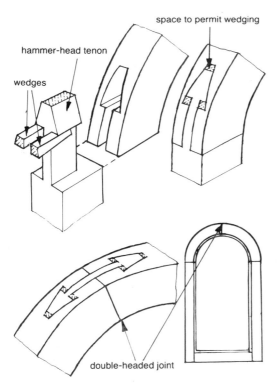

space to permit wedging

hammer-head tenon

wedges

double-headed joint

HAMMER-HEAD TENON

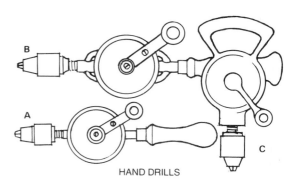

HAND DRILLS

handed   Items made in pairs, right- and left-hand. Also refers to fittings such as some locks and hinges which are right- and left-hand.

hand feed   Machines which have no automatic rollers for propelling the wood are known as hand-fed.

hand jointer   Also called a 'biscuit jointer'. This is a portable tool for enabling sheet material such as man-made boards to be joined end-to-end, edge-to-edge, at right angles, at right angled corners, or mitred corners. It has a motor unit and a flat base-plate on which it can be slid along. Parallel to the base-plate is a 4 in (200 mm) dia. TCT saw which cuts a groove 3.5 mm wide, and this is powered by the motor through a right-angled drive. At the front end of the base is a spring-loaded fence which is fixed at 90 degrees to it, and the saw lies behind this fence when not operating. When the fence contacts the work-piece it is pushed back and the saw emerges and cuts a crescent-shape groove or notch into which a key or 'biscuit' (hence the name) can be inserted. There are three sizes of keys and the saw must be pre-set to protrude the requisite depth for the size of key selected. The keys are made of compressed hardwood and are hygroscopic (that is, they will readily absorb moisture) and when adhesive is applied to the groove and the key inserted it will take up the moisture from the adhesive and swell to become immovable. One groove will only accept half of the key and when the protruding half is inserted into the mating groove (which has also had adhesive applied) it will, in its turn, swell up and the joint is accomplished. The keys are elliptical in shape, with pointed ends.

spring-loaded fence

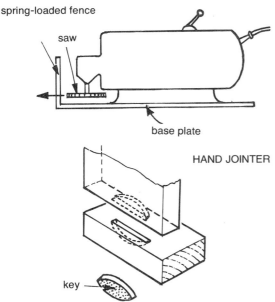

saw

base plate

HAND JOINTER

key

handkerchief table (USA) A single gate table with one flap. The bed and flap are triangular so that when the flap is up, the table-top is square; when the flap is down, it presents the appearance of a folded handkerchief (hence the name), and the table will fit into a corner. Invariably fitted with Queen Anne legs.

hand press Used in caul veneering. It may be a simple bed with cross-bearers, these being forced down by screws with wing nuts. A zinc with plywood or blockwood backing is generally used. Larger presses have a large centre screw which, by means of cross girders, presses down the whole thing in a single operation.

handrail The top horizontal member of a balustrade, or the sloping guide for the hand of a staircase.

hand rail bracket Used to fix a hand rail near to the wall but leaving space for the fingers to pass round. Fixed by plugging the wall and screwing.

hand rail bolt and punch Used in joinery to join sections of hand rails and other parts together in their length. The bolt itself passes into holes in both pieces. The square nut is dropped into a recess cut in one piece in line with the bolt, and the latter screwed into it. The round nut is placed in a slot in the other piece and revolved as the bolt is offered to it. Tightening is by means of the punch which engages with the slots in the round nut. Plain mitred joints in heavy timbers, as on curbs, are often strengthened with a hand rail bolt, and a dowel is also used in addition to prevent any twisting tendency.

handsaw General term for cross-cut, rip, and panel saw. (See under individual titles.)

hand screw Cramp for holding glued parts together temporarily and for securing wood to the bench for cutting, carving, etc. The wood type (A) consisting of beech chops and hornbeam screws is seldom made today. Overall jaw lengths are 8 in (203 mm), 10 in (254 mm) and 12 in (305 mm). (B) is the more useful type, having wooden chops and handles and metal screws which fit into pivoted centres. Thus, the chops are more adjustable and can be fitted to odd shapes so that the jaws clamp down at an angle. Jaws are quickly adjusted by holding a handle in each hand and revolving the one about the other. (Illustration on p. 90.)

hand vice Small vice, 4 in (102 mm) to 5 in (127 mm) long, enabling small pieces of metal, plastic material, etc, to be cut, filed or drilled, the jaws being tightened by a winged nut and opening by spring action as the nut is slackened. Often used by the cabinet maker, especially the furniture repairer, when making small metal fittings such as escutcheon plates. The hand vice simplifies filing and fitting, being more convenient than a steel bench vice or a metal sash cramp.

89

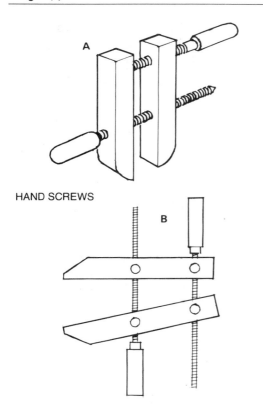

HAND SCREWS

hanger (1)   An upright fixed beneath a rail or top to support a member beneath. It is usually dovetailed.

hangers (2)   Metal sockets made in various designs to support joists, and to avoid the need for cutting joints. Some have a top flange which is built into the brickwork, or a cranked flange over the top of a beam. Stirrup type hangers allow joists to hang on both sides of a beam.

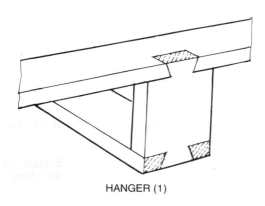

HANGER (1)

hanging   The operation of hingeing a door or sliding sash. The term also refers to a cabinet to hang on the wall rather than to stand on the floor, and sometimes to a wardrobe in which clothes are hung.

hanging stile   Stile of a door or gate to which the hinges are attached. Sometimes called the hingeing stile.

hardboard   Available in various sizes of panels and in thicknesses of about $\frac{1}{8}$ in (3 mm) and $\frac{3}{16}$ in (5 mm). A specially compressed and impregnated type also made, suitable for outdoor work. Perforated board with small holes at regular intervals is used for display stands, etc. Embossed patterns of various designs are produced for decorative effects.

hardener   Used in resin glues to cause setting. In some makes the powdered glue contains the hardener, and setting begins when water is added. In others the hardener is a separate liquid, and no setting begins until it is brought into contact with the glue. The usual method is to apply the glue to the one part and the hardener to the other. Hardeners of varying speeds can be obtained.

hardwood   Timber from deciduous broad-leaved trees which, in temperate climates, stand bare in water. On close examination, hardwoods are porous in that they have open cells (as distinct from self-contained cells) which carry moisture right through the tree. The cells are thus moisture-conducting rather than moisture absorbing. The term 'hard' has no bearing on the actual hardness of the wood. (See also *softwood*.)

harewood   Sycamore which has been turned grey by the use of sulphate of iron (green copperas).

Harlequin table   A table invented by Thomas Sheraton in which the centre part rises when the flaps are raised.

hasps and staples   There is a wide range of these. The commonest is (A), made from stamped steel and japanned finished. Some of the smaller sizes have no centre bolt holes. Such a bolt is advisable, as screws could be easily withdrawn. (B) is a type in which all screw heads are covered by the hasp, with a 'loose' staple which allows for inequalities in fixing. (C) is a locking-bar type suitable for double doors, one lock sufficing. (Illustration on p. 91.)

haster   An open-backed cabinet fitted with shelves and mounted on casters, with a door or doors on the front. Servants would fill the shelves with food and

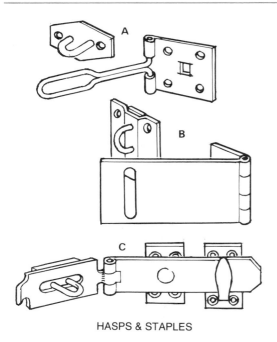

HASPS & STAPLES

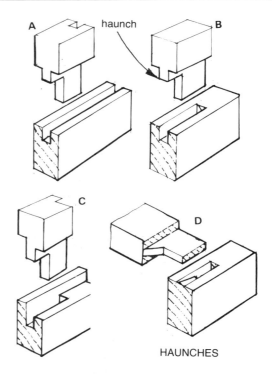

HAUNCHES

move the haster with the open back facing the fire to keep the food warm. The front doors could be opened to remove food for serving.

hatchment A term describing the painting of a deceased person's escutcheon or coat-of-arms on canvas stretched over a wooden frame which was hung on the front of his house for 6 to 12 months after his death. The hatchment also showed, by its design, the marital status of the deceased. They usually date back to the late seventeenth and eighteenth centuries, and often smaller hatchments were painted or carved on furniture, when they are referred to as palimpsest arms.

haunch A short projection at the side of a tenon. Its purpose is to resist any twisting tendency, and in some cases to fill up the gap caused by a groove ploughed in the stiles of a frame or door (A). Sometimes a concealed or secret haunch is used (B), this being cut at an angle so that it does not show. It is usually set in about $\frac{1}{12}$–$\frac{1}{16}$ in (1-2 mm) so that it does not show if the edge has to be trimmed. Also called a 'relish', or a 'haunchion'.

hauncher (see *horizontal spindle*).

hazel pine The sapwood of the American red gum (see *gum*) which used to be known as satin walnut (*q.v.*). The wood is not a pine.

head The upper member of a door; also the top part of a framing.

headboard Panel fitted at the head of a bed. May be quite simple or be in the form of a fitment with drawers, shelves, cupboards, etc. (See also *continental headboard*.)

headpiece The top horizontal member of a timber stud partition (*q.v.*).

headstock A fixed stock which is driven by a motor on a lathe. It can be fitted with a chuck which will hold one end of the work-piece, the other end being attached to the tailstock (*q.v.*). Alternatively, it can be fitted with a mandrel which will hold a face-plate for turning flat work such as bowls, platters, small table tops, etc. (See *face-plate, lathe, turning.*)

headway The clearance beneath an opening, or that of a staircase.

heart shake A radial shake beginning at the heart centre or pith.

heart side The side of a board which faces the centre of the log. Note that a board cut radially from a log as at (A) has no heart side.

HEART SHAKE

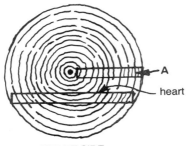

HEART SIDE

heartwood   That part of the wood between the pith and the sapwood. Since a tree grows by putting on a layer at the outside beneath the bark, it follows that all heartwood was at one time sapwood, but with the passing of time it has ceased to take any active part in the growth but remains as a firm core in supporting the tree. It is the most valuable part of the log for the conversion into timber for the woodworker.

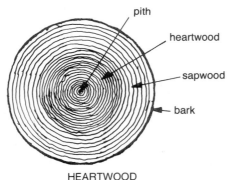

HEARTWOOD

heel   The wide end of a skew chisel or saw tooth, rear end of a plane, or the thick end of any item more or less pointed in shape. (See also *toe*.)

helical spring hinge   Hinge for door which opens both ways. Powerful helical (spiral) springs are contained within the cylinders. Some hinges have tension adjustment, other are fixed. (See *door closers*.)

hemlock   Eastern *tsuga canadensis*; Western *tsuga heterophylla*. Softwood from eastern Canada, British Columbia, north-west United States — weight 29-30 lb (465-481 kg). Pale brown colour and used for general utility purposes.

Herculaneum chairs   Refers to upholstered chairs of a particularly classical style; the term was used by Sheraton in his Cabinet Dictionary 1803.

Herma   Also 'herm'. A carved representation of the male head (usually the god, Hermes), mounted at the top of a pilaster or column.

herring-bone inlay   A form of decoration used widely in the walnut period of furniture. Often there were light or dark strings flanking the herring-bone centre. Sometimes the arrow effect was continuous round a top or drawer front. In other cases a centre joint was cut and the 'arrows' reversed at each side.

herring-bone strutting   Used to restrict lateral movement in the joists of a floor. Fixed with nails. Saw kerfs made at the ends help in avoiding splitting when nailing, and allow for a certain amount of movement in the event of shrinkage of the joists.

hessian   Material used in upholstery, manufactured from jute, and made in various qualities, weights, and widths. The threads are flat. For the upholsterer the 72 in (2 metres) width is the most popular. Best and heaviest quality is known as tarpaulin. A cheaper quality is known as scrim, being more open, and with round threads.

hewn   Timber which has been squared or roughly levelled with axe or adze.

hexagon   Most hexagons for woodwork are regular, having equal sides and angles. The usual way of setting out is to use the 60 deg set-square, as the figure is six-sided.

hickory   (*carya* various and *hicoria* various). From Canada and eastern USA, weight 46-47 lb (737-753 kg). Used chiefly for axe and hammer handles, oars, sports goods, etc. A strong, tough, and elastic hardwood. Colour varies from light yellow to light brown.

hidden mitred mortise and tenon   (USA) Corresponds to British 'mitred-bridle' (*q.v.*).

hidden spline mitre   (USA) Corresponds to British 'mitre, tongued' (*q.v.*).

hides   These include large cow hides; moroccos, the smaller skins of goats; and roans, the skins of sheep. They can be obtained dyed and specially finished to a fine, soft surface. Buffed hides are those with some defects which have been buffed with carborundum.

high chair   A chair specifically designed with a high seat for a child at the dining table. It always has legs with a pronounced splay for stability and is often fitted with a tray from which the child eats. Some models called 'convertibles' can also be folded to form low chairs.

highboy   (USA) A tall chest of drawers mounted on a 'low-boy' (*q.v.*). Although of plain design in New England, the design found its most ornate and elegant expression at the hands of Thomas Affleck (1740-1795), a Philadelphia cabinet maker; he used many Chippendale motifs such as very fine carving on the fascia and on the cabriole legs and apron. Other designs were based on Queen Anne or William and Mary styles, but the concept is purely American.

hingebound   Term applied to a door in which the hingeing stile binds as the door is closed. Generally due to the hinge recesses being too deep, to screws being of too large a gauge so that heads are not flush in countersinking, or to insufficient allowance for paint being made.

hinges   (see under individual types *acorn, back-flap, butt, card table, centre, clockcase, counter, cross-garnet, gate, lift-off, pin, pivot, quadrant, reflex, reversible, rising butts, rule joint, screen, step, stop, strap, strip, strut, etc.*).

hipped roof   Roof in which the ends slope as well as the sides. (See *hip rafter.*)

hip rafter   The corner rafters in a hipped roof.

Hitchcock rocker   (USA) A popular design of rocking chair produced by the firm of Hitchcock, Alford & Co. of Connecticut, USA. It has a shaped plank seat, scrolled arms and a scrolled comb; it is painted black with gold stencilled classical decoration. The back spindles are straight when the chair is new but take on the configuration of the occupant's back after a time.

Hogarth splat   Alternative name for 'fiddle-back' splat (*q.v.*).

hold up   Term used for the size of a piece of wood which is big enough to be worked to the required size.

hog saw   A saw fitted to an industrial machine to reduce offcuts to a size acceptable to the extraction system.

holdfast, bench   A cramping device enabling wood to be held down firmly on the bench. A hole slightly larger than the pillar diameter is bored right through the bench top. When the shoe is placed on the work and the screw tightened the pillar is levered over so enabling the pressure to be exerted. The pillar can be placed at any height to suit the wood being held. Some makes have a collar which is let into the bench top and held with bolts.

holding-down foot   A device sometimes fitted to a jig-saw to prevent the wood from rising at the up-stroke of the saw.

hole saw   (see *ring saw*).

hollow   Term with several applications. It may refer to a moulding of concave section, to a board which has warped so that it is 'hollow' one side and 'round' the other, to a moulding plane intended to work a rounded section, or in plywood, to a surface depression caused by a fallen knot or gap in the core.

hollow chisel   Used in a mortising machine. The chisel is hollowed out to receive the revolving auger, an escapement slot at the side enabling the chips to emerge. In use the chisel is set with its shoulder $\frac{1}{32}$ in (1mm) short of the seating, and the auger fixed. The chisel is then pushed right home, thus gaining clearance.

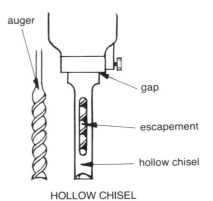

auger

gap

escapement

hollow chisel

HOLLOW CHISEL

hollow chisel mortiser   More accurately, the hollow square mortise chisel and auger bit. Essentially it comprises a square hollow chisel with four cutting edges at its lower end, inside which is mounted a revolving auger. The auger enters the wood first, making a hole which is converted to a square by the cutting edges of the chisel, which follows immediately behind the auger. Chip windows, which are open slots, are cut in the sides of the chisel and allow the shavings to escape. Normally only stub mortises and haunches can be cut with this machine, but it is possible to make through mortises by reversing the wood and cutting from both sides. Sizes of chisel vary from $\frac{1}{4}$ in (6mm) to 1 in (25mm).

hollow construction A framework with facing panels of plywood or hardboard as in a flush door.

hollow grinding This occurs to an extent on all grinding, but becomes marked when a wheel of small diameter is used. It requires less subsequent rubbing on the oilstone, but when a dry wheel is used care must be taken not to draw the temper.

hollow ground saw Circular saw which is slightly thinner at the middle than at the periphery. It thus has slight clearance. The teeth have no set and the saw leaves an extremely fine finish, almost equal to that of a planer. Sometimes known as the planer saw.

hollowing plane A plane which has a U-shaped sole, with a cutting edge to match; the blade is 1 in wide (25mm) and the overall length of the plane is $3\frac{1}{2}$ in (89mm). It is used for hollowing out flutes or contours, or cleaning up curved work such as mouldings.

holly (*ilex aquifolium*) European timber of 47 lb (753 kg) used chiefly for small items, turnery, inlay work, etc. White in colour but may become grey if conversion is delayed. It is close textured and works to a fine finish.

holm oak (*quercus ilex*) An evergreen oak, Europe generally. Seldom grown for conversion, rather as a decorative estate tree. It is a close-grained hard timber rather darker than English oak, weighing from 50 to 60 lb (801-961 kg).

Honduras mahogany (see *mahogany*).

honeycombing A fault in timber consisting of internal splits not visible on the surface, due usually to case hardening (*q.v.*) in which the surface of the timber dries too rapidly. The checks can be seen if a cross-section is taken through the wood.

honing Finishing an edge on the oilstone after the tool has been ground.

hood Alternative name for a bonnet-hood(*q.v.*).

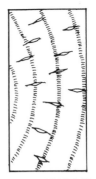
HONEYCOMBING

hoof foot The carved foot of some cabriole legs in the William and Mary and early Queen Anne periods.

hook joint Joint used between two doors or a door and the cabinet to form a dust-proof or air-tight joint as in a show case. Today they are machined, but originally pairs of moulding planes were made for the purpose.

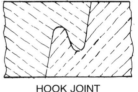
HOOK JOINT

hook, of teeth The angle that the front of a circular saw tooth makes with the radial line. The softer the wood the greater the degree of hook that can be given (A). Abrasive timbers may need no hook (B). The negative hook (C) is for cross-cutting.

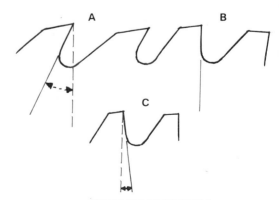
HOOK (OF SAW TEETH)

hoop pine (*Araucaria cunninghamii*) A softwood from Queensland, New South Wales, and New Guinea of 32 lb (513 kg) used as a general construction wood, being straight-grained and easily worked.

hope chest Colloquial term for a 'dower chest' (*q.v.*).

hopper Structure in which all four sides slope in at an angle.

hopper dovetails Through dovetails used in joining two parts which both slope at an angle. Ordinary methods of marking-out with the gauge cannot be used as the edges of the wood are at an angle. It is necessary to set out the angles and mark with knife and adjustable bevel.

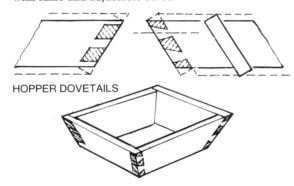

HOPPER DOVETAILS

Hoppus measurer A series of tables of ready reference for those in the timber trade. It covers round timber, cubic measure, superficial sizes, Petrograd standard, running feet in a square, etc. It is still occasionally used for measuring hardwoods.

horn Extra length allowed on a stile, partly to enable the mortise to be chopped without danger of splitting, to avoid displacement of the grain when a tenon is taken right through and is wedged, and to protect the corner of a framework when being handled before final fitting.

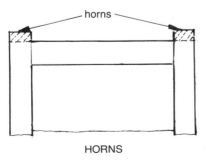

HORNS

hornbeam (*carpinus betulus*) A European hardwood of 43 lb (689 kg) weight, greenish white colour. It is strong and tough, difficult to split. Used in engineering, wood screws, planes (made in France), skittles, piano actions, etc.

horse chestnut (*aesculus hippocastanum*) European hardwood, of 36 lb (577 kg) light in colour. The tree is grown chiefly in parks or avenues and has little commercial use.

horse hair Excellent upholstery stuffing. Cheapest quality consists of short hairs which have little resiliency. After being washed and sterilised it is twisted into a rope, forming the curl which gives the springiness.

horseman's chair Alternative name for a reading chair (*q.v.*).

horse power (hp) The unit of power measurement. 1 hp equals 33,000 ft-lb of work per minute. The woodworker is usually more interested in the electrical equivalent of 746 W = 1 hp. As a general guide for circular saws it is generally reckoned that a motor needs $\frac{1}{2}$ hp for each 1 in (25 mm) depth of cut, though many saws have lower hp. When only thin wood or softwood is being sawn the motor can be of smaller hp.

horizontal spindle This is an industrial machine which has a rectangular metal frame from which a work-table projects on one side. This work-table carries any fences or jigs, and behind it is a horizontal spindle to which the cutter heads are fixed. The work is cramped or fixed to the work-table and the horizontal spindle with its cutters is brought down and cuts the work. Typical work includes corner locking and notching, small tenons, hinge recesses, leg tapers, etc. Also called a 'notcher', or a 'hauncher'.

hot-melt adhesives Thermoplastic adhesives which are melted in a heated applicator so that they spread easily and cure by cooling.

hot press Large machine press in which the plates can be heated to enable resin glues to be cured quickly, leaving the press free for other work.

house longhorn beetle (see *longhorn beetle*).

housed dovetail (see *dovetail housing*).

housed string Staircase string in which the risers and treads are housed in.

housing A joint in which one part is recessed into the other in a groove. The simplest is the through type (A) which shows at the front. The stopped housing (B) is concealed at the front edge. At (C) the top is shouldered so that any slackness is concealed by the shoulder. When the shouldered housing can be put together straightway the tongue can be parallel, but if the shelf has to be slipped in afterwards it should be slightly tapered so that it is a slack fit until pressed right home. (See also *dovetail housing*.)

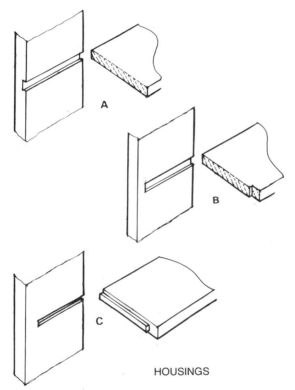

HOUSINGS

housing plane (see *dado plane*).

HSS High-speed steel. Used for saw blades, cutters, etc., but now largely superseded by tungsten-carbide tipped (*TCT*).

H underframing A form of chair underframing in which the side stretchers or rails are connected by a single cross-member placed centrally at right angles.

huntboard (USA) A kind of sideboard used in the southern states of America, its chief characteristic being its height which was usually about 39 in (990 mm), so that those people using it had to stand. It normally comprised a carcase containing two or three drawers flanked by a cupboard on either side, the whole being mounted on four square legs and tapered legs. Popular in the first half of the nineteenth century.

hunting chair An arm-chair in which the back seat and arms are filled with canework. Favoured by Thomas Chippendale the younger, circa 1816.

hunting table A horseshoe-shaped table placed in front of a fire so that all of the occupants had an equal share of the warmth. It was equipped with a cellarette containing decanters and this could be moved around the table on a track built into the top.

husks (see *bell flower*).

HUSKS

hutch Derived from the Norman-French word 'hunche' meaning a meal or grain tub. The term is now applied to a kind of chest raised on legs, with a table-top instead of a lid and often having pierced front panels providing ventilation for the storage of food.

hydrogen peroxide Used for bleaching. The 100 vol. is generally diluted with 2 parts water.

I

idigbo (*Terminalia ivorensis*) Hardwood from Ghana, Nigeria, and Gambia of 36 lb (577 kg) Used for plywood and general purposes. Sometimes known as black afara. Yellowish brown colour, rather coarse in grain. Stains and polishes well.

imbroiderer's chair (see *farthingale chair*.)

imbrication A term describing the carving of a surface to represent fish scales; a decoration much favoured in the early eighteenth century on chairs and tables, etc.

imbuya (*phoebe porosa*) Southern Brazilian hardwood of 45 lb (721 kg) used for furniture, veneers, plywood, and interior fitments. Similar to walnut but not a true walnut. Of fine texture sometimes with interlocked grain. Stands well when seasoned with slight tendency to warp and split during the process. Some workers find the dust irritant to nose and throat.

impact test Used to test the hardness of timber. A metal ball is dropped from a definite height, the diameter of the mark indicating the relative hardness of the wood.

impost The capital of a column or pilaster which marks the springing of an arch; also the part of a pillar upon which an arch rests.

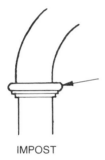

IMPOST

impregnation The forcing of a substance into the cells of wood. It may be a preservative, or a resin, in which case it is usually done in combination with compression in the manufacture of an extremely hard wood-based material akin to metal.

incipient decay The early stage of decay in wood due to fungi. Usually the wood becomes discoloured.

incising Form of carved decoration in which the pattern is cut into the surface rather than left standing with the background recessed.

increment teeth Ripsaw teeth which become progressively larger towards the handle. The advantage claimed is that the larger teeth come into operation at the strongest part of the stroke. They are not cut today.

independent chuck Lathe chuck with four jaws which can be moved independently of each other. Thus irregular objects can be held or cylindrical work

can be centred accurately. The jaws are reversible. Has limited use in wood turning.

ingyin (*pentacme suavis*) Hardwood from India, Burma, and Malaya of 52-54 lb (833-865 kg) Brownish colour, used for bridges, boats, carts, and sometimes furniture. Durable under water.

indigenous Term used for woods native to a particular country.

inlay Correctly speaking, the removal of part of the solid surface and the insertion of a different wood (or other material) in its place. Examples are the chopping out of solid wood, and inlaying of other woods to form floral, leafwork, and conventional patterns. Also the inlaying of narrow strings and bandings for which shallow grooves are channelled. The word 'inlay', however, is commonly used to cover marquetry cut in veneers. (See *marquetry*.)

inlay bandings and strings (see *bandings* and *strings*).

insecticide A timber insect pest destroyer.

inserted tooth Used on some circular saws. Advantages are that the teeth can be tempered harder than the main plate, the saw always maintains its full diameter, and a faster rate of feed can be maintained. When being retoothed the teeth should be changed one at a time otherwise the plate is liable to lose its tension.

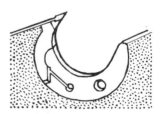

INSERTED TOOTH

inside ground gouge (see *scribing gouge*).

in situ Items made in the position for which they are intended, as distinct from being made elsewhere and brought to the job.

intaglio Form of decoration in which the ornament is engraved into the surface rather than raised from it. Not used much in woodwork, but sometimes found on brass inlay, particularly Boulle work.

intarsia Inlay decoration largely practised in Italy from the thirteenth century and onwards. Various coloured woods were used, also metals, ivory, mother of pearl, etc. The designs took many forms: architectural scenes, scrolls, arabesques, and fruit and floral motifs. Earlier examples were cut into the solid wood, but later took the form of marquetry in which patterns were cut in veneers with a fine saw and laid as a whole.

interlaced bow Windsor chair A type of Gothic Windsor chair (*q.v.*).

interlocked grain Grain in which the successive layers of growth are in the form of reversed spirals, so that in a quarter-cut board, the plane works with and against the grain in alternate streaks.

in the open Timber stacked without covering is said to be stacked in the open.

in the round Refers to felled logs which have not been squared or converted.

in the white Furniture or fitments in which construction is finished but which has not been stained or polished.

intrados The underside or inside of a curved arch.

inventory numbers Often found either painted or branded on French furniture made for the Crown or Royal Family of France and are mostly contained in the 'Journal du Garde Meuble de la Couronne.'

Ionic The second order of Grecian architecture, the name being derived from Ionia, in Greece.

Irish Chippendale A term used to describe furniture of Chippendale style made by Irish craftsmen in the middle of the eighteenth century. Characterised by flat and unconnected carving, very deep aprons, and other motifs being carved in relief against a punched ground with diaper patterns.

iroko (*chlorophora excelsa*) Nigerian hardwood of 42 lb (673 kg). Sometimes known as African teak but is not a true teak. Pale to dark brown colour. Used locally for general constructional work. Sometimes used as a substitute for teak for draining boards.

iron (1) Applied to a plane or machine cutter. It is in fact of steel.

iron (2) As well as being used for hinges, bandings, and handles, iron began to be used for furniture from

1840 onwards in Britain. The designs included chairs and tables for garden or public-house use, bedsteads, and even children's cots.

ironbark (*eucalyptus cebra*, etc.) Queensland hardwood, 63-77 lb (1009-1233 kg). Dense, heavy wood dark brown in colour, durable, and with great tensile strength. Used for girders, bridge work, sleepers, and general construction. There are many varieties of the wood.

Irwin bit A form of twist bit with nickers and cutters, but with single, rather than double, spiral.

IRWIN BIT

Isle of Man underframing Takes the form of three stretchers interlocked so that they resemble the arms of the Isle of Man.

isocyanate adhesive This is often called the 'Miracle' adhesive (or some such term) and has enormous strength: it will bond almost anything to anything and has a curing time of a few seconds after which the bond is complete.

isometric projection A pictorial form of drawing in which one corner of the object is nearest the observer and is vertical, the two sides sloping away at 30 deg with the horizontal. Actual or scale sizes can be drawn on all three lines. The projection is satisfactory for small objects, but on larger ones such as sideboards, etc. it gives a somewhat distorted appearance and the proportions appear wrong. It is used therefore on drawings intended to show working detail sizes, etc., rather than the actual appearance, though a compromise is sometimes made by drawing lines at 45 deg, marking measurements on these, and dropping vertical lines to cut the 30 deg lines. Even so this does not allow for the fact that parts farther away appear smaller than those near, even though they are in fact the same size. For pictorial appearance perspective is better.

isoscles triangle One which has two sides and two angles equal.

ivory black A black substance at one time made from charred bones or ivory and used for staining.

J

jacareuba *(calophyllum brasiliense)* Hardwood from Brazil, Central America, and West Indies of 38 lb (609 kg). Used for bridge and general construction work. Similar in colour and appearance to mahogany. May warp in seasoning.

jack plane Used before the smoothing plane or trying plane, the cutter — which is ground and sharpened to a slight curvature — being set coarse to quickly reduce the thickness of surfaces and edges. That at (A) has a steamed, quartered-beech body 16 in (406 mm) long. Cutter may be 1¾ in (44 mm) to 2¼ in (58 mm) wide. The metal type (B) is for general bench work, for trimming generally, and for short joints, etc. Metal jack planes are 14 in (356 mm) long with 2 in (51 mm) cutter, and 15 in (381 mm) long with 2¼ in (58 mm) cutter.

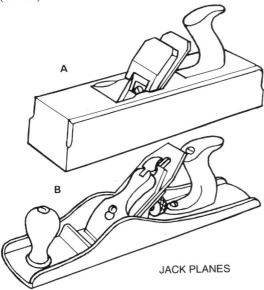

JACK PLANES

jack rafter A short rafter lining up with the common rafters but fitting between wall plate and hip rafter or between ridge and valley.

Jacobs chuck Used in the lathe, either in headstock or tailstock to hold morse drills. The three jaws are

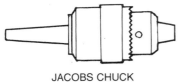

JACOBS CHUCK

automatically centred, and are closed by a rotating collar operated by a key.

jalousie An outer shutter consisting of sloping slats fitted between the uprights of a framework. (See also *louver*.)

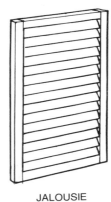

JALOUSIE

jambs In building, the sides of wall openings such as doorways and fireplaces. In carpentry the jambs are the stiles of doorway and other wall openings to which architrave or other woodwork is fixed.

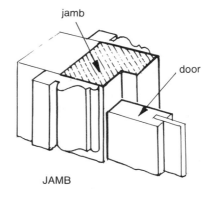

JAMB

Japan color (USA) A coloured pigment in powder form which is ground in hard-drying varnish. Its advantage is that it can be rubbed once it is dry.

Japan drier (USA) A gum varnish containing metallic salts such as salts of lead, cobalt, manganese, or zinc, which help rapid drying.

Japanese oak (see under *oak*).

Japanning A term used to describe the European and American techniques of imitating Oriental lacquer by applications of many layers of various paints and varnishes: it was popular in the late 17th and throughout the 18th century, and it was a favourtie pastime for ladies. Often it was embellished with raised gesso patterns and figures of a vaguely Oriental style, and these patterns were frequently gilded. The background of true Oriental lacquer work was always black, but japanned backgrounds could be blue, green, red or yellow. The methods were explained in a well-known book entitled 'A Treatise of Japanning and Varnishing' by John Stalker and George Parker published in 1688.

jardiniere A trough or open-topped box-like structure to receive growing plants.

jarrah *(eucalyptus marginata)* Western Australian hardwood of 57lb (913kg). Used for general construction work, sleepers, wood paving, etc. Deep red colour, with dense, hard grain. Sometimes used for panelling and furniture.

jaws The cramping faces of a vice. In a bench vice for woodwork they are invariably of wood screwed or bolted to the metal parts. Also refers to the gripping parts of a Jacobs, self-centering, or independent chuck.

jelly cupboard (USA) A small cupboard with two doors enclosing shelves; used for storing jelly ('jelly' corresponds to British 'jam').

jelutong *(dyera costulata)* Hardwood of 23lb (368kg) from Malay Peninsula. Pale yellow colour, will take stain or paint well, but not a good polishing wood.

Jennings bit Type of twist bit with nickers and cutters. May have double or single thread centre screw, or pyramid point. The original bit of this type was patented by Russell Jennings in 1855 in the USA.

JENNINGS BIT

jig Any device which acts as a guide for handwork or machining. It is invariably specially made for the job in hand. Thus for boring at a special angle a jig is made up; or for controlling movement at a special angle a jig is used; also for guiding movement of the wood in spindle moulding, etc.

jig saw A reciprocating machine saw for cutting internal shapes which the bandsaw could not reach. For the small workshop the bench model is used in which the throat distance is the limit the saw can operate from the edge of the wood. Larger trade machines are of the floor-to-ceiling type in which there is no throat restriction. Some machines have

spring plunger control of the saw; others the crossbow type spring.

In a portable jig saw or sabre saw a short, stiff blade is used. For woodwork jig saws operate at about 1,000 to 1,400 strokes per minute.

jigger (1) A tool similar in appearance to a spokeshave and used by coachmakers for side routing. Now obsolete.

jigger (2) (see *oscillating bit mortiser*).

jockey mortiser (see *oscillating bit mortiser*).

joggle A projection or horn left on the stile of a sliding sash or other window so that the mortise is not too close to the end where it would be liable to split. It is usually given an ornamental shaping.

JOGGLE

joined Refers to a carcase or frame employing joints instead of using solid planks. Also 'joyned'.

joiner The woodworker who is concerned with the wood finishings and fixings of a building as distinct from the carpenter whose work is mainly structural.

joiner's cramp Similar to a sash cramp *(q.v.)* but with the bar over 4ft (1220mm) long.

jointer (1) Also called a 'tracker'. A device fitted to some large planing machines with more than two cutters which allows an abrasive stone to be fed gradually towards the cutters (which are revolving at normal speed in the cutter block) until a thin silver highlight appears on each cutting edge (when the block is stopped).

jointer (2) Wood or metal plane used for shooting long joints or for planing any long edges. In wood it may be anything from 26in (660mm) to 30in (762mm) long. Metal jointers are usually from 22in (559mm) to 24in (609mm) long. Cutter width varies from $2\frac{3}{8}$ in (60 mm) up to $2\frac{3}{4}$ in (70 mm). The longer planes are seldom used today as large work is invariably machined.

jointer (3)   The term is also applied to the machine surface planer or edger in which the wood is passed over the rotating cutters when making straight joints.

jointer, tapeless   Machine used in jointing veneers. The veneers are glued and pressed together by a series of wheels mounted out of parallel. The application of heat causes the glue to set, and the parts are held together without tape, the advantage being that no time is spent removing the tape afterwards.

jointing   Technique for gluing together long narrow strips of wood side by side to form a wide panel. The adhesive is applied to the edges, which must be shot perfectly straight and very slightly concave in profile. The pieces are then cramped up and propped against a wall while the adhesive sets (do not lay them flat while the glue is setting).

joints   (see under individual headings).

joist hanger   Metal fitting fixed to a joist to take the end of another joist at right angles. It avoids cutting complicated joints. Also, a metal fitting attached to a brick wall into which joists can be fixed.

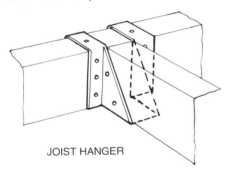

JOIST HANGER

joists   The main timbers supporting the flooring or ceilings. For the ground floor of a dwelling house they are usually spaced at 16 (406 mm) to 18 in (458 mm) centres, and to enable fairly narrow joists to be used honeycombed sleeper walls are built so that the clear span for the joists does not exceed 5 ft (1524 mm). Upper floors can have no intermediate support and deeper joists are needed.

joyned   Archaic term corresponding to 'joined' (*q.v.*).

kapok   A vegetable down from Java and the Dutch East Indies. Used as a filling for cushions and mattresses. Quality varies, cheaper grades being dusty and not always pure kapok.

kapur (*dryabalanops aromatica*)   Sometimes known as Borneo camphorwood. Reddish brown wood, dull in appearance. Fire-resistant. Used in furniture making and boat-building. 48 lb (769 kg) weight.

karri (*eucalyptus diversicolor*)   A gum wood from Western Australia, 53 lb (849 kg), dark red in colour and tough to work. A wavy or curly figuring is sometimes found in the grain. The wood is durable and resistant to fire. Used in general construction.

kas   (USA) A misspelling of the Dutch word 'kast' meaning a wardrobe or cupboard of the traditional farmhouse style. Made by Dutch settlers in America; they were bulky, with heavy cornice and mouldings, and supported by ball feet. Made during the 18th century.

katsura (*cercidiphyllum japonicum*)   Softwood of 22 lb (352 kg) from Japan. Light brown colour, even in grain, and with lustrous surface. Used for furniture, carving, and small items.

kauri pine (*agathis australis*)   A New Zealand and Queensland timber of light yellow-brown tint, particularly valuable when mottling or other figuring is present. 30-40 lb (481-641 kg) weight. Straight in the grain and strong; easily worked and almost entirely free from knots and other defects. The wood is reserved exclusively for high-class joinery. Great widths clear of heart are obtainable.

KD Furniture   Abbreviation for knock-down furniture (*q.v.*).

Kempas (*koompassia malaccensis*)   From Malaya, Sarawak, Borneo, 55 lb (881 kg). Pinkish when newly converted but becoming darker with exposure. Used mostly for structural work.

kerf   The cut made by a saw. When cutting tenons, dovetail pins, etc., in wood, the saw kerf must be made to the waste side of the guide lines, otherwise the resulting joint will be a loose fit.

kerosene oil   (USA) An illuminating oil, distilled from petroleum. Sometimes used in place of petrol for cleaning gummed-up oilstones, being rubbed on with a stiff brush. Another plan is to soak the stone in kerosene for a few days, then scrub it and wipe it dry. Corresponds to British paraffin *(q.v.)*. (See *resurfacing oilstones.*)

keruing *(dipterocarpus,* species) From Malaya, North Borneo, and Sarawak, 55 lb (881 kg) weight. Reddish brown colour, used mostly in construction work. Interlocked grain and non-lustrous surface. Does not polish well.

kettle stand Designed as an accessory for the habit of tea drinking which became popular in the late 17th century. There were three main types: (1) a small table with a circular top surrounded by a gallery or a deep rim and supported on a column with tripod legs: (2) a four-legged table in the late 18th century, frequently with a slide to hold the teapot: (3) a box-like structure lined with metal supported on four legs, the box having an opening to accommodate the kettle spout, while a slide was also provided for the teapot.

keyed tenon One which passes right through, the projection having a hole in it to receive a wedge or key. The inner face of the hole stands just inside the mortise so that the wedge draws the parts together.

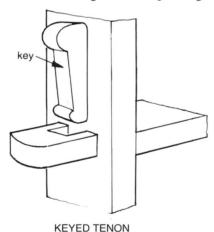

KEYED TENON

keyhole saw or padsaw Primarily used for slotting keyholes. Also for internal piercings. Blades are of springy steel, ground thin at the back, there being no set to the teeth which are usually 12 to 16 points to the inch; obtainable with special handle in which blade can be fixed at any desired projection. (See also *nest of saws.*)

keying (1) Method of strengthening a joint, usually a mitre, by the insertion of small keys or tongues. At (A) is veneer keying, and at (B) dovetail keying. Note

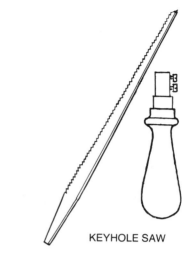

KEYHOLE SAW

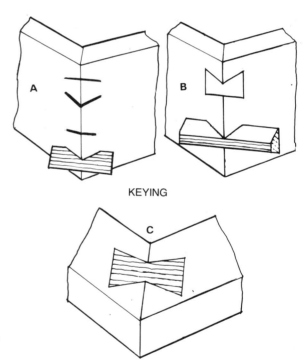

KEYING

that the key in the latter is slightly tapered so that it becomes tight when pressed in. At (C) the wood is mitred in its width and the key let in on its surface.

keying (2) Toothing or scarifying a surface to provide better adhesion when gluing or bonding a veneer or a plastic laminate to it.

keyplate Metal plate with centre hole, shaped similarly to a key and with screw holes. Fixed to the back of a fitment, etc., to enable the last named to be fixed by the slot-screw method. (See also *escutcheon*.)

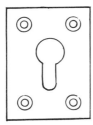

KEY PLATE

kick-back If work is introduced too quickly or if it is too heavy for a machine to cope with, it can be violently thrown aside. This is known as 'kick-back' and can be dangerous.

kicker In carcase work a rail fitted above a drawer runner to prevent dropping when the drawer is opened.

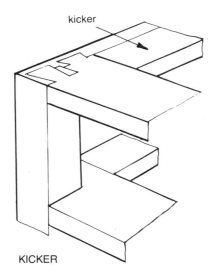

KICKER

kidney shape The plan shape of some writing and dressing tables. Although the outline can be drawn with compasses or radius rod (*q.v.*), the best shape is drawn freehand. A flowing line free from sudden changes in direction should be aimed at. Generally a fairly flat end shape is desirable to avoid waste space, though some wastage is unavoidable. Another way sometimes followed is to assume an ellipse and adjust the front curve.

kiln Structure used in drying timber. Its use enables drying times to be reduced considerably compared with natural air seasoning. All kilns have a means of heating, generally by coils of steam pipes; a system of introducing humidity by steam jets; and a free air circulation, either natural draught or by fans. Both temperature and humidity have to be varied as seasoning progresses, and the ratio between the two has to be altered during drying. Treatment for different woods varies, and schedules are available.

kiln dry Generally applied to wood which has been brought to a moisture content of 12% or less.

king-post roof trusses Span roof truss in which there is centre upright between tie beam and ridge. (See also *queen-post roof and princess post*.)

kingwood (*dalbergia cearensis*) Brazilian timber of 75-76 lb (1201-1217 kg) used mostly in veneer form. Is of a deep violet colour, hard and heavy. Also called 'Prince's wood'.

klismos chair A chair design of Ancient Greece; it inspired the design of several Regency period chairs, particularly those with sabre legs.

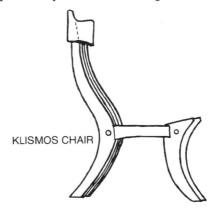

KLISMOS CHAIR

knee The top rounded part of a cabriole leg. Also a curved bracket or brace often used in boat building, sometimes known as a crook.

knee bend The members used in a staircase handrail where the direction changes from the horizontal to a downward slope.

knee hole The space between the side pedestals of a writing table or dressing table.

knee joint A simple open mortise and tenon joint in which the rounded ends are pivoted together with a

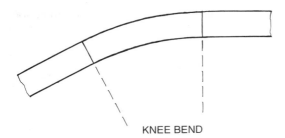

KNEE BEND

screw, dowel or bolt to allow movement to the maximum permitted by the shouldering of the mortise and tenon. The joint is often used for attaching the limbs of wooden puppets.

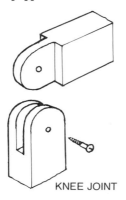

KNEE JOINT

knife   (see under individual headings).

knife case   A container for cutlery in general, not solely for knives. There are two distinct types — (1) a tall box with a sloping top and a convex front, the interior being divided into compartments for the various knives, forks, etc. (2) these were followed (in

KNIFE CASES

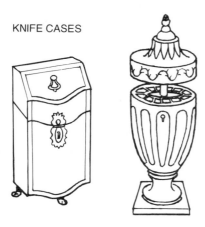

the late 18th century) by a vase-shaped container designed to stand on a pedestal at one end of a sideboard and being matched by a wine cooler at the other end. The top of the vase could be raised and lowered on a central shaft around which the cutlery compartments were arranged.

knife-cut veneer   Veneer which has been sliced with a wide knife rather than sawn. It may be rotary cut in which the log is mounted on a heavy lathe-like machine, the knife moving inwards at a predetermined rate which controls the thickness of the veneer. Most decorative veneers are flat sliced, the knife passing the wood in a straight path, or are cut by the half rotary slicing method *(q.v.)* or half-round slicing *(q.v.)*.

knock-down   Applied to furniture and fittings which are made to be taken apart for ease in conveyance or storing. Special fittings are used in construction rather than rigid joints, these usually working on the cam, screw, or wedge principle so drawing the parts together.

knop   A pronounced swelled member on a column or pillar; a term more often used for gold and silver ware.

knot   A defect found mainly in softwoods, produced by the saw cutting through a branch. On the surface of the wood the severed root of the branch shows in section, and is invariably dark in colour. Types of knots are distinguished under various names. A live knot is firm in the wood. A dead one is the result of a branch having died and shrunk, and may drop out. Both may be round or oval in shape according to the direction of the cut through them, or they may be spiked, that is, cut in line with the branch. Pin knots are those under $\frac{1}{4}$ in (6mm) in diam. The position and form of knots has to be carefully considered in structural timber as the strength of the member may be considerably reduced.

knotting   A solution of shellac in methylated spirit or commercial alcohol. It is used over knots before paint is applied, its purpose being to prevent the exudation of resin which, being soluble in paint media and thinners, would take place.

knuckle   The rounded centre part of a hinge through which the pin passes.

knuckle joint   Mechanical joint used chiefly for pivoting the fly rails of drop-leaf tables. A $\frac{3}{16}$ in (5mm) iron rod is used as the central pivot for wood $\frac{7}{8}$ in (23mm) or $1\frac{1}{4}$ in (32mm) thick. Usually the shoulders are cut at 45 deg, enabling the rail to move through 180 deg, though in most cases 90 deg is all that is needed. Apart from forming a stop the sloping shoulder avoids a feather edge *(q.v.)* to the socket.

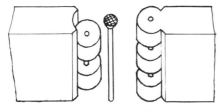

KNUCKLE JOINT

kokko *(albizzia lebbek)* From India, Sri Lanka, Burma, and Andaman Islands, of 47 lb (753 kg) weight. Used for furniture, boat-building, etc. Generally of golden brown colour. Sometimes known (incorrectly) as East Indian Walnut.

kokrodua *(afrormosia elata)* From West Africa, 44 lb (705 kg) weight. Is one of the Afrormosia species. Brownish yellow colour with darker streaks. Stands well when seasoned. Used for furniture, fitments, and general joinery.

krabak *(anisoptera,* species) From Malaya, Burma, Thailand, and Philippine Islands, of 35 lb (561 kg) weight. Yellowish brown, coarse textured, and does not polish well. Used in structural work, flooring, etc.

L

laburnum *(laburnum anagyroides)* European timber of 46-55 lb (737-881 kg). Seldom used in general woodworking, but sometimes cross-cut in veneer to form 'oysters' *(q.v.).* When cut at right angles the grain is circular in form, and when at an angle is elliptical.

lac (see *shellac).*

lacewood Wood of the plane tree *(q.v.)* when quarter-cut. The figure (medullary rays) is small and roughly resembles lace. Usually in veneer form.

lacquer (1) A hard varnish derived from the sap of the sumac tree, much used in the Far East as a varnish for wood, being applied in successive layers and allowed to harden. It is afterwards burnished and usually embellished with gold, or silver, mother-of-pearl, etc.

lacquer (2) Modern cellulose lacquer, however, is not the direct product of nature, but is commercial nitrocellulose. There are various types for both brushing and spraying and obtainable clear or in various colours for use on either wood or metal. It should not be applied over oil-painted surfaces, grease, dust, etc. Any dampness in wood is fatal to a good finish. Lacquer must be diluted when necessary with a special thinner made by the manufacturers. Owing to its extremely volatile nature, the vapour of which is highly inflammable, it should not be used near a naked flame.

lacquer (3) The two most widely-used lacquers are polyester and polyurethane. Polyester resin is used for the first, and this is an alkyd resin which is dissolved in styrene; the resulting coat is very hard and may even be belt-sanded. The lacquer also has such grain-filling qualities that normal fillers may be omitted; water stains are preferred for colouring the wood, as oil or naphtha stains will affect curing and bonding. The lacquer is not suitable for such timbers as iroko, mansonia, rosewood, and teak as they contain chemicals which inhibit the curing or bonding. Polyurethane lacquer (PU) is a synthetic finish and can be made to suit any particular purpose — thus, one used for exterior woodwork would be formulated to be weatherproof and flexible, while one for furniture would be hard enough to be rubbed and polished. It is a very tolerant finish and can be applied over all timbers, and most paints and lacquers, and over all stains excepting those containing linseed oil. It has good grain-filling properties, but if a full-grained burnished finish is required a special filler supplied by the manufacturer must be used as the lacquer will not bond with oil bound fillers. There are two types — the two-pack, which consists of the base and the hardener which need to be mixed, and the one-pack which is ready to use. The hardener (which is also called the catalyst, or the initiator) consists of a metallic salt in the case of polyester lacquer, and an isocyanate for PU lacquer. Some cellulose and melamine lacquers can be bought with the hardener already mixed in, called 'pre-catalysed' lacquer.

lacquer enamel A clear lacquer with coloured pigments added.

lacquer work True Oriental lacquer was a laborious and painstaking procedure. The object to be lacquered was smoothed and all joints filled, and then covered with cloth or paper to prevent sap from the wood from entering the lacquer and also to strengthen the structure. Up to 40 coats of lacquer were applied and rubbed down (working in a damp atmosphere). Decoration was then applied: it could be further coats of coloured lacquer incised to reveal the black ground or raised patterns which could be painted or gilded, and sometimes it included inlay. The lacquer was made from the sap of the lac tree (*rhus vernicifera*) which can cause serious rashes on bare skin.

ladder back   Term applied to late seventeenth century chairs in which there are several similar horizontal rails in the back similar in arrangement to the rungs of a ladder. Also used in some Chippendale period chairs as shown here.

LADDER-BACK

Lagos   Port in Nigeria from which many African timbers are shipped.

lagging   System used for building up shaped work. The lags are narrow strips screwed to ribs. Also used in making centres for forming brick arches.

L halving   Joint in which the ends of both parts are halved at right angles. (See *halving joint, A.*)

laid cord   A stout cord with the yarns laid together to prevent stretching. It is usually employed for lashing springs in place.

lambrequin   Originally a strip of cloth or fabric worn over a helmet to keep out the heat, but also applied to a short strip of ornamental drapery over a door, window, or shelf; it was sometimes imitated in wood or metal as a decorative motif.

lamb's tongue   A moulding often used in sashes and sash bars.

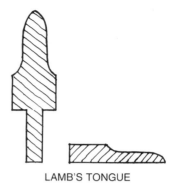

LAMB'S TONGUE

laminated beam   One made up of several thicknesses glued together. The chief value is in curved members since the grain runs longitudinally through the whole.

laminated construction   System in which several thicknesses are glued together. Since the grain is parallel with the direction of the member maximum strength is ensured, especially in curved work. Thus, shaped legs, rails, etc., of furniture can be made, and in building construction arches, shaped beams, roof members and so on can be formed without the weakness of short grain. In building work resin glue is invariably used.

laminboard or laminated board   A manufactured board similar to Clockboard and battenboard but with core strips not exceeding 7mm thick. The potential warping movement is small, hence its suitability as a groundwork for veneer. (See also *battenboard and blockboard.*)

LAMINBOARD

lamp black   A fine pigment powder used for making black stain or polish. A binder should be added for staining.

Lancashire ladder-back chair   A country style chair, circa 1785, with a rushed seat, turned front legs and underframe, and the ladder-rails of the same size and pattern throughout. Usually the front legs had club feet, which often terminated in turned balls.

Lancashire spindle-back chair   Similar in construction to the Lancashire ladder-back chair (*q.v.*) and with a rushed seat, but with rows of spindles instead of ladder-rails.

Lancashire Windsor chair Resembles a low-back chair *(q.v.)* with a bow, splat, and sticks surmounting the arm bow. Also made in Nottinghamshire.

lance tooth Long pointed saw tooth suitable for softwoods. Also known as *fleam tooth (q.v.).*

lancet arch A sharply pointed arch used widely in European medieval designs in both architecture and woodwork and probably derived from the Moorish arch found in Spain and Sicily, both countries having been invaded by the Moors. The radius of each curve is greater than the span.

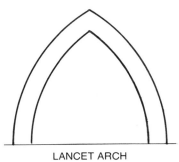

LANCET ARCH

lance-wood *(oxandra lanceolata)* From South America and West Indies; 62 lb (993 kg). Tough and elastic. Used for billiard cues, shooting sticks, bows, and shafts generally. Light yellow colour.

lancet Alternative name for a shoulder cutter *(q.v.)* in a tenoning machine, *(q.v.).*

landing Flat space between two flights or at the top of a single flight. (See also *half-space landing and quarter-space landing.*)

lantern light Raised roof-light with side windows and sloping top lights. Shape may be square, circular, or polygonal.

lapis lazuli A semi-precious stone greatly prized by the Ancient Egyptians and Romans. It is a rich ultramarine blue flecked with yellow pyrites and was used in inlay work in ancient times; 17th century Italian craftsmen painted an imitation lapis lazuli on chairs, chests, etc.

lap mitre Double-lapped joint in which both laps are mitred.

lapped dovetail Joint used widely in carcase, box, and drawer construction, in which the one part, usually with the pins, has a lap or covering piece so

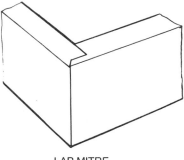

LAP MITRE

that the ends of the dovetails are concealed. Its particular value is in carcases in which the joint does not show on the one face. The lap is usually about one-third the thickness of the wood or a little less. (See also *double-lapped dovetail and drawer joints.*)

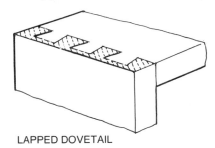

LAPPED DOVETAIL

lapped joint One in which the one piece is rebated so that it overlaps the other. The simple joint is invariably nailed as well as glued. The lap is also used in other joints such as the lapped dovetail *(q.v.).*

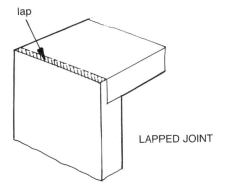

lap

LAPPED JOINT

lapping joint Used to joint beams, etc., in their length. Simplest form is shown, held together with bolts. Sometimes straps are used in place of bolts, and key wedges driven in to resist any sliding tendency.

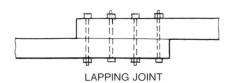

LAPPING JOINT

larch (*Larix decidua*) A strong, heavy, and most serviceable softwood used for outdoor woodwork of all kinds, including garden furnishings. Used also for piles, railway sleepers, telegraph poles, flooring, etc. Weight 47-48 lb (753-769 kg).

laser cutting Laser rays can be used to cut plywoods and timber, and essentially the process consists of fixing a drawing (black lines on white paper) to the face of the work-piece; a photocell then follows the lines. In doing so it feeds signals to the laser ray cutting-head which follows it round the drawing. The process can drill and cut extremely complicated patterns to an accuracy better than 0.13 mm; the cuts are parallel-sided and, for instance, are only 0.7 mm wide in 18 mm plywood. It will cut at the rate of 100 mm per minute in 50 mm thick softwood; 200 mm per minute in 18 mm thick oak; and 75 mm in 25 mm thick teak.

latex Natural latex is a milky viscous fluid which exudes from rubber trees when they are tapped. Can be processed to make latex foam rubber for upholstery padding and cushions: or it can be made into an adhesive by introducing ammonia or formaldehyde to prevent coagulation. Such adhesives are used for bonding fabrics.

lath Flat strip of small section used by slaters, plasterers, blind makers, and others. For specific purposes, they may be had from 1 in (25 mm) by $^3/_{16}$ in 5 mm up to 2 in (51 mm) by $^5/_8$ in (16 mm), or more. As a rule they are 3 ft (915 mm) or 4 ft (1219 mm) in length.

LATH NAILS (See next column)

lath-back Windsor chair A Windsor chair in which the sticks or spindles in the back are replaced by laths bent in a flat S shape; sometimes with a central splat.

lathe, wood turning A machine for turning wood to circular shape, almost always electrically driven. The size of the lathe is quoted as the 'bed size', which is the distance between the centres (*q.v.*) and governs the length of the work-piece. Typically, modern lathes range from 30 in (762 mm) up to 54 in (1372 mm).

The headstock is the one which is driven, the tailstock acting merely as a support; the headstock is normally fitted with a spindle which is hollow with a morse taper, but the outside is also threaded to take a face-plate and other chucks for special purposes. Flat work such as bowls, platters, small table tops, etc., can be fixed to the headstock by means of the face plate and turned (the tailstock is not used in this type of turning).

Some lathes are made to take attachments such as a circular saw, a bandsaw, a sander, or a small surfacer.

(See also *centres, face-plate, headstock, tailstock, mandrel, turning chisels, gouges,* and *turning, wood.*)

lathing hammer (see *hammer, G*).

lath nail A wire nail, $^3/_4$ in (19 mm) to $1^1/_4$ in (32 mm) long, galvanised to prevent rust. Used mainly for attaching plaster laths to joists, the large head ensuring a firm grip and the shank, owing to its slenderness, not tending to split the wood.

latten A high quality brass in sheet form, often incised and used to ornament chandeliers, sconces, etc.

lattice Criss-cross arrangement of slats, either diagonally or at right angles. (See also *trellis.*)

lattice roof One having trusses made of criss-cross laths as in the Belfast truss (*q.v.*).

lattice window One having diamond-shaped panes held in lead cames.

lauan (red, *shorea* species; white, *parashorea*) From Philippine Islands, 41 lb (657 kg). Red is dark, rather like African mahogany; white is pale. Fairly open in texture, used for furniture, boxes, etc.

laurel (*terminalia tomentosa*) From India and Burma, 50-70 lb (801-1121 kg). Similar to Italian walnut but harder. Works and polishes well. Used in general cabinet making.

laurel, Australian Alternative name given locally to Queensland walnut (*q.v.*).

lay-on hinges Special hinges for use on man-made materials such as chipboards, etc., where screwing near the edge is inadvisable. They screw direct to the surface. Their most important feature is that they allow the door to cover its hingeing stile. It is thus possible to have a row of doors which, then closed, hide all the hingeing stiles. They are usually sprung with an inbuilt latch; some open to 170°.

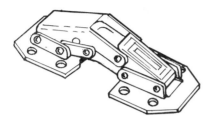

LAY-ON HINGE

Lawson's cypress (*Chamaecyparis lawsoniana*) Alternative name for Port Orford cedar. Creamy-white softwood which works well and is reliable. Has aromatic odour. Grown in this country largely for ornamental value.

lay-light A flat ceiling light which receives borrowed light from another window.

lazy Susan (USA) A dumbwaiter (*q.v.*).

leaded light Window or glazed door having grooved lead strips or cames in which the glass fits.

leaf The loose, sliding, or hinged part of a table top.

lean-to Applied to the single sloping roof of a shed or greenhouse. The term suggests that the building be erected against an existing wall, which supports the upper ends of the rafters.

leather Used throughout the centuries for upholstering chairs and couches and also as wall-hangings, when it was often gilt. First used in Britain in the 16th century. (See *hide*.)

lectern An ecclesiastical reading desk, or reading stand mounted on a column and base. Made in wood, brass, or stone.

ledge Cross batten nailed to boarding to hold the whole together. (See *ledged and braced door*.)

ledged and braced door Simple shed door consisting of upright boards, usually matching, held together with horizontal battens known as ledges, and with diagonal pieces termed braces, the whole nailed

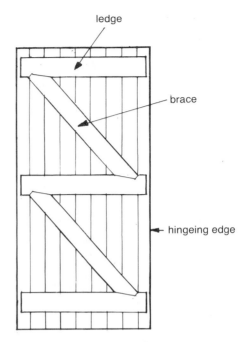

LEDGED & BRACED DOOR

together. Note that the braces should be notched into the ledges.

leg squares A term applied to prepared lengths of squared and dressed hardwood in different square sections for legs of tables, chairs, sideboards, cabinets, bedsteads, and similar work. These are often imported and are obtainable in beech, oak, mahogany, and other timbers.

lemon chrome Powder pigment used to mix with filler to kill whiteness of the latter when used on yellowish woods.

lemonwood Alternative name for degame (*q.v.*).

lengthening bar Extension bar for a cramp.

lever cap Fitted to a metal plane to hold the cutter in place of the wedge used in a wood plane.

lever lock One in which the bolt is held by levers which have to be lifted before the bolt can be shot.

library steps Used in the libraries of large houses in the 18th century. There are two principal designs: (1) fixed steps, often with a hand rail, and mounted on castors for easy movement: (2) folding steps which frequently convert to chairs, tables, etc.

109

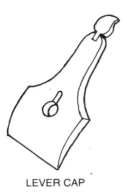

LEVER CAP

lid stay A wide range is available. (A) is the friction type with fibre washers which hold the lid in any required position. At (B) is a combined hinge and stay for bureau lids. (C) is automatic, locking and unlocking by movement of the lid. The rule-joint stay (D) fits in a confined space and the simple type (E) is used when the stay can pass through the shelf. For radio and similar cabinets the pneumatic type ensures quiet and joltless closing.

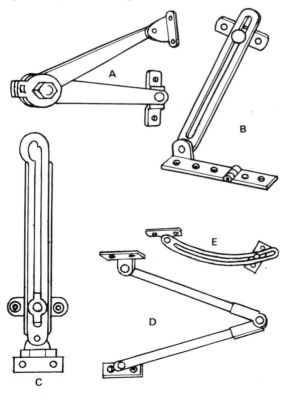

LID STAYS

lifting The penetration and softening of one film by the solvents of another, resulting in the raising and wrinkling of the surface. Also, veneers and plastic laminates lift as a result of poor bonding.

lift-off butt hinges Enable the door to be lifted off when required. Made right and left hand, and in small sizes in brass for cabinet work, and in larger sizes in iron for room doors. That at (B) enables door to swing clear of any projections.

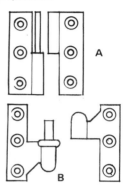

LIFT-OFF BUTT HINGES

lignin One of the components of wood. Its purpose is to stiffen the cellulose of the cell walls, and to bind them together.

lignum vitae (*guaiacum officinale*) The heaviest of all commercial timbers. It was used for bowling-green bowls, and during the seventeenth and eighteenth centuries it was in demand for loving cups and other drinking vessels; it was also used in the late Stuart period for oyster veneers. It was believed to have medicinal qualities, hence the name. Its colour is dark brown, streaked with black, and it comes from the West Indies and Central America. Weight 73-80 lb (1169-1281 kg).

lime (*tilia vulgaris*) European hardwood, of 37-38 lb (593-609 kg). Light coloured wood with little figure marking. Fairly soft yet crisp to cut, making it excellent for wood carving. Used also for piano actions and keys.

limed oak Liming is suitable only for open-grained woods such as oak. The effect is to leave a white deposit in the open grain, the main surface of the wood being either left natural or stained. Proprietary liming compounds are available, or flat white paint can be used. Yet another method is to use whiting mixed to a thick paste with water. Sometimes zinc white powder is added to wax polish made with bleached wax. The traditional method of using slaked lime in water is seldom used today.

Lindermann joint A tapered dovetail joint which can only be made by a special machine. The dovetail locks the joint, and is very slightly tapered in its length to avoid friction when sliding the adjoining boards (or panels) together. Assembly is done by machine; the joint is glued but needs no cramping.

line Inlay strip from bare $\frac{1}{16}$ in (2 mm) up to about $\frac{1}{8}$ in (3 mm) wide, usually in ebony or boxwood, but can be in any wood. Alternative name is string.

linear measure Measurement of length only as compared with superficial measure *(q.v.)* and cubic measure *(q.v.)*.

linear speed Term applied to machine speeds, and in particular to the bandsaw. It is the speed at which any one tooth moves in metres or feet per minute.

linenfold panel A feature of early oak woodwork. In the true linenfold the wood is carved in the form of folded linen as at (A), the folds being traceable throughout, but other patterns (B) consist rather of a moulded section with the top and bottom cut away to a flat background.

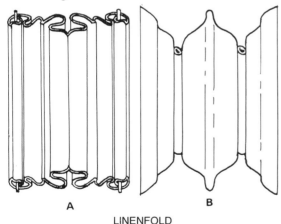

LINENFOLD

linen press Consists of a base with a standard at opposite ends — they are joined across the top by a stout rail, in the centre of which is a length of screw-threaded studding. By turning the studding, a board can be raised or lowered to exert pressure on damp linen placed in it.

lingue *(persea lingue)* Chilean hardwood of 35 lb (561 kg), pale reddish brown with interlocked grain. Furniture, fitments, etc.

lining Usually refers to the casing or rebated framework for a door, or to the grooved front and back parts of the framing of a sliding sash window, when they are known as the outside lining and the inside lining. May also refer to the leather covering fixed to a writing table, or to the material glued to the inside of drawers, etc.

lining up A term synonymous with thickening up; e.g. a moulded frame screwed underneath a top to strengthen it and to increase the thickness.

link plate lock Used for a door which closes over the face of the cabinet, the lock being let in flush at the back of the door, and the link plate at the closing edge of the cabinet. As the bolt shoots both right and left the lock can be used both right and left hand.

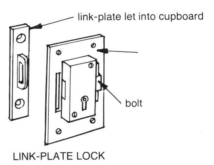

link-plate let into cupboard

bolt

LINK-PLATE LOCK

linseed oil Extracted from the crushed seeds of flax. Raw oil is medium brown in colour, and is sometimes used on bare wood to enhance the grain, sometimes with a little oil-soluble aniline Bismarck added to warm the shade. It is a drying oil and is used as a lubricant to the rubber in French polishing, and to kill the whiteness of plaster filling. Boiled oil dries more rapidly and is used in oil polishing with the addition of a little terebine to act as a drier. It should never be used on an oilstone as it chokes the pores as it dries out.

linters Fibres left after processing cotton bolls. They are formed into pads or continuous rolls which are used for upholstery. (See *white flock.*)

lintel Beam fitted horizontally at the head of a wall opening to support the wall above.

lint-free Free of lint (loose particles) or fluff.

lipping Narrow strips of good quality wood applied to the edge of a top, shelf, end, etc., of cheaper wood or to plywood or blockboard. It is usually tongued on.

111

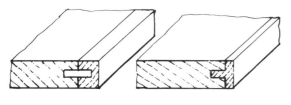

LIPPINGS

liquid glue Term refers to any glue sold as a liquid rather than in cake or powder form. Such glues may be fish, polyvinyl, some animal glues and some resisn.

lists Trade name for thin turned rods, similar to dowels, used (for instance) in the side of a drop-side cot.

list or listel Narrow square moulding member, more generally known as a fillet.

litharge Fused form of lead monoxide. Pinkish in colour and used in colouring. Also used in oil paints as a drier and for its hardening properties.

live centre The lathe centre which revolves the wood as distinct from the dead centre which is stationary and upon which the wood revolves. (See *centres.*)

live knot One which is firm as distinct from a dead knot which is loose. (See *knot.*)

livery cupboards These were small cupboards which often stood in bedrooms during the sixteenth and seventeenth centuries and contained bread, beer, and candles for the use of members of the family or their guests or retainers. There does not seem to have been any basic type and there is a wide variety of designs.

load Term for 50 cubic feet of timber.

loafers Archaic name for lopers *(q.v.).*

lobate Also called auricular *(q.v.)* as some of the decorative motifs resemble human ears, or ear lobes. A mid-17th century style of furniture which was short-lived. It was developed by Friedrich Unteutsch, and a few examples exist in South Germany and Switzerland; they are characterised by chair backs carved with grotesque faces, contorted human figures, sea-creatures, shells, etc. The presence of shell decoration leads some authorities to consider the style to be a link between the late Renaissance and the ensuing Baroque era.

lobby A vestibule or anteroom giving access to several main rooms.

lobby chest Described by Sheraton as 'a kind of half chest of drawers, adapted for the use of a small study, lobby, etc.

lock block Wood block fixed between the faces of a flush door to give a fixing for the lock.

locked mitre A joint which can be used in solid wood, MDF, or plywood. When made up, the joint is hidden externally and it also has the advantage that it only needs cramping up in one direction.

locking stile That stile of a door upon which a lock is fixed.

lock plate The front plate of a lock; also applied to an escutcheon.

lock rail Centre door rail opposite which the lock is fitted. Usually made extra wide.

locking bar Fitting used on gates and exterior doors. The bars slide within keepers, the end being pivoted to enable it to fit over a staple. A padlock is used to secure it.

locks There are many types of locks designed for specific purposes. The commonest for furniture are: Cut lock (A), for which the wood has to be cut away to enable the entire thing to finish flush. Made for both doors and drawers, the former right and left hand. To tell the type needed, if the lock is needed for the left-

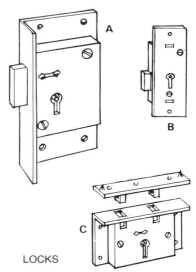

LOCKS

hand stile when viewed from the outside a left-hand lock is needed. Straight lock (B) is merely screwed to the back of the door without being let in. Usually the bolt shoots both ways so that the lock can be right or left hand. Box lock (C) has a lid plate with hooked projections, the bolt in the lock engaging with these. (See also *link plate, mortise, rim, roll-top, sliding door, yale locks.*)

log The stem of a felled tree. Also applies to (A) the same when cut into two or more lengths; (B) to heavy logs which have been roughly squared for shipping; (C) to larger limbs of substantial girth.

log conversion Spoken of as 'breaking the log'. Conversion means the sawing of logs into, say, planks, deals, battens, boards, etc., according to commercial requirements.

log rule One used for round timber. It usually has tables showing the quantity of timber to be obtained from a log.

log saw Frame or bandsaw used in sawing up logs.

logwood Originally used to make stains. The heartwood of this Central American tree was cut into chips and boiled. It was, however, variable, ranging from black, purple, red, to straw. Not used today.

London ladder-back chair Originally a country design adopted by London chair makers in the middle of the eighteenth century. The front legs were usually square and straight although later designs incorporated cabriole-style legs.

London pattern hammer (see *hammer*).

London pattern screwdriver One in which the blade is a flat metal bar. The handle has characteristic flat sides.

LONDON SCREWDRIVER

long-and-short shoulder joint Mortise and tenon joint used for a rebated framework, the back shoulder which reaches into the rebate being longer than that at the front. Also called a 'stepped shoulder joint'.

long-and-strong chisel and gouge Turning tools more robustly built than the normal and used in heavy turning.

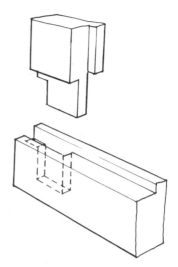

LONG-AND-SHORT JOINT

longcase clocks Tall clocks which derive their motive power from falling weights: the actual motion is controlled by a pendulum working in conjunction with an escapement. The first ones were made in Holland in 1656 by Christaan Huygens, who had adapted Galileo's theories of the rate of oscillation of a suspended body to the longcase clock. In England the first designs were produced in 1658 by Ahasuerus Fromanteel. Commonly called 'Grandfather clocks' from an allusion to them in a popular music hall song in the late nineteenth century.

long-cornered chisel Turning chisel in which the edge slopes at an angle.

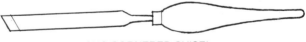

LONG CORNERED CHISEL

long-hole borer A special attachment which can be fitted to a lathe enabling a long hole to be bored in (for instance) the column of a standard lamp.

longhorn beetle (*hylotrupes bajulus*) Attacks seasoned soft-woods, especially in the south of England. Beetle is usually black and is $\frac{2}{5}$ to $\frac{4}{5}$ in (10 to 18 mm) long. Fully grown larva is about $1\frac{1}{4}$ in (32 mm) long. Beetles emerge from boring in June, July and September. Treatment usually calls for expert advice.

long oil A varnish which has a large proportion of linseed oil in its composition.

long pod Tapered chisel or gouge used by woodcarvers in the finishing stages of work. (See *carver's chisel (E)* and *gouge (F)*.)

long spade Tapered chisel and gouge used by woodcarvers. (See *carver's chisel (F)* and *gouge (G)*.)

loo table A table with a circular top mounted on a heavy pillar which is, in turn, supported by tripod feet or a polyfonal base with turned bun feet. Popular in the Regency era for playing the French game of loo; later, in Victorian times, they were used as dining tables. (See *drum table.*)

loose-leaf table One in which there is an entirely free, separate leaf. In some cases there may be more than one leaf.

loose seat Separate frame used chiefly in dining chairs. The seat frame is usually halved together at the corners. There should be $\frac{1}{8}$ in (3 mm) clearance all round for the material, and all sharp corners and edges removed.

loose tongue Tongue which is quite separate. Has grain running straight across square, or sloping. Often plywood is used for the tongue.

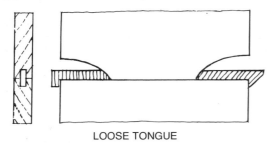

LOOSE TONGUE

lopers The slides which support the fall-front of a bureau or the draw-leaves of an extension table. In the case of a bureau special stays are available to provide for the lopers to slide forward and back automatically with the drop and rise of the fall-flap.

lost head nail Wire nail similar to a French nail, but with small head. It has less holding power, but is not so unsightly.

LOST-HEAD NAIL

louvers (or louver boards) A series of laths or slats fitted to a hinged frame in front of a window to give ventilation whilst excluding sunshine. Also sometimes fitted to a meteorological instrument container, and to some musical instruments to regulate sound. They may be fixed or pivoted to open or close. (See also *jalousie.*)

love seat A two-seater settee with four legs and usually without an underframe.

low-angle plane Metal plane having cutter set at 12 degrees. Used chiefly for trimming end grain. There is no back iron, and cutter has bevel uppermost. Some block planes have low angle.

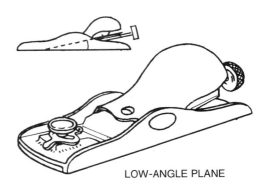

LOW-ANGLE PLANE

low-back Windsor chair A Windsor chair which has the same type of seat and underframing as the standard bow-back design but has a U-shaped arm mounted on spindles. The smoker, firehouse, and captain's chairs *(q.v.)* are all low-back. They probably developed from the Queen Anne style writing chair of the early eighteenth century; in the USA, Philadelphia low-backs appeared as early as 1725.

lowboy (USA) An American design based on the British flat-top dressing table with drawers, with an admixture of the French commode. It was made in three styles — William and Mary, Queen Anne, and Chippendale — and was normally made en suite with a tallboy *(q.v.)*.

low relief A term applied to raised and/or carved ornament which does not stand up very proud of the groundwork. (See also *bas relief.*)

lozenge Diamond-shaped decoration, usually carved. Used widely in early seventeenth century woodwork.

lug A projection to provide a fixing, or to provide temporary seating for cramps in shaped work.

lumber The US and Canadian term for converted timber.

lunette Decoration, usually carved, consisting of a series of semi-circular shapes, often interlaced. Used widely in late sixteenth century and first half of the seventeenth century.

LUNETTES

lustrine Also called 'lustring'. A glossy silk fabric with a ribbed pattern; popular for upholstering furniture in the 16th and 17th centuries.

lyctus (see *powder post beetle*).

lyre A very ancient form of a harp frequently used as the main design motif for chair backs and sofa table ends. Both Hepplewhite and Sheraton used it, as did the American cabinet maker, Duncan Phyfe.

LYRE MOTIF

M

macaroni tool Used by wood carvers. It is of channel section.

macassar ebony (*diospyros macassar*) From the Celebes, of varying shades of brown with light and dark streaks. 62-64 lb (993-1025 kg) weight. Usually available in veneer form only.

Macclesfield chair A ladder-back chair similar in design to the Lancashire ladder-back (*q.v.*).

Maco templet An adjustable device which, by means of sliding brass strips, registers the contours of mouldings. Also called a 'templet former'.

madison formula A wax-oil finish originally formulated as a finish for Western Red Cedar. It consists of: paraffin wax, zinc stearate, white spirit, boiled linseed oil, pentachlorophenol concentrate, burnt sienna pigment in oil, and raw umber pigment in oil. It should hold its colour for at least three years when, after washing off any grime, a further coat can be applied.

magnetic catches For use on cupboard doors. They are in two parts, one of which is a plain metal plate while the other contains a small magnet. When the door is closed the two parts magnetically attract each other and keep it closed. Can be obtained in various strengths.

magnolia (*magnolia acuminata*) Yellow-grey colour, of 36-37 lb (577-593 kg) from USA. Seldom available. Has several alternative names: southern whitewood, cucumber, sweet bay, evergreen magnolia.

mahogany There are many varieties of which the chief are: Cuban (*swietenia mahogoni*). From the West Indies of 40 lb (641 kg) weight. Fine quality wood, somewhat brittle, with white deposit in the grain. Excellent furniture wood. Dark reddish brown colour.

Honduras (*swietenia macrophylla*). From central America, of 34-39 lb (545-625 kg). Another excellent quality furniture wood, rather lighter in colour and less brittle.

Costa Rica (*swietenia macrophylla*). Similar to Cuban mahogany.

African (*khaya ivorensis, etc.*). Many varieties from tropical West Africa. Is not so reliable or so richly figured as American mahogany, but is widely used. Weight from 30-48 lb (481-769 kg).

Australian (*dysoxylum fraseranum*). Dense rich red hardwood, sometimes with gummy veins. It is an entirely distinct timber from those of tropical America.

mahogany stain There are many excellent proprietary stains on the market which cover all shades of colour. A home-made stain can be produced by using bichromate of potash (*q.v.*).

major axis The longer of two axes used in setting out an ellipse. (See *ellipse*.)

Maka swing chisel mortiser This is a patented system which is based on a swinging chisel which enters the wood, cutting and clearing away the chips during its swing. The amount of swing is imparted and controlled by an eccentric shaft which projects through a circular disc. This, in turn, moves a beam on which the cutting chisel is bolted. As the eccentric shaft rotates it raises and lowers the cutting chisel and also moves it from side to side, so that the forming of the mortise is accomplished by a series of arcs. This creates a mortise with a rippled bottom which is, however, flat enough for all practical purposes. The cutting chisel (illustrated) is fitted with a chip-breaker tooth, a stabbing tooth, and serrated teeth on the leading edge to remove chips. A combined haunching and mortising chisel is also available.

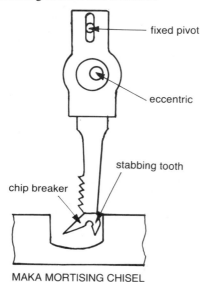

MAKA MORTISING CHISEL

makarati (*burkea africana*) Tropical African hardwood of 57 lb (913 kg), golden brown colour. Hard and strong but difficult to work. Used chiefly for constructional work.

making good Term used in repair or renovation work for the replacement of faulty parts, etc.

makore (*mimusops heckelii*) From Africa, of 45 lb (721 kg) weight, used in cabinet work, especially veneers. Varies from pink to purple-brown shade. Stains and polishes well.

malachite A semi-precious stone which is an ore of copper and sometimes called 'jasper'. It is green in colour and Venetian craftsmen were skilled in imitating it in paint.

mallet A typical woodworker's mallet is shown at (A) with beech head and ash handle. Latter is usually tapered so that it tends to become tighter in use. The head varies from 4 in to 7 in (102–170 mm) long. Useful all-round size is 6½ in (165 mm), the whole weighing about 2½ lb (1.1 kg). It is used for striking wooden-handled chisels, etc., or when the use of a hammer would tend to damage wood, as when assembling parts together. (B) is a carver's mallet, with rounded beech, lignum vitae, or boxwood head which enables it to be used at any angle against the carving tool.

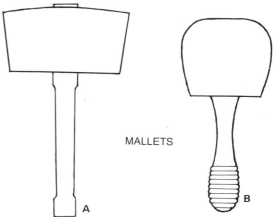

MALLETS

manchich Alternative name for black cabbage bark (*lonchocarpus castilloi*). Hardwood from Central America of 57 lb (913 kg). Heavy dark brown timber. Used chiefly for structural work but is a good turning wood and polishes well.

mandio (*qualea* various) Hardwood of 50 lb (801 kg) from Brazil and Amazon basin. Pink-brown or purplish wood with interlocked grain. Used for joinery and furniture. Alternative name is mandioquiera.

mandioquiera (see *mandio*).

mandrel The revolving spindle of a lathe or circular saw. In a lathe it is threaded to take a face plate or chuck, and is also usually hollow with morse taper (q.v.) to receive various chucks. The term also refers to a cylindrical or tapered wood rod of circular section held between centres in a lathe to support a hollow item whilst being turned.

manio (*podocarpus chilensis, etc.*) Softwood from Chile of 35 lb (561 kg). Light yellow timber with straight grain. Used for joinery, flooring, and plywood.

mansard roof One of double pitch which enables extra space to be obtained beneath the roof.

mansonia (*mansonia altissima*) Hardwood of 38 lb (609 kg) from Nigeria and Ghana. Brown wood, tough and durable. Used for cabinet work and carpentry.

maple (*acer*, various) Uses are chiefly for furniture (particularly in the USA), billiard cues, and sometimes musical instruments such as violins. A variety, richly mottled (*Acer saccharum*) is known as 'bird's eye maple' (*q.v.*).

maple, bird's-eye (see *bird's eye*, also under *maple*).

maple silkwood (*flindersia brayleyana*) Hardwood of 35-40 lb (561-641 kg) from Queensland, New South Wales. Sometimes called Queensland maple. Rather like mahogany in colour. Used for furniture, veneers, etc.

marble-wood (*diospyros marmorata*) Hardwood of 45 lb (721 kg) from Andaman Islands. Grey-black and yellow stripes. Polishes well, but does not hold glue satisfactorily. Used for small items. Also known as zebra wood.

margin templet A strip of wood used in staircase work to gauge the distances from the intersection of the riser face and top of tread to the edge of the string.

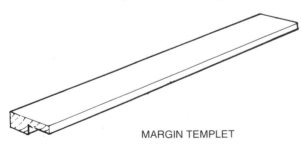

MARGIN TEMPLET

marking awl Pointed tool used when marking out cabinet work and joinery. A particular use is in marking the pins from the dovetails or vice versa. See also: *birdcage maker's awl, bradawl*, and *marking knife*.

marking gauge Gauge with pin marker rather tan a cutter. Is used for marking *with* the grain or on end grain, but for cross-grain marking the cutting gauge is used (*q.v.*). The fence may be plain wood or with inset brass strips to reduce wear. *Other gauges are butt gauge, grasshopper gauge, and panel gauge (q.v.).*

marking knife A knife with the bevel ground one side of the blade only and used for marking out joints, etc, particularly when marks are across the grain where the marking awl would merely scratch. A specific use is in cutting shoulder marks. It should always be used in preference to the pencil unless the mark would appear as a blemish, as in a chamfer. Combined marking knives and awls are obtainable. (See also *marking awl, marking gauge*, and *cutting gauge.*)

Marlborough leg A design of leg employed by Thomas Affleck of Philadelphia, USA; it consists of a square or square-tapered leg terminating in a block or plinth. The derivation of the name is uncertain but Chippendale is known to have recommended it as an alternative to the cabriole leg.

marquetry Decorative inlaying of various woods in veneer. It may be carried out with a fine saw on the marquetry cutter's donkey (*q.v.*), or with the knife. The former is generally used in trade work, the veneers being in packs to be cut several at a time. Two methods are used. In the first each part of the design is cut separately from 'prickings', and the whole then assembled. In the second, called the 'window' method and normally used today, the sheets of different woods are held together and the cut made through both simultaneously. The parts can be interchanged afterwards, and there are thus two forms of the same design, one the counterpart of the other.

marquetry cutter's donkey (see *donkey*).

Martha Washington chair (USA) An armchair with open arms, a shallow upholstered stuffover seat, and an upholstered back with a serpentine top rail. The legs are square, and the general appearance is reminiscent of some Chippendale chairs. The chair is reputed to have been used by Martha Washington at Mount Vernon.

Martha Washington sewing table (USA) A design of workbox with an oval top and carcase, and a hinged top; the legs are normally square and tapered. Reputed to have been used by Martha Washington at Mount Vernon.

Masonite Trade name (in Britain and the USA) for an oil-tempered hardboard which is extremely tough and can be used out-of-doors provided the edges are sealed and the faces painted. Available in $\frac{3}{16}$ in (6 mm) thickness.

mason's mitre   Used chiefly in oak joinery, mainly of the early period. The mitre is cut in the solid and has the advantage of not opening in the event of shrinkage. Against this the moulding in the one part cannot be worked with the moulding plane, but has to be stopped short of the joint and finished with carving tools. It is copied from stone masonry which is carved in this way. Dowels are shown in this particular joint, but the mortise and tenon joint was more usual. (See also *mitre*.)

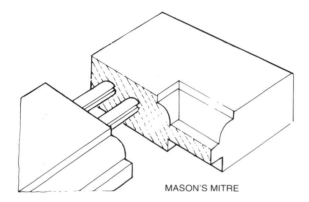

MASON'S MITRE

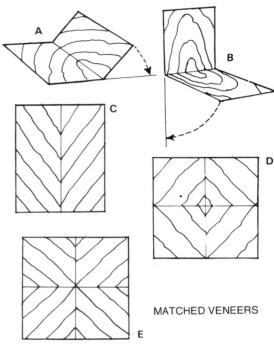

MATCHED VENEERS

mastic   A resinous gum used in varnish making. Pale yellow in colour when fresh, but inclining to darken when kept. Also a material used for gap filling (for instance, between a window frame and the surrounding brickwork). Such mastics are usually compounded to be waterproof and flexible; they can be applied with a putty knife or extruded from a special gun. Most are mixtures of reclaimed rubber, silicones, and a petroleum-based solvent.

matai *(podocarpus spicatus)*   A softwood of 39lb (625 kg) from New Zealand used locally in general building work.

match boarding   Machined boards tongued at one side and grooved at the other, with or without a bead or chamfer. (See *tongued and grooved boards*.)

match planes   Pairs of planes, one of which forms a tongue, and the other a groove, enabling tongued and grooved matching to be made by hand.

matched   Term often used in veneering in which consecutive leaves of veneer are used to give a balanced effect. Some of the arrangements are shown. In book matching (A) the one leaf is turned over sideways much as a book is opened. Butt or end matching (B) is similar but the leaf is turned at the end rather than at the side. (C) shows V or herring

bone matching; (D) is diamond matching; and (E) is reverse diamond matching.

matcher   The operative who prepares matched or other built-up patterns in veneer.

matching   Term often used in staining and polishing, and refers to the toning of parts to an even shade. More generally known as colouring *(q.v.)*.

matt finish   Polished or cellulosed finish which has no more than an eggshell gloss.

mattresses   These were filled with a variety of materials. Early ones in medieval times could be stuffed with straw and were known as 'palliases' or 'pallets'; the nobility, however, slept on feather or swans' down mattresses. In the seventeenth century, wool or flock mattresses were common, although in 1664 Evelyn was recommending beech leaves!

Modern mattresses can be interior-sprung, plastic foam or latex rubber. Interior-sprung mattresses contain many small coil springs rivetted to metal laths which form a framework; in the best examples the springs are 'pocketed' individually in a fabric covering to avoid any grinding between them.

MDF   (see *medium density fibreboard*).

measure Timber is measured (a) by cubic content, (b) by superficial area, and (c) by linear metre or foot. Certain hardwoods and fancy timbers of slender girth are sold by weight; dense tropical woods are obviously heavier than those from more temperate zones.

Cubic content is calculated by multiplying the length by the width by the thickness; superficial area by multiplying the length by the width; and linear measure is the number of running metres or feet. In the trade, a set of tables known as a 'Hoppus Measurer' *(q.v.)* is used to calculate cubic content quickly if imperial measurements are being used. In all calculations it is important to ensure that all measurements are in the same denomination, e.g. all metres, or all feet.

All softwoods are sold in metric; hardwoods are sold either by cubic metres or cubic feet. One cubic metre = 35.315 cubic feet. (See also *load, Petrograd standard, square.*)

mechanical joint One in which movement occurs. (See *finger, knee, knuckle, rule, secretaire joints.*)

medium-density fibreboard MDF is the recognised abbreviation for this. A man-made fibreboard developed in the USA during the 1960s. Basically it consists of timber which has been reduced to a fibrous condition by steaming and grinding; the fibres are then dried and impregnated with synthetic resin binders. The panels are put through heated steel rollers and then pressed before being cut to size.

The density is about the same as a medium-weight hardwood, and it has a uniform consistency throughout. It can be worked with hand tools, but machining gives excellent results, especially if TCT cutters are used. The edges can be worked (unlike other man-made boards) and can be spindle-moulded or dovetailed. It is also a first-class groundwork or substrate for veneers and plastic laminates. The final colour is usually pale straw, and it can be stained and polished. Thicknesses range from $\frac{1}{4}$ in (bare) to $1\frac{3}{4}$ in (6 mm to 45 mm), although $\frac{1}{2}$ in to $\frac{7}{8}$ in (12 to 22 mm) is the normal range.

medium hardboard A middle-grade hardboard, not suitable for exterior use.

medulla Botanical name for pith *(q.v.)*.

medullary rays These radiate from the pith of a tree trunk and are responsible for the characteristic figure in quarter-cut oak, beech, and silky oak boards.

meeting rails The two sliding sash rails which meet when the window sashes are closed.

meeting stiles In a pair of doors or gates the two uprights or stiles which meet when the doors are closed.

melamine finish This a a lacquer based on melamine which is condensed with formaldehyde to form a resin, which is transparent, heat-, water-, and abrasion resistant. The final product is usually a mixture of melamine resin, urea resin, and plasticisers in a suitable solvent and can be obtained as cold-cured, or acid-catalysed, and clear or pigmented. Each type can be applied with brush or spray.

melamine-formaldehyde resin A thermosetting resin prepared by the condensation of melamine with formaldehyde which results in a resin which is highly resistant to water and heat; decorative laminates are bonded with it.

melawis Identical with ramin *(q.v.)*.

melon bulb Alternative name for the cup-and-cover bulbous leg *(q.v.)*.

Mendlesham chair A design of Windsor chair originating in Mendlesham in Suffolk and reputed to have been made in the early 19th century by the local wheelwright, Daniel Day. The chairs are usually made of fruitwood or yew, have a saddle seat in elm, and the back tapers from top to bottom with an ornamental splat flanked by two or three spindles at each side. The splat terminates in a curved back stay which has a curved and turned stay beneath it, the two being connected by two or three turned balls. The whole construction is lighter and more elegant than the ordinary Windsor chair.

menuisier French term for a maker of furniture which is not veneered, such as chairs, settees, etc. (See *ébéniste.*)

meranti *(Shorea,* various) Hardwood from Malaya and Sarawak of 40-41 lb (641-657 kg). Two varieties, red or reddish-brown colour, and yellow or pale straw shade. A strong timber used for joinery, furniture, etc.

mercury gilding A gilding technique for bronze, now obsolete (and illegal, owing to the toxicity of mercury); also called 'fire gilding'. The bronze was coated with a paste of gold and heated mercury; the object was then heated in a furnace to remove the mercury as vapour, leaving the gold deposited on the bronze, when it could be either left matt or burnished.

merulius lacrymans The deadly fungus which initiates dry rot. (See *dry rot.*)

mess Windsor chair A scroll-back Windsor chair *(q.v.)* which has only one arm (the right-hand one as you face the chair), the other arm being omitted to leave room for the occupant's sword and scabbard.

metal dowel Metal rod used in fixing the foot of door posts when there is no cill. The projecting ends fit into the floor boards or into holes in a concrete floor.

methyl alcohol (USA) This is methanol or wood alcohol and corresponds to British 'industrial alcohol'. Used in lacquer thinners, paint removers, and aniline wood stains. It is not recommended for amateur use as its vapours are toxic and can be absorbed through the skin.

methylated finish (see *methylated spirits*).

methylated spirits This is used mostly for making french polish and stains. It is ordinary alcohol with wood spirit, etc. added to make it undrinkable, in which form it is sold free of duty. There are several kinds of mixtures produced for various purposes permitted by the Customs and Excise, and they are all subject to regulations. French polish manufacturers use industrial methylated spirits, known as 'I.M.S.', but this is not obtainable by the general public. That sold in oil shops is coloured and is made further unpalatable by the addition of wood spirit, mineral spirit, pyridine, and methyl violet dye. French polish can be made with this successfully because the colouring effect is small and soon fades. A better method, however, is to use 'methylated finish'. This is colourless, but contains three ounces of resin per gallon. This resin may be common rosin (this is the more usual, as it is a cheaper substance) or it may be white lac. For the purpose of polish making 'methylated spirit white lac' is more suitable, and can generally be obtained if specified.

mezzo-relievo A term applied to carved relief work where the projection of the carving is equal to half to the real proportions. (See also *alto-relievo* and *bas-relief*.)

mill work Joinery and other items manufactured in quantity in a factory ready for use in a building. Doors, windows, and staircases are obvious examples.

milled timber As distinct from boards, planks, squares, etc. timber which is delivered from the mills in a partially manufactured state, such as floor boards, skirting, sash stuff, T and G boards, etc.

mineral oil, white Light liquid paraffin used to lubricate the rubber when polishing.

mineral spirits (USA) Distilled from petroleum, these correspond to British 'white spirit' (also called 'turpentine substitute').

minor axis The shorter of two axes used in setting out an ellipse. (See *ellipse*.)

mirrors Early mirrors in medieval times were made of polished steel although Italian and French glass mirrors were imported in the Tudor period. English production was started in 1615 by Robert Mansell at Lambeth in London. The glass was blown and cut as described under glass *(q.v.)* and silvered by being floated over a thin coating of tin; there were two disadvantages, one being that the 'silvering' was liable to rust; the other that size was strictly limited. From 1663 the Duke of Buckingham was granted a monopoly for 14 years. Cast glass was invented about 1690 in France and was introduced into Britain in 1773 although it had been imported for many years previously. Modern silvering techniques appeared in early Victorian times. As well as hanging mirrors there are cheval mirrors, pier glasses, and toilet glasses *(q.q.v.)*. The alternative term for mirror is 'looking glass'.

mirror plates Small brass or chromium plate for hanging mirrors and fitments, etc. Also called glass plates.

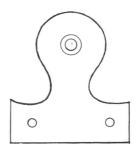

MIRROR (GLASS) PLATE

mirror stand Similar to a pole-screen *(q.v.)*, this design had a mirror mounted on a slim column, and it could slide up or down. Popular towards the end of the 18th century.

misericord These are small seats provided for old or infirm members of the clergy to rest on during long services in church. They can be wooden or stone, and consist of a bracket seat mounted on a corbel, often with side carvings called 'supporters'. Do not confuse with *miserere* which is a musical rendition of the 51st Psalm.

mitre A joint formed by the intersection of two mouldings or two plain pieces of wood. The angle at which the moulding is cut should halve the overall angle of the joining pieces. Most mouldings join at right.angles, and the mitreing angle is, therefore, 45 degrees (A). Other odd mitres are shown at (B) and

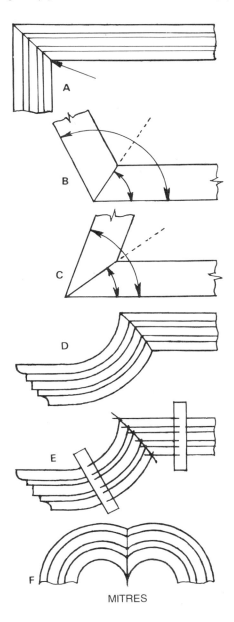

MITRES

(C). When a curved moulding joins a straight moulding of the same section, the mitre must be curved (D). To find the curve, draw in both mouldings full size, marking the position of all the members and making sure that they are in exactly the same position in both. A slip of paper can be used for marking, as shown at (E). Draw in a line where the members intersect, thus forming the mitre curve. When two mouldings curved to equal radii meet, both curving in the same direction, the mitre is straight (F).

mitre box and block The box consists of a base and upright side pieces cut to give a right and left 45 deg mitreing angle; also a 90 deg right-angle cut for squaring ends of mouldings, etc. In the case of hexagonal-shaped frames, 60 deg mitreing cuts are required. The cuts are a guide for the tenon saw, and in some cases, the cuts are reinforced with metal guide clips. The box is used when dealing with fairly large mouldings, particularly cornice or sloping lid mouldings, it being essential that the square edges of the moulding lie flat against the side and bed of the mitre box, with waste wood underneath, plus a packing of wood to prevent slipping whilst sawing. The mitre block is a form of bench hook, provided with mitreing guide cuts in its fence piece. It is used for the smaller mouldings. A more universal appliance in the trade is the metal mitre-cutter which is fitted with saw guides adjustable to various angles. A length stop is also provided.

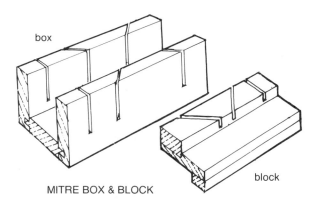

box

block

MITRE BOX & BLOCK

mitre and scribe Joint in which about one half is mitred and the other scribed. It is used on large sections in which a complete scribe would leave the wood so thin as to be unmanageable.

mitre bridle Useful particularly when the edge has a shallow moulding. The tenon is visible on one surface only. When the inner edge has to be rebated as well as moulded the slot is set up accordingly.

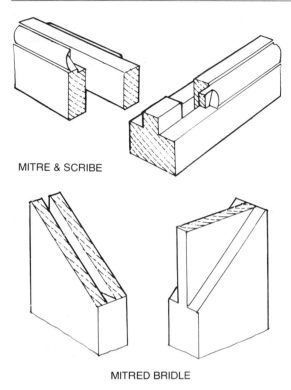

MITRE & SCRIBE

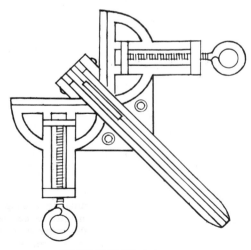

MITRED BRIDLE

Sometimes a dovetail, either through or stopped, is used rather than a tenon.

mitre cutter Used by picture framers, with calibrated bed and adjustable stop. Cuts or trims both mitres in one operation. Blades have slicing cut, and

can cut entire width of fairly narrow mouldings in one cut. Wider mouldings need two or three cuts. Pedal operated, knives being returned to up position by a spring; industrial models are motorised.

mitre cutting tool and cramp This grips the moulding whilst being sawn. It takes mouldings up to 4 in (102 mm) wide. It can also be used as a cramp when glueing and nailing picture moulding, etc. together.

mitre dovetail A corner joint in which the dovetail is entirely concealed. Used in good-class cabinet work, chiefly for outside joints, plinths, and all show work in which it is desired to hide the joint. It is essential that the pins are cut first and the tails marked from them. It is impracticable to reverse the procedure because the lap makes it impossible to mark the pins. (See *double-lap dovetail*.)

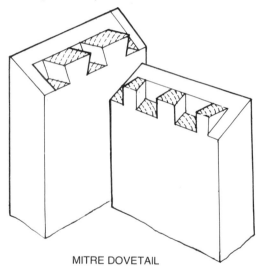

MITRE DOVETAIL

mitre, dowelled A means of strengthening a plain mitre. The dowel near the heel can be longer than the other.

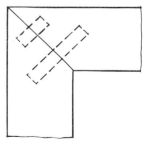

MITRE, DOWELLED

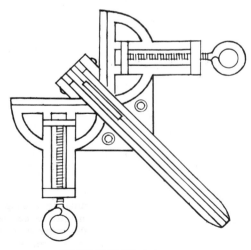

MITRE CUTTER & CRAMPS

mitre gauge Appliance used on circular saw, bandsaw, disc sander, etc. The bar slides along a groove in the table, and the fence is adjustable to right angles or to any odd angle.

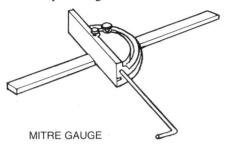

MITRE GAUGE

mitred half-lap Halving joint when the one surface must show as a mitre, particularly useful when edge has to be moulded (dotted line).

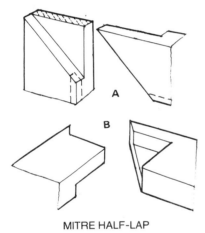

MITRE HALF-LAP

mitre keying (see *keying (1)*).

mitred lap Used when lap must not show on either surface.

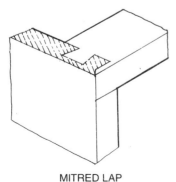

MITRED LAP

mitred lip Dovetail or tongued joint sometimes used on carcases in which the lip (or lap) is mitred.

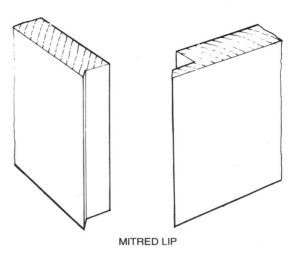

MITRED LIP

mitre saw Appliance used for sawing mitres and square cuts. The saw is held by adjustable guides and can be set to cut any angle from 45 deg to 90 deg. A length gauge is also fitted. Made in three sizes.

mitre shooting-block The purpose of this appliance is much the same as that of the mitre shooting-board, except that it enables heavier mouldings to be trimmed, either at a 45 deg angle or a 90 deg angle. It consists of a bed which is secured in a bench vice, with a fixed face block and a movable face block operated by a threaded screw.

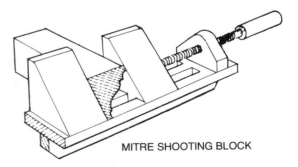

MITRE SHOOTING BLOCK

mitre shooting-board This is similar to a straight shooting-board (*q.v.*) except that the stop is central and cut so that its edges slope at 45 deg mitre angle. It is used for trimming mitres at ends of small mouldings with a plane. (See also *donkey's ear shooting board*.)

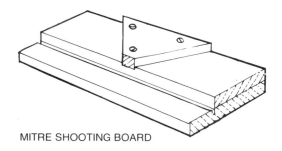

MITRE SHOOTING BOARD

mitre square Similar to a try square but with the blade central and fixed at 45 deg with the stock. Used for marking mitre lines or for testing mitres. An alternative is the combined try and mitre square with sliding stem.

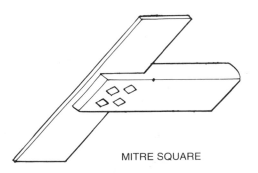

MITRE SQUARE

mitre templet Stuck mouldings, i.e. mouldings worked in the solid on framings, sash bead moulding bar, etc., require to be cut to meet in a mitre at the corners. Wooden or metal templets enable a chisel to be used to pare the wood to a true mitre angle, the template serving as a guide and support when placed over the moulding edge.

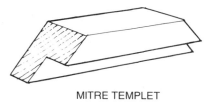

MITRE TEMPLET

mitred tenons Used for tenons of rails which meet at right angles in the thickness of a leg, the ends being cut at 45 deg, thus giving maximum tenon length without leaving a gap. The mitred ends, however, should not make a close fit.

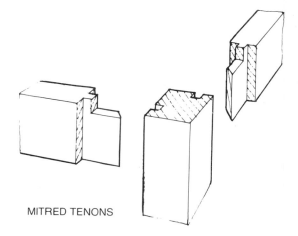

MITRED TENONS

mitre, tongued When wood is mitred in its width the joint is as at (A), though it could be stopped if preferred. For wood mitred in thickness the joint is that at (B). Note that the tongue is nearer the heel than the toe so that it has maximum depth without cutting too deeply across the wood.

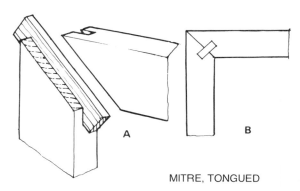

MITRE, TONGUED

mitre trimmer Appliance used to trim mitres or make square cuts. The knives are operated by a lever and have a slicing cut. Adjustable fences are provided enabling wood to be trimmed at any angle. Note that it is intended for trimming only, not for cutting mitres.

modelling Term used by wood carvers. It may refer to the making of a model in clay as a preliminary stage to the actual carving, or to the roughing-in or bosting-in of the main form, all detail being ignored, except that enough wood is left for it.

modillion A bracket usually carved and of scroll form, supporting the upper members of a cornice moulding. (See *dentils and mutule*.)

MODILLION

module A measure of proportion in classical architecture. It is the radius of a column measured at its widest part.

moisture content The amount of moisture in timber expressed as a percentage of the dry weight (oven-dry). Thus if the original weight is 12 lb (5.4 kg) and the dry weight 10 lb (4.5 kg), $\frac{1}{5} \times 100$ gives 20 per cent of the dry weight.

moisture-resistant plywood Classed as MR, these use urea-formaldehyde resin adhesive. The boards will survive out-of-doors in moderate conditions, but are not resistant to extreme weather; they are immune to attack by fungi.

monkey-tail bolt Used chiefly on garage doors at the top. Has a long handle enabling it to be reached easily.

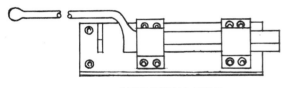

MONKEY TAIL BOLT

monk's bench A settle-table, the back being made to pivot and slide. It is a misnomer in that it has no

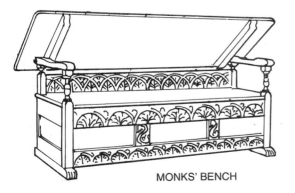

MONKS' BENCH

connection with monks, as such pieces were not made until after the Dissolution of the Monasteries about 1540. Possibly it arose in some association with the misericord.

monopodium A table (usually with a circular top) supported on a single pillar or column, as in a drum table, or a capstan table *(q.q.v.)*.

monoxylon (See *dug-out chest*.)

moon stone A man-made oil stone which is extremely hard; it is comparable to a white Arkansas stone.

moquette Upholstery material of velvety pile used in easy chairs, settees, etc.

mora *(mora excelsa)* Close-grained wood of 60 lb (961 kg) or more, dark or light brown colour. From British and Dutch Guiana. Used in ship building, railway work, etc.

morocco Skin used in the best upholstery. It is a selected goat skin, the superior coming from mid-Europe, and the cheapest from Persia and India.

Morris chair (see *Sussex chair*).

morse drill Although intended primarily for metal, these drills are useful for some jobs. They are particularly effective for wood if specially ground as shown.

MORSE DRILL

morse taper Slow taper often made in the hollow mandrel of a lathe to receive either centres for turning or a Jacobs chuck *(q.v.)*. *Various sizes are made, but the degree of taper is standard for each number.*

mortise and tenon joint One in which a projection on the one piece (the tenon) fits into a corresponding recess (the mortise). Used mainly for framings, etc. There are many varieties to suit the details of the item being made.

mortise bolt Consisting of a cylindrical bolt fitting closely in a sleeve to which is fixed a face plate. The whole is let in flush. Key and key plate is also fitted. Used chiefly for house doors.

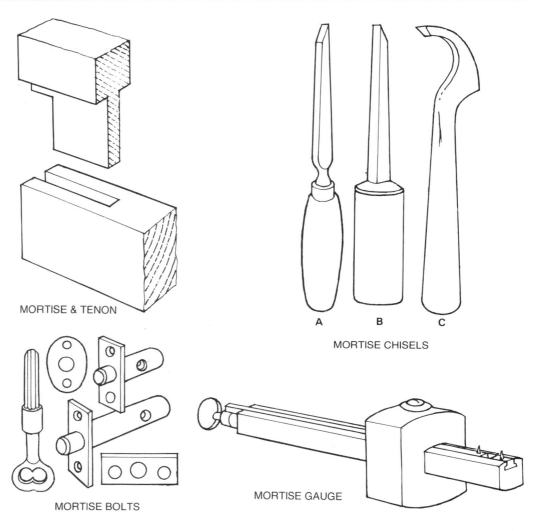

MORTISE & TENON

MORTISE CHISELS

A   B   C

MORTISE BOLTS

MORTISE GAUGE

mortise chisels There are three principal types. (A) is a light type for softwoods, called a sash mortise chisel; (B) is a heavier type, usually bolstered at the handle with a leather washer; (C) is a swan-neck type, especially suited for chopping a mortise in a room or street door stile for the lock. The hook shape acts as a fulcrum against the edge walls of a partly formed mortise and thus simplifies the removal of waste wood at the bottom. (See also *hollow chisel.*)

mortise gauge With two pins to mark each side of mortise. One of the pin markers is a fixture, the other being adjusted to the mortise width and set by an adjustment screw. The same setting serves to mark the lines of the tenon thickness. All marking off should be done from the face side of rails and stiles so

that, even though the mortises and tenons are not central, the framing will go together flush.

mortise lock Let in flush at the edge of a door, the whole thing being sunk bodily into the thickness of the wood. Simpler type is tubular and requires only a hole to be bored for the body and shallow recess for the face plate.

mortises, types of machined There are five types of mortise which can be machined by (1) the chain mortiser; (2) the hollow chisel; (3) the oscillating bit; (4) the Maka; and (5) the Alternax. (See under individual machines.)

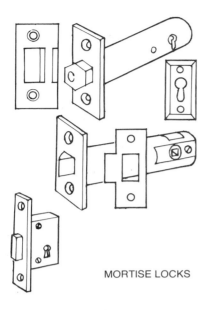

MORTISE LOCKS

mosaic Decoration composed of very small pieces of wood or stone; Tunbridge ware is a good example.

mother of pearl The internal layer substance of the oyster shell. Varies in quality, the more expensive being delicately coloured. In woodwork it is used chiefly for inlays, escutcheons, etc. Can be cut with a fine fretsaw, but should be backed with stiff paper as it is extremely fragile. Should not be cramped as it may easily break. A weight on top is sufficient. Underside should be scored to help adhesion, and a little plaster of Paris should be added to hot glue. To level it when necessary use fine file lightly then *flour* glasspaper, finishing with tripoli powder.

mottle Highly figured wood, the appearance of which is caused by interlocked or undulating grain. Light plays an important part, and the effect varies in accordance with the angle from which the wood is viewed. Although the surface is quite flat it appears to undulate, sometimes in irregular dimples and sometimes as ripples.

mould A templet used to mark out shapes. (See *face* and *falling mould.*) Also refers to a reverse pattern in moulding plastic materials. A third meaning refers to a fungus that forms on wood when in a damp atmosphere. It may also be the term for male and female shaped parts cramped together when making moulded plywood.

moulder and planer (see *four-sided moulder and planer*).

moulded plywood Single or double curvature plywood formed to shape between moulds during the assembly stage. Generally resin glue is used as the adhesive.

moulding box A long box with parallel sides used when moulding long square-tapered or rounded items such as a column. A spindle passes through one end on which the work is centred. At the outside is a disc with equidistantly spaced holes enabling the work to be revolved an exact distance. At the other end of the box is a large screw which centres the work and holds it. When in position the box can be passed across a spindle moulder, or the moulding can be worked with the scratch stock or electric router. The shape of the box may have to be varied in accordance with the method being used.

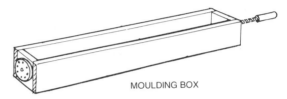

MOULDING BOX

moulding planes Some planes have a fence (as fitted to the ogee plane) which is worked along the edge of the wood. Others (rounds and hollows) have no fence, as the angle at which they are used varies, being often used in positions in which a fence would be impracticable. English pattern planes have usually to be held at an angle (see illustration) whereas most Continental moulding planes are held upright. In use, the plane is best started at the far end of the work, and brought a little farther back at each successive stroke. If moulding the edges of a table top, the ends should be planed first to eliminate splintering at the corners. Hollows and rounds are numbered in pairs, and 18 pairs make a full set.

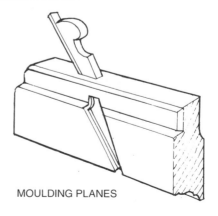

MOULDING PLANES

moulding rubbers   Used in cleaning up mouldings, and consisting of wood blocks of various shapes cut to a reverse of the moulding. The abrasive paper is wrapped round the block. Each member of a large moulding is dealt with separately. The purpose is to avoid dubbing over the edges.

mouldings   These may be of a single member or a combination of them. When worked in the solid they are referred to as 'stuck'; when fixed separately they are 'applied' or 'planted'. A large moulding may be of a single piece or be built up separately; or in some cases it may have a backing of softwood. (See also *architrave, astragal, bolection, cavetto, cyma recta, cyma reversa, dado, drawer bottom slip, embossed, fillet, hollow, lid, listel, ogee, picture frame, picture rail, roundel, sash bead, scotia, torus.*)

moulmein cedar *(cedrela toona)*   Also known as toon or Burma cedar. Hardwood from India and Burma of 30-40 lb (481-641 kg). A mild red timber with fragrant smell. Used for cigar boxes and general domestic purposes.

mountain ash   Two varieties, peppermint and giant gum. Both are Australian eucalyptii.

mounts   These comprise: hinges, locks and handles; protective mounts for edges, corners, and decoration liable to be damaged; and constructional fittings such as bandings. They can be in iron, brass, ormolu, or precious metals.

mouth   Opening in the sole of a plane to allow shavings to pass through. Also refers to a hardwood piece recessed into the sole to reduce the mouth width when the latter has become too wide, the result of repeated truing. Some metal planes have adjustable mouths. The term is used for the opening in any tool through which shavings have to pass.

muhimbi *(cynometra alexandri)*   Hardwood from Uganda of 55 lb (881 kg) weight. Brownish or reddish colour often streaked. Used for local structural work, turnery, and sometimes veneers.

mulberry   The European mulberries, *morus alba* (golden brown with dark streaks) and *morus nigra* (dark brown), were used in the early 18th century as veneers for case furniture. In 1609 James I encouraged the planting of mulberries in the Midlands to help the English silk trade (silk-worms feed exclusively on mulberry leaves).

mule chest   An intermediate or hybrid design (hence the name) which is halfway between a chest and a chest of drawers in that one long drawer or two short ones were built under the chest section. It first appeared in the first half of the 17th century.

mullet   A grooved piece of wood used to test the edges of a panel to fit into a groove. It is invariably made from an offcut of the same grooved material.

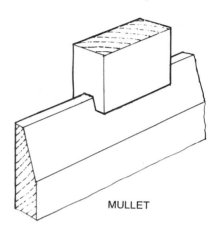

MULLET

mullion   The upright division between the lights of a window or other opening, often applied also to the vertical sash bar and to an upright division between panels.

multi-plate press   Large machine press used chiefly in making veneered panels. The plates are thermostatically controlled, and pressure is usually hydraulic. Many panels can be pressed in one operation, and by using resin adhesive and applying heat the panels are quickly set, releasing the press for another batch of work.

multi-ply   Plywood built up to over ¼ in (6 mm) thick by more than three layers of veneers. (See *plywood.*)

muninga *(pterocarpus angolensis)*   Hardwood of 40 lb (641 kg) from Rhodesia, South Africa. Golden brown colour usually streaked. Used for furniture, panelling, etc.

muntin   Vertical division in a framed door contained between horizontal rails. Also applied to the rail running from front to back in a large drawer to avoid sagging. The archaic word was 'munting'.

mural clocks   A general term which includes 'Act of Parliament' tavern, stage-coach, and similar clocks *(q.q.v.).*

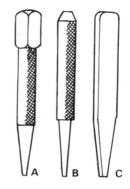

NAIL PUNCHES

music stool   Seat used by a pianist. Height may be adjustable, but if fixed it is usually 22 in (558 mm).

mutules   Architectural term used in woodwork to describe the rectangular blocks placed below the soffit of a cornice, which are sometimes called 'dentils' or 'modillions' *(q.q.v.)*.

N

nails   (see under individual types *clout, corrugated, cut, finishing pin, French, gimp pin, lath, lost-head, needle points, oval panel pin, roofing, screw nail, sprig, square, tack, veneer pin, wire*).

nails   (USA) The lengths of nails in the USA are designated by the 'penny' system (abbreviated to 'd'); nails less than a 2d are measured in fractions of an inch, and over 20d they are called 'spikes' and measured in inches. The thickness of a nail increases and the number of nails per pound-weight decreases with the penny size.

nail pull   Tool used to withdraw large nails. Used mainly to de-nail old wood. A hand-operated ram forces the jaws into the wood which grip automatically as the tool is levered over on to the foot.

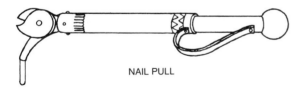

NAIL PULL

nail punch   Small steel tool for driving nails beneath the surface of the wood. Obtainable in various sizes, and either square (for cut nails) or round (for wire nails). Hollow point is best for wire nails as it is less liable to jump out of position. Sometimes known as a nail set.

naphtha   A volatile liquid, colourless or pale yellow colour, used in some stains, and sometimes in the varnishing process. (See *staining*.)

nargusta (*terminalia amazonia***)**   Hardwood from British Honduras and Trinidad of 50 lb (801 kg). A brownish-yellow timber which is resistant to fungal attack. Sometimes known as 'white olivier'. Used for furniture, plywood, veneers, and structural work. Not easy to work, but stains and polishes well.

natural oil stone   One which is quarried and prepared to shape as distinct from an artificial or manufactured stone. (See *oilstone*.)

natural seasoning   The drying of wood in the open. It is specially stacked to allow air to circulate freely, with cover above to protect against rain and sun. (See also *kiln*.)

neats-foot oil   Pale yellow oil used chiefly as a lubricant for an oil stone. Made by boiling the feet and shin bones of cattle.

neck   Narrow part at the top of a column or other turning joining two wider parts.

needle   Short horizontal beam passed through a hole in a wall to support the weight above during alterations. The ends of the needle are held by dead shoring, the latter consisting of stout timbers adjusted by folding wedges or by special adjustable metal supports.

needle point   Virtually a needle without the eye, and used mainly in the veneering process to position marquetry; also for fixing small mouldings, etc.

needles   (A) is a half-round needle, made 3 in (76 mm) up to 6 in (152 mm) for sewing in springs. (B) is an upholsterer's straight, double-pointed, single-eyed, type, made 8 in (204 mm) to 10 in (254 mm) by 14 gauge. (C) is a smooth, oval eye, packing needle. (D) is a triangular-pointed, round-eyed, carpet needle, 2½ in (63 mm) to 2¾ in (70 mm) long. (E) is a 2 in (51 mm) sail needle.

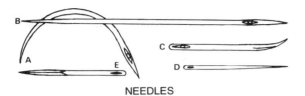

NEEDLES

negoro nuri A form of lacquer originated by Japanese monks in the fourteenth century. The object was first given a coat of black lacquer, followed by a red one; the red lacquer was polished away either deliberately or by constant handling in use to reveal the black.

Nelson Windsor chair A scroll-back Windsor chair *(q.v.)* with the yoke or crest rail carved to represent a twisted rope. Also called a Trafalgar *(q.v.)* chair.

neoprene A synthetic rubber used in adhesives for bonding fabrics or PVC to wood.

nest of saws Set of three saw blades with one interchangeable handle. Smallest is the keyhole saw (A), middle size (B) compass, and largest pruning saw (C), usually about 18 in (457 mm) long.

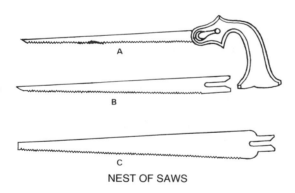

NEST OF SAWS

nest of tables Set of small occasional tables so designed that they fit one beneath the other; they only occupy the space of the largest when not in use. In the 18th century, a set of three tables was called a 'trio', *(q.v.)* and a set of four, a 'quartetto' *(q.v.)*

newel The main post of a staircase carrying the handrail. In the case of a spiral staircase in which the treads meet at the centre, it is the centre pillar holding the steps.

newel cap A capping piece planted above a newel post.

niangon (see *nyankom*).

nib of saw The small bead-like feature found on the back of some handsaws near the toe. Various theories have been propounded to account for its origin, some considering it to be purely decorative, others considering that its emergence from the kerf is an indication that the blade has nearly been withdrawn to its full extent.

nibs Small specks of dust, etc., which settle on a wet polished, painted, or varnished surface, and which must be removed or flattened down by rubbing very lightly with the finest grade of abrasive or, preferably, wet-and-dry paper. (See '*de-nib*'.)

niche A recess, usually semicircular, in a wall to receive a bust or statuette.

nicker In a centre bit the knife edge which cuts the circular path before the cutter removes the wood. In a twist bit there are two nickers and two cutters.

night latch Lock with slide knob fitted bolt on inside. Opened with key from outside.

nitric acid Sometimes used for removing ink marks on a polished surface; also in the pickling process on pine.

nitrile rubber An adhesive containing copolymers of butadiene and acrylonitrile and blended with vinyl chloride copolymers to produce an adhesive which will bond vinyl sheets, leather, and fabrics to wood.

nitrocellulose A substance derived from natural raw cellulose and nitroglycerine but subjected to considerable treatment in chemical baths. It is the basis of cellulose polishes or lacquers. (See *lacquers (2)*.)

nitrostain (see *staining*).

nog Wood insert built into a wall to provide a fixing.

NOGGING PIECES

nogging pieces   Short timbers fitted between the studs of a partition or similar wall. In horizontal nogging the pieces are staggered to allow through nailing. Diagonal nogging is skew nailed. (See *timber stud partion.*)

nominal size   The size of sawn timber before being planed. Thus 1 in (25 mm) nominal only finishes about $\frac{7}{8}$ in (22 mm).

Nonsuch   A term referring to a late 16th century style of inlaid decoration applied (mainly) to chests, and displaying conventional representations of buildings. The name derives from the name of the architect (Toto del Nunziata) of the palace built by Henry VIII at Cheam.

Norfolk latch   Used chiefly on shed and similar doors of the ledged and braced type. Operated from the outside by the thumb. Also known as a thumb or Suffolk latch.

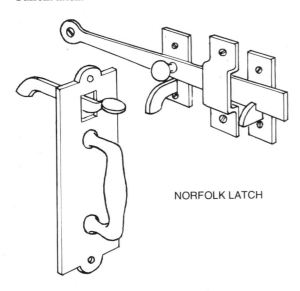

NORFOLK LATCH

normalised steel   Strip steel $\frac{3}{16}$ in (4 mm) or $\frac{1}{4}$ in (6 mm) thick used in making cutters for the French spindle. It is relatively soft, enabling it to be filed at the edge to be turned up.

North Wales dresser   A dresser with cupboards in the base, surmounted by a dresser top.

nose bit   A form of shell bit (*q.v.*) but with turned-over cutting edge. It is more satisfactory for end grain boring. Furthermore the turned-over end withdraws the core as the bit is withdrawn.

NOSE BIT

nosing   Any rounded projecting edge such as that on a staircase tread.

notched joint   Used chiefly in carpentry. It is usually skew-nailed. The notch gives definite position and resists side strain, the nails serving chiefly to hold the parts together. Single notch (A) resists stress in one direction; double notch (B) in two directions. Cogged and notched (C) is used chiefly in flooring joists, the cogging avoiding weakening the main beam as it would if a notch were cut right across.

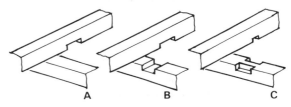

NOTCHED JOINT

notcher   (see *horizontal spindle*).

notched tenons   Sometimes used when rails have to be inserted at the same level at opposite sides of an upright. The opposing tenons are halved in thickness towards the end so that they lie side by side. The root of both tenons is of full thickness.

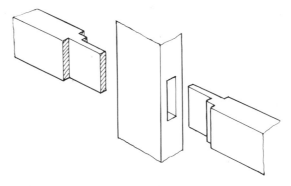

NOTCHED TENONS

novelty saw   Circular saw having a batch of cross-cutting teeth followed by a large gullet. Sometimes a raker tooth is included, this being square-topped and of slightly less projection than the other teeth. Its purpose is to clear the kerf. Sometimes known as a

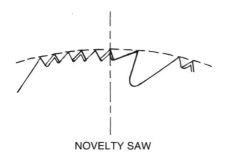

NOVELTY SAW

combination saw. Novelty saws are intended for both ripping and cross-cutting.

nulling Form of rounded carved decoration worked on the torus moulding, usually with separating darts as shown. Used often on table and other tops in the mid-eighteenth century.

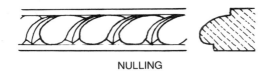

NULLING

nursing chair A design of chair with a low seat and no arm to make it comfortable for a nursing mother.

nyankom *(tarrietia utilis)* Hardwood from Ghana, Ivory Coast, and Sierra Leone of 40 lb (641 kg) weight. Somewhat like mahogany in colour, sometimes slightly purple. Has attractive grain when quarter-cut, stands well when fully seasoned, but liable to twist unless fully dry. Used for furniture, fitments, and structural work.

oak *(quercus robur)* British oak is the heaviest and strongest of world oaks, weighing from 45-52 lb per cu ft (721-833 kg per cubic metre). American white oak *quercus alba)* has a weight of 41-48 lb (657-769 kg). American red oak *(quercus borealis* and *q. rubra)* is slightly heavier. The uses of oak are: high-class furniture and fittings, church woodwork, building, railway carriage and wagon construction, ship, boat, and barge building, gates, agricultural implements, wheel spokes, garden furnishing, etc. Among other oaks are: Japanese *(quercus monogolica)* and Indian

(quercus spicata). Australia has two oaks of a different family: shee oak and silky oak *(q.v.);* the latter is widely used in this country, but is not a true oak.

Brown oak is the English oak which is of a fine golden brown shade due to fungal attack in the early life of the tree. Bog oak is the fossilised wood sometimes found embedded in bogs, and is of a shining black colour. Difficult to work and often brittle.

Both Russian oak and Austrian oak are the *Quercus robur* and yield valuable timber.

oak, silky *(cardwellia sublimis)* An Australian timber in demand for cabinet work, interior fittings and general purposes. It shows a marked ray figure when quarter-cut.

obeche *(triplochiton scleroxylon)* Hardwood from the Cameroons of 20-25 lb (320-400 kg). It is of light colour, somewhat open in the grain. Sometimes known as Nigerian whitewood, white mahogany, arere, or wawa. Stains and polishes well to resemble mahogany. Used chiefly in cabinet work and plywood.

oblique Applied to members, joints, lines, etc. which are arranged at an angle other than a right angle.

oblique joint One in which the joining members meet at an angle other than a right angle.

oblique mortise and tenon Joint used chiefly in carpentry in roof work. The tenoned member meets the horizontal at an angle, the end of the sloping notch taking the side thrust. The stub-tenon prevents lateral movement.

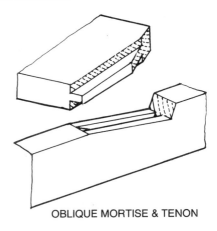

OBLIQUE MORTISE & TENON

oblique projection Pictorial representation of an object in which an elevation (or plan) is drawn in normal fashion, and one side and top shown at an angle. The latter is usually 30 deg or 45 deg, set squares being used. It is a quick and convenient way of showing joints and small items pictorially, but gives a false idea of proportions and appearance, especially in large items, since all corresponding lines are parallel. Perspective is better for pictorial appearance. (See also *isometric projection* and *orthographic projection*.)

obtuse Applied to an angle which is greater than 90 deg. An acute angle is less than 90 deg.

occasional table A small table standing about 24 in (609 mm) high, with a rectangular, circular, or octagonal top. Usually intended to stand against the wall.

octagon This eight-sided figure sometimes features in woodwork, possibly as a table top or a panel. It is usually regular — that is with all sides of equal length. Angles are of 135 deg and mitreing angles of 67½ deg.

odoko (*scottellia coriacea*) West African hardwood of 40 lb (641 kg) weight. It is of yellow-brown colour, the quarter-cut wood having ray flecking. Sometimes known as emufohai or olusare. Used for furniture, turnery, carving, etc.

offcuts Waste pieces resulting from cutting up timber; corresponds to US 'cut-off'. (See also *hog saw*.)

ogea (*daniellia ogea*) West African hardwood of 29 lb (465 kg) weight. Heartwood is pale red-brown colour with darker streaks, and unusually wide sapwood of whitish colour. Used for general interior joinery.

ogee moulding One of serpentine shape. Curves may be based on the circle or be elliptical. (See also: *cyma recta* and *cyma reversa*.)

A   B

OGEE MOULDING

oil (see under *camphorated, linseed, neatsfoot, olive, paraffin, poppy, red, white mineral*).

oil gilding A method of applying gold leaf using gold size. The surface is prepared with two or three coats of gesso followed by yellow clay. In cheaper

work the wood is simply given two to three coats of paint priming. When dry the surface is painted over with gold size and left until the work is just tacky. Gold leaf is put on either with the tip, in which case loose-leaf gold is used; or is pressed on, transfer gold (which is backed with tissue paper) being used. When dry any loose leaf is dusted off. Oil gilding cannot be burnished.

oil, oilstone A thin, clear oil should always be used on oilstones. Neatsfoot or sewing machine oil is usual. A drying oil such as linseed oil must be avoided, as it chokes the pores in the stone and creates a slimy, slippery scum which has to be removed. Oil, apart from acting as a lubricant, serves to carry away small steel particles and prevents the cutting edges of tools becoming over-heated through friction. Paraffin oil is generally used for cleaning.

oil polish Gives an eggshell shine to wood, and is largely resistant to heat, water, and spirit marking. Raw linseed oil with a little driers such as terebine added is used. Calls for intensive rubbing with drying intervals. Needs no special skill.

oil stain (see *staining*).

oilstone Used to give a keen finishing edge to edge tools. There are two main types, natural and artificial. Of the natural stones the Washita is the most generally used by the woodworker, being reasonably fast-cutting and giving a good quality edge. There seems to be an element of luck in it, however, some Washita stones tending to become hard in use and failing to cut. Another natural stone giving an extremely fine edge is the Arkansas. It is used chiefly for finishing off an edge, and by wood carvers. It is extremely expensive. Some years ago the Charnley Forest stone, a natural stone quarried in the Midlands, was popular, but it was slow cutting and is seldom seen today.

The artificial stones are quick-cutting and are available in three grades: fine, medium, and coarse. There is also a combination stone, coarse one side and fine the other. An advantage of the artificial stone is its constant quality. It never becomes hard or gummy unless an unsuitable oil is used. It is generally considered that neatsfoot oil is the best for lubricating the stone, but any fairly thin oil is suitable. Stones are made in various sizes. A case for a stone should be made straightway, partly to protect it from dust, but also because a loose stone seldom survives a fall, especially on a hard floor.

In addition to regular oilstones are oilstone slips in various shapes and sizes. They are used chiefly for sharpening gouges, mouldplane cutters, etc. Made in various grades.

oilstone box Most woodworkers prefer to make their own oilstone box from hardwood. The stone is sunk into a recess about $\frac{1}{2}$ in (12 mm) deep. To prevent it from shifting in use it is usual to either stick a strip of leather at each end at the underside, or to knock in a panel pin at each end, nip it off with about $\frac{1}{16}$ in (2 mm) projection, and file to a point.

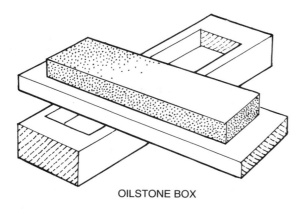

OILSTONE BOX

oil varnish Class of durable varnishes based on oil and drying by oxidation. Many types available, and best are slow drying but are resistant to outdoor conditions.

okan *(cylicodiscus gabunensis)* Hardwood of 78 lb (1249 kg) from West Africa. Sometimes known as African greenheart, though it is not a true greenheart. Yellowish-brown in colour, sometimes greenish, and toning to a dark brown. A dense wood not easy to work. Resistant to decay, and used in heavy construction work.

okoumé In France the more correct name for gaboon *(q.v.)*.

okwen *(brachystegia species)* West African hardwood of 39 lb (625 kg), light to medium brown in colour with dark lines. Resistant to beetle and fungal attack. Turns well and is suitable for carving. Used chiefly for furniture, veneers, etc.

old woman's tooth A hand router with a single narrow cutter for cleaning out the bottoms of grooves. The projecting cutter resembles a tooth — hence the name.

olive, East African *(olea hochstetteri)* Hardwood from Kenya and Abyssinia of 56-60 lb (897-961 kg). Dark brown with greyish markings used in fancy work. A European variety *(olea europea)*, yellowish-brown colour, sometimes used in fancy goods.

olive oil Sometimes rubbed over varnished work to avoid blooming.

olusare Alternative name for odoko *(q.v.)*.

one-third lap joint Used chiefly by pattern makers. Sometimes forms the intersection of a six-spoke wheel. The parts join with a form of halving joint, but the 'halvings' are cut to one third depth rather than one half.

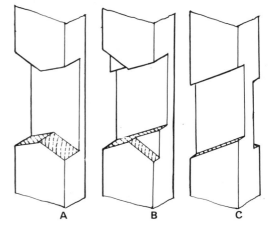

A   B   C

ONE-THIRD LAP JOINT

onion foot A design of foot used on some Windsor chairs about 1900; it consists of a pronounced swell or protruberance immediately below the ring.

open-bine twist A spiral turning in which the bines or spiral bits are separated from each other. Twist turnings have a single, double, or triple bine. They were first made in this country in the 17th century. In hand work the lathe plays a secondary part. The spirals are cut with carving tools, rasps, files, etc. Nowadays, twists can be mass produced entirely by machinery. In the case of the open-bine twist, double or triple, however, the making is still largely a combination of turning and carving. This entails correct setting out. The triple open-bine twist is the more difficult to cut because, whereas in the double-bine the tool can be taken straight through between the bines, there is always one bine to prevent this in the triple bine. Although open-bine spirals are highly decorative, they lack the strength of the solid type.

open grain In timber grain which shows large pores; also called coarse grain.

opening In the sawmill 'opening a log' refers to the first cut. The result may affect subsequent conversion.

open mortise A mortise occurring at the extreme end of a member without any setting in.

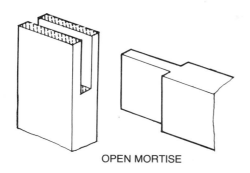

OPEN MORTISE

open newel staircase One in which a well or opening is formed between the flights.

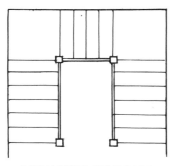

OPEN NEWEL STAIRCASE

open string A staircase string which is cut to follow the line of the treads and risers. Also known as a cut string. It is the converse of a closed string *(q.v.)* where the treads and risers are housed into the actual string.

opepe *(sarcocephalus diderrichii)* Timber of 46 lb (737 kg) from Nigeria, Ghana and West Africa. Yellow-brown colour, sometimes with ribbon stripe figure. Resists fungal attack. Used in cabinet work, flooring, fittings, etc.

orange peel A granular effect sometimes affecting cellulose finishes and produced either by spraying at too low a pressure, by having the wrong air/liquid mix in the spray gun, or by too-rapid drying. It can often be eliminated by a pull-over *(q.v.)*.

orange polish French polish made with orange shellac. Gives a golden brown colour to the wood. (See also *button, garnet, transparent,* and *white polishes.*)

orbital sander An electric portable sander in which the abrasive granules move in a very small circle (about $\frac{3}{16}$ in or $\frac{1}{4}$ in (4 mm-6 mm). Used for the fine finish of work for polishing. Is specially useful for surfaces with many joints and for work with no definite direction to the grain as burr walnut. The pad over which the abrasive paper is fixed retains its same direction but, instead of moving back and forth as in a reciprocating sander, has a circular movement. Thus any individual granule moves in a small circular path, and can leave fine circular scratches.

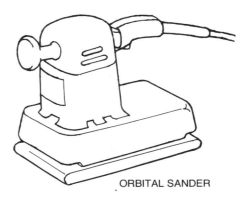

ORBITAL SANDER

orders Applied to the classical styles of architecture, Doric, Ionic, Corinthian, Composite, and Tuscan; and referring to the column, base, capital, and entablature, the proportions of which are established.

Oregon pine Alternative name for Douglas fir *(q.v.)*.

oriel Window of bow or bay plan projecting from the wall and supported by brackets.

ormolu The term derives from the French *bronze dorée d'or moulu,* and the material is gilt bronze. It was in use from the middle 18th century in France and most ormolu found on English furniture is of French origin. The process was, briefly, to make a wooden model from which a bronze casting was produced; this was then tooled and chased to perfection and gilded by the mercury process *(q.v.)*. Ormolu mounts were used to strengthen construction and protect vulnerable parts, as well as being purely ornamental.

oro Alternative name for antiaris *(q.v.)*.

orthographic projection Drawing of an object as seen square from the front, side, or from above. Thus elevations and plans are in orthographic projection.

oscillating bit mortiser This consists essentially of a rotating bit opposite a work-table, both being mounted on a pedestal stand. As the bit rotates it also oscillates from side to side, the whole length of the bit moving and rolling so that it is at right angles to the work throughout the motion. This creates a stub mortise with rounded ends and a flat bottom; a through mortise can also be cut, with care. The slotting bit has specially ground cutting edges, and some also have one edge of the bit serrated for chip removal. Also called a 'slotter', 'jigger' or 'jockey' mortiser.

ottoman An upholstered, box-like seat, with a hinged lid covering a bottom compartment in which linen, etc. can be stored. It is used much the same as a sofa or couch, or a small, temporary bed for a child.

outer string The staircase string which is farthest from the wall.

out of truth Term applied to a frame, carcase, or any structure which is not square or is in winding.

out of wind Applied to a framework or carcase in which the corresponding opposite members are truly in the same plane, or to a surface of a board which is not twisted or warped.

outside-ground gouge A firmer gouge *(q.v.)*.

oval back chair Type which became popular in the Hepplewhite and Adam periods towards the end of the eighteenth century.

oval nails These have the advantage of making only a small hole, and, because of the oval shape of the shanks, the wood is not so liable to split. The common nail (A) is obtainable ½ in (12 mm) to 6 in (152 mm) long. The lost-head nail (B) is similar, but finer, and obtainable 1½ in (38 mm) to 4 in (102 mm) long. (See also *lost-head nails.*)

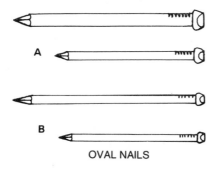

OVAL NAILS

oven dry Term used in ascertaining moisture content *(q.v.)* and referring to oven-dried timber which ceases to give up moisture after heating for a specified time. Microwaving timber for turning is an innovative process, giving a new meaning to the term!

over-all size Dimension of an item which includes all projections such as mouldings, tenons, etc.

over-door Decorative item such as a pediment positioned above a door frame.

overhand planer (see *surface planer*).

overhand ripping Method of ripping used widely by cabinet makers for ripping timber on the bench rather than on trestles. The wood is held down with cramps with the line of cut overhanging the bench edge. After one or two cuts with the point of the saw sloping upwards to start the saw, the latter is held as shown. Many consider it less back-aching, and the labour is borne by both arms.

OVERHAND RIPPING

overhead router A fixed floor-standing machine with an overhead arm which caries the motor and the collet in which the cutter is held; there is also a table with a central guide pin. The table and the motor heights are adjustable. The work to be routed is fixed temporarily to a jig and the guide pin follows this as the work is moved round the table; the cutter necessarily follows and routs out the pattern. Fences can also be used instead of the guide pin and are particularly useful when (say) routing a panel to size.

It is a high-speed machine (up to 27,000 rpm) and can be employed for such work as moulding, grooving, rebating, chamfering, and recessing. There are many different cutters with a wide range of profiles. Latest designs are computer-numerically-controlled (CNC) and can be programmed for various routing operations.

overlapping drawer The drawer front is larger than the opening and is rebated at the inner side and moulded at the front. Apart from appearance, an advantage is that it helps to keep out dust. Sometimes doors have a similar treatment. Sometimes known as a lipped drawer.

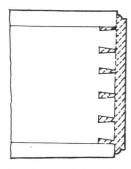

OVERLAPPING DRAWER

overlay A thin facing, usually fretted to a decorative outline, fixed to a panel, framework, etc.

oversailing floor One which projects out from the ground floor walls. Many old timber buildings had the first and second floors cantilevered out in this way.

ovolo Moulding of quarter-circular or quarter-elliptical shape, with quirks at each side.

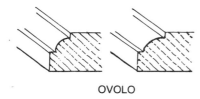

OVOLO

oxalic acid A poisonous acid used chiefly in woodwork as a mild bleach. The crystals are dissolved in water and applied with a rag, several applications being given if necessary. When dry it is neutralised by wiping over the surface with an alkali such as borax, otherwise it may attack any finish subsequently applied.

oxbow curve A reverse serpentine shaped curve.

ox gall Used sometimes as a burnish in the acid finish of french polishing.

Oxford frame One in which the sides cross each other and project at each corner.

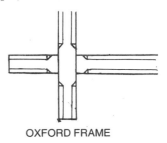

OXFORD FRAME

oyster shell For the substance see *mother of pearl*. The term also refers to a form of veneering, practised chiefly in the late seventeenth and early eighteenth century, in which the veneers consist of cross-cuts, either at right-angles or sloping at an angle, of tree branches. The wood is usually laburnum and sometimes yew, walnut or similar decorative timber. The pieces are squared up and jointed together side by side. The right-angle cuts give a circular grain, and the oblique cuts an elliptical effect. Invariably it is necessary to flat the veneers owing to their liability to cockle as moisture dries out, and they need to be sized because of the end grain.

ozokerite wax A natural earth wax sometimes used with beeswax in making wax polish.

P

packaged furniture Alternative name for knock-down furniture *(q.v.)*.

packing Odd material used to fill a space or to make an item solid.

padauk *(pterocarpus dalbergioides)* A rich-coloured hardwood, varying from yellowish-brown and purplish-red to dark claret red and bright red, streaked with black, according to the locality of growth, which may be India, Burma, and the Andaman Isles. Weight 54-59 lb (865-945 kg). The padauk exported from these isles is bright crimson colour, with maroon or dark streaks but tends to lose its brilliant colour on exposure. The figuring in most cases is conspicuous and attractive, often showing roe, mottle, curl, and blister effects. The wood is hard, and sharp tools are required, as the grain varies. It is used in good class furniture, inlaying, etc.

pad foot　A chair foot shaped to resemble an animal's paw. (See *paw foot.*)

padding stain　(USA) A special stain used in antiquing *(q.v.)*; it is applied with a pad.

pad, stuffing　Ready-made pads used by the upholsterer, obtainable by the yard or cut to size. They can be hair, coco fibre, black fibre, or sisal woven into hessian.

pad tool　(see *tool, pad*).

padsaw　(see *keyhole saw*).

pad, tool　Handle with chuck grip enabling various tools to be held — chisel, knife, saw, screwdriver, bradawl, etc.

paint remover　(see *stripper*).

paired　The right hand and left hand of two otherwise similar parts. Also called 'handed'.

pale　A narrow board used in fencing.

palimpsest arms　(see *hatchment*).

palisade　Fencing consisting of pointed poles or pales usually held together with wire.

pallet　Piece of wood built into the joints of brickwork or breeze block to enable fixings to be made, usually for door frames.

palm planes　Tiny planes used for delicate work by cabinet makers, model makers, and musical instrument makers. They are supplied with convex, concave or square cutting edges. The plane bodies are usually $1\frac{3}{4}$ in (45 mm) long.

PALM PLANE

palu (*mimusops hexandra*)　Hardwood of 70 lb (1121 kg) of a warm purple colour, from India and Ceylon. Used for tool handles and other turnery.

panel　The enclosed part of a door or framework. It fits in grooves or rebates (A) and (B) and is usually recessed, but may be either flush (C) or raised (D). When in solid wood it is never glued but must be free to shrink or swell.

In cabinet work the term panel is freely applied to any enclosed feature; hence the terms pilaster panel, frieze panel, carved, inlaid, etc. (See also *fielded, flush, linenfold, raised*, etc..)

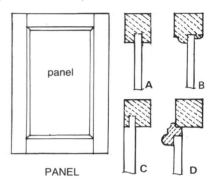

PANEL

panel board　A flat board on which to place thin stuff when planing. To form a stop either screws are driven in at the end, the heads standing proud, or a thin strip is glued or pinned on at the end. Screws are generally better in that they bite into the wood and help to hold it.

panel gauge　With long stem and wide rebated fence. Used to gauge width of any wide stuff — panels, tops, ends, etc.

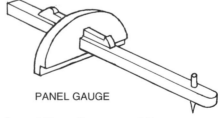

PANEL GAUGE

panel moulding　Loose moulding in joinery to mitre round the edge of a framework or door to enclose the panel. It forms a rebate for the latter.

panel pin　Wire nail with small tapered head used for holding light stuff. Leaves only a small hole to be filled in. Sizes range from $\frac{3}{8}$ in (9 mm) to 2 in (51 mm).

panel plane　Usually refers to the metal plane with wood lining formerly made by Norris or Spiers. From $13\frac{1}{2}$ to $15\frac{1}{2}$ in (343–394 mm) long. Used for planing joints, end grain, and for fine work generally.

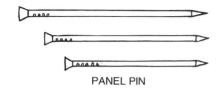

PANEL PIN

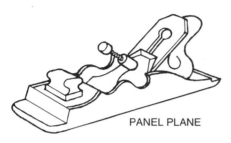

PANEL PLANE

Used for planing joints, end grain, and for fine work generally.

panel planer   (see *thicknesser*).

panel saw   A handsaw similar to a cross-cut *(q.v.)* but smaller. Sizes range from 18 to 22 in (457-559 mm), with teeth of 10-12 points per inch (25 mm). Average size for cabinet work is 20 in (508 mm) long with 11 points. Used for cutting thin stuff and for the larger tenons, etc.

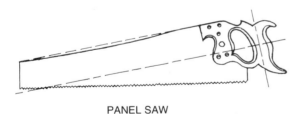

PANEL SAW

panelled frame   Any framework with one or more panels contained in a framework of stiles, rails, and possibly muntins.

panelled linings   When a door or window is set deeply into a wall the inner surface is often panelled. It applies also to panelling around the edge of a deep opening in a wall.

panelling   Applies to any system of rails, stiles, and muntins with filling panels, but more particularly to wood wall linings. Early panelling had narrow panels, no wider than could be cut from an average tree, but in later work the panels were much wider, being jointed to give the width.

panic bolt   Fitted to the inside of public building doors, and requiring only pressure at the bar at the door to enable the latter to open quickly in the event of fire or panic.

pao santa *(zollernia)*   Brazilian hardwood of 81-83 lb (1297-1330 kg). Dark, almost black colour and difficult to work. Used in heavy construction work.

paper joint   Plain rubbed or butt joint with newspaper interposed, enabling it to be broken easily when work on it is finished. Split turnings *(q.v.)* are made in this way.

papier mache   Substances made largely from paper pulp. It was used largely in Victorian times and finished with black oriental lacquer. Furniture made from it was displayed at the Great Exhibition of 1851.

parabola   Curve obtained by cutting a cone parallel with its side.

parabolic arch   Pointed   arch   based   on   the parabola.

paraffin, medicinal   Occasionally   used   as   a lubricant when french polishing. Also called white mineral oil.

paraffin oil   An illuminating oil, or cleansing oil, unsuitable for lubricating purposes. It may, on occasion, however, be applied to oilstones, especially artificial stones, by way of a lubricant and cleaner. The oil has great penetrating properties, and is ideal for slackening screws rusted in wood, loosening stiff, rusty hinges, and cleaning driving chains thick with dirt and old oil. Corresponds to USA Kerosine.

paraffin wax   Sometimes used with beeswax to lower the cost of wax polish.

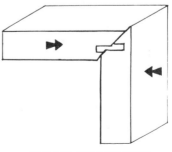

PARALLEL SPLINE MITRE

parallel spline mitre (USA) Used only on plywood, clamps only being needed one direction. Note that the slots for the spline are very minutely offset.

parallel strips Two pieces of wood with perfectly parallel sides. One usually has an inlaid line of contrasting wood near the top. Their purpose is to test whether wood is free from winding. The inlaid one is placed near the back, the other at the front, and a sight taken across them. Also known as winding strips.

parana pine *(araucaria angustifolia)* A choice Brazilian timber, warm yellowish brown or cream in colour, with close grain, sometimes showing pinkish brown and greenish streaks. The sapwood is white. It is easily worked and when planed has a satin sheen. The wood is liable to break and crumble, as when dovetailing, unless tool edges are quite sharp. In view of the characteristic beauty of the wood, a natural finish is highly desirable. It is a conifer and therefore classed as a softwood.

parasite A growth such as dry rot which feeds on the substance of wood.

parcel Term used loosely for a quantity of timber or veneers.

parcel gilt Partially gilt.

parchment panel A linefold panel *(q.v.)*.

parchment size Used in the gilding process in making gesso. Parchment cuttings are cut into small pieces, covered with water and left overnight. In the morning the water is thrown away and the cuttings transferred to a double kettle and water to about three times the volume of the cuttings. It is simmered for about three hours, strained and allowed to cool. (See also *gesso.*)

parclose screen These are used to separate private chapels from the main body of the church and are made of stone or wood. The most common wooden screens are square-framed; the arched type is rare.

parenchyma This is a tissue composed of thin-walled brick-shaped cells originally functioning as food storage elements in the living tree which, when lying horizontally, are found in the wood forming the ray tissue (as in figured oak). They are also found singly or in groups of vertical strands which can often be seen on the cut cross-section. They contribute very little to the strength of the tree.

paring chisel Lightly built chisel intended for fine paring work, never for striking with the mallet. Generally it is bevel-edged, and longer than the general bench chisel.

PARING CHISEL

parliament hinge One fitted to a room door, and having a projecting knuckle less than the plate in length. When fitted the knuckle should stand out from the door face slightly more than half the greatest projection of any skirting or architrave. It enables the door to fold back flat against the wall.

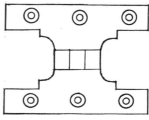

PARLIAMENT HINGE

parlour chair A term describing a side chair which is intended for use in the parlour (now called the sitting room or lounge) as distinct from a dining chair.

parquetry The craft of covering a surface or a floor with a geometrical mosaic of woods to make a pattern; different grain patterns and natural and applied colours create or enhance the effect.

particle boards These are man-made boards manufactured from specially prepared particles of ligno-cellulosic materials such as wood, flax, hemp, and bagasse (residue from sugar cane after the extraction of the syrup); they are bonded with synthetic resins or other organic binders. They are graded for thermal conductivity, surface spread of flame, minimum strength properties, moisture content, and freedom from foreign particles. Typical uses (according to grade): built-in fitments furniture panels, roof decking, flooring, door cores, and substrates for plastic or veneered face boards. (See also *chipboard, hardboard and MDF.*)

parting bead The thin beaded slip which separates the sliding sashes of a window. The term 'parting slip' is applied to the bead which keeps the weights apart.

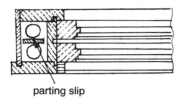

PARTING BEAD

parting slip

parting tool (1) A V-shaped tool used by wood carvers. Made in various widths and in three angles of about 60, 90, and 110 deg.

parting tool (2) Used by wood turners for several purposes, among them the marking out of diameters along a cylinder, cutting ribs, or turning small pins. Note that the blade is ground away (or 'relieved') behind the bevel to avoid binding when making deep cuts.

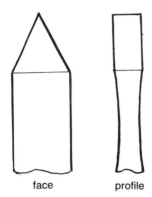

face   profile

PARTING TOOL

partridge wood *(caesalpinia granadillo)* Hardwood of 75-80 lb (1201-1281 kg) from Brazil and Venezuela. Dark brown colour. Also known as granadillo or brown ebony. Sometimes used for walking sticks and umbrella shafts.

paste filler (see *filler, grain*).

pastiglia A type of gesso used by sixteenth century Italian craftsmen. Also called 'tempera'.

patera A circular or elliptical ornament worked in relief or inlaid into a frieze, pilaster, or other part. A feature frequently found on furniture in the Adam style.

patina The gloss acquired by woodwork by years of polishing.

pattern A wooden model from which metal castings are made.

pattern maker's hammer Similar to the Warrington pattern but lighter. (See *hammer (M)*.

pattern veneering Refers to patterns made up either in different woods or varying grain arrangements of the same wood. Usually the veneers are pieced together dry with gummed tape and laid as a whole with a caul.

patternwood Alternative for alstonia *(q.v.)*.

pawfoot Chair, stool, table, or stand leg of cabriole type with foot carved in imitation of an animal's paw, usually a lion. Used widely in the eighteenth and early nineteenth centuries. (See *pad foot*.)

PAW FOOT

pear drop handle Drawer or door handle in brass used in seventeenth century.

pearl ash A whitish powder (crude potassium carbonate) sometimes used for stripping off old French polish.

pearl essence (USA) Very fine pulverised particles of fish scales (quanin) held in suspension in a clear lacquer, thus producing pearl lacquers. It is also made synthetically from mercuric chloride.

pear-wood *(pyrus communis)* Known for its extensive use for T-squares, set squares, straight-edges, draughtsman's curves, etc. 47-48 lb (753-769 kg). Close grained and excellent for carving.

pecan nut Sometimes used by the French polisher to disguise scratches in polish. The nut is broken and rubbed over the part so that oil exudes.

pedestal In furniture applied to pieces such as a writing table, sideboard, or dressing table, which are built in two carcases with a connecting drawer part above. The term also denotes the base for a column, statue, vase, or other ornament; may also refer to a single cupboard such as a bedside pedestal cupboard. (See also Socle.)

pedestal table A table supported by a single column or shaft.

pediment A triangular or otherwise shaped frontal head feature to a doorway, clockcase, or a tall piece of furniture such as a wardrobe or bookcase. Now rarely seen, these pediments were a feature in British, French, and other furniture of the late eighteenth and early and mid nineteenth centuries.

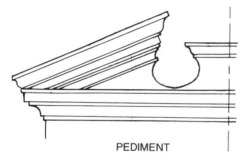

PEDIMENT

peeler A lathe-like machine for cutting rotary veneer.

peen The narrow, tapered end of a London, Exeter, Warrington, or pattern maker's hammer (see *hammer*). For woodwork it is at right angles with the shaft, and is used for starting small nails, and for rubbing down narrow cross bandings and inlay lines. Also spelt pene or pein.

pegboard A type of hardboard which has a regular pattern of holes drilled over its surface. This allows pegboard fittings (*q.v.*) to be inserted, and this facility is particularly useful for display stands in shops, etc.

pegboard fittings These can be inserted into the holes in pegboard (*q.v.*). They are usually made from stout wire and are useful for shop display stands, etc.

peg leg A design of leg which is completely plain except for a slight tapering in the length; the top end is reduced to enter a solid chair seat.

pegged joints Method of locking a joint by passing a peg through both mortise sides and tenon so that the latter cannot be withdrawn. Dowels of $\frac{1}{4}$ in (6 mm) or

$\frac{3}{8}$ in (9 mm) diameter are mostly used today, but originally the pegs were roughly shaped squares sometimes with the corners taken off, and tapered. (See also *draw-boring*.)

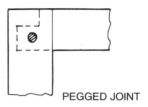

PEGGED JOINT

pegtooth (see *fleam teeth*).

pelleting A method of hiding screw heads. Today they are often called 'plugs' and are formed by using a plug-cutter in an electric drill which will remove a core or pellet from a piece of matching wood. The recess for the screw head is drilled out to a depth of $\frac{1}{4}$ in or $\frac{3}{8}$ in (6 mm to 9 mm) and the pellet glued in. Another method of making them is to turn them up on a lathe from a long strip of matching timber and cut them off; only a few can be turned at any one time as they are liable to snap off.

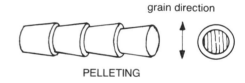

grain direction

PELLETING

pelmet Covering at the head of a window to hide curtain fittings. It may be of soft material (valance) or of plywood, hardboard, etc.

Pembroke table Small table with a flap at each end, these being supported by brackets which might be either hinged or pivoted on finger or knuckle joints. Either one or two drawers are fitted beneath the top. It is generally thought to have received its name either from the Duchess of Pembroke who first ordered one, or from the Earl of Pembroke who was supposed to have originated the type. A popular table in the late eighteenth and early nineteenth centuries.

pencil brush Small round pointed brush used by the polisher to touch up small blemishes such as filled-in nail holes, discoloured parts, etc.

pencil, carpenter's Oval pencil with wide, large lead. Used to mark out carpentry work. The large lead lasts much longer without sharpening afresh.

pencil cedar *(juniperis virginiana)* Softwood from USA and West Indies. Pale yellow to deep pinkish colour, 26-34 lb (416-545 kg). Used almost entirely in pencil making. The East African pencil cedar *(juniperis procera)* is similar in characteristics, and is also used in pencil making and for chest linings.

pencil post (USA) A column or shaft which is tapered and octagonal in section throughout its length; often used as bed-posts.

pendant Any decorative detail hanging beneath a post or under a rail or beam. Also applied to a suspended light.

pendulum saw A circular saw used for cross-cutting. It is suspended from above on a long arm and is passed across the wood with pendulum-like movement.

penetration Refers to the resistance of wood to the penetration of a liquid. In particular it is used in connection with veneers and their liability to penetration by glue; also to solid wood in connection with preservative liquids.

Pen Farrell guard A guard used on a spindle moulder *(q.v.)*.

pen painting A technique devised in the late eighteenth century and popular for many years which sought to imitate the patterns of incised ivory laid over ebony. Most often applied to small objects such as tea caddies, trinket-boxes, and the like.

pentagon Five-sided regular polygon. The quickest way to draw it is to draw a circle and step five times round it with dividers, adjusting by trial and error until the stepping is exact. Radial lines are drawn from the points to the centre of the circle and, with the same centre, a second circle is drawn which gives the required size of pentagon.

peppermint A variety of the Australian mountain ash.

per cube Measurement according to cubic contents irrespective of length, width, and thickness. Since metrication timber is measured by the cubic metre, 35.315 cu ft equalling one cubic metre.

perch Alternative name for a bracket.

peripheral speed The speed at which any one tooth of a circular saw is moving. The optimum speed for a circular saw is based on a peripheral speed of 9,500 ft per minute, and its rpm will vary with its diameter. When the rpm of a saw is known, the peripheral speed can be calculated as follows:

rpm × saw diam × $3\frac{1}{7}$. Thus if the rpm of a 10 in saw is 3,500 rpm the calculation is:

$$\frac{10 \times 3,500 \times 3\frac{1}{7}}{12 \text{ (to bring ins. to ft)}} = 9,166 \text{ FPM approx.}$$

To convert feet per minute to metres per minute multiply by 0.3048.

permanganate of potash Chemical in crystal form which, dissolved in water, is used to stain oak, and softwoods. It gives a rich, deep brown shade but is not really satisfactory as the colour is fugitive.

periwig chair Alternative name for a barber's chair *(q.v.)*. So-called because the scrolls and carving on the crest of the extended splat resembled the periwigs of the period (circa 1720).

peroba rosa *(aspidosperma peroba)* Brazilian hardwood, 44-53 lb (705-849 kg). Used in building, joinery, and for sleepers, etc. Resistant to decay.

perron Outside staircase with landing at the top.

persimmon *(diospyros virginiana)* Hardwood from USA, 49 lb (785 kg). Sapwood tree in which heartwood shows only in very old trees. When it occurs it is nearly black, but sapwood is whitish brown with green patches. Dense wood used in turnery, shuttles, etc.

perspective Type of drawing used in giving a pictorial view of an object. More realistic than any of the projections such as isometric and oblique in that the lines vanish or converge, parts farther away from the observer being smaller. There are rules for correct drawing in perspective, but these are seldom followed completely, a simplified version being all that is needed.

Petrograd standard Old-style measurement representing 165 cubic feet, or 120 pieces (or their equivalent) 12 ft × 11 in × $1\frac{1}{2}$ in.

pew hinge One with large projecting knuckle like a parliament hinge *(q.v.)* but usually with a decorative knuckle.

pheasantwood Alternative name for angelin *(q.v.)*.

phenol-formaldehyde (PF) (see under *resin glue*).

phenolic lacquer A synthetic lacquer made from phenol and formaldehyde. The lacquer gives a heat-, spirit-, and water-proof finish.

phenolic-neoprene adhesives These are based on blends of phenolic resins with neoprene rubbers: they include contact adhesives for bonding fabrics, plastics, rubber, etc., to wood.

Phillips screws The heads of these screws have four-way cruciform slots into which a special screwdriver fits. Now superseded by Mastadriv and Pozidriv designs which are more sophisticated versions. (See *Reed and Prince screws*.)

PHILLIPS SCREW

phloem The botanical name for bark *(q.v.)*.

piano finish A mirror-like finish obtained by applying many coats of rubbing varnish, each coat being lightly rubbed down with fine abrasive paper (e.g. wet-and-dry paper).

piano leg A design of leg used on some chairs, circa 1870. It consisted of a very long tapered shank, a vase-shaped swell surmounted by several rings and a ball. All the turnings were exaggerated to give a dramatic and ponderous effect.

piano stool Recognised height is 22 in (559 mm), but those used by professionals are usually adjustable in height. Sometimes the seat encloses a box or well to contain music, the size being fixed by that of sheet music.

piano strip hinge Long, narrow hinge as used on the fall and lid of a piano. Apart from those made specially for a piano, strip hinges are made in 3 ft (1 metre) lengths and can be cut down to whatever is needed. Brass, chromium, and plastic hinges are available.

picking up Refers to the liability of some woods with difficult grain to tear out or break away at the pores leaving little pockets when passing through the machine planer.

pickling A process used in some antique finishes. The pickle may consist of lime, caustic soda, and ammonia, etc. Painted furniture was often pickled, the paint being stripped off and leaving an attractive finish often tinged by the colour of the paint originally used.

pictorial marquetry That in which pictures such as landscapes, portraits, etc., are formed rather than ornamental designs. (See *marquetry*.)

picture frame moulding Made in a wide range of sizes, sections, woods, and finishes. The common feature is the provision of a rebate to receive the glass, picture, and backing.

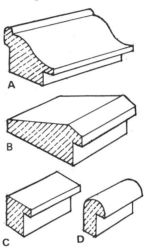

PICTURE-FRAME MOULDINGS

picture frames There are few records of picture frames before 1600, as early paintings were generally executed on solid wood, the panel and the frame being one piece. Frames became popular around 1630 and there are, of course, many different styles.

picture rail This usually marks the junction line between wall and frieze. Milled moulding material for the purpose is supplied in widths from 1 in (25 mm) to 3 in (76 mm). The mouldings are rounded on top to engage the picture hooks. Sometimes a tongue is machined at the top to fit into a groove worked in a plate shelf.

pie-crust edging A decorative raised edging used on small circular table tops in the eighteenth century. In the best work the whole thing is cut in the solid, the bulk of the centre waste being removed by turning, and the actual edging carved. In cheap work it is often applied, the moulding being spindled.

pierced panel One in which the decoration or other design is pierced right through rather than recessed.

Gothic tracery panels were often treated in this way, sometimes to give ventilation to a food cupboard.

pier glass   A tall mirror which was fixed to the wall immediately above a pier table; any form of lighting placed on the latter would be reflected into the room.

pier table   A table designed to be fixed to the wall on the pier between two windows; it had only two front legs, the back being attached to the wall. In the USA the term is used to describe any table which is designed to stand against the wall.

pie safe   (USA) A cupboard standing on four plain legs, and with two or four drawers above and below; the door panels (and often the side panels as well) were filled with pierced tin sheets to allow air to circulate around the food without the risk of flies entering. The pierced holes were punched in definite patterns, such as stars, eagles, or floral motifs.

pietre dure   Literally, 'hard stone'. The technique of creating a pattern of coloured stones bonded to a marble base with plaster; practised by Florentine craftsmen, circa 1600.

pigeon hole   Small space formed in bureaux, desks, etc., to store stationery. Pigeon-hole piling is the stacking of timber for seasoning with spaces left between the pieces to assist drying.

pigment   Finely divided and insoluble particles of a coloured base added to paint, etc., to obtain colour.

pilaster   A flat squared pier partly built into and projecting from the face of a wall. In furniture it takes the form of a similar pier fixed to front edge of carcase end. Frequently narrow strips of thin wood are planted on the hanging stiles of doors to convey the effect of pilasters, the stiles being cut wider to permit this.

piling   The method of stacking wood for drying. Various systems are followed. In 'Bristol' piling the pieces are stacked with alternate layers at right angles, spaces being left between the boards in each layer. 'Cabinet' piling has the lengths shorter towards the top. In close piling the items lie directly on each other without skids (q.v.) and is bad practice as it does not allow air circulation and may cause staining. Pigeon-hole piling has spaces at each side of the boards. (See *stacking*.)

piling sticks   Placed vertically in line between the boards about 2ft (610mm) apart in a stack for seasoning. Also known as stickers.

pillar   A detached column sometimes occurring in joinery but seldom in cabinet work. It is usually in one of the classical styles: Doric, Tuscan, Ionic, Corinthian, Composite. Such columns are invariably hollow, being coopered together (q.v.).

pillar and claw table   An alternative name for a tripod table with a carved pie-crust top which could be circular, octagonal, or oval. The actual foot was a pad foot, circa 1730, followed by the claw and ball about 1740 to 1760, and finally with a lion's paw in the early nineteenth century.

pillar drill   (see *drilling machine and drill stand*).

pillar table   Small table, usually circular, with centre turned shaft or pillar supported by tripod legs. More often known as a tripod table (q.v.).

pillarwood (*cassipourea malosana*)   Pale yellow hardwood, 46lb (737kg) from East Africa. Used in turnery, structural work, and is often stained to resemble other hardwoods.

pin bit   (see *shell bit*).

pincers   A nail extracting tool available in various sizes. Usual patterns are the Tower (A) and the Lancashire (B).

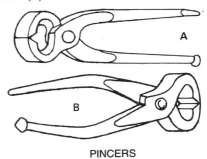

PINCERS

pinch bar   A lever used for moving heavy objects.

pincushion seat   One in which the padded upholstery is on top of the frame with a margin of wood all round. Usually rounded in shape.

pinch dog   (see *dog, joiner's*).

pin driver   (see *push pin* and *rampin*).

pine (*pinus sylvestris*)   This is the premier softwood, known to commerce as Red Baltic or (in this country) Scots pine. It is known also under such designations as Scots fir, redwood, red pine, etc. The uses of pine comprise all branches of sound joinery and carpentry, indoor fittings of every kind, and kitchen furniture. Other pines are: (1) the yellow or white pine of Canada and the NE United States *(pinus strobus)*, known also as Quebec pine and (to arborculturists) Weymouth pine; (2) pitch pine *(pinus palustris)*, a heavy constructional timber; (3) The Kauri pine of New Zealand and Australia, the Parana pine, and the New Zealand rimu.

pin hinge   Alternative name for centre hinges. Made in straight form (A), and cranked (B) in pairs. The hinge used at the bottom of the door must either have a raised seating to enable the door to clear, or it must have a washer over the pin.

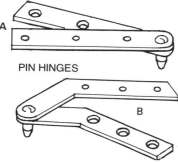

PIN HINGES

pin hole   Small round hole made by pinhole borer. Not bigger than $\frac{1}{16}$ in (2 mm) diameter.

pinhole borer   These are beetles which attack freshly felled logs, and are found chiefly in tropical and sub-tropical regions. They do not continue working in seasoned timber. The bore holes indicate past infestation, but the wood can be used in the knowledge that there is no risk of recurrence.

pinholing   A pimply surface found on varnish film and caused by the presence of moisture or trapped solvent. It often occurs when coats are applied on top of each other without sufficient time being allowed for the solvents to evaporate.

pin knot   Small knot $\frac{1}{4}$ in (6 mm) or less in diameter.

pincers   A nail extracting tool available in various sizes. Usual patterns are the Tower (A) and the Lancashire (B).

pins   (see under individual headings).

pin vise   (USA) A tool with a knurled steel body which can be rotated between thumb and forefinger; one end has a chuck which accepts small-size drills, scribers, and similar tools.

pipe clamp   (USA) Comprises a length of tubing with a flange at the lower end which is fixed to the bench top; a threaded collar at the top enables a clamp jaw to be screwed down on to the work. Fulfils the same function as the British bench holdfast. (See *holdfast.*)

piping   Narrow pipe-like detail used in upholstery in joining material at the edges. It consists of cord covered with material. Corresponds to US 'cording'.

pitch   The angle at which the plane iron meets the work when the iron is in its normal position in the plane. With a bench plane it is usually 45 degrees; with a block plane or any similar plane which is used with the bevel of the cutting iron uppermost, it is 20 degrees or even (on low-angle planes) 12 degrees. There is also a 'York' pitch *(q.v.)* used by some cabinet makers for smoothing planes which varies between 30 and 53 degrees.

pith   (see *medulla*).

pivot hinge   A primitive hinge used until the fifteenth century on plank chests.

plain sawing   (USA) A method of converting lumber which includes heart wood boards.

planer formulae   Peripheral cutting speed in metres per minute = 3.14 × D (cutter block dia. in mm) × R (rpm), divided by 1,000 (to convert mm to metres). The rpm (R) can be obtained by transposing the factors thus: R = 1,000 × P, divided by 3.14 × D.
   The pitch of a cutter may be ascertained from the following formula: P (pitch of cutter mark in mm) = 1,000 × F (feed speed in metres per minute), divided by N (number of cutters) × R (rpm of cutter block).

planes   (see under individual headings).

plane, London   *(platanus acerifolia)* The tree almost always grows in urban areas (hence the name) and its timber is rarely used commercially, although when quarter-cut it shows an attractive figure known as 'lacewood' *(q.v.).*

plank seat   (USA) A type of solid seat used on American Windsor chairs. Sometimes it was 'bottomed' *(q.v.)* but only lightly; the front edge was rounded off.

plank stool   A stool made from roughly-adzed planks, pegged together.

planted When referring to mouldings, means those mitred and fixed separately from the framework or groundwork, and not stuck on the solid.

plaque A circular or oval medallion, usually of porcelain, used as decoration.

plastic laminate A thin, tough veneer made of cellulose-based paper treated with phenol-formaldehyde resin; this is overlaid with the photo-reproduction of the desired pattern and this is coated with malamine formaldehyde to give a surface which is heat, water, and chemical proof.

plastic wood A proprietary filler made from wood flour; can be obtained in different colours to match various woods.

plateau An ornamental stand (resembling an epergne) on a shallow plinch or feet; it was placed on a table top to display silverware, etc. Fashionable from the end of the eighteenth century and through the Regency period. Often made in brass, but also of japanned wood.

plate pail A receptable resembling a pail used for carrying plates from the kitchen to the dining room in a large house. Usually polygonally sided, with one side left open so that the plates could be grasped easily.

Plectaneum chairs A range of patented designs of folding chairs and stools, unupholstered; produced by Edwin Skull of High Wycombe, circa 1865.

pliers These tools are made in various styles and sizes to perform such diverse operations as cutting metal or holding small and delicate articles. (See under individual names.)

pliers saw-set A tool which bends saw teeth to the correct angle when setting. It resembles a pair of pliers and it is applied to the saw teeth so that they are inserted one by one between an anvil and a plunger. When the pliers are squeezed the plunger pushes the saw tooth on to the anvil to impart the correct angle. The anvil itself is 'stepped' so that it can be adjusted to form different angles. (See *saw-set*.)

plinth The base of a piece of case furniture which rests on the floor.

ploughing The cutting out of grooves, etc. Terms such as trenching, channelling, and housing are also used.

plug Wood filling of wedge shape driven into brickwork, stone, etc., to enable a fixing to be made. Chief types are shown, the flat one being driven into the joints. The tapered shape gives a twist to the plug which increases the grip. Also applied to wood pieces used to fill in the blemishes in groundwork of veneered work, or plywood. (See also *pelleting*.)

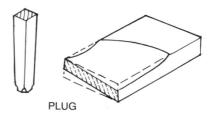

PLUG

plug tenon A stub or short tenon, used when required on the top of a post or table leg to guard against the risk of lateral movement. (See *spur tenon*.)

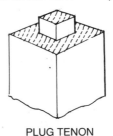

PLUG TENON

plum (*prunus domestica*) European hardwood, 50-53 lb (801-849 kg). Used in turning, tool handles, inlay work, etc.

plunge router A portable router with a built-in electric motor which operates at about 24,000 rpm. It differs from the overhead router (*q.v.*) in that it is taken to the work and the routing is achieved without the use of a guide-pin; various attachments allow the router to describe curves, circles, straight lines, etc., and it can also be used freehand. Most of the operations which can be executed on the overhead router can also be undertaken on the plunge router, and there is an equally large number of different bits available. There is a special plunging device which allows the router to be placed on the work with the motor running and which allows the bit to be lowered and commence cutting.

plywood Boards made of veneers, the grain of which is at right angles in the alternate layers. Most plies have three layers, either of equal thickness or with a thicker centre layer known as stout heart. In addition there is multi-ply with 5, 7, 9 or more layers.

The complete number is always odd. Usually thicknesses are given in millimetres. The first size is always in line with the grain of the outer layers, the second at right angles to it. Various woods are used and they are invariably rotary cut; alder, birch, ash, obechi, Oregon pine, beech, etc. For decorative purposes a flat sliced veneer may be added at the surface. The adhesive varies with the quality; it may be animal, casein, soya bean, resin, etc. For plywood liable to be exposed to damp conditions a waterproof cement is essential. Plywood is also graded according to its freedom from knots, but the system varies according to the country of origin.

pneumatic tools These are normally used only in large concerns as they are more expensive than electrically-driven tools and demand a complicated back-up system. They can be made smaller than electric tools for comparable work, and are simpler in design and therefore need less maintenance. For woodwork, the tools are mainly drills, sanders, and screwdrivers. Air tools are quite safe and no damage occurs if they stall due to excessive loading. However, they do accelerate very rapidly and for this reason initial contact with the work-piece should be light.

pocket Opening in the pulley stile of a sash window frame to enable the weights to be withdrawn and replaced. Often the ends are notched, the top being cut at an angle so that it is retained in position. The bottom may be screwed but is frequently just tapped into position.

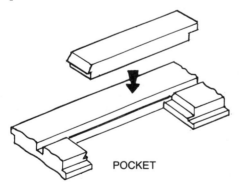

POCKET

pocket screwing Concealed slant-screwing by means of a gouged thumb slot. The top of a table may be screwed from below by gouging a slot or pocket in inside face of rail and driving in the screw aslant.

pocketed spring upholstery Consisting of small spiral springs encased in calico or hessian. The spring is usually sewn in the calico and each unit held to its neighbour with steel clips or twine. Hessian types may

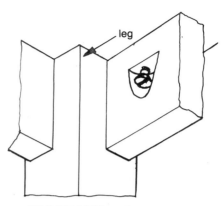

leg

POCKET SCREWING

be walled, having partitions of hessian between the springs. (See *spring-interior mattress.*)

pod bit Alternative name for a nose bit *(q.v.)*.

poker work (see *pyrography*).

points The size of saw teeth. The number of points in an inch (25.4 mm) are counted including those at both ends. Average sizes are: ripsaw 3-4 points, cross-cut 5-8 points, panel-saw 7-12 points, tenon saw 12-14 points, dovetail saw 16-22 points, and light hacksaw 24-32 points.

90°   60°

POINTS

pole In forestry, a felled stem from a tree of slender girth, usually under 8 in (203 mm) in diameter. Hence, telephone poles, etc. Also applied to long cylindrical material, generally.

pole lathe An old and now obsolete lathe used chiefly for turning Windsor chair legs and spindles. It had a bed of two squares of timber and one fixed and one adjustable centre. A long springy pole was fixed at one end with its thin free end suspended above the lathe. A cord was attached to this free end and taken down to the treadle. The cord was given a twist around the wood to be turned and the latter held between the centres. As the power stroke was made with the foot, the pole sprang back, reversing the rotation. The turner (known as a bodger) became extremely quick, a detail being completed in a matter of seconds.

pole plate Horizontal beam which carries the feet of rafters.

pole screen   (see *fire screens*).

polish   (see under separate entries: *cellulose lacquer, French polish, oil polish, wax polish, etc.*).

pollard   Tree in which the top and boughs have been polled to encourage fresh growth. This causes a wild and varied grain which yields valuable veneers such as burr walnut.

polyethylene glycol (PEG)   A stabiliser for wood as it replaces the natural moisture in the wood. The wood is totally immersed in a PEG solution and left for several weeks and then removed and left to dry for several weeks more.

polygon   Figure with more than four straight sides: pentagon 5, hexagon 6, septagon 7, octagon 8, nonagon 9, decagon 10, dodecagon 12.

polyurethane foam   Form of interior filling for upholstery. The foam may be in bulk to cut to shape, or in specially moulded shapes.

polyurethane lacquer   Also called 'urethane' lacquer. A synthetic resin varnish obtainable either as a one-can air-drying type, or a two-can type which sets by catalytic action. It is heat, water, and chemical resistant, and is one of the most widely used finishes.

polyvinyl acetate glue   One of the modern adhesives, generally known as PVA. A white glue used cold and with many advantages; it is, however, not waterproof. It is at its best in close-fitting joints as it is not normally regarded as a joint filler. It does not become brittle hard and is therefore not hard on cleaning-up tools. The glue has great tensile strength, but under the sheer test has a lower reading than some other glues. It does not cause staining. (See *resin glue (synthetic.)*

pommel   A terminal feature, generally ovoid in shape, found on the uprights of upholstered chairs, circa 1550. They are usually gilt wood, or copper, but in the early Stuart period they were often covered with the same fabric as the upholstery of the chair.

poon   (*calophyllum tomentosum*)   Hardwood from India, Burma, and Andaman Islands of mahogany colour, often well figured. Used in cabinet making and general building construction.

poplar   (*populus* various)   Hardwood of 31-35 lb (497-561 kg) from Europe, Canada, USA. The black, grey, and white poplars yield sound timber but the Lombardy poplar has no value as a timber tree. Not widely used.

poppyhead   A term describing the finials on bench-ends in cathedrals and churches; they date back to the end of the fourteenth century. The word has no connection with the poppy flower, but probably derives from the French *poupée* meaning a puppet or figurehead.

POPPY-HEAD

poppy oil   Pale yellow liquid sometimes used as a lubricant when French polishing; also in the manufacture of some paints and varnishes.

pores   The pores (or vessels) of a timber are composed of thin-walled cells joined end-to-end to form a long chain throughout the tree and are connected to each other by open ends. They are responsible for the upward movement of water and mineral salts in the living tree. Having thinner walls, they contribute less to the strength of the tree than the fibres (*q.v.*).

porphyry   A hard semi-precious stone which takes a high polish and is red-purple in colour. However, the term has now been extended to include green (Greece), brown (Norway and Sweden), violet and light green (France). They were imitated by Italian craftsmen in paintwork.

post-and-panel construction   (USA) A form of construction utilising posts, rails, and panels to create a framed-up carcase as opposed to one built up from solid components.

posts   Applied loosely to any upright, but often particularised in connection with a door, King, Queen, Princess, sign, corner, bed, etc.

pot board   Name given to a shelf used in the lower part of a dresser. It rested upon the bottom or stretcher rails.

potash, American rock (*crude caustic potash* (*q.v.*)) Used for weathering oak, turning the wood deep brown. With later treatment of chloride of lime the wood becomes grey. Is both poisonous and harmful to touch.

potash, bichromate of   (see *bichromate of potash*).

potash, permanganate of   (see *permanganate of potash*).

potence   A T-shaped cross; also a gallows-shaped frame. (See *gallows bracket.*)

pot life   The maximum time for which a mixed adhesive remains usable.

pouch table   Work table having a soft material bag suspended beneath the top. Popular in the first half of the nineteenth century.

pouffe   Low seat or stool without a back and made entirely of soft material.

pounce bag   Used in the acid finish in French polishing. Made up of two thicknesses of muslin and filled with Vienna chalk. It is dabbed over the surface so that a deposit of chalk is left. (See *acid finish.*) A pounce bag is also sometimes filled with the finest pumice powder and used to remove stubborn rubber marks.

powder post beetle (*lyctidae*) Found in some unseasoned or newly dried hardwoods — oak, ash, elm, sweet chestnut. Only the sapwood is attacked. The beetles are about $\frac{1}{5}$ in (5 mm) long and vary from reddish brown to black. The larvae are white, about $\frac{1}{4}$ in (6 mm) long when fully grown. The beetles emerge usually in April and can fly. Treatment is largely preventive, the timber being sprayed with an insecticide toxic to the larvae. Both benzene hexachloride and DDT have been used.

powered plane   A portable electric plane with rotary cutters. It is used for the rapid reduction of wood to the required size.

powder stains   Stains in powder form which are mixed with water, oil, or alcohol to produce a wood stain.

power tools   A term used to describe the range of tools which contain their own motive power (either an electric motor or compressed air); they are thus completely portable and can be taken to the work as opposed to the work being brought to them. Thus a portable saw is a power tool; a static saw table is not. The term is generally used as referring to electric drills (*q.v.*).

pre-catalysed lacquer   (see *lacquer* (3)).

preservation of timber   There are three principal preservatives for timber: tar oils, water-borne, and solvent-based.

Creosote is the main tar oil; it results from the distillation of coal tar. If properly applied by pressure impregnation or hot and cold tank steeping it gives excellent durability. It has an initial stickiness and smell which soon disappears, and provided it is re-surfaced from time to time it needs no further maintenance. It cannot be painted over until several years have elapsed and even then a sealer such as a metallic wood primer must be applied first. It is almost exclusively for exterior use.

Water-borne preservatives consist of such chemicals as salts of copper, mercury, sodium, and zinc dissolved in water, and are suitable for indoor and outdoor use. Treated timber may be painted or varnished, and may even be glued, but the adhesive to be used should be approved by the manufacturer. Preferably for interior use; although the constituents are poisonous, there is no risk of food contamination once the preservative is dry.

Organic solvents. These are based on pentachlorophenol, or copper or zinc naphthenates which are dissolved in white spirit, naphtha, or light petroleum distillates; these solvents evaporate quickly although there is sometimes a strong smell during application. They penetrate the wood better than other preservatives and so can be brushed on, or sprayed, but best results come from dipping or pressure impregnation.

In addition there are exterior stain finishes of several different kinds. They either leave a definite film on the surface or penetrate the surface layers of the wood. Although most give a matt or semi-matt finish, full gloss is available; some offer a range of colours and allow the wood grain to show through, while others are pigmented and give a completely opaque finish. Generally speaking, the more pigment such stains contain the longer their life; it also helps if the wood is first treated with a water-repellent preservative. A preservative incorporating the Madison formula (*q.v.*) can be used for Western Red Cedar.

Varnishes can also be used although it should be remembered that an initial application of four or five coats is required to give two years' protection; the surface should then be given two coats of varnish every year. A recent development has been the incorporation of ingredients which absorb the ultraviolet rays in daylight, which is one of the chief causes of surface breakdown.

As well as conventional varnishes, there is now a type called 'micro-porous' which is formulated to allow the timber to expand and contract although the surface film remains unbroken.

press An apparatus for pressing veneers, making flush doors, and manufacturing man-made boards. (See also: *hand press, multi-plate, vacuum press.*)

press bedstead An eighteenth century design of collapsible bed which could be folded back into a cupboard or mock chest of drawers when not in use.

press cupboard A cupboard fitted with drawers to contain linen and often with pegs on which clothes could hang; they seem to have become popular about 1550, and gradually developed into wardrobes.

pressure bar A metal bar fitted in a planing machine to hold the timber against the table and avoid chatter. The pressure bars are set in vertical slideways and are held by strong springs.

pressure pad A flat pad used with a belt sanding machine. It is used to press down on to the moving belt.

pricking Paper sheet used by the marquetry cutter to enable a design to be repeated. A series of fine needle holes is made close together all round the outline of the design. This is held over a sheet of paper and fine asphaltum powder dusted through the holes. The paper is then heated, the asphaltum powder leaving a permanent brown mark. Any number of exact replicas can be made in this way.

prie-dieu Early examples from Italy date back to the sixteenth century and consisted of a padded base to kneel on, with a backboard or shallow cupboard, surmounted by a shelf. A more ornate design was popular from about 1840, and was virtually a low-seated chair (on which one knelt) and a tall back with a shelf across the top; both seat and shelf were padded.

prima vera (*tabebuia donnellsmithii*) Yellowish-white timber with striped figure when quarter cut 31 lb (497 kg). Works and finishes well. Used for interior fittings, veneers, furniture.

prime Term applied to best quality timber.

priming Applied to the first coat of paint on woodwork, its function being to close the pores. It is

advisable to use the type recommended by the maker of the following undercoat and gloss paint.

princess post Short post used in a queen post roof truss.

Prince of Wales feathers Details often used in chair backs of the late eighteenth century, notably in Hepplewhite work. The splat was pierced and carved in the characteristic shape of the three feathers.

Prince of Wales Windsor chair A Windsor chair incorporating the Prince of Wales' feathers as a decorative feature in the splat.

prince's wood A term used in seventeenth and eighteenth centuries for Kingwood (*q.v.*).

principal The chief rafters of a roof truss.

print marking Term used in polishing in connection with soft French polish which fails to harden completely so that an impression is left on the surface by any object placed upon it for a few hours.

profile The cross-section of a moulding, but also more generally applied to the outline of any object.

profile box Templet used for marking the shoulders of moulded items such as handrails. It is of box-like form, the inside shaped to a reverse of the moulding, with square and sometimes angled ends.

prong chuck The chuck commonly used for between-centres turning. There is a centre point of circular section with a small gap at each side and two fangs bevelled on one side only. It may have either morse taper or screw fixing.

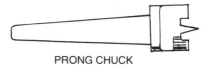

PRONG CHUCK

proof spirit (USA) The classification applied to mixtures of water and grain alcohol in equal proportions; thus 100 per cent proof comprises 50 per cent alcohol by volume, and 188 proof contains 94 per cent alcohol by volume.

pull Term often used in veneering to describe how veneer 'pulls' a panel hollow. Also applied to drawer handles.

pulley Used to transmit power in machines. They are of two main types; for flat belt and for V belt. The last named are generally used for small machines. Flat belt pulleys may be of metal or wood and are made in a wide range of sizes and widths. The split type of metal pulley has its advantages in that it can be added to the shaft without any dismantling of the machine. Pulleys of the V type are made with single, double, triple, and quadruple grooves There are also stepped pulleys with two or more sizes to enable speeds to be varied by passing the belt from one groove to another.

pull-over Process used in the cellulose finish. A pad of cotton waste, covered with wash leather, is damped with a pull-over liquid which has a mildly solvent action on nitro-cellulose. It has the effect of removing all irregularities in the finish. The term is also sometimes used in French polishing and refers to the use of the rubber with large circular or figure-of-eight movements to take out ridges or ropiness caused by working the rubber along the grain.

pulvenated frieze Another name for a barrel moulding *(q.v.)*.

pumice powder A fine powder in various grades used chiefly in a pounce bag in the French polishing process to take out rubber marks caused by the use of too wet a rubber. A little powder is sprinkled beneath the rag of the rubber, the latter being known as a grinder *(q.v.)*.

pummel Square part left on a turning. It is usually needed to enable mortises to be cut to receive rails.

pump screwdriver Name sometimes given to a spiral screwdriver *(q.v.)*.

punch (see *centre punch, nail punch*). Punches are also made in various patterns for embossing the background in some carved wood. The carver also files up special punches (usually from French nails) for finishing awkward recesses which would be difficult to cut entirely with carving tools.

puncheon A short upright timber used for supporting a roof or a platform: they were also used as roof supports in mines.

punch, handrail (see *handrail bolt and punch*).

punch, veneer Used in replacing blemished parts of veneer leaves, particularly woods with curly grains such as burrs. The cutting edge is of curved and often irregular shape and a cut is made through both the leaf and a piece of sound veneer in one cut and the parts interchanged.

PUNCH, VENEER

punky Term sometimes used to describe spongy wood or wood in early stages of decay.

purfling Narrow lines inlaid around the edges of the back of a violin.

Puritan (USA) A term applied to the seventeenth century furniture made by the early settlers.

purlin Beams parallel with the ridge plate of a roof and lying on the principal rafters. They carry the common rafters.

purpleheart *(peltogyne pubescens)* Hardwood of 62 lb (993 kg) from the West Indies and tropical South America. Pale brown when first cut but changing rapidly to vivid purple. Used for inlaying, fancy goods, turnery. Dries slowly with a tendency to split. Sometimes sold as amaranth, purple wood, or violet wood.

push block A notched or stepped block with handle. Used on the circular saw, planer, or spindle moulder to enable the end of wood to be passed over the cutters without danger to the hand. It varies in shape and details according to the work it has to do.

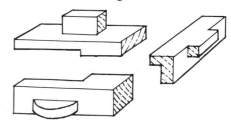

PUSH BLOCK

push drill One which revolves the drill by means of a reciprocating movement of the handle. Various sizes of drills can be fitted. (See *Archimedean drill.*)

push-pin A tool for inserting small nails such as veneer pins. It comprises a long tube fitted into a normal handle, and at the open end of the tube is a

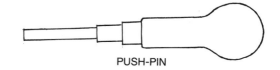

PUSH-PIN

spring-loaded plunger. The pin is inserted in the open end, head upwards, and when the handle is pressed down the pin is driven into the wood.

push stick   Wood strip with notched end to enable wood to be pushed in its entirety over the circular saw without the hand approaching closely to the saw. For the spindle moulder, the push stick frequently has a needle point or forked end. (See also *push block*.)

putti   (see *boys* and *crowns*).

putty   Used in glazing to hold glass in the rebate and for filling holes in wood to be painted. For polished cabinet work, the putty is coloured by the addition of dry pigment, burnt umber for dark oak, or red ochre for mahogany. Putty is usually bought ready made, but can be made from whiting and linseed oil well kneaded together. A small amount of gold size added when kneading makes a hard putty which is very suitable for glazing cabinets.

pycnanthus *(pycnanthus kombo)*   From West Africa, of 30 lb (481 kg). Featureless timber of greyish oatmeal shade. Liable to insect and fungal attack. Interior work generally.

pyinkado *(xylia dolabriformis)*   Timber from Burma, 62 lb (993 kg). One of the iron woods. Reddish brown, hard, and durable. Used for flooring, sleepers, and heavy constructional work.

pyinma   (see *benteak*).

pyrogallic acid   Sometimes used before fuming with ammonia. It gives a warmer shade and speeds up the process. Obtainable in crystal form.

pyrography   Method producing a design on wood by means of a hot needle or points. The wood is burnt or scorched. Various shapes of points can be fitted according to the effect required, some being flat for general shading.

quadrant   The quarter of a circle. The term is also applied to some fanlight stays, though the term is somewhat a misnomer in that the curve is invariably far less than a quarter-circle.

quadrant cellaret fitting   Seldom used today but found in some older sideboards. The quadrant fitting for bottles is fixed to the back of the door and opens with it.

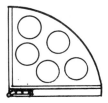

QUADRANT
CELLARETTE FITTING

quadrant drawer   Small drawer, sometimes found in eighteenth century writing desks, toilet tables, etc. The parts are dovetailed together (lap or through according to position) and pivoted at the right-angled corner.

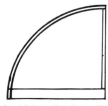

QUADRANT DRAWER

quadrant hinge   Hinges having a stay of quarter-circle shape which enables it to open up to, but no more than, 90 deg. Used chiefly for secretaire flaps. Made both right and left hand. It can be used only in positions where there is clearance for the stay or when the wood can be cut away to receive it.

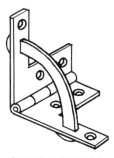

QUADRANT HINGE

quadrant iron   Seldom seen today, but once a feature of cylinder fall desks. Invariably has to be specially made to suit the radius of the fall. The pivot plate needs carefully centreing to ensure correct movements.

quadrant stay One of quarter-circle shape, used to limit the movement of and to support a secretaire or similar fall. Some patterns have a spring in the plate which has to be pressed before the flap can be moved. The side of the wood has to be channelled to receive the quadrant and this must be struck from the same centre as the latter.

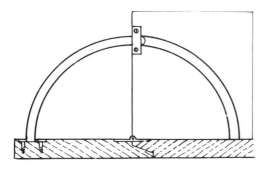

QUADRANT STAY

quadrilateral Plane figure with four sides — square, rectangle, rhombus, rhomboid, trapezoid, trapezium (*q.v.*).

Quaker chair (see *round back chair*).

quanin (see *pearl essence*).

quartered Term applied to a log which has been sawn into quarters with radial cuts. The resulting figure of the wood is affected by it, especially those woods which have pronounced medullary rays. The last named are radial to the log and are fully exposed.

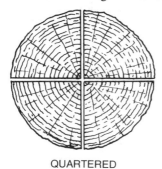

QUARTERED

quartered panel Veneered panel in which the four consecutive leaves of veneer are laid in decorative form.

quarter-girth Term used in round measurement of a log. It is assumed that the log is square, not round, and one-quarter of the girth taken as one side

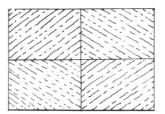

QUATERED PANEL

of the square. The girth is taken at the middle of the log to allow for taper. Thus if the girth is 48 in (1219 mm) the square is taken as having 12 in (305 mm) sides giving 144 sq in (92903 sq mm). This, multiplied by the log length, gives the cubic contents.

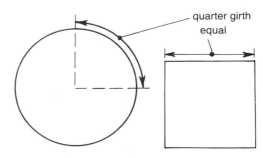

QUARTER-GIRTH

quarterings A term applied variously. (1) It denotes square stuff of scantling size used for studs of a lathe and plaster partition. (2) Similar stuff cut from a plank or deal. (3) For rough field or hill side fencing, round stuff quartered for the stobs or posts.

quarter-round Sometimes applied to a moulding of quarter-round shape. Alternatively known as a quadrant moulding.

quarter-sawn A term applied to boards sawn radially from the log. In the case of beech, oak, and woods with marked medullary rays (*q.v.*), the figure is prominent since the cuts are parallel with the rays.

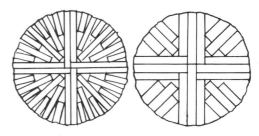

QUARTER-SAWN

quarter-sliced Knife-cut veneer which is sliced radially. In any quartered timber only a few leaves are truly quarter-sliced, the figure lessening as the cuts run across rather than parallel with the medullary rays. (See also *quarter-sawn.*)

quarter space landing A landing which is half the overall width of a dog-legged staircase or the width of a flight in an open-newel staircase. A quarter turn of winders is also shown in the illustration.

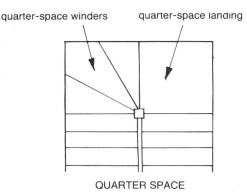

quarter-space winders quarter-space landing

QUARTER SPACE

quartetto tables A nest of four tables, each graduated in size so that they fitted, or nested, into each other. The most popular design was for tables with trestle ends comprising two pillars set into a foot block at each end; stretchers joined the pillars of each table. The period 1760 to 1840 was their hey-day. They were also called 'quarto' tables. (See *nest of tables.*)

quaruba, red (*vochysia* species) Hardwood from the Amazon district of 32 lb (513 kg) used in general joinery and for construction purposes. Light pinkish-brown, whitish in the sap. Tends to be woolly in the grain and not a specially good polishing timber.

quatrefoil Ornamental feature of Gothic work consisting of four part-circles contained within a

QUATREFOIL

circle. Sometimes the 'points' formed by the circular shapes are cusped in the form of carved leafwork. A simpler alternative is a chamfered cusping, the point being cut away at an angle.

Quebec birch The American variety of birch from Canada. (See also *birch.*)

quebracho (*schinopsis lorentzii*) Hardwood from South America of 72 lb (1153 kg), used in heavy structural work, bridge building, and for sleepers. Light red and darkening on exposure. Resists decay. Extremely hard and has to be pre-bored for nailing.

Queen post roof One in which there are two main posts to the truss. (See also *king post roof truss.*)

Queensland walnut (*endiandra palmerstonii*) Hardwood of 46 lb (737 kg) from Queensland used for furniture, veneers, joinery, etc. Fine and even in the grain but difficult to work as tools blunt rapidly. Takes stain and polish well. Has rather unpleasant smell.

quill bit Alternative name for a shell bit (*q.v.*).

quilted figure Refers to the rich figuring found in some woods, giving an undulating appearance.

quirk A narrow, flat recessed member of a moulding.

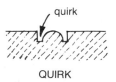

quirk

QUIRK

quirked bead (see *bead*).

quirk router An almost obsolete tool used chiefly by coach builders for working a quirk or square recess around a curved edge.

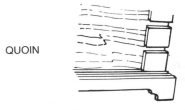

QUOIN

quoin An architectural motif sometimes used on the corners of highboys and longcase clocks; it was often 'rusticated' (*q.v.*).

R

rabbet (USA) Corresponds to British rebate *(q.v.)*.

rabbit skin glue Frequently used by the gilder in making gesso *(q.v.)*.

race knife Hooked knife for marking the cubic contents of logs.

racking Side pressure, first in one direction then the other, causing a carcase or framework to go out of square.

rack saw Large circular saw with moving table for the log.

radial arm router This consists essentially of a beam which is pivoted at its centre and free to slide through it, and it is also able (by being pivoted) to cover a given circular area from either of its ends. The cutter moves around the work and the machine is suitable for large panels, door edges, table tops, etc. In practice, the templet is fixed to a base and is followed round by a roller mounted on, or above, the cutter; contact is maintained by hand-pressure. Close stair strings can also be routed, using a suitable templet.

radial square Used on circular work to mark radial lines.

RADIAL SQUARE

radial step (see *winder*).

radio-frequency heating (RF) More exactly, high-frequency electronic or dielectric heating which requires an electrolyte to be included in the adhesive. It is a method of heating a glue line to shorten the setting time. It is only suitable for industrial use and is commonly employed for furniture assembly.

radius rod Used for marking or testing circular arcs. In addition to uses in woodwork, it is often made by the carpenter for use by the bricklayer in making semi-circular openings.

radial In timber language that which pertains to the medullary rays, these being in the nature of radii.

A radial section of a tree is a vertical section passing through the centre. Radial cutting is approximately parallel with the rays and at right-angles with the annual rings.

radial arm A vertical arm fitted to a power-fed machine. It extends down to a gearbox with variable feed.

radial arm saw Circular saw directly attached to the motor and underslung beneath an arm upon which it travels. The arm can be raised or lowered, and can turn through any angle. The saw itself can also be pivoted. Used chiefly for cross-cutting, mitreing, compound angle cutting, etc.

radial shake One which starts at the outside of a log and runs radially towards the centre.

RADIAL SHAKE

rafter The sloping timber of a roof running from eaves to ridge. (See also *jack rafter*).

rafter shoe Metal socket fitted to the foot of the principal rafter of a roof.

rail The horizontal member of a door, gate, panelling, or other framework. Also applies to the horizontal members in carcase work; e.g., top rails, bearer rails, drawer rails, apron rails, etc.

raised-head screw One which has a counter-sunk head but with slightly domed top. Often used with a screw cup. Also called a 'mushroom head' screw.

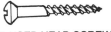

RAISED HEAD SCREW

raised lid Any lid having a superimposed panel. Sometimes it is merely an applied panel; in other cases a moulding may be planted on the lid proper, and a panel fitted to this.

raised panel (see *fielded panel*).

rake   In furniture this refers to the backward slope of a chair back.

raker tooth   A tooth in a combination circular saw which does not reach to the periphery of the other teeth, its purpose being to clear the sawdust. (See *circular saw*.)

raking   An item, such as a moulding, pitched out of the vertical.

raking moulding   One which slopes at an angle to the horizontal but with horizontal returns. It is often found in the pediment of a classical door or above the cornice of a bookcase.

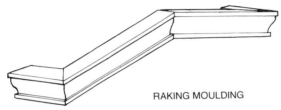

RAKING MOULDING

raking riser   One which slopes inwards on stairs to give greater foot space. Sometimes used in winders.

raking shore   Sloping shore to support a wall. Lower end rests on the ground, and the upper end is bedded against a wall piece which spreads the thrust over a large area.

ramin   (*gonystylus* species) Hardwood from Sarawak of 42 lb (673 kg). Used for furniture making, plywood, and light structural work. Light yellow colour, darkening slightly with age. Mild working and somewhat coarse textured. Splinters can cause irritation.

ramp   The vertical curve of a handrail at the newel post.

ram pin   Tool used for driving panel pins, etc., in awkward places. It consists of a spring-loaded tube, within which is a magnetised steel ram which prevents the pin from falling out. Pressure on the handle drives the pin into the wood. (See also *pushpin*.)

random widths   Timber bought in bulk, the widths of which vary.

ranging down   Bringing the teeth of a circular saw to the same height so that all cut equally. It is done by pressing a piece of old grindstone against the revolving teeth until all are just touched. The stone is held flat on the sawing table.

rasp   Tool rather like file but with separate projecting teeth. Used mainly for the preliminary finishing of shaped edges. Usual type is half-round. It removes waste quickly but leaves a coarse finish. Generally followed by the file. (See also *file, float, riffler, shaper*.)

rata   (*metrosideros robusta*) New Zealand timber seldom found in this country.

ratchet brace   Brace with a device which leaves the bit stationary when the handle is turned in one direction. Its advantage is that only part of the sweep need be used when working in a restricted position. It is also useful when boring a large hole in a hard wood in that only the most powerful part of the movement need be used. (See also *brace*.)

ratchet screwdriver   One in which there can be positive drive in one direction only, the blade remaining stationary when the handle is resolved the other way. It can also be locked for use as a normal screwdriver. Its chief advantage is in hingeing a door in that the latter can be supported by one hand, the other being merely rotated back and forth without the grip on the tool handle being altered. (See also *spiral ratchet screwdriver*.)

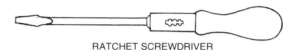

RATCHET SCREWDRIVER

rate of feed   The speed in feet (or metres) per minute that the wood passes through a machine.

rat-tail file   A light round file tapered towards one end like a rat's tail, hence the name. It is used for enlarging holes, filing edges of hollow-shaped parts, making tapered holes for the pegs of musical instruments, etc.

rauli beech   (*nothofagus procera*) Hardwood from southern Chile of 38 lb (609 kg) used for furniture making, turnery, etc. Light red-brown colour, fine textured, and of straight grain. Slight tendency to warp in air drying.

raw sienna   Powder pigment used in tinting plaster of Paris when used as a filler.

raw umber   Light brown pigment used in tinting plaster of Paris when used as a filler.

rays   (see *medullary rays*).

reading chair One in which the reader sits astride facing the chair back, his arms resting on the top. A book rest is provided, and there are sometimes pivoted trays which can be pulled out from beneath the yoke, these holding pencils and other small items. In some cases a sconce for a candle is fitted. Used fairly early in the eighteenth century and later. Also called a 'cockfighting' or 'horseman's' chair.

reamer For enlarging a hole. The half-round type gives a cleaner finish for wood. It may also be used to make a hole taper-shaped to receive a bung or spigot. Also known as a rimer. (See also *taper bit*.)

rebate A recess worked on the edge of a piece of wood over part of its thickness to form a bed for another part. Although widely used in Britain, it is a corruption of the correct word 'rabbet' *(q.v.)*.

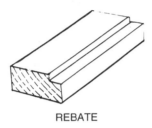

REBATE

rebating block (see *spindle moulder*).

rebate plane One in which the cutter reaches to both sides. Cutter may be square or skew, the latter cutting more easily and tending to keep the plane pressed sideways into the rebate. It is pitched at 50 deg. Originally made in widths from ¼in (6 mm) up to 2 in (51 mm) but available only in a few sizes today. There is also the carriage maker's rebate plane which is in metal, is adjustable, and fitted with a back iron. (See also *T rebate plane and fillister plane*.)

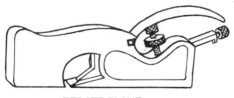

REBATE PLANE

rebating table Extension at the side of an edger (planer) on which the wood rests during rebating.

receding cornice One which slopes backwards rather than projects.

recessed panel One which is set back from the general face of the surface. Usually the term is applied to a panel cut in the solid wood.

reciprocating saw A large saw which cuts horizontally through a log; it consists of a wide blade which moves backwards and forwards.

rectangle Four-sided figure with opposite sides equal in length and all angles right angles.

red deal A loose term to express red Baltic pine (Scots pine) cut into recognised deal dimensions.

red ochre Red pigment added to plaster of Paris to tint the latter when used as a filler for mahogany and other red-toned woods.

red oil Used to enhance the colour of mahogany. Originally it was made by steeping bruised alkanet root *(q.v.)* in linseed oil but today oil-soluble red aniline dye is used.

red sanders *(pterocarpus santalinus)* Hardwood of 70 lb (1121 kg) from southern India, used for turnery, inlaying, etc. Deep red colour sometimes known as ruby wood.

red tulip oak *(argyodendron perastal)* Hardwood from Queensland of 45 to 58 lb (721 to 929 kg). Used for veneers, bentwood, and decorative purposes.

redwood The pine exported from the Baltic. More generally known as red Baltic pine, or (in this country) Scots pine. Weight 26 lb (417 kg). Used in all branches of joinery, carpentry, and for kitchen furniture, etc. (See also *sequoia*.)

red zebra *(melanorrhoea* species) Hardwood from India, Burma, and Malaya. Little has reached this country, and it is used locally for bridge and other construction work. Timber is dark red with yellow and sometimes black streaks. Sometimes known as rengas or Borneo rosewood.

Reed and Prince screw (USA) Corresponds to British recessed head screw *(q.v.)* This is similar to the Phillips screw *(q.v.)* but each type requires its own screwdriver. The Reed and Prince screw has straight, pointed walls between the slots while the Phillips has

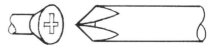

REED & PRINCE SCREW

bevelled walls. As regards screwdrivers, the Reed and Prince has a sharp, pointed end; on the other hand, the Phillips has a blunt, shallow-angle end.

reeds or reeding   A series of beads worked on the face of a feature such as a pilaster or around the edge of a table top. The reeds are half-round in section.

refectory table   One of the earliest types of dining table, the name originating in its association with the meals or 'refections' of monastic days. Constructed on the lines of a high bench, the earliest examples had heavy solid ends connected by a stout stretcher. The ends were frequently mounted on massive shoes.

reflex hinges   Lift-off hinges often used for the wing mirrors of a dressing table. Made right and left hand.

registered chisel   Heavily-built chisel with metal ferrules at both ends of the handle, and sometimes with leather washer beneath the shoulder. Made in sizes from $\frac{1}{4}$ in (6 mm) up to $1\frac{1}{2}$ in (37 mm) Used in heavy chopping work.

REGISTERED CHISEL

reglet   Small square moulding or fillet. (See *list*.)

regulator   Used by the upholsterer to regulate or even-out stuffing, particularly when stitching an edge to give shape to the upholstery. Sizes vary from 8 in (203 mm) to 12 in (305 mm).

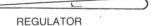

REGULATOR

regulator clocks   These clocks were originally designed so that clock makers could use them as standard timekeepers against which other clocks could be checked, and so were fitted with special types of pendulums which allowed for change in temperature and humidity. However, two popular designs evolved, namely the 'Laterndluhr' or 'Vienna' regulator and the 'Biedermeir' regulator, both of which are used today as decorative domestic clocks.

rejects   Pieces of timber or worked parts that fall below the required standard.

relief   Generally applied to wood carving, and referring to the depth to which the carving is taken. Also used in relation to a fret or other planted-on ornament. (See *alto-relievo, bas-relief, mezzo-relievo*.)

relief carving   Ornament and detail projected from the background. It is said to be in high relief when the detail projects more than half its natural circumference; low relief when the recessing is shallow.

reliquary chest   A chest used during the early Medieval period to contain the remains of King or Queen.

relishing   A term sometimes applied to haunching *(q.v.)*.

remouthing   Applied to a wood plane the mouth of which has become enlarged from repeated truing of the sole. A piece of hardwood is let into the latter to diminish the mouth size.

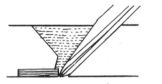

RE-MOUTHING

rengas   Alternative name for red zebra *(q.v.)*.

rent table   Similar in style to a drum table *(q.v.)* but having drawers in the drum top; either seven for the days of the week, or twelve for the months of the year. Often a saucer-like depression was incorporated in the centre of the top to receive money. They appeared about 1760 and were widely used by land agents and rent collectors during the late eighteenth and early nineteenth century.

rep   A fine cord-like material used as a cover in upholstery.

repair plates   Sometimes used in mending broken furniture and other woodwork. Most good repairers

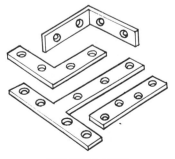

REPAIR PLATES

avoid them when possible, but they are sometimes unavoidable. When used on furniture they should never be visible, and should always be recessed flush.

reredos A screen behind the alter in a cathedral or church.

re-saw To rip into smaller sizes wood which has already been converted from the log.

resin glue (synthetic) Used widely in the wood-working trades generally. Chief types are:

phenol-formaldehyde. The hot-pressing type needs a thermostatically controlled press. The cold-setting glue is critical in application. Both are used in trade workshops only.

urea-formaldehyde. Available for both hot and cold application. The latter is the type for the small user. It is available in various forms. One type consists of a thick syrup which is the glue proper, and a hardener. The syrup remains liquid until brought into contact with the hardener. Various hardeners are available: fast, medium, and slow. Temperature largely affects the rate of setting, however, heat accelerating it. As the syrup remains usable for about three months only, the glue is also supplied in powder form, and if kept in an airtight container will remain usable for a year or more. When mixed with water it becomes the syrup glue already mentioned. Another form of powdered glue already contains the hardener, and needs only to be mixed with water.

polyvinyl-acetate glue A cold-application glue in the form of a white liquid, used as it is without a hardener. In common with other resin glues, it is stain-free, but some glues turn a brown colour when in contact with certain woods.

resorcinol-formaldehyde resin A glue used for work exposed to damp, and of great durability. Capable of withstanding immersion in boiling water. Can be used for wood, asbestos, rubber, plastics, and porcelain. More costly than resin glues.

resorcinol-formaldehyde (RF) Adhesive. (See *resin glue (synthetic.)*

respond One of a pair of pilasters.

rest Horizontal bar on which the tool rests in turning.

restoration The repair and/or renewal of a piece of furniture or woodwork, having regard to the need to avoid faking; also materials such as glues and finishes

used must be reversible, that is capable of being removed at any time without damage to the piece.

resurfacing an oilstone Necessary when the surface wears out of true. Natural stones can generally be trued by rubbing on a piece of flat paving stone or marble, using a mixture of silver sand and water as an abrasive. For artificial stones it is necessary to substitute carborundum powder for sand.

return A length of applied moulding which is continued on to an adjoining surface, as a rule at right angles. It also refers to the end of a length of moulding which is worked to the same contour as the moulding itself. In this case it is known as 'returned at the ends in the solid'.

reveal The side of an opening in a wall for window or door, between the frame and the outer surface.

reverse ogee (see *cyma-reversa*).

reversible hinge One which opens both ways and used mainly for a screen. The centres between the pins must be equal to or slightly greater than the thickness of the wood, otherwise the hinge will bind.

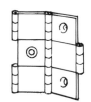

REVERSIBLE HINGE

reviver Used to restore a faded and dull polished surface. The following are effective:
(a) One part linseed oil, one part vinegar.
(b) Equal parts linseed oil, vinegar, and methylated spirit.
(c) Four parts linseed oil, one part terebine, 12 parts vinegar.

revolving bookcase One which is pivoted on a centre upright. The bookcase portion is boxed out around the upright and can be revolved. (See *bookcases.*)

revolving bracket Short length of wood cut into the top rail of a table and free to be twisted so that it supports a iight flap. It rotates on an iron pin (often a screw) the inner end bearing beneath the top. The ends are cut at an angle to give clearance.

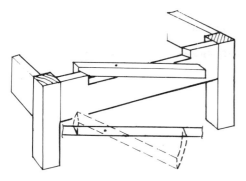

REVOLVING BRACKET

revolving centre   Back centre of a lathe which revolves with the work.

REVOLVING CENTRE

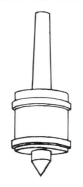

revolving chair action   Made of heavy iron with ball-bearing plate and cross-shaped plate. The former is fixed beneath the seat and the latter to the legs. Smooth in action, it takes apart for cleaning, etc. Used chiefly for piano stools and office chairs.

revolving door   One having four wings which are free to rotate together on a common centre. The whole thing turns in a shaped framework so that, no matter what the position, two wings always close the aperture, so avoiding all draught. The wings can be also be folded back flat against each other when through ventilation is needed in hot weather.

rewa-rewa *(knightia excelsa)*   New Zealand timber of 45 lb (721 kg) used for interior fitments and furniture. Dark red colour.

rhomboid   Figure with unequal adjacent sides but equal opposite sides. Opposite angles are equal but not right angles.

rhombus   Geometrical figure with equal sides and opposite angles equal but not right angles.

rhus vernicifera   This is the lac tree, which is a member of the Sumach family. 14- and 15-year-old trees are tapped with horizontal incisions in the bark, and the sap which exudes is the basis of true lacquer. When exposed to the air, it gradually turns black in colour. The lac is very toxic and should not be allowed to touch the bare skin. Incidentally, the tree grows well in southern England but is usually confined to an arboretum because of its toxicity.

rib   Refers loosely to any constructional member used in shaped work.

riband back   The back of a Chippendale chair fretted and carved in imitation of knotted and interlaced ribbon.

ribbing   A sort of rough spiral effect caused when turning long, slender work. Generally due to the wood bouncing up over the tool edge. Often the only cure is the use of a steady *(q.v.), though altering the rpm of the lathe sometimes helps.*

ribbon and leaf   Decorative motif frequently used by carvers in the eighteenth century for the enrichment of table edgings, etc.

RIBBON-AND-LEAF

ribbon and stick carving   Repetition carving of a moulding in imitation of a ribbon wrapped spiral-wise around a stick.

RIBBON-ON-STICK

RIB PANEL

161

rib panel A carved panel popular in the late fifteenth and early sixteenth centuries. The edges of the ribs were often ornamented with leafwork, cusps, etc.

riffler A form of bent file for finishing special curves and shapes in wood where an ordinary straight file would be unsuitable. Rifflers are made in various shapes and sections.

RIFFLER

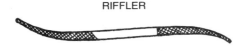

rift sawn Another term for quarter sawn *(q.v.)*.

rim Circular, elliptical, or kidney-shaped structure forming the top part of a table to which the legs are bridle jointed. It may be built up brick fashion (A) or laminated (B). The outer surface is veneered.

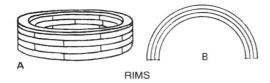

RIMS

rimer (see *reamer*).

rim lock Name given to a room door lock which screws upon the lock rail with the box staple sunk into the jamb post in alignment. It is made in a variety of sizes, and R and L hand; also reversible. To find which lock is required stand outside the room. The closing stile indicates the hand required. When a door opens outwards a 'reverse' bolt lock should be used. In some locks the bolt can be reversed.

rimu *(dacrydium cupressinum)* Softwood from New Zealand, used in building and furniture making. Rich red-brown colour. Not often exported to this country.

ring centre Used as a back centre when turning between centres. (See *centres.*)

ring fence This is not only a safety feature but also a guide when profiling mouldings or shaping edges on a spindle moulder. It consists of a steel ring, the hole being eccentric, and it can be fixed at any height in relation to the table and at any position near the spindle. It can be used in conjunction with a templet temporarily fixed to the work, which is guided by the contact of the templet with the ring fence. The set-up has the advantage that if a heavy moulding is being worked it can be fed up to the wider side of the ring,

which reduces the depth of the cut; by subsequently bringing the work round to the thinner part of the ring, the cut will gradually be increased to the maximum, thus obviating any chance of a 'kick-back' *(q.v.)* occurring.

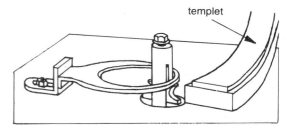

templet

RING FENCE

ring porous Term used in timber identification. When the end section of a ring-porous wood is examined the pores of the early wood are large and are formed into a clearly defined ring, one or more pores wide. The change between early and late wood is abrupt. (See also *diffuse porous.*)

RING POROUS

ring saw Also called a 'hole' saw. Used in a drilling machine or a portable electric drill. It consists of a small toothed blade bent into a circle which revolves on a central twist drill; its chief advantage is that it can cut larger holes than either drills or bits. It is also available with a disc mounted on the central twist drill; the disc is grooved to take several sizes of saws and the tool is then called a 'nest' of ring saws.

ring shake (see *cup shake*).

rings (see *annual rings*).

ripping Sawing lengthwise in the direction of the grain.

ripping chisel Used to remove old tacks when stripping off worn upholstery, the edge being placed against the tack head and the handle struck with the hammer.

ripping fence An adjustable straight guide fitted to a circular saw to enable cuts parallel to an edge to be made. It is often faced with wood.

ripple Figuring in some timbers giving the appearance of an undulating surface. The markings run across the grain and the effect is often known as fiddle back figure *(q.v.)*. It occurs in such woods as sycamore and sapele.

ripple mouldings Usually these were made in ebony or an ebonised hardwood. The surface of the moulding was chiselled into a series of shallow facets which reflected the light to give a ripple effect. The style was popular in the middle of the seventeenth century, particularly in Germany, Holland, and Portugal. In Germany it was known as *wellenschrank*, and in Portugal as *tremidos*.

rip saw Handsaw or circular saw blade used for heavy ripping with the grain. Teeth are large — four-five points per inch (25.4mm) — and they are filed straight across so that they present a series of chisel-like edges to the wood. Ripsaw teeth of circular saws are filed as at (A) for softwood, and as at (B) for hardwood.

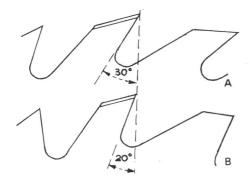

RIP SAW TEETH

rise The vertical height between the top surfaces of two adjoining steps of a staircase.

rise and fall Refers to the movement of a circular saw which can be adjusted in height in relation to the table. Either the saw itself or the table may be made to adjust vertically.

riser The vertical member of a step.

rising butt Form of helical knuckle hinge which lifts the door as it is opened, enabling it to clear a carpet or uneven floor. Made right and left hand. To tell which hand is required stand outside the door. If hinges are to the right then right-hand hinges are needed. When fitted to new work the top rebate of the casing is sloped to give clearance. When fitted to an existing square rebate casing the corner of the door facing the rebate needs to be rounded to give clearance. Also called a screw-butt hinge.

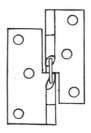

RISING BUTT

rising sun A favourite decorative motif on both British and American furniture of the late eighteenth century. It represents a half-sun with divergent rays; it is occasionally called a 'setting sun'.

rive To split wood along the natural line of its grain as distinct from sawing it. Fencing timbers in oak are sometimes riven and are stronger than when sawn in that there is no short grain.

rivets Used for pivoting card table, ironing table, and deck chair legs, etc. They may be round head or flat head They are burred over washers and are usually of copper. Various lengths and thicknesses are made. Bifurcated or split rivets are for fixing leather and sometimes plywood.

riving knife A steel blade fitted behind a circular saw to prevent the sawn wood closing into the saw and so jamming it. The knife is also known as a 'river'. It should be slightly thicker than the gauge of the saw. The term is also applied to a tool used in riving or cleaving wood for fencing or laths.

roan A sheepskin used in an upholstery cover. It has not the durability of morocco but is cheaper, and is sometimes used on the outsides of chairs where wear is not so great.

robinia *(robinia pseudoacacia)* The accepted name for the acacia, a hardwood of 40-50lb (641-801kg) from Europe and America. A strong, durable timber, but the tree is grown more for its ornamental qualities than for its timber.

rocker Curved rail at the bottom of a rocking chair or cradle.

rocker-arm jigsaw   Usually used for fretwork. The arms holding the saw-blade are pivoted near the back giving the saw a reciprocating movement.

rod   (see *skid*).

roey   Striped figure in some hardwoods when quarter-sawn. It shows as alternate strips of light and dark wood.

roll   A firm edging formed in upholstery by stitching right through and pulling tight. In carpentry it is member rounded at the top and fixed to a roof. Zinc or lead is dressed over it.

roller feed   Applied to machines in which the wood is fed through by means of rollers.

roller gauge   One having a sharp-edged wheel in place of the usual marker or cutter. Makes light marks on wood, but it is doubtful whether it is as effective as the marking or cutting gauge.

ROLLER GAUGE

roll-top desk   A form of writing secretaire with pedestal ends and a tambour rolling shutter which closes over the upper pigeon hole fitment. A spring closing four-levered lock is usually fitted.

roll-top desk lock   A spring lock fitted to the tambour of a desk. It has latches which project sideways and engage with a metal plate recessed into the writing top.

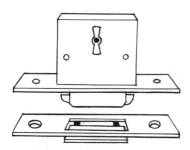

ROLL-TOP DESK LOCK

Roman spindles   These were used in the backs of Windsor chairs and usually had baluster-turned shaping with additional rings.

romayne panel   A carved representation of a male head (often that of Erasmus) used as a medallion in the centre of chest panels in the sixteenth century throughout Europe. Popular in England during the reign of Henry VIII.

rood beam   The beam in a cathedral or a church which supports the rood, which is a large wooden crucifix with the attendant figures of the Virgin Mary and St John.

roofing nail   One with a twist along its length for holding corrugated iron or plastic sheeting, $2\frac{1}{2}$ in (63 mm) long. It is driven in with the hammer and turns as it passes into the wood. The large head gives a wide grip over the metal.

roofing square   (see *square, roofing*).

room divider   Tall item generally used to separate the dining area of a room from the lounge portion. As it is seen from both sides it has to be finished equally well on both sides.

rope moulding   (see *cable moulding*).

rose countersink   For use on brass. Sometimes made with wood handle, but usually in bit form for use with the brace, or with plain shank for fitting in the drill chuck. Woodworkers often need the rose countersink for enlarging the countersinking of hinges and other fittings. (See also *countersink*.)

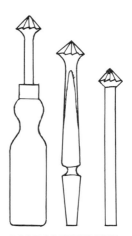

ROSE COUNTERSINK

rose mahogany   *(dysoxylum fraseranum)*   Hardwood of 50 lb (801 kg) from New South Wales. Also known as Australian mahogany. Close, interlocked grain, rich red in colour. Difficult to work owing to the presence of gummy veins.

rose pink Pigment in powder form sometimes added to plaster of Paris when used as a filler for mahogany.

rosette Patera carved in the form of a conventional rose.

rosin Also spelt 'resin'. A natural gum resulting from the distillation of pure turpentine from pine trees. It can be obtained either as a coarse powder or in lump form. Used to harden wax polishes, or as an ingredient in hard stopping. (See *beaumontage*.)

rosewood (*dalbergia*, various) A heavy dark-coloured wood at one time prized for the highest-class furniture and for pianoforte cases. Owing to the restricted supply it is now rarely seen except in veneer form. The finest quality was the Brazilian known as Rio. The East Indies and British Honduras also produce timber listed as rosewood.

rot (see *dry rot*, *wet rot*).

rotary-cut veneer As the name implies, these veneers are sliced from the round log in a continuous strip, from the outer circumference to the pith, a fixed cutter being fed by degrees to the slowly revolving log. The cutting blade is parallel to the wood and the veneers are cut to a precise thickness. The grain of the resulting veneer is of a wild and uninteresting character. The method is extensively used for plywood manufacture. (See also *half-rotary slicing*.)

rotary cutting (see *rotary-cut veneers*).

rotary miller bit Used for mortising, grooving, and sometimes rebating. It can cut both in the direction of its length and laterally. The ends of the mortise are necessarily rounded and have to be finished square by hand unless the sides of the tenon can be correspondingly rounded. (See *oscillating bit mortiser*.)

ROTARY MILLER BIT

rottenstone (see *tripoli powder*).

rough Unplaned timber direct from the saw.

roughing out The preliminary removal of the waste when carving, working a moulding, turning, or cutting a shape.

round-back chair Victorian bedroom chair with open rounded back. Seat is usually caned but sometimes has stuff-over upholstery. (See *Quaker chair*).

round, carving in the Carving that has to be viewed from all sides as in a bust, animal, or figure carving, and in some types of ornament carving.

round file (see *file*).

round-head screw One having a rounded top with cylindrical shoulder beneath.

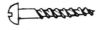

ROUND-HEAD SCREW

round-nose turning chisel Flat chisel with rounded edge sometimes used for flat hollows in turning, but not widely used.

ROUND-NOSE TURNING CHISEL

round plane One with rounded sole to plane a hollow moulding. It has no fence and is held at the required angle by judgment. Usually it is started on a chamfer. Made in many sizes and degrees of curvature, often in pair with hollow planes (*q.v.*).

round step (see *bullnose step*).

round timber The log before conversion. Tree tops and branches of serviceable size are sometimes termed 'round wood'.

rounded edge The edge, such as that of a stair tread or furniture top, which has been rounded to a half circle. (See *nosing*.)

rounded-end tenoner (see *tenoners*).

roundel Any item of circular shape, but more generally referring to a small round carved or inlaid decorative panel, or to a round window.

rounding cradle A wooden appliance used when it is necessary to plane a flat surface on a rounded piece of wood, or to round a piece of wood. Also handy when making triangular strips such as carpet rods or corner blocking fillets. The cradle consists of two pieces of wood glued and screwed together, the top edges planed at 45 deg to form a 90 deg trough. A

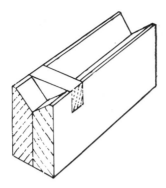

ROUNDING CRADLE

wood stop is fitted at one end, and the cradle is used against the bench stop or held in the vice.

routers (see under individual headings as, *hand, overhead,* and *plunge*).

router (hand) The wood type is sometimes known as an old woman's tooth because of the tooth-like cutter. The latter is set at a high angle and scrapes rather than cuts. The metal type, one of which is shown, has a cranked cutter which chisels out the waste wood. It has an adjustable fence, and the cutters, ¼ in (6 mm) and ½ in (12 mm) wide, also smoothing cutter, are adjustable by screw feed. In addition, there is an adjustable shoe for closing the throat, and a gauge for regulating the thickness of the shaving. Routers are used for making channels in wood for housing the ends of shelves, etc., the side of

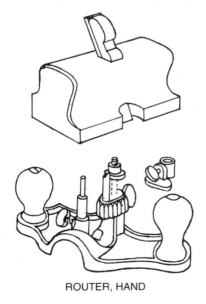

ROUTER, HAND

the grooves being cut beforehand with the tenon saw. The router serves to cut away the waste wood to an exact depth. The metal type is also made with closed mouth.

router cutters These are used in routing machines and are, preferably, tungsten-carbide-tipped (TCT) although they are also obtainable in high speed steel (HSS). They are made in a very wide variety of shapes and sizes; among the most widely used are single flutes (for profiling), double flutes (for recessing), moulding cutters, dovetailing bits, rebating cutters, panel cutters for cleaning up the edges of panels, and shaper cutters.

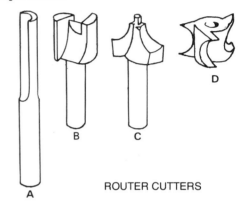

ROUTER CUTTERS

routing Forming a recessed surface with the router (*q.v.*).

rpm Revolutions per minute of a machine or motor. To find pulley sizes the rpm of the motor and desired rpm of the machine must be known. The ratio between these gives the relative sizes of the pulleys. If a motor turns at 1,450 rpm and the machine is required to run at 2,000 rpm the ratio is

$$\frac{1,450 : 29,}{2,000 : 40} \text{ say } \frac{3}{4}$$

Consequently the motor needs a pulley of 4 in (102 mm) diam and the machine one of 3 in (76 mm) or any other two sizes having the same ratio. When the motor already has a pulley and it is required to know the size of the machine pulley the calculation is:

$$\frac{\text{rpm motor} \times \text{diam motor pulley}}{\text{rpm machine}}$$

When the machine already has a pulley and it is required to know the motor pulley size the calculation is:

$$\frac{\text{rpm machine} \times \text{diam machine pulley}}{\text{rpm motor}}$$

rubbed finish   A semi-matt, smooth finish obtained by rubbing the surface with pumice powder or the finest grade of wet-and-dry abrasive paper.

rubbed joint   Butt joint in which two pieces are glued together side by side to make up width. There is no mechanical shaping, the glue alone holding the parts together. Joints up to about 3 ft (1 metre) can be planed to a true fit, and, after glueing, rubbed together (hence the name). When testing, the parts are swivelled together one above the other, and there should be friction at the ends. Longer joints are planed slightly hollow and one or more cramps put on at the middle. Alternative names are slayped or glued joints *(q.q.v.)*. (See also *stacking joints*).

rubber   Used in French polishing, and consisting of unbleached wadding with a covering rag such as fine-grained linen.

rubber-based adhesives   Also known as contact adhesives. Generally used for fixing a plastic panel to a wood base. Both surfaces are coated and left for a time which varies with the make. When the two are brought together the hold is immediate (although thixotropic types allow a short time for adjustments), and the position of the one in relation to the other cannot be altered. Sometimes used for small veneered parts and for repair work over which it is difficult to apply cramps. (See *nitrile rubber.*)

rubberised abrasives   These comprise grinding wheels, discs, and blocks, and are made of silicon-carbide particles embedded in neoprene rubber. They are resistant to oil and water and, it is claimed, they will not harden or soften with age.

rubber, moulding   Slip of wood worked to a reverse of a moulding, and used for cleaning up the latter. Abrasive paper is wrapped around it and held with the fingers. (See *moulding rubber.*)

rubber webbing   Used in place of spiral or tension springs. Made in widths of $^3/_4$ in (19 mm), $1^3/_8$ in (35 mm), $1^1/_2$ in (38 mm), 2 in (51 mm), and $2^1/_4$ in (58 mm). Fixed with either tacks or steel or wire clips. Also called 'resilient webbing.'

rubbing compound   (USA) An abrasive in paste form used for rubbing down lacquered surfaces which is supplied in various grades of fineness.

rubbing varnish   A hard varnish that can be friction-polished to a high gloss with a fine abrasive.

ruching   Form of gimp or decorative strip used to finish the edges of upholstery.

Rudd table   An elaborate form of dressing table used in the late eighteenth century, with drawers, swing mirrors, folding top, and quadrant drawers, the whole folding away out of sight when not in use. The original table was made for Margaret Caroline Rudd (1745-99), a well-known courtesan.

rule   A device for measuring dimensions. It can be made of wood, steel, or plastic, and calibrated with either metric or imperial dimensions, or a combination of both. Folding hinged rules are also made, either with two or three folding sections, and in addition there is a zig-zag type in which the sections swivel outwards. But one of most popular designs is the flexible metal rule which can be pulled out from the case which contains it; it can be retracted either by hand or by actuating a spring.

rule joint   An edge joint used mainly for the leaves of a gate-leg table. Special hinges are needed in which the countersinking of the screw holes is on the reverse side from the knuckle. Special planes are made for working the sections, but the shapes can be worked with a rebate plane and round moulding plane. A pair of cutters fixed in the scratch-stock will complete the sections; or the edge can be spindle-moulded.

The idea of the rule joint is that, with the extension leaf hanging down, an ovolo edge is seen. This becomes invisible when the leaf is raised. The name is derived from its similarity to the brass joint of a rule.

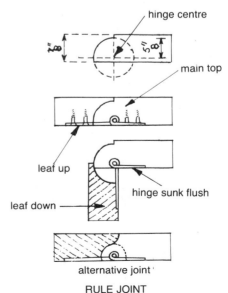

RULE JOINT

It is imperative that the knuckle centre of the hinge coincides with the centre from which the joint is struck, otherwise a gap or binding will result. In the case of $\frac{7}{8}$ in (23 mm) wood the knuckle of the hinge is recessed in the main top $\frac{5}{8}$ in (16 mm) from the edge, and it must be immediately beneath the top square. Some allowance must be made for the polished surface. If it should squeak it can be cured by rubbing candle grease along it after polishing.

rule joint hinges   Used for a table with double top, the upper of which opens out flat to form an extension. The knuckle projects at the top since the centre is in line with the upper surfaces of the tops when opened out, and can only be used in positions where this does not matter. It is not used for the rule joint of a gate-leg table, and receives its name from its resemblance to the metal hinge of a folding rule.

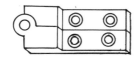

RULE-JOINT HINGE

rule joint stays   Two types are shown with flat fixing plates or one flat and one bent plate. Used for the opening lids of tables, music stools, etc. (See *lid stay* and *quadrant stays.*)

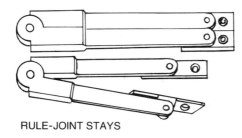

RULE-JOINT STAYS

rung   Commonly a stave of a ladder, but in chair-making a turned tie-rail between the legs of a chair is frequently referred to as a rung.

runner   (see *drawer runner*).

runners   Used as a track for sliding doors. They may be of hardwood fibre, metal, or plastic. (See also *drawer runners.*)

run out   Term applied to a moulding or chamfer which, instead of finishing at a stop or mitre, or running right through, gradually fades out to the surface. This is sometimes necessary to stop the moulding short of the shoulder of a rail.

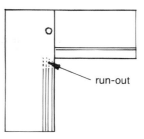

RUN-OUT

rush chair   One with plaited rush seating. Rushes have been used for the purpose from earliest times.

Russell-Jennings bit   The original form of American auger or twist bit.

Russian tallow   Added sparingly when making gilder's gesso. It was also used as a filler when polishing but has the disadvantage of never drying out really hard and is thus unsuitable for good class permanent work.

rustication   An architectural motif involving the deepening of joints between blocks to make them stand out; the edges are often chamfered as well. The treatment is sometimes found in the quoin blocks (*q.v.*) on the corners of eighteenth century tallboys and longcase clocks.

rye flour   Sometimes added to resin glue when used for veneering to extend it and cheapen the cost.

S

sabicu (*lysiloma latisiliqua*)   Hardwood of 60-61 lb (962 kg) from Cuba. Similar to Cuban mahogany but less red. Used for good-quality furniture.

sabre leg   Chair leg which curves backwards. It tapers towards the foot and is rectangular in section. Became popular towards the end of the eighteenth century. Also known as the Waterloo leg on chairs made after 1815. Alternative name is the swept leg. Some authorities consider the design was derived from the klismos chair (*q.v.*). It was also used by Duncan Phyfe, the noted American maker.

sabre saw Reciprocating saw of the jigsaw type (*q.v.*). It is gripped in the lower jaw of the machine only and is heavier and wider than the normal jigsaw blade. It is usually used for curves which are not too severe. A sabre saw is also used on the portable jigsaw. The teeth are pointed towards the body of the tool so that it draws the wood towards its sole on the power stroke.

sack-back Windsor chair (USA) A Windsor chair with an almost circular seat and an arm bow with the ends of the upper bow brought forward into it; the back contains spindles.

saddle (1) A block to support shaped work when being spindle-moulded. Also used for special shaped work on the bandsaw.

saddle (2) A thin strip fixed to the floor beneath a room door. It gives clearance to the door over carpets, and reduces draught. Frequently it is bevelled at one or both edges, depending upon whether or not the carpet reaches right to the edge.

saddle (3) A device which bridges across the work, and used to give a fixing for cramps in assembling items of awkward shape.

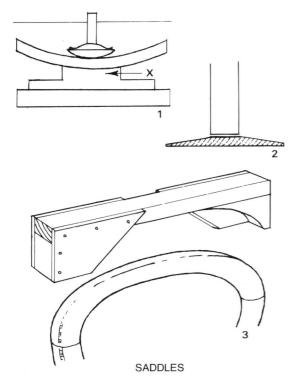

SADDLES

saddle (4) A support for shaped work when being caul veneered. It approximates to the shape of the back of the groundwork, so supporting it during cramping.

saddle bar Grooved bar screwed up beneath the box bar of a showcase top. It secures the glass and strengthens the top.

SADDLE BAR

saddle-cheek chair An upholstered easy chair with small wings fixed at either side of the back. Illustrated in Hepplewhite's 'Guide' 1788.

saddle joint Used by carpenters where a vertical timber is V-notched at the foot to engage a correspondingly shaped horizontal member.

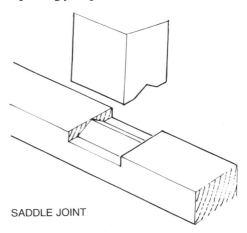

SADDLE JOINT

saddle seat Solid wood seat used particularly in Windsor chairs. Hollowed out with two depressions leaving a raised and rounded centre ridge or 'cod' which flattens out towards the rear.

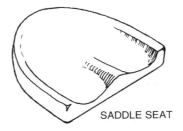

SADDLE SEAT

safe-edged A file having a plain edge free from serrations.

sal (*Shorea robusta*) Indian hardwood of 55 lb (881 kg) Pale brown colour and used for sleepers and other purposes where durability is essential.

Salem rocking chair (USA) A variation of a Windsor chair with a low back. Made in Salem, Massachusetts, in the early nineteenth century.

Salem secretary (USA) A design resembling a Sheraton-style secretaire with a china cabinet upper part.

salient angle One which projects outwards at any angle less than 180 degrees.

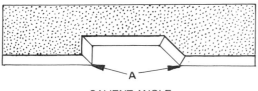

SALIENT ANGLE

Salisbury glue Name sometimes applied to a high-grade animal glue made from skins rather than bones. It is generally clearer in colour than ordinary Scotch glue.

saltire A construction in the form of St Andrew's cross; usually refers to cross-underframes. (See *X-stretcher.*)

salver stand An eighteenth century stand which supported plates or salvers; they were placed in the turned spirals and rested against the upright back.

sandalwood (*santalum album*) Indian wood of 55 lb (881 kg) also found in Western Australia. Yellow colour with fragrant scent and used chiefly for decorative boxes, turnery, and ornamental work generally.

sandarac A gum used in making some varnishes.

sand bag Used when veneering shaped work, especially parts of double curvature for which a reverse caul would be difficult to make. A bag is part-filled with silver sand, heated, and placed in an open box, and pressed or thumped to the approximate shape. The work is then cramped down, the sandbag taking up the reverse shape, and ensuring even pressure over the whole surface. In some cases the box

may not be necessary, the sandbag being cramped directly over the work, battens being used to take the cramp shoes.

sand blasting Technique sometimes applied to plywood or some softwoods (such as pine) which has the effect of removing the softer parts, leaving the figuring in relief.

sand, for shading Used for a shaded effect in veneers and marquetry. Silver sand is heated and satinwood or boxwood veneers dipped into it to give a brown shaded effect. By partly immersing the veneer a graduated effect can be given. (See *sand shading.*)

sander Machine for finishing wood, or, in some cases, for trimming it. Chief types are:

A. Belt. The abrasive cloth is continuous and passes round two drums. In the small bench type there is a table to support the top of the belt, the work being held over the whole. Usually there is a vertical stop to enable the work to be kept steady and held square (diagram A). In the larger machines the wood is held beneath the lower part of the belt, and pressure applied by a pad held over the belt. Also used in some portable hand machines, and in floor sanders.

B. Bobbin. A small revolving cylinder covered with abrasive cloth or paper used for finishing acute concave shapes.

C. Disc, rigid. Used for trimming mitres, square ends, projecting tenons, etc., rather than for finishing.
D. Disc, flexible. Used only in portable sanders for rough cleaning off paint, etc.

E. Drum. May be the large industrial machine with big revolving drum, or several drums, each with successively finer abrasive. The work passes beneath. There is also a smaller drum sander which is virtually a form of drum bobbin sander but larger, used for concave shapes. Yet another type is pneumatic. It gives to the work so that items of compound curvature such as a cabriole leg can be sanded. A flexible shaft sander is simply a small drum sander at the end of a flexible shaft.

F. Orbital A small portable type used for flat work. The pad remains pointed in the same direction but is vibrated in a series of small orbits of about $\frac{1}{8}$ in (3 mm) diam at high speed. Thus a pencil mark made on the pad would appear as a small circle when the machine is put into action.

G. Reciprocating Again a portable machine. There are two pads which move towards and away from each other in a reciprocating movement. Thus the abrasive marks are in a straight line. Used for flat work.

Some small bench sanders are universal, and can be used for belt, drum, and bobbin sanding.

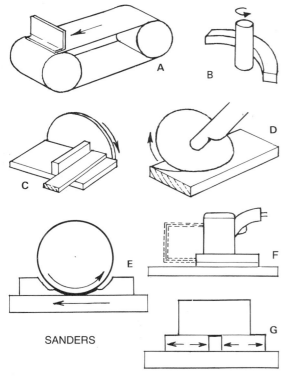

SANDERS

sanding belt   Continuous abrasive belt of cloth or paper used in a belt sanding machine. Can be obtained in various sizes and grades of abrasive.

sanding block   A block, suitably shaped to fit the hand, around which a piece of abrasive paper is wrapped. Can be made of wood, cork, or hard composition rubber; or in the form of a plastic foam block with the abrasive incorporated in the face — this kind is washable.

sanding, pattern   Method of finishing outlines of convex shapes, using a pattern or master, thus ensuring all being alike.

sanding planes (USA)   These consist of an aluminium base fixed to a wooden handle. A strip of abrasive paper is clipped to the base and the tool is used in much the same way as a sanding block *(q.v.)*.

sanding sealer   A coat of diluted shellac applied to bare wood to seal the surface before sanding. A

specially formulated sealer is used when spray-finishing with cellulose lacquers.

San Domingo mahogany *(swietenia mahogani)* Fine-quality dark mahogany often known as Spanish or Cuban, 40 lb (641 kg) in weight and used in high-class furniture and fitments. Has a white deposit in the open grain, and shavings tend to flake up rather than to be continuous. Somewhat brittle but capable of a fine finish.

sandpaper   A term which is a misnomer sand is not used as an abrasive. Curiously, however, for machine woodwork the terms 'sanding' and 'sander' are retained. (See *abrasive paper, glasspaper, garnet paper, and silicon carbide.*)

sand shading   Method of darkening veneer locally by dipping it into hot sand. By only partly immersing it a shaded effect is produced. Used widely in the eighteenth century, particularly on light woods such as satinwood and holly. Sometimes walnut was also shaded. (See *sand.*)

sandwich   Term used for work which is built up in layers. Thus in blockboard the centre core is 'sandwiched' between the face veneers. Some roof trusses are also sandwiched, the sloping and horizontal beams having upright and diagonal members contained between them.

sap   The fluid contained in the living tree responsible for its growth and continued life. (A) indicates sapwood; (B) heartwood.

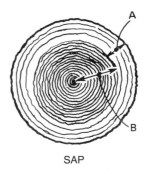

SAP

sapele *(entandrophragma cylindricum)* West African hardwood of 44 lb (705 kg), used for veneer, furniture, panelling, etc. A hard, close-grained wood, reddish brown in colour. Frequently has a stripy roe figuring. Used chiefly for veneers and furniture and interior fittings.

sap stain Result of fungi attack leaving blue patches. The strength is not affected and the timber can be used if the appearance does not matter.

sap streak (USA) Patches of natural resin sometimes exposed when working softwoods; they must be sealed with shellac (knotting) as paint films will not harden over them.

sarcenet A silken fabric first imported into Britain during the thirteenth century. The name derives from its being made by the Saracens, and no doubt returning Crusaders introduced the material.

sarcophagus In Ancient Greece, a coffin made of special stone which was supposed to consume the flesh of a person buried in it. The shape, which is that of a rectangular hopper, was used as a design for commodes, caskets, and wine-coolers.

Sargent planes Range of bench planes made by the American company of that name. They were fully adjustable and were made all-metal with wood body and metal adjustment frame. The all-metal type was similar to the Stanley plane. As a rule the term 'Sargent' is generally taken as referring to the wood-metal type, although the firm made both kinds.

SARGENT PLANE

sarking Roof lining of thin boards. Also the boarding to hold tiles or slates.

sash and frame Window having a sash boxed frame and pair of sliding sashes.

sash beads Those fitted to the frame of a sliding sash, and consisting of the inner or retaining bead, and the parting bead (q.v.).

sash cramp Used in assembling frames of all kinds, glueing width joints, and in carcase work. Made in lengths from 24 in (610 mm) to 48 in (1220 mm) and in both light and heavy patterns. Length is that of the bar, not the cramping capacity. (See also *T bar cramp, cramp head and joiners cramp.*)

SASH CRAMP

sash door Bookcase door having moulded bars dividing the whole into rectangular panes.

SASH DOOR

sash fillister plane A plane for working the rebates of sash timbers. The rebate is worked on the far side, the fence bearing against the face side. As the moulding is worked from the face side both are perfectly uniform, irrespective of whether the thickness varies, and accurate mitres, etc., are ensured. In use, the plane is started at the far end of the work, being brought back at each successive stroke until a full run is obtained, this being maintained until stopped by the depth gauge. A universal metal plane can be obtained which works both rebate and moulding in one operation.

sash lining The inside and outside members of a sash box frame; also the back lining. (See illustrations under *sash and frame*.)

sash mortise chisel (see *mortise chisel*).

sash pocket chisel Thin chisel, usually bevelled both sides, and used when cutting the pockets for a sliding sash window. As the wood cut in making the hole is used as a cover it is desirable for the chisel to be thin so that a thick cut is avoided.

satin First imported from China during the thirteenth century, satin is silk-like fabric with a glossy surface.

satinay *(syncarpia hillii)* Queensland timber of 46-56 lb (737-897 kg). Pale strawberry colour. Hard and strong and not difficult to work, though tough. Used locally for general purposes.

satin finish A finish which has a soft sheen.

satin walnut or *(correctly)* **American red gum** *(liquidambar styraciflua)* Uses generally are for inexpensive bedroom furniture, panelling, toys, stripwood, fretwork, etc. For long much confusion has arisen through the application of the names 'satin walnut' and 'hazel walnut' to the timber. In the trade 'American red gum' is now accepted as the correct designation. Weight 37-38 lb (593-609 kg). Colour cold brown. Seldom seen in the United Kingdom since the 1939-45 war.

satinwood, East Indian *(chloroxylon swietenia)* Hardwood of 59 lb (945 kg) found chiefly in Sri Lanka and India. Used chiefly in veneer form and for ornamental work. Much of it is finely figured and it was widely used in the late eighteenth century and later for good-quality furniture.

saturated solution Liquid charged with something to a point when no more can be absorbed.

satyr mask Form of carved decoration used on the cabriole legs of chairs and tables during the first half of the eighteenth century.

saucer edge Circular table top or tray with raised edging, usually circular and turned. The term is sometimes applied to a pie-crust top *(q.v.)*.

SAUCER EDGE

sausage turning A double-swell design of turning which is often used on the underframing of Windsor chairs.

Savanarola chair An X-chair named after Ciralamo Savanarola, a Dominican friar who was violently opposed to Renaissance influences in Italy; he was executed as a heretic in 1498. The chair folded, and consisted of sets of identical leg frames which were fixed behind each other; it had flat arms and sledge feet *(q.v.)*.

saw (see under *back, band, bead, betty (chair-maker's), bow, chairmaker's, circular, combination, compass, coping, cross-cut, dado head, donkey, dovetail,*

drunken, flooring, frame, fret, hand, jeweller's (see bead), jig, keyhole (see pad), nest of, novelty, pad, panel, rip, scroll, tenon, veneer).

saw anvil A small device used by the professional saw sharpener, being a piece of steel, with a bevel along one edge (sometimes both edges). The saw is held over the anvil so that the teeth overhang the bevel evenly; each alternate tooth is given a sharp tap with the cross-peen of a hammer, thereby knocking it down on the bevel and setting it. By reversing the saw and repeating the process, the teeth are all set to the same degree. The beginner is advised to fit a wooden jig to such an anvil, with a small fence to keep the saw teeth in alignment with the bevel, the teeth being tapped with a flat nail punch rather than the cross-peen of a hammer. (See also *saw set and pliers saw set.*)

saw bench The framework, usually metal, on which the bearings and other parts of a circular saw are mounted. Usually refers to the machine in its entirety.

sawbuck table (USA) A design of table with an X-shaped frame; usually found in the New England states.

saw chops Appliance used to hold a saw blade whilst sharpening. It is generally held in the bench vice. It is also made in metal with attached thumbscrews for fixing to the bench. The wood types shown are usually home-made. That at (A) is for handsaws and backsaws. (B) is for circular saws.

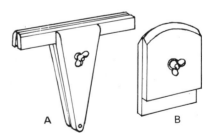

A   B

SAW CHOPS

saw-cut veneer Veneer which is sawn as distinct from being sliced. Originally all veneer was hand sawn and was anything up to $\frac{1}{8}$ in (3 mm) thick. Later a large circular saw was used which reduced the thickness to $\frac{1}{16}$ in (2 mm) or less. It is a costly method since more wood is lost in sawdust than is used in veneer, and it is almost unobtainable today. When it is used the circular marks on the underside should be taken out with the toothing plane, as otherwise glue is held in the spaces, and as this shrinks it pulls the veneer, leaving a faint replica of the marks on the surface.

saw doctor Tradesman who specialises in putting saws into condition, particularly the tensioning of the blade and correcting distortion.

sawdust Fine sawdust mixed with an adhesive makes badigeon *(q.v.)* which can be used as a stopping for cracks in floor boards, etc. Wood flour (the finest sawdust) can be mixed with cellulose-based wallpaper paste, or paint, to make a kind of plastic wood.

saw files Used for sharpening. Pattern for most saws is three-cornered, giving a filing angle of 60 deg. Files may be plain tapered, slim tapered, double ended, mill, and round-gulleting.

saw guides Device built into a bandsaw to prevent lateral movement of the saw. There are two; one above, and the other below the table. The lower one is fixed in height, but the other can be adjusted to enable it to be fixed as close to the work as possible yet giving clearance and adequate view. There are adjustable blocks at each side of the saw, and these may be of metal or of hardwood.

sawing fence A metal arm which reaches from the front edge of a circular saw table or bandsaw table up to the saw blade. Its purpose is to enable cuts parallel with an edge to be made. For grooving, rebating, and some tenoning operations it is necessary to add a wood fence which reaches beyond the saw so that the work has support throughout the whole of the cut. (See also *fence.*)

sawing horse Structure to hold logs whilst being cross-cut. A pair of intermediate supports is sometimes added to give support when a short log is being sawn.

sawing stool (see *trestle*).

saw kerf (see *kerf*).

sawn Applied to timber which has been sawn but not planed.

saw pit Used years ago before the days of power saws for the conversion of logs into usable sizes. It consisted of an oblong-shaped hole in the ground across which the log was laid. Two men used a pit saw one standing on the log and the other down in the pit, being top sawyer and pit-man respectively.

saw set The pliers type is shown at (A). Teeth are pressed against a graduated anvil showing the correct angle for teeth 4 to 12 points to the inch. The simple form shown at (B) consists of a slotted blade with handle. In use, each alternate tooth is gripped in one of the slots, i.e. the slot suiting the thickness of the plate, and the tooth bent over to the desired angle of set. A gauge is sometimes fitted, this bearing against the side of the saw, so regulating the degree of set. (See *pliers sawset* and *saw anvil*.)

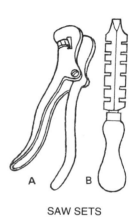

SAW SETS

saw set gauge A metal plate used to test the amount of set given to circular saw teeth. The four corners are filed to give the varying degrees of set. Nicks filed at the corners give quick identification of the degree of set.

saw teeth (see *teeth, saw*).

saw tooth rack Device to support shelves in adjustable positions. They are screwed to the cabinet ends and the cross pieces placed loosely in the notches.

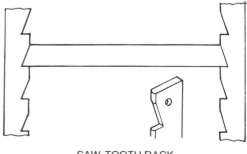

SAW-TOOTH RACK

saw vice   (see *saw chops*).

say   A fine, thin serge-like fabric; also a kind of silk or satin.

scagliola   A composition consisting of plaster of Paris, glue, and small pieces of alabaster, marble, or porphyry, etc., mixed together and highly polished to resemble a slab of one or other of the minerals mentioned. Extensively used in the eighteenth century for table tops.

scale   Used in making reduced or scale drawings. Can be obtained in boxwood or ivorine or printed on card. Alternatively the ordinary rule can be used. Useful scales for woodwork are $1\frac{1}{2}$ in to the foot or one-eigth. The advantage of this is that each $\frac{1}{8}$ in on the rule represents 1 in in actual size.
in actual size.

scalene triangle   One which has all its sides and angles unequal.

scaling   (see *'imbrication'*).

scallop   (see *escallop*).

scalloped edge   (A) A small series of small arcs cut at the edge of thin material by way of simple decoration. (B) the wavy and rounded edge of a table top.

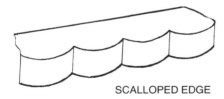

SCALLOPED EDGE

scant   Term used for material which is of bare measure.

scantling   Lengths of small square-edged timber. Limits: width 2 in (51 mm) to $4\frac{1}{2}$ in (115 mm); thickness, 2 in (51 mm) to 4 in (102 mm).

scarf   Joint used in lengthening timber, mostly in carpentry though a simple version is sometimes needed in furniture repair work. There are many variations, some requiring screwing or nailing, others of an interlocking form held together with wedges. In some cases fish plates (q.v.) are used with bolts to hold the parts together. A simple form is given at (A), the parts being nailed. That at (B) is sometimes used for long wall plates, the weight of the roof members

bearing down and so making the dovetail shape effective. Joint (C) resists a bending strain by virtue of its sloping ends and is strong in that the root, which takes the main strain, is thick. At (D) the folding wedges force the parts together, and the tenoned projections prevent lateral movement.

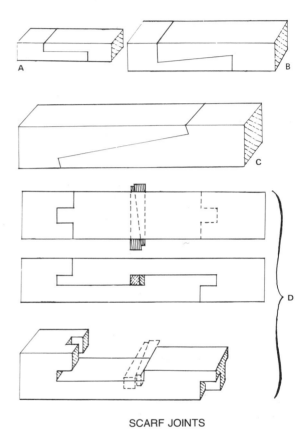

SCARF JOINTS

sciapod   A carved representation of a one-legged monster, sometimes found on church bench-ends.

scissors truss   Roof truss in which the rafters are strengthened with a pair of scissors beams of X form with a tie rod at the intersection.

sconces   The term includes a variety of lighting arrangements such as movable lanterns, candle-holders fixed to the wall, with or without screens. In 1755 Dr Johnson defined the word as meaning 'a pensile candlestick, generally with a looking-glass to reflect the light' (pensile means hanging or suspended). (See also *girandole*.)

175

scotia A concave moulding derived from the classical styles.

Scotch bit An auger bit with normal cutters but no side nickers or spurs. Used for rough boring.

scraper, cabinet Used in the cleaning-up process of hardwood to take out plane or other tool marks, and to remove tears (pronounced 'tares') from woods with difficult grains. Also in cleaning up veneered surfaces. The rectangular type (A) used for cleaning up flat and convex surfaces is from 4 in (102 mm) to 6 in (153 mm) long and about $\frac{1}{16}$ in (1.5 mm) thick. A thin scraper heats up quickly and is uncomfortable to use, whereas a thick one is difficult to bend and is consequently tiring in use. For shaped work types (B) and (C) are used — in fact in some cases it is necessary to file a special shape to suit the work. To sharpen the tool the edges are filed straight and square and finished on the oilstone. A hard rounded steel tool known as a ticketer (q.v.) (a gouge does equally well) is used to turn up the four edges, being held at a slight angle. The edges can be turned back and resharpened two or three times; but re-filing and honing is then needed.

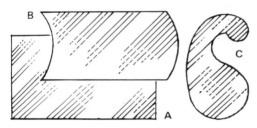

SCRAPERS, CABINET

scraper, handled Used by some woodworkers for cleaning up, though most craftsmen prefer the simple scraper. Its chief advantage is in cleaning woods with hard and soft grain, such as figured oak, as it is not liable to cut into the soft parts leaving the figuring standing proud. The thumbscrew at the back gives a slight bend to the blade so that the corners do not dig in, and at the same time gives support behind the cutting edge. The edge is filed and honed at an angle of about 45 deg, and turned back to about 15 deg in

SCRAPER, HANDLED

about three stages, the angle being lessened in each stage.

scraper plane A large edition of the handled scraper but of plane form. Some types have the cutter reaching to the sides so that rebates can be cleaned up.

scraping tools Used by the wood turner for extra hard woods. Their action is that of scraping as distinct from cutting. The tool is used almost radially to the revolving wood but with the handle slightly raised. Made in many shapes, and often ground from old files with the serrations ground away. For some woods the edge is turned up with a ticketer (q.v.).

scratch To work a moulding or other detail with the scratch stock (q.v.).

scratch stock Used to work mouldings, cut grooves for inlays, etc. It can be used on both straight and curved edges, and the cutter can be filed to any desired shape to suit the section required. Another advantage is that the moulding can be stopped if need be. It is invariably made in the workshop from two pieces of wood screwed together and with a notch cut as shown. The cutter is held between the two by tightening the screws. An important detail is that the lower side of the notch is slightly rounded (B) because the tool has often to be tilted at the start of the cut.

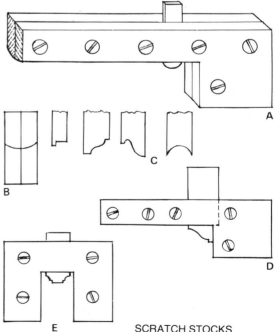

SCRATCH STOCKS

Curvature on the upright edge is only necessary when the tool has to be worked around a concave edge. Since the scratch stock is worked in both directions the cutter is filed square. For a large moulding requiring deep projections the side should if possible continue into the notch so that it is supported (D).

screeds   Strips of wood used as a guide to thickness when plastering.

screen hinge   (see *reversible hinge*).

screen, pole   Small firescreen which slides up or down on a rod. (See *pole screen.*)

screens   The portable folding screen, consisting of 2, 4 or 6 panels linked together have been recorded in Britain since the early fifteenth century. Although some were made of wicker, many were covered with expensive fabrics or embroidery.

Exceptionally, screens with up to 12 panels decorated with oriental lacquer were being imported about 1700. Smaller fire-screens began to appear in the late seventeeth century. (See *cheval, pole screens.*)

screen size   Screens with accurately spaced square openings are employed to grade grits for abrasive papers, and the grit size is known by the number of holes in the smallest mesh it has passed through. The following are current screen sizes for the various abrasives used in woodwork: 40 (= $1\frac{1}{2}$); 50 (= 1); 60 (= $\frac{1}{2}$); 100 (= 2/0); 120 (= 3/0); 180 (= 5/0); 220 (= 6/0); 240 (= 7/0). Screen numbers 40 and 50 are coarse; 60 and 100 medium; 120 and 180 fine; 220 and 240 extra-fine.

screen stick   Alternative name for pole screen (*q.v.*).

screw box and tap   Made in pairs for cutting a thread in wood. The box has a cutter of V section, and

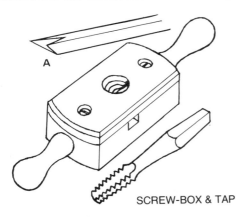

SCREW-BOX & TAP

an important detail is that the point of the V must slope back from the corners so that the periphery of the wood is cut before the root of the V. Otherwise it is liable to crumble the thread. Used mainly in making handscrews, wood screws for the mitre shooting block, and wood cramps; also in turnery for jointing long items. The tap is of metal and is tapered. It is used in making the screw box.

screw, carver's   Appliance to enable the wood carver to hold work stationary on the bench. One end has a tapered wood screw to enable it to be driven into the wood. At the other end is a square spigot which will engage with the square holes in the curved nut piece. The latter acts as a spanner in tightening the screw, which is passed through a hole in the bench, and the nut tightened from below.

screw castor   One with wood screw for fixing. Small screws driven through the plate prevent it from unscrewing. (See also *castor.*)

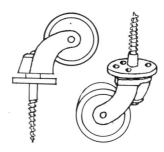

SCREW CASTOR

screw cups   Made in two forms, raised (A) and flush (B). They look much neater than a plain screw head, especially on show work. They are useful also in positions on which screws have to be withdrawn and replaced from time to time since there is no tendency for the head to bite too far into the wood.

SCREW CUPS

screwdriver   Made in many sizes and patterns. Illustration shows the cabinet pattern. The Phillips type is also shown (C), this engaging with a reversed cruciform depression rather than a slot. (See also

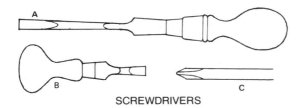

SCREWDRIVERS

London, ratchet, and spiral-ratchet types.) A cranked screwdriver is also made for use with screws above which there is no clearance for an ordinary screwdriver.

screwdriver bit   Used in the brace to enable extra leverage to be obtained for difficult screws; also for the rapid driving of screws. Constant pressure must be given to avoid slipping from and burring over the slot. Made in various sizes.

screw nail   In Scotland this often refers to an ordinary wood screw. Sometimes the term is applied to a roofing nail *(q.v.)* which is of spiral form and revolves as it is driven in.

screw-on bolt   One which does not need to be recessed into the wood but has simply to be screwed on.

SCREW-ON BOLT

screw plate   Useful for fixing under-shelves to legs, table tops to their framing, etc. Made of bright steel, in various sizes. A fitting somewhat resembling it is the packing case bolt, used to hold down a lid temporarily.

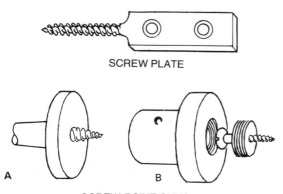

SCREW PLATE

SCREW-POINT CHUCK

screw-point chuck   Used in the lathe to hold small items such as egg cups, bowls, etc., whilst turning. Normal pattern is shown at (A). The special pattern (B) utilises a separate wood screw, the advantage being that it is not liable to break off, and that varying lengths of screw can be used. It may be of the Morse taper type or have screw fixing on the mandrel.

screws   Used for joining wood parts together, or for fixing metal fittings such as hinges. They are classified primarily by their types, as follow: (A) countersunk, (B) roundhead, (C) raised head, (D) dowel, (E) twin-thread, (F) steep pitch, and (G) chipboard. With the exception of the dowel screw, the remainder are further classified by their length and gauge. The length of each screw is shown in the illustration; the gauge is the diameter of the shank. (See also *screw finishes, screws – brief history.*)

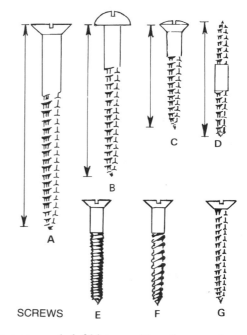

SCREWS   E   F   G

screws — brief history   Tapering metal screws with slotted heads and threaded shanks date back to the late seventeenth century. Early examples were usually brass and had hand-filed threads which were more or less horizontal in profile. Lathe-turned screws with a more pronounced taper appeared from 1760, and were made in steel as well as brass. Present-day types of machine-made screws with gimlet tips came into use about 1850.

screw finishes   These are normal steel (for general woodworking purposes but should not be used in oak which causes corrosion); bright zinc plate (bright protective coating — for all dry interior uses and outdoors where a paint finish is to be applied); zinc-sheradised (dull grey protective coating which may turn brown unless painted — for exterior work and can be painted); nickel-plate (bright reflective finish which can tarnish — for dry interior work); chromium-plate (bright reflective finish — uses as nickel plate); electro-brassed plate (reflective bright yellow finish — interior work only); bronze metal antique (dark brown finish — for use with oxidised copper fittings); dark Florentine bronze (near-black finish — uses as bronze metal antique); antique copper bronze (uniform bronze colour — for interior use with copper, bronze, and matching timber finishes); black japanned (overall black enamelled finish — interior work but can be painted for exterior use); Berlin blacked (overall black enamel finish but duller than japanned — uses as black japanned); steel blued and oiled (dark blue/black oxide coating, protective lubricating oil finish — needs painting); solid brass (uniform bright yellow, does not rust but can become brittle after a long period in extreme circumstances out of doors); silicon bronze (uniform dark colour — ideal for all exterior work, particularly marine work, as it does not corrode); aluminium alloy, anodised (matt silver grey finish — for fastening aluminium articles); stainless steel (bright steel finish — for all uses where long-term durability, strength, and freedom from rusting is essential. May be used with aluminium components).

scribed joint An alternative to the mitred joint *(q.v.)* for some internal mitres. External or salient joints cannot be scribed. It is often used by carpenters in fitting skirtings around a room as at (A). To find the scribing line a mitre is cut first (C) and the wood cut away square to the line of the mitre (D). It is sometimes used in a moulded and rebated framework (E) here again the mitre being cut first and the outline cut in square with gouge and chisel. Its advantage appears only in wide mouldings liable to shrink, as a mitre might open (F) whereas a scribe pulls along the moulding (G). Any moulding which slopes inwards in general direction can be scribed (H) (I) (J) but not one which in part slopes outwards (K). The term corresponds to the US coping *(q.v.)*.

scriber A marking awl *(q.v.)*.

scribing cutter Used on the tenoning machine to scribe the front shoulder over a moulding.

scribing gouge One which has its bevel inside the curve. Also called an inside cannelled gouge. Used when the hollow shape has to be cut in square as in a

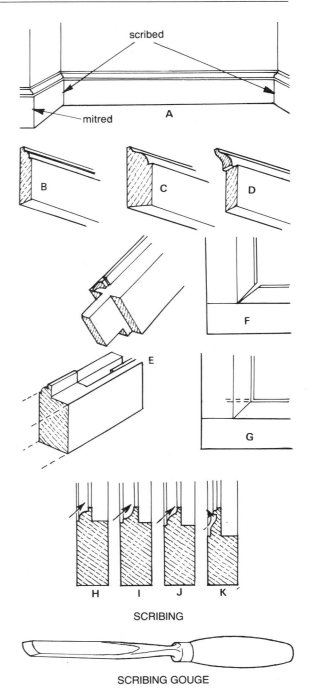

SCRIBING

SCRIBING GOUGE

scribed joint. It needs to be sharpened with an oilstone slip. (See *oilstone*.) Made in widths of $\frac{1}{8}$ in (3 mm) to $1\frac{1}{4}$ in (32 mm) and in varying sweeps.

scribing piece   Vertical piece of wood fixed to a cabinet and scribed to fit over the skirting. It may also be added to a fitment to enable it to fit closely to an uneven wall. Often a bead is worked along the joining edge.

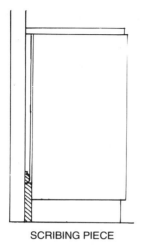

SCRIBING PIECE

scrim   Material used in upholstery made in many qualities and widths from jute. It is of fairly open weave with round threads. (See also *hessian.*)

scriptoire   (see *scrutoire*).

scroll   Term referring to any spiral detail. In particular it is applied to some furniture feet, that at (A) being late seventeenth century and (B) the French scrolled foot of about 1760. The term is also used to describe the spiral termination of a stair hand rail (C).

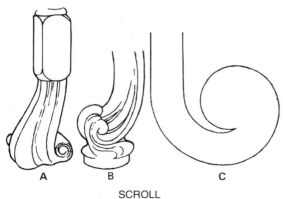

SCROLL

scroll-back Windsor chair   A Windsor chair which has no bow, comb, or splat, the back consisting of a slightly curved top rail and a stay, plus the back

stands which are serpentine curved and terminate in a plain scroll — hence the name.

scroll chuck   (see *self-centring device chuck*).

scroll leg   A form of double scroll sometimes used for tables and stands in the second half of the seventeenth century. Usually it was square in section and frequently veneered.

scroll saw   A fret machine *(q.v.)*.

scrolled marquetry   (see *seaweed marquetry*).

scrolled pediment   (see *swan-neck pediment*).

scroll-over arm   Chair arm popular in the early years of the eighteenth century and onwards. The arm itself widened out towards the back and was relatively flat but was circular in section at the scrolled front. The front support or stump was jointed to the arm proper at the middle of the front scroll, and invariably set back from front legs.

scrub plane   The name given to a metal plane with single cutter 1¼ in (32 mm) or 1½ in (38 mm) wide. The cutting edge is rounded so that the corners do not dig in, and the plane is used for the preliminary planing of rough surfaces. The corresponding wood plane usually has a front handle or toat after the style of a Continental plane. Also called a 'roughing' or 'scurfing' plane.

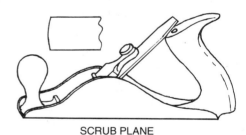

SCRUB PLANE

scrutoire   Archaic term describing an enclosed writing cabinet or table; now called an 'escritoire' *(q.v.)* It had a vertical flap as opposed to a sloping one.

scumble   A type of glaze *(q.v.)* which is specially compounded to remain in a workable state long enough to be mottled, blended, or figured.

scurfing plane   *(see scrub plane)*.

scutcheon   An escutcheon *(q.v.)*.

sealed bed The correct name for a four-poster bedstead.

sealer A coat used in cellulose polishing to seal stained and filled timber, and to provide a smooth surface for subsequent operations. Also used to fix stains and fillers in French polishing. Sealers are also widely used on floors.

seasoning The drying of timber to bring it to a moisture content suitable for the conditions in which it is to be used. There are two main methods; natural or air seasoning, and kiln seasoning. The latter may supplement the former. In air drying the timber is stacked in such a way that air can circulate on all sides, and it gradually gives up its moisture, the time taken depending upon the particular timber and its thickness. It can, however, only lose moisture until it is in equilibrium with the atmosphere, and timber thus seasoned in the open is still too wet for many purposes. Kiln seasoning will reduce the moisture content still further, and by this means it can be brought to whatever content is needed to suit the purpose for which it is required. Today kiln seasoning is often used for green wood (though for some species preliminary air drying is essential), and when properly done is perfectly successful. It does require careful treatment, however, which varies with the species. Heat alone would be disastrous because the rate of evaporation would be too great, and it is necessary to make the air humid. In some progressive kilns the interior is divided up into bays of varying temperature, and the stacks of timber are moved on trolleys from the cooler to the hotter. In compartment kilns the timber remains stationary, and the air is heated and dried as the moisture is evaporated. (See also *second seasoning*.)

seating Level surface or bed upon which another member has to rest.

seat, pincushion Chair or stool seat with its rails lying flat to the top of which the upholstery is tacked but does not reach right to the edges. Gimp is usually tacked around the edges of the covering.

seat rails Rails of a chair or settee to which the upholstery is tacked, or on which the loose seat rests.

seat, stuff-over Chair or settee in which the seat covering is taken over and around the seat rails thus hiding them. The covering may be tacked beneath but more usually is tacked at, or just above, the bottom edge and the raw edges hidden by gimp. (See also *loose seat.*)

seaweed marquetry Type of marquetry which became popular in the late seventeenth and early eighteenth centuries, consisting of fine, intricate, and scrolled arabesque work. As both background and scrolls were cut simultaneously and the parts interchanged, it follows that the cutting produced one pattern of light scrolls on a dark background, and another in reverse. In fact several veneers were cut in a pack so that many corresponding sheets of marquetry were produced, half of them being counter to the other. Also called arabesque, or scrolled endive marquetry.

secondary beam Large sectioned beam supporting the common joists in a double floor.

second fixings Items of woodwork such as handrails, skirtings, picture rails, etc., that are added after plastering has been completed.

second seasoning The final kilning of timber to the moisture content of the conditions in which it is to be used, 10 to 14% for dome.

secretaire Piece of furniture for writing, with writing top which pulls out and is enclosed by a vertical front which drops down flat when in use. Widely used in the eighteenth century. Also called scriptor, scrutoire. (See *bureau.*)

secretaire joint Used for the fall front of a secretaire. Its advantage is that the fall is flush with the main writing top when lowered, yet shows no gap at the front when in the up position. As the thinness of the material occasioned by the rebates limits the length of screws that could be used with butt hinges, the fall front may be pivoted on dolphin hinges fitted to the sides. Quadrant stays (*q.v.*) are fitted to prevent lowering to more than the horizontal. Though square rebates are sometimes used, the sloping rebates shown are more satisfactory in that the root of the joint is

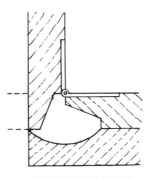

SECRETAIRE JOINT

thicker and stronger. When there is a fixed rail beneath the fall it is necessary for it to be hollowed at the top as shown to give clearance.

secret fixing   Method of fixing fitments, panelling, etc., so that no screws, nails, or plates are visible. Chief methods are slot-screwing (B), and the use of rebated grounds plugged to the wall with which correspondingly rebated battens at the back of the fitment engage (A).

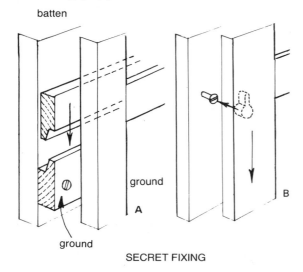

SECRET FIXING

secret mitre dovetail   (see *mitre dovetail*).

secret nailing   One method (A) is to raise a chip from the wood without detaching it, using a chisel, drive in the nail, and glue back the chip. The term also applies to the fixing of tongued flooring in which the nails are driven into the tongues (B).

SECRET NAILING

section   Shape and details of a wood item, whether a piece of wood or a built-up construction, obtained by an imaginary cross-cut at right angles. Its purpose is to clarify construction and details. It shows the relative positions of parts, and reveals details such as moulding, rebates, grooves, etc.

section mould   Shape cut in thin material to the section needed and placed at the end of material,

enabling it to be marked. Its special use is in items which vary in section along their length, another section mould being cut for the second end.

sector   The area of a circle bounded by two radii and part of the circumference.

sedilia   These are seats provided near the altar in a cathedral or church for the priest, deacon, sub-deacon, and sometimes the clerk. They are usually built in stone but a few are in wood, notably a four-seater (circa 1300) in Westminster Abbey.

seed lac   (see *shellac*).

segment   Part of a circle bounded by a chord and part of the circumference.

segmental arch   One in which the curve is an arc less than a semicircle.

SEGMENTAL ARCH

sekondi *(khaya ivorensis)*   One of the African mahoganies from the Gold Coast of 47-48 lb (769 kg). Has good mahogany colour, and is a reliable furniture wood.

selected stuff   The best grade of timber.

selects and No 1 common   Hardwood grading next below firsts *(q.v.)*.

select merchantable   US equivalent to British unsorted joinery softwood *(q.v.)*.

self-centreing chuck   A three-jaw chuck used in the lathe. A key operates all three jaws simultaneously

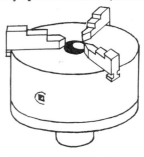

SELF-CENTREING CHUCK

so that round wood is centred automatically. There are two sets of stepped jaws, the steps facing inwards in the one, and outwards in the other.

semi-circle   Half a circle.

semi-circular head   Top part of a window or door frame shaped to a semi-circular shape. A joint used for such a head is shown under *hammer-head tenon*.

Sepa hinge   Complicated hinge let into the edges of wood and having no projecting knuckle. Can only be used for wood more than 1 in (25 mm) thick. Made in 1 in (25 mm) and 2 in (51 mm) sizes.

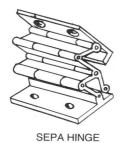

SEPA HINGE

separator   Packing between two bolted pieces of timber.

sequoia *(sequoia sempervirens)*   Softwood from California and Oregon of 25 lb (400 kg). Generally known in America as redwood. Soft in texture and straight in the grain, it is also durable when buried in the earth. It lacks strength, however, and this limits its usefulness. The giant sequoia *(Sequoia gigantea)* may reach a girth of 95 ft (29 m) or more. Some treees have reached an age of 4,000 years.

seraya *(shorea)*   Hardwood from North Borneo of 22-23 lb (352-368 kg); straw to reddish brown in colour. Used for cigar boxes, ship building, and to an extent for furniture. Has a silky lustre, but grain tends to be interlocked.

serge   Woollen twilled fabric made on a loom; used in late seventeenth and eighteenth centuries as a furniture covering.

serif   The ends of a letter which project laterally. In incised V lettering the sides curve outwards into the terminating cross strokes.

serpentine front   Applied to an item such as a sideboard, commode, chest of drawers, etc., having a symmetrical plan shape of a reverse curve, the centre convex and the ends concave. Sometimes the curves are broken by short straight parts formed by the legs, but in the better pieces the shaping is continuous, and may be repeated at the ends. To reduce costs, however, the ends are often kept flat.

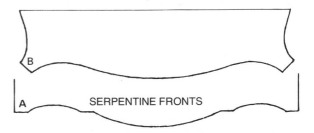

SERPENTINE FRONTS

serpentine marble   A painted wood finish rendered to resemble the skin of a serpent.

serpentine stretcher   One of double curvature forming an X shape. Depending upon period, it might be flat and veneered, moulded, or of simple square section.

SERPENTINE STRETCHERS

serving table   Side table to hold plates, etc., whilst a meal is served.

set (1)   Refers to the bending over of alternate saw teeth in opposite directions so that the saw cuts a kerf slightly wider than the thickness of the saw plate, so avoiding binding (see also *spring setting and swage setting*).

set (2)   Also refers to the adjustment of a plane (see *setting*), or to any other tool or machine.

set (3)   The drying or hardening of an adhesive, a paint, or a varnish is known as its setting time; also the drying period of steamed and bent timber.

set (4)   A nail punch is also known as a set (see *nail punch*).

settee   A seat with a back and arms for two or more persons, almost invariably having six or more legs.

setting (1)   Adjusting a plane. It includes fixing the back iron at the correct distance from the cutting edge and giving the necessary projection of the latter from the sole. In a machine planer it involves giving all cutters the same projection. In general it applies to any tool or machine having adjustable cutters. (For *saws* see under *set.*)

setting (2)   The hardening or drying of glue after assembling.

setting (3)   The period of drying out of steamed and bent timber, ensuring that it stays in shape.

setting in   Process in wood carving in which the outline of the pattern or motif is cut downwards with chisels and gouges. In hardwood this can offer considerable resistance and usually necessitates a trough being cut round on the waste side so that the chips crumble away to the side when setting in follows.

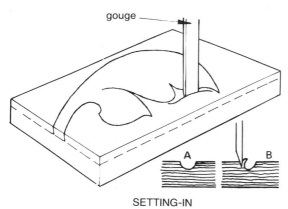

SETTING-IN

setting out   The preparation of working drawings, full sizings, skids *(q.v.)*, etc.

setting out rods or skids   (see *skids*).

settle   Seat for two or more people with panelled back and either open arms or panelled ends. Sometimes with box or locker seat. In use from earliest times. Seat was usually of wood, sometimes with squab cushion. Belonged chiefly to the farmhouse or inn. First designs appeared circa 1450.

settle-table   Settle in which the back can be pivoted over and slid forward to form a table top. (See *monk's bench.*)

set-up   Term for the general arrangement of guides, supports, stops, etc., necessary for a machining, assembling, or other working process.

sewing table   Small table with suspended pouch for needlework and with drawers. Sometimes with pivoted top. Alternative term is pouch table.

shag   A cloth with a long coarse nap used in upholstery and for wall hangings.

shagreen   A kind of leather with a granular surface prepared from the skins of horses, asses, or camels. Also prepared from shark or ray skins, and highly polished. Used in Jacobean times for covering desks and small boxes, and also in the eighteenth century for tea caddies, knife boxes, etc.

Shaker pegs and knobs   Special designs used by the Shakers, who were an American religious sect.

shakes   Defects in timber resulting in splits. Sometimes due to wind damage or lack of sustenance in growth, or more frequently to faults in seasoning. Defects known as checks may be major or minor. Surface or end splits may affect only a small portion of the board. Through checks, however, run from one surface to the other. Heart shakes result from old age shrinkage; star shakes are often caused by faulty artificial seasoning. Ring shakes are termed round, or, if only partial, cup. The terms check and shake frequently refer to the same type of defect. (See *cup shake, heart shake, star shake, thunder shake.*)

shangie   A handle sometimes attached to the toe of a long handsaw to enable two men to use it. Its chief value is in sawing thick stuff as it enables the man holding it to follow the line at the back of the wood, as well as giving increased power.

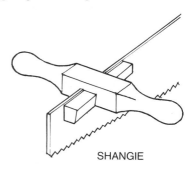

SHANGIE

shaped work   This in cabinet work is generally taken as referring to pieces of furniture that are shaped in plan as in the case of a bow-front or serpentine cabinet, as distinct from the mere shaping of edges.

shaper (1) Form of rasp or file in which the cutting parts are formed by holes or slots with the sharp edges of the metal bent down. Thus the waste passes right through and clogging is avoided. The tool is available straight and flat or rounded in either length or width.

shaper (2) (USA) A spindle moulder (*q.v.*).

shaper (3) This is an industrial machine which uses the principle of the spindle moulder to shape a wide variety of wooden parts, including chair arms, legs, seats, and rails; table legs, rails, and tops; window sash sizing and rebating, and such diverse items as gun stocks and brush handles. A spindle with a cutting tool on its lower end is mounted on a pivoted arm which is free to swing either inwards or outwards relative to the work-piece. The latter has a templet fixed to its underside and the set-up is mounted on a large rotating table. There is a roller collar beneath the cutting tool which follows the templet during the cut, and as it does so the pivoted arms swing inwards or outwards. There are larger machines which have two swinging arms and cutter heads.

shaping block, circular Used on larger spindle moulders with the ring fence (*q.v.*), a templet of the shape being attached to the work.

shaping Curved parts which are cut on the bandsaw, jigsaw, or with bow or similar narrow-bladed saw. Can also refer to work accomplished on the spindle moulder (*q.v.*).

shaving table Used in the mid eighteenth century with wash basin, cupboard, or drawers beneath, and shaving glass at the top.

Shaw guard Guard for use on the spindle moulder (*q.v.*).

shawl-back Windsor chair A Windsor chair in which the comb is sharply curved forward at each end; this enables a shawl to be thrown over the back without slipping off, and thus ward off draughts.

shear force One which produces a tendency for one part to slide along another.

shear plate connectors Similar to a toothed connector (*q.v.*) except that they have solid rims instead of teeth, and these require pre-cut grooves to house them. They are used for strong wood-to-metal fastenings and can be employed back-to-back for demountable structures.

sheathing Generally refers to the technique of covering a framework with panels of plywood, blockboard, etc., as distinct from its having grooved-in or rebated-in panels. The whole gives a flush effect. In some cases, however, light panelled frames are fixed over heavier structural members.

sheath leaf Detail of carved leafwork in which the leaf folds back over the stalk and protects it.

shed Applied loosely to outdoor buildings such as those for garden tools, wood, coal, cycles, etc., or for working purposes.

shelf A board fixed horizontally on which articles such as books, crockery, and ornaments can be placed. A shelf may be attached to the wall by means of brackets, or there may be several of them built into a framework with an open front and with, or without, a back and top.

shelf life The period of time during which a packaged adhesive can be stored, unopened and in the correct conditions, and still be usable. Also called 'storage life'.

shelf supports Although there are several ways to support shelves by means of wooden battens, struts, etc., special fittings can be obtained. One popular type is called 'Tonk's strip' and comprises a metal rack with slots cut into it to receive hooked-clip shelf supports. One style (A) can be screwed directly to the surface and needs no letting in, while another (B) requires to be recessed in to accept the thickness of the strip, with a deeper central groove to enable the hooked clips to be inserted (C) is an all-wood rack type.

There are also several kinds of stud fittings. One type (D) needs holes bored in the ends of the cabinet with shallow holes bored in the underside of the shelves; another (E) needs no holes in the shelves but a groove is usually cut in the cabinet ends to allow a vertical flat part to sink in flush. Additionally there are other designs which are variations of those mentioned.

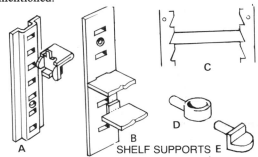

SHELF SUPPORTS

shelf thickness formula This is an approximate guide and states: shelf thickness = shelf length in metres × W, divided by 100 (to convert metres to mm). The result is the thickness of the shelf in millimetres. The value of W varies, typical examples being: for ash, beech, mahogany, and teak, 2.0; for cedar, elm, and red deal, 3.0; for veneered chipboard, 4.4.

shell Alternative name for a furniture or fitment carcase *(q.v.)*.

shellac The basis of french polish. It is an animal substance derived from an insect, the *laccifer lacca,* which flourishes in India. The insect feeds on the young shoots of trees and forms a secretion which covers the swarm and hardens. The hard mass is crushed, separated from the twigs, and washed. It passes through purifying, stretching, and other processes, and for some purposes is dewaxed. The following are the chief types: bleached and dewaxed lac, used for transparent polish; bleached lac, for white polish; seed lac, unstretched for button polish; TN or factory shellac, stretched, for orange polish; flake shellac with original dye, for garnet polish.

shell carving A popular motif of decoration in the early eighteenth century. It appeared on the knees of cabriole legs, seat and table rails, in broken pediments, and elsewhere. (See illustration under *escallop.*)

shell, spoon, nose and gimlet bits These are used chiefly for boring screw holes. Shell bits (D) are slow cutting but not liable to split the wood. Except for the gimlet bit (A), sometimes termed a half-twist bit, the bits form a core. The nose bit (B) removes this more readily when withdrawn. The spoon bit (C) is of spoon formation at the tip, and is the type formerly widely used by Windsor chair makers. The shell bit (D) is often a worn spoon or nose bit with sharpened tip.

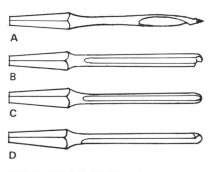

A

B

C

D

SHELL, SPOON, NOSE, & GIMLET BITS

Apart from making screw holes the shell bit is useful for removing broken screw shanks from wood, its edge cutting around the screw, thereby freeing it from the wood. The gimlet bit (A) bores easily without great pressure, but if used near the edge might cause a split. Bits normally range in size from $\frac{1}{16}$ in (2 mm) up to $\frac{5}{8}$ in (16 mm) but some of the larger sizes may be difficult to obtain as they have largely been replaced by bits used in the electric drill.

she oak *(casuarina fraseriana)* Western Australian timber of 42 lb (673 kg) used for veneers, turnery, roof shingles, etc. It is not a true oak, and is of a yellowish red colour.

sheveret Another name for a cheveret *(q.v.)*.

shield-back chair Popular type from 1780 to 1790 and chiefly associated with the Hepplewhite style. Mahogany was invariably used.

shims Thin metal packing pieces used in some bullnose and shoulder planes having a detachable nose piece, the shims fitting between the fore end of the plane body and the nose to regulate the size of the mouth. Also used as distance pieces.

shingle A roofing tile in wood. It may be in oak, in which case it is usually riven; or of western red cedar, tapered in length.

ship lap Weather boards rebated at one edge and thinned down at the other so that they fit together flush. (See also *weather boarding for other sections.*)

SHIPLAP

shive The bung of a cask.

shoe Term applied to the feet of a trestle table, sideboard, dresser, or other piece of furniture. It is the horizontal member to which the ends or legs are fitted at floor level.

shoe piece A small slotted projection on the back seat rail of a chair which is intended to receive the base of the splat which, prior to 1700, was not fixed to the seat.

shoot To plane an edge straight and square, or to plane a joint. Sometimes spelt shute.

shooting block, mitre (see *mitre shooting block*).

shooting board An appliance used for planing the edges of thin wood to avoid wobble in the plane, and for squaring the ends of wood. Made in any length fronm 18 in (457 mm) to 4 ft (1219 mm) or 5 ft (1524 mm). It is usually made in the workshop. A simple type is shown in the drawing. Essential features are that the upper board is of equal thickness throughout, has its edge straight and square, with a dust groove at the bottom corner. The stop is of wedge shape so that it can be tapped in if it becomes loose.

For trimming the end of wood the latter is held against the stop and gradually fed up to the plane. The latter is worked back and forth against the edge of the upper board. When the edge of thin wood is being planed straight or a joint being made, the wood is placed to overhang about $\frac{1}{8}$ in (2 mm). The edge is made straight by virtue of the truth of the plane sole. The plane does not touch the edge of the upper board. In the case of planing a joint the one piece is placed with the face side uppermost and the other with it facing downwards. If the plane side should not be quite square with the sole the two parts will still go together in alignment. An odd angle can be trimmed by placing a tapered block against the stop. (See also *donkey's ear shooting board, and mitre shooting board*.)

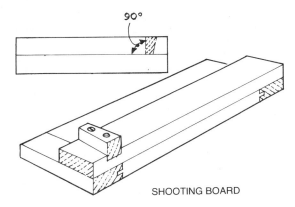

SHOOTING BOARD

shooting plane Alternative name for a jointer plane *(q.v.)*.

shore (see under *dead shore and raking shore*). A flying shore is one having no direct support from the ground.

shoring Method of supporting a building whilst alterations or repairs are carried out. Types are dead shoring, flying shoring, raking shoring, double raking shoring, treble raking shoring.

short ends Relatively short length of timber, no more than 5 ft 6 in (1675 mm) long in various widths.

short grain Applied to a narrow piece of wood or narrow part of the work where the grain runs crosswise with the length.

short oil varnish The converse to long oil *(q.v.)*. The term refers to a varnish containing only a small quantity of linseed oil; all rubbing varnishes fall into this category.

shorts Timber generally which is less than 6 ft (2 m) long. Used in the timber trade for pieces which are shorter than the general run.

shoulder The bearing parts of a tenoned or similar joint are known as the shoulders. Also applied to a supporting projection.

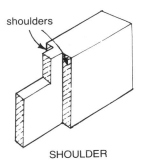

SHOULDER

shoulder cutter (see *tenoner*).

shouldered dovetail housing Joint used mostly for shelves. It is usually stopped at the front. The taper in its length has the advantage that the joint is quite loose until nearly home, and is thus much easier to fit than a parallel joint. A barefaced dovetail housing has the dovetail slope at one edge only.

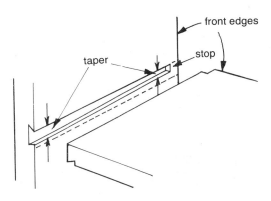

SHOULDERED DOVETAIL HOUSING

shoulder plane   A form of rebate plane used mainly for trimming wide shoulders, though it can be used for finishing any rebates. It is specially useful for end grain. The cutter is usually set at 18 deg with the bevel uppermost. Thus it is supported close up to the cutting edge. The plane is of metal and is adjustable. The illustration shows the combination type enabling it to be used as a bullnose with the short front fitted, or as a chisel plane with both fronts omitted. Formerly a wood lined plane was also made but this is no longer available today. Some planes were all-steel, others of gun metal with steel face.

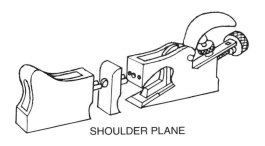

SHOULDER PLANE

show-case   (see *china cabinet*).

showcase joint   A mitred joint for joining three rails at a corner.

show-wood   A term applied to upholstered furniture which has some of the wooden parts deliberately showing.

Shropshire dresser   A dresser with a cupboard, or two, built into the shelving.

shut bed   A bunk bed which fitted into an alcove in a wall: used in Saxon times.

side   The wide face of a board.

side axe   One which has its bevel on one side only. Used largely by coopers in fashioning the staves of a barrel; also used by wheelwrights at one time.

side-cutting pliers   These have jaws which are hollowed out on one side, with cutting edges opposite.

sideboard   In its original application this was a side serving table, but in its present meaning it became the rather specialised piece developed in the second half of the eighteenth century with drawers and cupboards. Recognised height for comfortable use was 36-38 in (914-965 mm), but today they are frequently made lower. Length varies from 2 ft 6 in (762 mm) to 5 ft

(1524 mm) but many modern sideboards are made much longer. Drawers and cupboards are an obvious necessity.

sideboard table   Rather massive side table, often with marble top, used in the first half of the eighteenth century. It became the side table of the Adam period with flanking pedestals and urns, and developed into the sideboard.

side dresser   Tool used in making even the sides of saw teeth when swage setting.

side dressing   Making the sides of saw teeth even when setting. In the case of spring setting it is usually known as side filing *(q.v.)*.

side filing   Operation to correct any unevenness in the set of saw teeth. Either a fine file or a hone is used after setting but before sharpening is begun. Light rubs in each direction are given, both sides being treated alike.

side grain   The grain on the surfaces of wood as distinct from that at the ends.

side rebate plane   Used for trimming the sides of grooves and sometimes rebates, or for the sloping side of a dovetailed housing. In some older patterns separate right-hand and left-hand planes were made. The nose is removable to enable it to work right into a corner. The tool is specially useful for widening a groove to receive a polished shelf or a veneered part which could not be reduced in thickness.

side table   Large table flanked with pedestals with urns used in the dining room in the late eighteenth century. It has now a more general application to any table intended to stand against the wall instead of being in the middle of the room. (See *sideboard.*)

side thrust   A fault in hollow chisel mortising caused by the cut being stepped down in one direction only. It may deflect the hollow chisel and even crack it. Correctly the cuts should be started from each end and worked towards each other.

siding   (see *slab*).

sight size   That part of the glass that can be actually seen in a mirror frame. It applies also to the length and width of the glass that is visible in a glazed door, taking no account of rebate depth.

silex   Silicon oxide used in making paste filler.

silica (see *silex*).

silicon carbide This is the abrasive material used on wet-and-dry paper *(q.v.)*. It is man-made from silica with added carbon (in the form of coke) heated in an electric furnace, the resulting fusion creating a hard crystalline rock. When this is pulverised into grit, the particles are hard but brittle, and tend to lose their sharp points easily. In use it has a very high cutting ability provided it is not applied heavily; the waterproof grade can be used wet with soap as a lubricant, or with wax.

silk A fabric woven from the cocoon of the silk moth *(bombyx mori)*; it originated in China and was introduced into Constantinople about the sixth century. In Britain the manufacture of silk began in 1585 as a result of an influx of Flemish weavers.

silking Parallel hair-like striations in a painted or varnished film.

silkwood, maple *(flindersia brayleyana)* Australian timber of 35-40 lb (561-641 kg). Used for furniture, plywood, veneers, etc. Somewhat like mahogany with fine grain qualities.

silky oak *(cardwellia sublimis)* Australian timber of 37 lb (593 kg). Used for furniture, turnery, interior fitments, etc. Has prominent medullary rays, but is not a true oak. Pinkish brown colour.

sill Bottom member of a window frame or other structure. Sometimes spelt cill. Also the horizontal bottom member of a stud wall; it is fixed to the floor.

silvan Pertaining to trees, woods, etc.

silver furniture Type that became popular with wealthy people in the second half of the seventeenth century. It was made with sheets of thin silver mounted on a wood ground and with ornamental parts of cast silver.

silver grain Oak figuring produced by cutting the log parallel with the medullary rays.

silver greywood *(terminalia bialata)* From the Andaman Islands, 40 lb (641 kg) weight. Used for veneer, cabinet work, panelling, etc. A timber of widely varying appearance. One is plain and unfigured and is known as white chuglam. Another is lightish brown, finely figured with darker streaks. Stains and polishes well.

silver sand (see *sand, for shading*).

silver spruce *(Picea sitchensis)* The sitka spruce of western Canada and USA.

silverwood In the eighteenth century this term appears to have been applied to harewood *(q.v.)*.

simple-angled dovetails (USA) Dovetails which are cut at angle of 45 degrees, but with one side square. The pins are cut at an angle of 80 degrees from the surface as in straight dovetailing, and parallel to the outside edge.

singerie French term for the use of monkeys as a decorative motif.

single-end tenoner (see *tenoners*).

single iron Plane cutter with no back iron *(q.v.)*.

sinking (1) A shallow recess cut in the solid. Frequently applied to work such as sunk paterae, fluting, gouge cuts, etc.

sinking (2) The liability of some polishes, varnishes, and other finishes to be absorbed by porous woods.

sisal fibre Used in some spring-interior mattresses and cushions as stuffing, but now largely replaced by plastic materials.

sissoo *(dalbergia sissoo)* Indian hardwood of 48 lb (769 mm), somewhat like rosewood. Has close grain and seasons well.

sitka spruce (see *spruce, sitka*).

six cutter Large machine which has six revolving cutter heads, enabling it to cut complicated sections in one operation, including grooving, rebating, moulding, etc.

size Thin glue used on softwoods before veneering and on end grain before gluing. It helps to prevent undue absorption of glue.

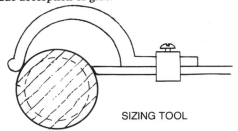

SIZING TOOL

sizing tool   Used by wood turners to cut grooves or spigots to uniform size.

Skarsten scraper   A proprietary scraper made in various patterns used for cleaning up wood surfaces. Blades are replaceable and are sharpened with a fine file. There is also a toothed pattern for breaking up a tough surface which has been painted. For floor work a long-handled tool is available.

skeleton   Term sometimes used as an alternative to carcase *(q.v.)*. Often applied to floors and framings before boarding is added.

skeleton framework   The main structural parts of an item, including legs, rails, stiles, etc., before panelling or other cladding is added.

skew   Applied to items which are not square. Also to nailing or screwing out of square.

skew-back saw   Handsaw having its back edge shaped to a hollow curve. (See *illustration under panel saw.*)

skew-butt hinge   (see *rising butt*).

skew chisel   Alternative name for a corner chisel. (See under *carver's chisels.*) Also another name for the long-cornered chisel *(q.v.)* used by wood turners.

skew cutter   Plane cutter which is set obliquely across the sole instead of being square. Usually confined to rebate and badger planes *(q.v.)*.

skewer, upholsterer's   Used by the upholsterer to hold down hessian, covers, etc., temporarily during the tacking-down process.

skew fillet   (see *tilting fillet*).

skew nailing   Driving nails at an angle instead of square. Sometimes needed when nailing in a corner, or to clear a detail.

SKEW NAILING

skid (1)   A piece of softwood about $\frac{1}{4}$ in (5mm) thick and 11 in (280mm) wide on which sections and details of an item are drawn. It is usually long enough for the entire height of the job to be drawn, and the whole thing is put in in full size, including mouldings, rails, doors, etc. An exception is when a deep job is to be shown, in which case broken lines are put in and the actual size marked with arrows. Enough information should be given to enable someone to prepare cutting lists and to make the job. Both edges of the board should be planed straight. Lines parallel with the edge are put in using the rule and finger method, and those at right angles drawn with the T-square or try-square. In some cases a plan skid of the job is also needed. An alternative name is a rod.

skid (2)   The term also refers to short seasoned sticks, 1 in (25mm) or less thick, used for stacking converted timber when seasoning. They are also known as stickers *(q.v.)*. It is important that they are placed vertically one above the other. (See *piling and stacking.*)

skin glue   Animal glue made from skins rather than bones. (See *Salisbury glue.*)

skin   Applied loosely to the surface covering of a structure, or to the outer layers of a built-up substance.

skinning in   Alternative name for fadding *(q.v.)*.

skin for upholstery   These include cow hide, morocco (goat skin), roan (sheep skins).

skirting   The plinth board, usually moulded on its top edge, which runs around the bottom of an inside wall. In best class work it is tongued at the bottom edge to fit into a groove worked in the floor boards.

skirting piece   (see *apron piece*).

skived joint   Used in joining the ends of a sanding belt.

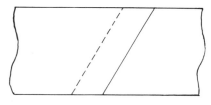

SKIVED JOINT

skiver   Cheap form of leather made from split sheepskin. Often used for table tops.

slab The outside slice from a log which is being squared or cut into boards. One side is rounded. Also known as a siding. It is usually discarded as firewood or used to cover timber stacks.

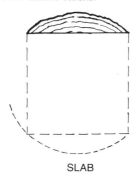

SLAB

slab leg Table support in place of legs in the form: of a single flat piece, usually shaped at the edges. (See *trestle table*.)

slamming strip The upright door stop fixed at the closing side to form a rebate. (See *door stop*.)

slant-front desk (USA) Corresponds to British 'bureau' (*q.v.*).

slash sawn (see *flat sawn*).

slat Rail in a chair back, usually thinner than the rest of the framework, but also used loosely for any narrow, thin rails.

slat-back chair Sometimes applied to a simple form of ladder back chair (*q.v.*), but with plain flat slats.

slate stone, Welsh Sometimes used for honing tools. Quality and capacity to cut varies.

slating batten (see *tiling batten*).

slats Any narrow, thin strip stuff used in making shutters, Venetian blinds, etc. Also the intermediate back rails of a chair.

slayped joint Alternative name for a glued joint (*q.v.*). Also known as a rubbed joint.

sledge foot Normally used on chairs and settles, this kind of foot consists of a block of wood into which both front and back legs are housed; it is usually relieved on the underside.

sleeper Apart from its association with railway track, the term sleeper indicates the heavy horizontal bottom piece which in larger outdoor structures supports the vertical timbers.

sleeper plate The wall plate used in a honeycombed wall supporting the joists.

sleigh bed An American bed resembling a sleigh in shape and exhibiting French Empire influence.

sleigh bench (USA) A bench seat which could either be mounted on sleigh runners or stand on its own, thus being dual-purpose. The bench ends are solid and have hand-holes to facilitate lifting, and the construction was tenoned and pegged. The design was favoured by the Amish, a religious sect in the northeastern USA.

slicer Heavy slicing machine for cutting veneers. In flat slicing the log is held stationary on a bed, and the knife, which is mounted on a carriage, moves across it at right angles with grain. In some machines the knife is stationary, the log moving. The finest figure is produced by this method. The knife is set at a slight angle so that it has a slicing cut, and moves towards the log after each cut by a distance equal to the required thickness of veneer. Except in cases in which the colour would suffer (as in sycamore) the log is steamed beforehand. (See also *half-rotary, half-round slicing, and rotary cut veneer*.)

slicer, tapeless veneer Machine which joins veneers edgewise. A series of wheels set at an angle force the veneers together. The edges of the veneer are pressed against a disc which is kept moist with resin glue, which, as a result of electrical heating, sets immediately.

slicing, half-rotary (see *half-rotary slicing*).

slicing, half-round (see *half-round slicing*).

slick bit One for use with the electrical drill. Cutters are for holes from $\frac{1}{2}$ in (12 mm) up to $1\frac{1}{4}$ in (32 mm) and are interchangeable on a common $\frac{1}{4}$ in (6 mm) shank. They give a clean finish, and snatch is avoided by the grinding bevel which is only a few degrees from a right angle. For a through hole a spare piece of wood should be cramped beneath and the hole taken right through to this.

SLICK BIT

191

slide A small shelf which can be pulled out from a table, bureau, or similar piece and used as a temporary rest for a book or other item. Sometimes known as a slider.

slider Alternative name for a loper *(q.v.)*, or for a slide.

sliding bevel (see *bevel, sliding*).

sliding door Light doors are usually carried on gliders working on a fibre track, or, in the case of a heavier door, on a ball-bearing fitting running on a metal track. Most room-size sliding doors run hanging from an overhead track. When the door is of glass it generally runs in a special metal or plastic channelling.

sliding door locks A suitable type for a wood door is shown at (A). It has a three-way keyhole which enables the lock to be used in any required position. The body fits into a recess with plates sunk in flush. Plate glass doors require a special lock (B), the overlap of the closed doors being held by a Z-shaped bolt. When unlocked the doors are free to slide over the lock plate. The lock body is let into either top or bottom of the cabinet.

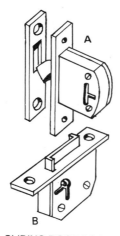

SLIDING DOOR LOCKS

sliding door runners and track There are two kinds, gliding and ball-bearing. Of the former type (A) has a track consisting of a strip of hard fibre with rounded top edge, and is let into a groove. The runner is of a greasy nature and is self-lubricating. Another kind, (B) for glass, consists of a double channel in either metal or plastic.

Ball-bearing runners (C) require to be recessed in.

The track is in various lengths and may be of a simple pattern to fit into a groove, or of T shape for screwing.

To enable glass doors to be inserted and removed the top grooves must be double the depth of those at the bottom to allow the doors to be lifted upwards and dropped into their grooves, or similarly removed.

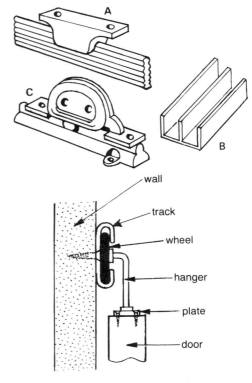

TOP HANGING TRACK

SLIDING DOOR RUNNERS & TRACK

sliding dovetail (USA) Corresponds to British *'dovetail housing joint' (q.v.)*.

sliding sash One which can be moved up and down, and which has counter-weights held on cords or chains. Other sashes are fixed, pivoted, or hinged. (See also *sash and frame.*)

sliding T-bevel (USA) Corresponds to British *'bevel, sliding' (q.v.)*.

slip, belt Sometimes occurs in a flat belt and is often caused by the belt having become hard and dry. Periodic dressing will keep it in condition. A sticky dressing will sometimes cure slip, but it should not be necessary if dressed, say, once a month.

slip dovetail   Alternative name for a dovetail key (see *keying*). Also an alternative name for a slot-dovetail *(q.v.)*.

slip feather   Loose tongue with the grain running diagonally. It enables the tongues to be cut in longer strips than when the grain is at right angles. It is also an alternative name for a veneer key *(q.v.)*.

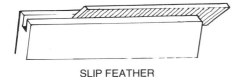

SLIP FEATHER

slip joint   (USA) Corresponds to British *'open mortise and tenon' (q.v.)*.

slip key   (see *keying*).

slip, oilstone   (see under *oilstone*).

slip seat   Alternative name for a loose seat *(q.v.)*.

slitting cutter   Fitted to some plough and multi-planes to enable thin wood to be slit into narrow strips. A depth stop is provided, this being fixed outside the cutter. The cut is made halfway down from each side.

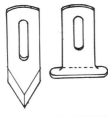

SLITTING CUTTERS

sliver   Thin piece of wood split from a board.

slot-dovetail   Form of dovetail joint fitting in a groove with one or both sides sloping. When the dovetail slope occurs on the side only it is known as a bare-faced dovetail slot (B). It may run right through or, more usually, stopped at one edge (C). (See also *housing joint.*)

slot mortise   Usually refers to one cut with a rotary miller bit and consequently having rounded ends.

slot-screwing   A method of screwing two pieces of wood together where the shrinkage of one could cause

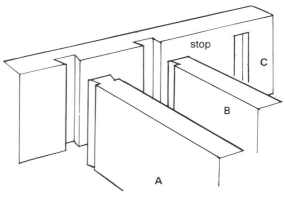

SLOT DOVETAIL

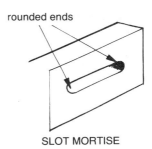

SLOT MORTISE

splitting; the screw passes through a slot instead of a hole and thus allows a certain amount of lateral movement. It can be used to fix drawer runners to solid carcase ends, or to bearers which are fixed across several pieces as on the underside of a drawing board.

slot screw joint   A joint used in place of dowels to strengthen butt-jointed boards. The screw positions are squared across the edges of the board, but with one board staggered about $\frac{1}{2}$ in (12 mm) in relation to

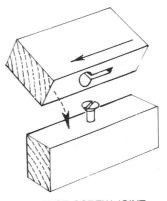

SLOT-SCREW JOINT

the other. Gauge marks are made on both edges from the face side and countersunk screws are driven into the edge of one board to project about $\frac{3}{8}$ in (10mm). Holes to suit the diameter of the screw heads are bored full $\frac{3}{8}$ in (10mm) deep in the edge of the second board, and slots to suit the screw shank size cut at one side. A cramp is applied at a slight angle, and the one board knocked along with the mallet until the ends are level, thus causing the screw heads to bite into the slots and, by their entry, pull the boards tightly and firmly together. When satisfactory the parts are separated and the screws tightened half a turn. Glue is applied and the assembly process repeated.

slotted-collar block   (see *spindle moulder*).

slotter (1)   This is a cutter for a spindle moulder head and comprises two circular toothed plates held apart by shims of various thicknesses to make up the thickness of the slot required.

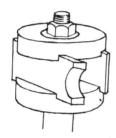

SLOTTED COLLAR BLOCK

slotter (2)   (see *oscillating bit mortiser*).

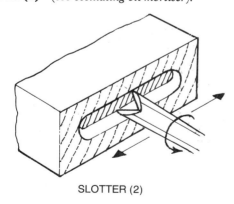

SLOTTER (2)

Sloyd knife   (USA) A craft knife with a curved cutting edge to the blade and a pointed tip; used for whittling.

small knot   One of $\frac{1}{2}$in (12mm) to $\frac{3}{4}$in (19mm) dia. (See *knots*.)

smoker's bow chair   A low-back Windsor chair probably based on the American Philadelphian low-back of 1725; it first became popular in Britain about 1820 and is still widely used today. It has heavy turned baluster legs, a D-shaped seat, an arm bow with flaring sides, and a deep scrolled top piece mounted centrally on the arm bow. Sometimes there was a shelf under the seat for a spittoon.

smoothing plane   Bench plane of wood (A) or metal (B), used primarily for the final cleaning up of timber after truing with a longer plane, but also required for planing small pieces and for bench work generally. Originally there was also the ebony or rosewood-lined steel plane in cutter widths of 2in (51mm) to 2$\frac{1}{4}$ in (58mm) made by Spiers and Norris. Although no longer made there are still many of them in use.

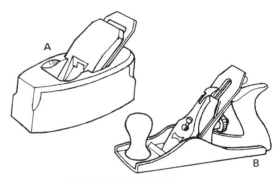

SMOOTHING PLANES

smutting   (USA) Refers to the operation of dusting rottenstone powder over a wax film to simulate age.

snail or snail-horn countersink   (see *countersink*).

snake hinge   Decorative hinge often used on secretaire joints (*q.v.*). Alternative names: dolphin hinge, and cock's-head hinge (USA)

SNAIL COUNTERSINK

snakewood (*piratinera guianensis*)   Hardwood from central and tropical South America of 77-83lb (1233-1329kg). Dense wood, chocolate brown in colour. Available only in small pieces, and used chiefly for inlaying, violin bows, and small items.

snape A bifurcated fastener (like a large paper fastener) used to fix drop handles in the seventeenth century.

snipe's bill A form of moulding plane used for trimming a recessed moulding. Made R and L hand to suit the run of the grain.

sociable A sofa or ottoman.

sockets The cavities at the sides of the pins in a dovetail joint. Also any opening into which another part fits.

socket castor Made either round or square to fit over the end of a table or chair leg, the end of the latter being shaped to fit the socket. (See *castor*.)

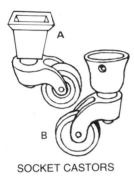

SOCKET CASTORS

socket chisel, gouge, bruzze, etc. Any cutting tool having a tapered socket into which the handle fits, as distinct from having tang fixing. (See *illustration C, mortise chisel*.)

socle The plinth or base of a column, usually moulded.

sodium perborate Sometimes used in bleaching wood.

sofa Similar in construction to a settee but usually larger; it is intended for reclining, and has a roll arm at each end. (See *sociable*.)

sofa table Oblong table introduced towards the end of the eighteenth century, and continued in the following century. Its long shape made it suitable for use beside a sofa. Generally there were flaps at the ends supported by hinged brackets, and two drawers at one side. Frequently the other side has dummy drawer fronts. Average height is 25 in (635 mm) and top width 12 in (305 mm) to 14 in (356 mm).

soffit Underside of an opening, arch, stair, etc.

softwood Timber of the coniferous or cone-bearing trees with needle-pointed leaves. Also known as non-porous woods in that the cells are not open-ended as in hardwoods, the sap passing from cell to cell through fragile party walls. The term 'softwood' is generally convenient but does not necessarily relate to actual softness since some softwoods are harder and heavier than some hardwoods. (See also *hardwood*.)

soldier Upright member used in carpentry. In particular the term refers to short uprights providing a fixing for a skirting, and also to those used in strutting excavations.

sole Applied to the working face of a plane, portable electric saw, electric router, etc.

sole plate (1) A horizontal or near-horizontal wood beam at the foot of a raking shore to spread the load. It is also applied to the buried base member of a gate post having sloping struts at each side.

sole plate (2) The lowest horizontal member of a timber stud partition wall *(q.v.)* which is fixed to the floor. It is also called a 'sill'.

solid colour Polish which has been made opaque with colouring matter. Used when plain areas have to be grained or painted out.

solid door One which is made up of a single slab or of two or more pieces butt-jointed side by side, as distinct from having framed construction.

solid, in the Usually refers to a detail such as a moulding which is cut in the substance of the item itself as distinct from one which is applied.

solid moulding One worked or stuck in the substance of the item, that is, not applied.

solid nose bit A twist bit in which the ends of the double twist are joined, and are pierced to form cutting edges. It is stronger than the similar Gedge bit *(q.v.)*. (See also *Irwin, Russell-Jennings, and Scotch nose bit*.)

SOLID-NOSE BIT

solid profile cutter (see *spindle moulder*.)

solid step One which consists of a single piece of timber rather than being built up from separate treads and risers. It may also be laminated to increase fire-resistance.

solid strutting Vertical timbers fixed between floor joints to give stiffness.

soss hinge One which enables parts to be hinged together without any projecting knuckles. Card templets are issued with the hinges, but it is more accurate to mark out with gauge and square.

sounding board A canopy erected over a pulpit in such a way that it acted as a tympanum and helped to carry the preacher's voice. Also called a tester *(q.v.)* from its resemblance to that object.

sound knot Alternative term to live knot *(q.v.)*.

south Wales dresser These are distinguished from the North Wales dresser by having a pot-board underneath a row of drawers; the Northern style normally has enclosed cupboards. A dresser top with shelves is common to both.

spacing piece Item of wood or metal to hold items apart by a required distance. It may take the form of a collar. (See also *distance piece*.)

spade carving gouge (see *carver's gouges*).

spade chisel (see *carver's chisels*).

spade toe The lower termination of a square tapered leg. Sometimes known as a thurmed toe, but in furniture such feet were always cut by hand methods. They were never 'thurmed'. (See *thurm*.)

SPADE TOE

spade gouge (see *carving gouges*).

spalt Term sometimes used for wood which is brittle as a result of decay, over-dryness, or short grain; it is usually a light brown colour.

span The distance between two supporting items such as pillars, pilasters, walls, etc.

spandrel or spandril The enclosed space between the curve of an arch and the rectangular top and sides. In cabinet work the term also refers to a curved top rail between uprights. Sometimes known as a span rail. In staircase work it refers to a triangular filling beneath the string to bring to an even line.

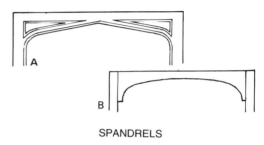

SPANDRELS

spanish foot (USA) Corresponds to British *'Braganza foot' (q.v.)*.

spanish or sweet chestnut (see *chestnut*).

span rail Alternative name for a spandrel *(q.v.)*.

span roof Common type of roof like an inverted V with equal pitch at each side.

spar varnish A specially durable waterproof varnish used on the exterior of yachts, boats, etc.

sparver Originally a bed curtain, but later a fabric canopy over a bed instead of a tester *(q.v.)*. Used in Britain from fifteenth century onwards.

spearfast cross cut Handsaw with teeth specially shaped for rapid cutting. Particularly suitable for softwood and for green timber. It cuts on both strokes. It is too coarse for fine cabinet and joinery work, but excellent for carpentry.

SPEARFAST CROSSCUT

species Term for classifying timbers into groups. It is done on a botanical basis. The main group is the 'family', of which there may be more than one 'genus'; and in the latter there may be several 'species'. In the Latin scientific name the first is the generic name and is given with an initial capital letter; the second is the species with small initial. Thus an oak may be *Quercus alba*, or *Quercus robur*, etc.

specification Statement of the quality, weight, finish, etc., of work to be executed.

speed In woodwork refers to the speed at which a machine operates. It is usually expressed in rpm (revolutions per minute), and may be that of the driving motor, the spindle to which the cutter(s) is fixed, or (in a lathe) the revolutions of the work. It may also refer to peripheral speed which is the rate at which teeth or cutters are moving.

spelching A term describing the breakthrough of the saw teeth when cutting a work-piece on the saw-bench.

spider bevel Tool originally used by coachmakers. It has adjustable blades which can be fixed at varying angles.

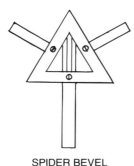

SPIDER BEVEL

spider gauge Alternative name for a grasshopper gauge *(q.v.)*.

spider leg Leg made up of three or four slender turned columns dowelled into squares or blocks. They were often used in the eighteenth century for side tables to hold silver and other items. Sometimes known as the cluster leg *(q.v.)*.

spiers of Ayr Well-known Scottish firm of tool makers. Planes were a speciality, and were of steel lined with hardwood. The firm began to make planes about 1840, and listed smoothers, panel, and larger planes.

spigot The projection at the end of a turning to fit into a corresponding recess in another turning. Also refers to a plug used for a cask.

spike A large nail, usually more than 4 in (102 mm) long.

spike grid connector For connecting large pieces of timber such as baulks, posts, etc., used on piers, jetties and the like. They are installed by being inserted between the timbers to be joined and embedded by applying pressure by means of a through bolt.

SPIKED GRID CONNECTOR

spike knot One which is exposed when cut through in line with the branch, so having a spike-like appearance.

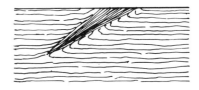

SPIKE KNOT

spiling Method of reproducing a curved or odd shape when direct measurement would be difficult or awkward. It is useful in fitting, say, a hardboard or plywood panel up to a moulded projection. A piece of stiff paper with straight edge is placed against the wall or other surface, its edge cut to clear the projection. A pointed item such as a set-square is placed in various positions all round, its point touching the projection, and a pencil line drawn on the paper around it. The paper is removed and placed on the board to be cut, the straight edges coinciding. The set square is placed in line with each pair of pencil lines, and a pencil run along each side towards the point. A line faired through the points gives the outline to be cut.

Another method of arriving at the same result is to place the actual panel against the greatest projection, the edge parallel with the wall or whatever it may be. A series of lines is drawn at right angles with the edge. A pointed stick is cut to the widest gap between panel and wall, held against each line in turn, and a mark made on the panel at the end of the stick. The marks so made are points along the shape to be cut, and a line passing through them is faired in. The stick must be parallel with the squared lines.

197

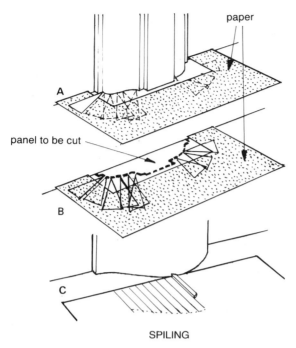

paper

panel to be cut

A

B

C

SPILING

spill plane One specially designed to produce spiral shavings for use as spills. It resembles a skew rebate plane, but the cutter is set at a more acute angle to give a more pronounced curl to the shavings.

spindle Small turned member contained between rails. It occurs in some table and sideboard galleries, chair backs, etc.

spindle-back Windsor chair A Windsor chair which has spindles in the back. The spindles are turned rods with a slight swell about one-third of the way up.

spindle moulder Machine having a horizontal table with a revolving spindle projecting through it; used for making mouldings, grooving, rebating, and so on. There are several types of cutting head, the simplest being the French head. In this the cutter passes radially through a slot in the spindle head and is ground at each end to an exact reverse of the required profile. The edge is turned over and ticketed, and the action is more of scraping than cutting, as the cutting edge is not bevelled. The 'Whitehill' block is a steel disc with a central hole to accept the spindle and small HSS cutters are bolted into slots in the periphery. Most have two cutters, but some have four. 'Safety' blocks such as those by Leitz have wedge-shaped slots to hold the cutters in. The solid profile cutter is made all in one piece, and is made in HSS.

The two-wing 'throw-away' tipped cutter has two TCT blades fixed opposite each other; when worn out they are discarded. There is also a shear-cutting rebating block which is fitted with small spurs mounted in the top and bottom faces and these cut the bottoms of rebates or the tops and bottoms of grooves, as the case may be. Last, there is a slotted-collar block in which a pair of balanced cutters are fixed. All types need careful setting-up to ensure dynamic balance.

Fences and guards are needed for safe operation, and the latter comprise the Shaw guard; the 'cage' or 'bonnet', which is a hood which encloses the head and cutters but with an aperture allowing the wood to be cut (if the cage or bonnet guard is combined with an anti-snatch-back spring-loaded pressure shoe it is known as the 'Yarwood'); the 'Pen Farrell' guard is a steel pressure ring that surrounds the head and bears down on the wood and has a vertical flange to shield the cutting tool — it should be used in conjunction with the cage or bonnet guard. The ring fence *(q.v.)* is not intended primarily as a guard but as a guide for pieces being worked.

spindle turning (see *turning, wood*).

spiral A line which recedes from a centre point as it revolves around it. Its practical application is in a scroll as in a handrail. (See *scroll.*)

spiral balance (see *spring balance*).

spiral-ratchet screwdriver One having a spindle with double spiral groove enabling screws to be inserted or withdrawn by the pump action of the handle. It may have spring return or be free. The tool may also be locked in the down position enabling it to be used as either a ratchet screwdriver or as a simple rigid type. Usually a second and sometimes a third blade is available, being held by a chuck operated by a spring collar. Countersink and drills are also made. It is also known as a 'Yankee' screwdriver.

SPIRAL RATCHET SCREWDRIVER

spiral turning (see *twist turning*).

spirit To woodworkers this is methylated spirit *(q.v.)*.

spirit case A wooden oblong casket, usually in mahogany and often with silver mounts; fitted for bottles of spirits and placed on a sideboard or side-table.

spirit colours (black, green, mahogany, etc.). Spirit-soluble powders used in making spirit stains and for colouring French polish.

spiriting off One of the methods of finishing in French polishing. The work, having been bodied to a full gloss, is left to harden. A rubber, known as a ghost, is made from cotton wool with cloth facing, and is charged with no more than a drop of methylated spirit. It is worked over the surface in long parallel strokes, as first with a light touch, the pressure gradually increasing as the moisture evaporates. It has the effect of removing the oil. A fresh part of the rag covering is used as it becomes greasy. On no account must the rubber be damp with spirit. It should merely be cold when pressed against the cheek.

spirit level An instrument for determining the absolute truth of a horizontal part. Particularly useful when fixing wall fitments, shelving picture rails, etc. Body may be of wood, usually with brass facing, or of metal. Lengths for joinery and carpentry range from 6 in (152 mm) to 12 in (305 mm). For long surfaces the level is placed on a long wood batten with parallel edges. Longer levels up to 3 ft 6 in (1067 mm) or so are also made but are usually associated with bricklaying.

spirits of camphor Used in making some polish revivers. A colourless liquid. A dose larger than half a teaspoonful may be poisonous.

spirit stain (see *staining*).

spirit varnish One with methylated spirit used as a medium. Thus French polishes are a form of spirit varnish. Except when used as part of the French polishing process, spirit varnish is usually associated with cheaper work. It is brittle and has not the resistance to wear of oil varnish *(q.v.)*, and is of no value for outdoor work. It should never be applied over oil varnish as it is liable to cause crazing. It is seldom used these days.

splad (see *splat*).

splat A wide upright member fitted between two back rails of a chair or settee. Sometimes called a splad *(q.v.)*.

splay An outward slope. An example of its application is in a Windsor chair which has splayed legs.

splayed work The development of inclined surfaces. It largely involves compound angles and cuts

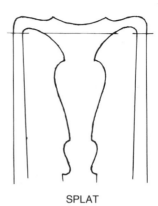

SPLAT

as in roof work, linings around window and door openings, staircase work, and so on.

splay knot (see *spike knot*).

splayed edges A bevel *(q.v.)*.

splayed joint (see *spliced joint*).

splice Usually refers to a scarf joint, or to the joint in the handle of a billiard cue.

spliced joint One in which two pieces are jointed lengthwise with a sloping joint rather than being butted straight across. Also known as a splayed joint. There are several variations of it. (See also *scarf joint.*)

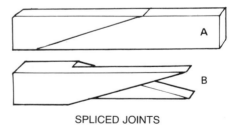

SPLICED JOINTS

spline A long flexible wood strip used by draughtsmen in setting out curves, particularly those which are not part of a circle. Usually the ends are somewhat thinner than the centre as otherwise most bending takes place in the middle producing an ugly curve. The spline is held down in position by special weights as shown.
    The term is also applied to a loose tongue *(q.v.)*.

spline (USA) Corresponds to British 'tongue' *(q.v.)*.

spline miter (USA) Corresponds to British 'tongued mitre' *(q.v.)*.

splint seat (USA) A chair seat made of interlaced thin strips of hickory or oak, popular during the eighteenth century.

split handle Drop handle found in some Queen Anne furniture rounded at the front only and usually hollow at the back.

split-ring connector Split circular steel bands which are embedded in pre-cut circular grooves in the pieces being joined, half the depth of the ring being housed in each piece of timber. It is used for wood-to-wood joints only, and develops a very strong joint.

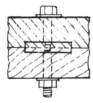

SPLIT-RING CONNECTOR

splitting wedges Used in riving logs. They can only be used for woods suitable for splitting such as oak. They are knocked into the wood in line with the medullary rays. In some cases wooden wedges follow the preliminary insertion, their advantage being that they follow the natural line of cleavage, whereas a steel wedge would be liable to cut through the grain.

split turning A half-turning consisting of an ornament split in half lengthwise and planted on a pilaster or panel. It was a feature of the Jacobean and seventeenth century Flemish periods. To make split turnings two pieces are put together with thin glue with newspaper interposed. After turning they are split apart with a thin chisel.

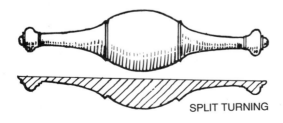

SPLIT TURNING

spokeshave Used mostly nowadays for trimming the shaped edges of wood, making shaped legs, etc.

Made in both wood and metal and choice is largely one of personal preference. Wood types are apt to wear quickly, particularly at the mouth, and some have a brass mouth plate to prevent this. Usually the cutter is held by its tangs in holes in the stock, but some have screw fixing which simplifies adjustment. The cutter is sharpened on the narrow edge of an oilstone or with an oilstone slip. Cutters are sometimes adjustable.

SPOKESHAVES

spool (USA) A decorative motif in turning corresponding to British 'reel' *(q.v.)*.

spoon-back chair Term sometimes used for a chair back with double curvature in the uprights; circa 1720-1730. The back often had a crest rail at the top and this rail usually had a dip in the centre to accommodate the queue of the occupant's wig. (See *bended-back chair* and *writing chair*.)

spoon bit (see under *shell, spoon, nose, and gimlet bits*).

spoon chisel Also known as an entering chisel. (See under *carvers' chisels*.)

spoon foot (USA) Corresponds to British 'club foot' *(q.v.)*.

spray gun Used for spraying paint, lacquer, distemper, etc. A high-pressure gun usually requires an air-compressing unit with air-balancing chamber, and fitted with pressure gauge.

spraying Method of finishing woodwork using a spray gun *(q.v.)*. Specially suitable for lacquers having a highly volatile medium which would make brush application difficult. The gun should be worked with a movement parallel with the job to ensure even build-up. (See also *flatting, pull-over, and lacquer*.)

Spraytex Proprietary name of a decorative powdered fibre in various colours, giving a suede-like finish. It is used as a substitute for baize in lining cutlery drawers, instrument cases, etc. The powder is applied by a special gun on to an adhesive.

sprig Tapered cut nail without a head. Used for picture backs, fixing lino, and for glazing. Made ½in (12mm) to ¾in (19mm).

spring Term sometimes used in connection with thin wood has to be fitted into holes or mortises between two fixed surfaces. It is bent or sprung to reduce its length, enabling it to enter the recesses.

spring (see *spring, upholstery*).

spring balance A coil spring contained in a tube which is located in the groove between a sliding sash and its frame; it eliminates the need for a box sash frame, weights, and cords.

spring base The main frame of a divan bed on which the spring mattress lies.

spring catch One in which the bolt is bevelled so that it recedes as the door is closed but springs out when the latter is fully closed.

spring corner cramp A nearly circular piece of spring steel, pointed at the ends, used mostly to hold mitres together whilst the glue sets. Also useful in repair work for holding items of odd shape. Sometimes known as a spring dog.

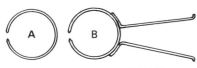

SPRING CORNER CRAMP

spring hinge One used for a swing door. It is fixed by a shoe to the bottom of the door with a spindle passing into a box let into the floor and controlled by a spring.

SPRING HINGE

spring setting Method of setting a saw in which the teeth are bent over alternatively right and left to give clearance. (See also *swage setting.*)

sprung upholstery This did not come into general use until the middle years of the nineteenth century. Early springs were much the same as the spiral double-cone springs in use today.

spring unit Combinations of springs ready assembled on a wire mesh or base of steel laths ready for tacking to the frame.

springwood The early growth of the annual rings. Each year the tree adds a new ring to its growth. In spring the new wood is rather more open and is lighter in colour than the denser and darker summer wood.

springing The horizontal line from whch the curve of an arch springs. See also *spring*, which refers to the bending of material to enable it to be slipped into place.

springs, holding down Used on the spindle moulder when a medium or heavy cut is taken on narrow stuff. Springs should bear on the wood with fair pressure, but not be so tight that the friction makes moving the wood difficult.

spring, upholstery These were not used in chairs, settees, etc., until the nineteenth century. The oldest type were coil (A) and were stitched to the webbing or hessian, or sometimes stapled to the woodwork. Tension springs (C) are held with nails, screws, or hooks and are ⅜in (10mm) or ½in (12mm) diameter. They are fixed at a tension of 1½in (38mm) to 2in (51mm) on an 18in (457mm) length. Pocketed springs in sets encased in material are also made, and there are ready-made units of spiral springs on metal laths in single or double layer. There is also the zig-zag type (B) for dining chairs; it is also called serpentine springing.

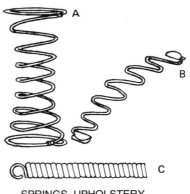

SPRINGS, UPHOLSTERY

sprocket piece   Tapered piece of wood fixed at the end of a rafter to give a tilt at the lower end of a roof and compensate for tile thickness.

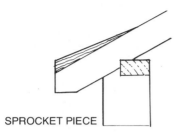

SPROCKET PIECE

spruce *(Picea abies)*   Softwood timber of 28-34 lb (449-545 kg) to which the term whitewood is usually applied. Soft and light in weight, it is extensively used for interior joinery, ladders, spars, packing cases, etc. Not generally used for outdoor construction work. The Sitka or silver spruce of Canada and western USA *(Picea sitchensis)* is widely used in general construction.

spruce, black   (see *spruce, Canadian*).

spruce, Canadian *(picea glauca)*   Softwood from Canada, USA, and Europe of 28 lb (449 kg). In Canada three species of the Sitka spruce are recognised; white spruce *(picea glauca)*, black spruce *(picea mariana)*, and red spruce *(picea rubra)*. For all practical purposes the three may be grouped. Used for building, packing cases, and pulp.

spruce, Himalayan *(picea smithiana)*   From India, of 31 lb (497 kg). Similar to European spruce.

spruce, red   (see *spruce, Canadian*).

spruce, silver   (see *sitka spruce*).

spruce, Sitka *(picea sitchensis)*   Giant tree in western Canada and USA. Moderately durable, and employed for house construction, masts, general carpentry, and pulp. It is also used for the soundboards of flat-fronted musical instruments such as guitars.

spruce, white   (see *spruce, Canadian*).

sprung moulding (1)   A term sometimes applied to a curved moulding; also, a thin piece of moulding used for cornices and attached to blocks or brackets fixed to the cornice frame.

sprung moulding (2)   Alternative term for a pitched moulding *(q.v.)*.

spud   Metal rod or dowel projecting from the lower end of a door post. The term also refers to a tool used in de-barking.

spur   A small tooth fitted to an adjustable metal fillister plane in front of the cutter, used when working *across* the grain so that wood is scribed so avoiding splitting the grain at each side. It can be turned to a neutral position when the tool is used *with* the grain. It is also used on some plough planes when used for trenching across the grain. A dado plane *(q.v.)* is also fitted with a double spur for cutting both sides of the groove, again when used *across* the grain.

SPUR

spur knife   Small knife mounted on a veneer-peeling machine. It cuts the veneer to length as the log revolves.

spur stretcher   Another name for the cow-horn stretcher *(q.v.)*.

spur tenon   (see *plug tenon*).

squab cushion   Small, thin cushion used on a chair with wooden seat.

square (1)   Tool used for marking or testing timber. Usual woodworker's pattern is of wood-metal (A), the parts being riveted together and with flush brass washer pieces. An improved pattern has the metal tongue of L shape passing right through the butt and is therefore quite rigid.

Today the engineer's pattern (B) is widely used. It has the advantage that only the required tongue projection need be given, this having the advantage that a rebate can be marked or tested for squareness. The tongue is invariably calibrated. The butt also has a 45 deg shoulder for mitres, and a spirit level is frequently fitted. For large work the wood square (C) is generally used, and is often made by the craftsman himself. A mitre square is given at (D) and is used for 45 deg mitres. (See also *bevel, sliding, and steel square.*

square (2)   Another meaning is a length of wood which is square in section with sides from 1 in (25 mm) up to 6 in (152 mm). Hardwood squares are widely sold for the furniture trade in lengths for chairs, tables, and sideboards.

square (3)   In general the term is used in the testing of carcases, frames, etc., which are said to be square when tested and found truly rectangular.

square (4) A term describing 100 superficial feet (square feet) of boards.

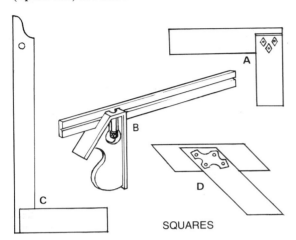

SQUARES

square cutter block Used on some of the larger spindle moulding machines. Its advantage over the French head is that it has more of a cutting action as distinct from that of scraping. Cutters are bolted on to opposite faces of the head, and sometimes all four faces can have cutters, each pair (on opposite faces) cutting a different member of the moulding. The cutters cannot be ground to an exact reverse of the required section owing to the angle at which they approach the work, and in any case clearance for the bolts is necessary.

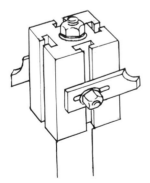

SQUARE CUTTER BLOCK

square dovetails A machine-cut corner joint used mainly for boxes in which the interlocking members are all of equal size.

square edged Timber with edges at right angles to the faces.

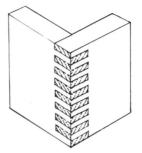

SQUARE DOVETAILS

square leg Leg of square section (A), sometimes with the outer faces moulded (B), or with a moulding at the outer corner (C), and sometimes an inner bevel (D). Used on chairs, tables, etc. An innovation during the Chippendale period, though square legs had been used on some heavy pieces of the early oak period.

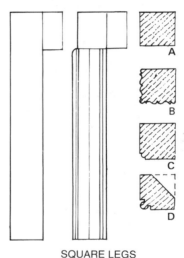

SQUARE LEGS

square log (see *baulk*).

square nails Used mainly in general ship work and boat building. (A) is made of copper or galvanised

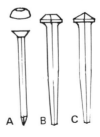

SQUARE NAILS

iron, for hull planks, the points being riveted over roves. Holes the size of the nail shank thickness are drilled first so that the corners bite into the wood. (B) is a deck spike, made from steel, copper, or galvanised iron. (C) is a rose head spike for general use.

square, roofing Alternatively known as a steel square, rafter, or framing square, and used to obtain the various bevels, or cuts as they are called; also to enable the lengths of rafters to be ascertained. Different makes vary as to the tables and markings, but the method of marking angles is much the same in all. The long blade is 24 in (610 mm) and the other, or tongue, 16 in (407 mm). On one side both blade and tongue are divided into sixteenths at the outer edge, and into eighths at the inner edge. On the reverse side the outer edges are marked in twelfths, the inner edge of the blade into thirty-seconds, and the inner edge of the tongue into tenths. Scales are marked on the centre. It functions on the principle of the right-angle triangle.

square turning (see *thurming*).

squaring rod (see *diagonal rod*).

stabiliser An ingredient included in the formulation of some adhesives to assist in maintaining their properties during their processing and service life.

stable Applied to timber that is practically free of movement due to the giving-up or absorption of moisture.

stacking The piling of timber for seasoning, leaving spaces to give free access or air. Skids *(q.v.)* or stickers

are placed vertically above each other to support the timber and to afford ventilation. (See *piling*.)

stacking furniture A term applied to chairs and tables which nest into each other for space-saving storage. It is often possible to stack three or four chairs on top of each other and occupy little more space than one chair — a great advantage in the assembly halls where they are usually found.

stacking joints Method of stacking rubbed joints after glueing. Each joint rests at a slight angle upon a batten leant against the wall. Long joints usually need two battens.

staff bead (1) One which is worked at both sides of a salient angle. Also known as a return bead.

staff bead (2) The inner (room-side) beading piece around a sash window frame against which the inner or lower frame slides.

STAFF BEAD (1)

staggered The arrangement of any items that are not in line. Thus the width joints in the top and bottom of a carcase are staggered with those of the ends.

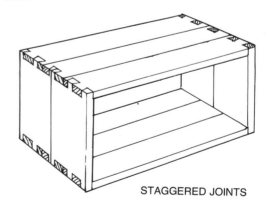

STAGGERED JOINTS

stain (see *oil, spirit, varnish, and water stain*).

staining Used widely for furniture, fitments, joinery, etc., either to deepen the colour of some hardwoods or to colour an inferior wood in imitation of a better one. Colouring may be by pigment or by the use of a chemical which alters the tone of the

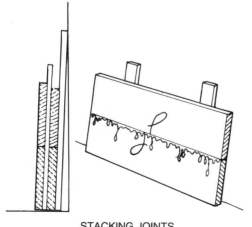

STACKING JOINTS

wood. Ammonia *(q.v.)* is often used to fume oak, and can be added to pigment stain to deepen the shade and drive it deeper into the grain. Sulphate of iron (green copperas) can be used to give grey tone to oak and sycamore (the latter is then called 'harewood' *(q.v.)*. Whenever water stain is used (either with chemicals or aniline dyes) the wood should be wiped over beforehand with clean, warm water to raise the grain, and papered smooth when dry. This reduces the subsequent liability of the grain to rise.

Oil stains are a popular method of staining and are white-spirit based and can therefore be diluted with it. They are compatible with all finishes except those which are white-spirit or oil-based, when the stain will tend to bleed through into the finish. Oil stains have a tar-based substance in them to give the colour (particularly in darker shades) and occasionally this rises to the surface and precipitates out; this can prevent a subsequent finish from bonding properly. To prevent this, wipe the surface over after staining with a clean, white rag to remove any residue, first allowing the stained surface to become touch-dry.

Naphtha stains are based on oil stains, plus a large proportion of liquid naphtha. They penetrate the wood deeply, evaporate quickly, and do not raise the grain — they do smell strongly until evaporated and you should avoid inhaling this. Always thin down with naphtha thinners.

Spirit stains are available either ready-mixed or as spirit-soluble aniline powders which can be dissolved in white spirit (approximately 120 grams to 5 litres). Certain colours are available as Alcovar powders which produce a stain that is resistant to ultraviolet light.

Nitrostains are oil stains which can be diluted with white spirit; they are compatible with all finishes although care must be taken when using them in conjunction with oil-based varnishes and lacquers which have the same base; the stain must be completely dry before applying the finish. Always wipe over the stained surface with a clean, white rag before applying further finishes.

Oil or naphtha stains will affect the curing and bonding of polyester lacquers, and water stains are to be preferred; polyurethane lacquers are tolerant of all stains except those containing linseed oil. In all cases, it is always best to follow the manufacturer's instructions carefully.

staining wax This is a compound of several different waxes blended together with organic colouring matter and pigments. The different shades of wax are intermiscible and can be applied coat-on-coat to create a complete finish.

staking out Driving pegs into the ground when laying a concrete base to a shed, outhouse, etc.

Stalker and Parker The authors of a book on 'Lackering' published in 1688, and since republished.

stand Term for any framework supporting a cabinet or cupboard of some kind. Alternatively known as a stool. (See also *stands.*)

standard (1) A post or upright as, for instance, the supports of a toilet mirror.

standard (2) A measured quantity of softwood; the most widely used was the Petrograd standard *(q.v.)*.

standard chest A large iron-bound chest used in the fifteenth century for the transport of household goods. They usually had domed or canted lids and were covered in cloth or leather.

standard hardboard Lowest grade of hardboard; not suitable for exterior use or situations where any degree of strength is required. Normally used for cladding.

stand, carver's Robustly built stand with three legs and solid wood top with centre hole on which the carver fixes the wood when carving three-dimensional work (that is, in the round) such as busts, figures, etc. It enables the carver to view his work from all angles. The centre hole is to enable a carver's screw (see *screw, carver's)* to be passed through.

standing timber Growing trees of suitable size and kind for commercial use.

standish A small stand for a writing table and containing inks, pens, and other writing accessories. Later (1773) referred to as 'inkstands'.

stands Supports for various articles such as: candles, china, cutlery, flower, kettle, lamp, mirror, music, pedestal, plate, teapot, term and wig.

staple Double-pointed nail of U shape for fixing wire fencing, for use with a hook catch, and sometimes for fixing upholstery springs to wood battens.

star shake One which is wider towards the outside of a log and tapers towards the pith.

stationery nest Box-like structure with divisions for stationery, and often with small drawers. Fitted behind the fall of a bureau or secretaire.

stave Parts forming the walls of a cask, but also applied to the parts of any similar structure. Also refers to the rungs of a ladder.

stay-back Windsor chair   A design of scroll-back Windsor chair *(q.v.)* in which the back-stay is given prominence by being carved, fretcut, or composed of turned spindles.

stay-log slicing   Method of slicing veneer (see *half-round slicing*).

stays   Used to support a lid, fall, door, or window, and desinged specially for the purpose. Many types are dealt with under lid stays *(q.v.)*. (See also *quadrant stay, quadrant hinge, and rule joint stay*.) There is also the wardrobe stay (A), the purpose of which is to prevent a door from opening more than a required amount; and the casement stay (B) with holes along it to enable it to slip over a peg fixed to the framework, and hinged to enable it to be lifted. A pneumatic stay (C) is used for record players. The lid can be dropped, when it will close to within an inch and then shut silently. The cocktail cabinet stay (D) enables both a lid and a fall to be moved simultaneously together.

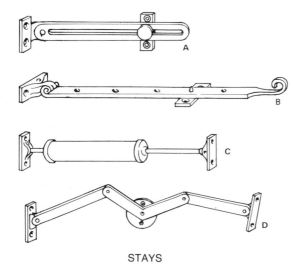

STAYS

stay-set cap iron   Back iron in two separate parts for an adjustable metal plane. The end part can be lifted away enabling the cutter to be sharpened a few times without unscrewing the bolt and detaching the upper part of the back iron.

steady   Used by the wood turner when turning long, slender work between centres. Many versions exist: common 'home-made' versions take the form of a sort of 3-sided open box to which a notched bearing piece is pivoted. A wedge at the back, dropping by its own weight, keeps the bearing piece up against the work, so supporting it. Turning can take place right opposite

the steady since the device automatically takes up to the reduced size of turning.

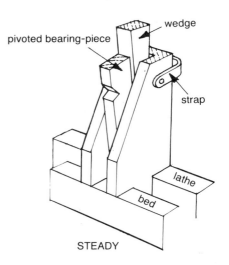

STEADY

steam chest   A container into which timber is placed and through which steam is passed prior to bending. Either top or end is detachable to enable wood to be placed inside. It also refers to a metal water container with holes in it to receive glue pots.

steaming   A process to which some timbers are subjected to soften them before bending or slicing into veneers.

steel furniture   Probably the earliest steel was made in the Tula Ironworks in central Russia in 1725. During the reign of Catherine the Great armchairs on X-shaped supports and occasional tables were being produced. Modern steel furniture was introduced by a Munich designer, August Endell, at the end of the nineteenth century, but it did not really come into its own until the 1930s when a considerable number of steel and tubular chairs, armchairs, and tables were produced in both Britain and the USA. The *Bauhaus* movement was probably the main inspiration in Germany during the 1920's and many of the students fled to other countries following the rise of the Nazi regime, and took their ideas with them.

steel square   (see *square, roofing*).

steel wool   Fine strands of steel bundled into wads which can be used for removing rust, burnishing metal articles, and rubbing down painted or lacquered surfaces (only the very finest grades are used for this). Grades are: Nos. 5, 4, 3, 2, 1, 0, 00, 000, and 0000 (the finest).

steeping The immersion of timber in a preservative, the pieces being stacked in a tank with stickers to keep them apart and allow free movement of the liquid.

Steers bit Expansion bit in which the moving cutter can be adjusted by means of a screw. The latter also serves to lock the cutter and prevent movement during use.

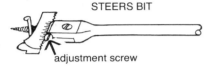

STEERS BIT

adjustment screw

stem The tree trunk. Also referred to as the bole, shaft, mast, etc.

stencil Used by wood carvers to mark out repeat patterns as when carving a moulding. It can be of flexible foil to fold around a curved surface or of stout brown paper; those used for creating patterns in paint or lacquer are best cut from thin sheet metal. Early American furniture employed stencilled and painted motifs frequently.

step Applied to the use of dividers when a distance is 'stepped out' into equal distances. (See *stepping out*.)

step-ladder hinge Made specially for step ladders.

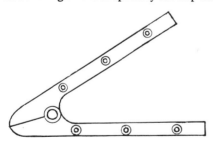

STEP-LADDER HINGE

step joint A notched joint often used in roof work. (A) is the single step, and (B) the double step.

stepped shoulder joint (see *long-and-short shoulder joint*).

stepping out Process using dividers when marking a number of equidistant positions. The setting of the dividers is ascertained by trial and error, the distance being 'stepped out' until the legs exactly coincide with the marks.

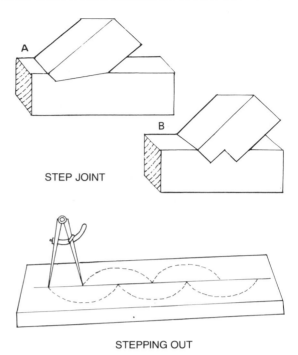

STEP JOINT

STEPPING OUT

stepped string A staircase string cut at the top to the shape of the steps. Also called a cut string.

steward's table Table with drawers and often a folding top for the use of the steward in a large country mansion. It was used for writing, keeping accounts, holding cash for the payment of wages or when received on rent days, storing plans, and so on.

stick-back Windsor chair A Windsor chair with a box-back containing sticks (or 'lists', *q.v.*) but no splat.

stickers Strips of wood interposed between planks in a stack. They should be inserted at regular intervals along the length and located vertically above each other so that the planks cannot bend or be distorted owing to uneven support. Preferably they should be of the same wood as the planks; softwood should always be avoided as knots may bleed resin in hot sunshine and mark the planks. Sometimes called 'skids' (*q.v.*).

sticking Working a moulding in the solid as distinct from applying it.

sticking board A board having in it a series of grooves, rebates, etc., on which wood is held whilst being rebated or moulded by hand. The planing process is known as sticking *(q.v.)*. In particular window and door bars are worked on the sticking board. The stages in working both rebates and mouldings are shown. It is assumed that the sash fillister plane *(q.v.)* is used for rebating. This works on the far side of the wood so that the width of wood left for moulding remains constant. A projecting screw acts as a stop. The board may be varied in accordance with the work to be done.

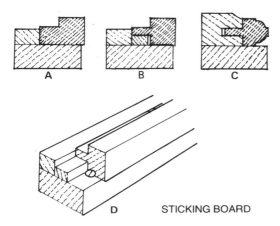

STICKING BOARD

sticking pieces　Oddments of the same section as the wood to be machined. They are used as trial pieces and used to test the setting of the machine before the actual job is started.

stick shellac　Also called 'shellac stick'. It is shellac in solid stick form, with pigments added to match a wide variety of wood colours; it is used to fill blemishes and imperfections.

stiffer　The rubber used in the stiffing process in french polishing *(q.v.)*.

stiffing　One of the methods used for finishing in the french polishing process. After bodying the rubber is dipped up half-and-half polish and spirit and the sole made perfectly smooth. There should be enough polish to flow freely but not to run. It is glided on in straight strokes with a slight overlap. This is repeated three times, leaving the surface clear and bright. A light touch is needed and straight strokes are essential. (See also *spiriting off*.)

stile　Term applied to the upright members of a framework or door. Stiles always run the full length of the door frame, rails being fitted between them. In a door the stiles may be particularised as hanging or hingeing stile, and closing or shutting stile; or, in the case of double doors, meeting stiles. In a horizontal

item such as a framed top the pieces which run the full length are invariably known as the stiles, the rails being contained between them.

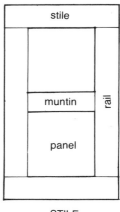

STILE

stinkwood *(ocotea bullata)*　Reddish brown timber of 46 lb (737 kg) used locally for panelling, etc. From South Africa.

stock　The main body part of a tool.

stool　Apart from its application to a seat without back, or to a footrest, the stool is the lower independent structure of a cabinet, bookcase, or similar item. It is made up of legs and rails. Also applied to a night stool or commode.

stool wood　Alstonia *(q.v.)*.

stop (1)　The end of a chamfer or moulding which does not run right through. It may be finished in various ways. At (A) it is run out from the spindle moulder, (B) is a plain chiselled stop, and (C) is a decorative stop. Sometimes mouldings are stopped.

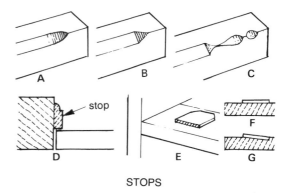

STOPS

stop (2) The term is also applied to a projection at the head of a bench to hold wood stationary whilst being planed (see *stop, bench*).

stop (3) Another application is that of a rebate against which a door closes (D).

stop (4) It also refers to the thin applied block fixed to a drawer rail to prevent a drawer from being pushed in too far (E). This is usually glued and pinned on (F), but in better work is let into a sloping groove (G).

stop, bench Projection from a bench top to hold wood stationary whilst being planed. Usually it is of wood and fits by friction in a square hole (A), but sometimes has a bolt and wing nut (B), or a cam device may be fitted to hold it in position. Some manufacturerd stops have a pronged metal plate. When a tail vice is fitted to the bench the stop may be an iron bar with side spring to hold it in position (D).

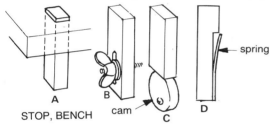

STOP, BENCH

stop-butt hinge Small steel hinge (A) for the lid of an attache case, portable record player, etc., enabling the lid to remain upright when opened, thus dispensing with a lid stay. Another type with wire strut is shown at (B). Another type found on old boxes and caskets is that at (C).

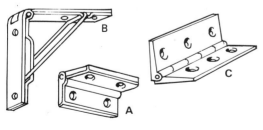

STOP BUTT HINGE

stop chamfer templet For cutting the stop of a chamfer, either square or at an angle. The chisel lies flat on the sloping part or is held flat against the square stop.

stopped chamfer (see *chamfer*).

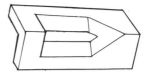

STOP CHAMFER TEMPLET

stopped dovetail housing A dovetail housing, either bare-faced (A) or shouldered both sides (B), in which the recess does not reach through to the front. Also known as a stopped slot dovetail. It is an advantage to make the dovetail slightly tapered in its length so that it is an easy fit from the back, and is not tight until pushed home. (See *dovetail housing joint.*)

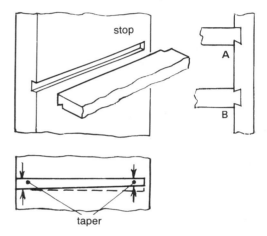

STOPPED DOVETAIL HOUSING

stopped housing A housed or grooved joint in which the groove does not reach through to the front edge.

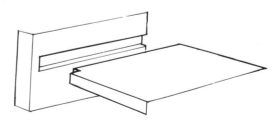

STOPPED HOUSING

stopped rebating One which does not run right through. When this is done on the spindle moulder an operation known as dropping-on may be needed. This can cause the cutters to snatch the wood, and could be dangerous. It is therefore essential to fit a stop to the

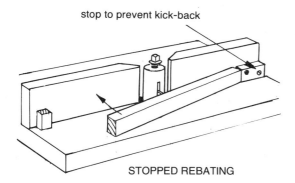

STOPPED REBATING

fence to resist any such trouble. A second stop is fitted to the far end when the rebate is stopped at both ends to limit the amount of travel.

stop rabbet plane (USA) Also called a 'chisel plane'. The cutting iron projects at the front end of the body and enables it to get into corners.

stopping Flexible material used to fill in nail holes, etc. Many proprietary stoppings are made, but the best workshop material is beaumontage (*q.v.*).

stop rod Rod with its end cranked at right angles and fitted to a mitre gauge to enable items to be sawn or sanded to exact length.

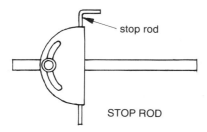

STOP ROD

storage life An alternative term to shelf life (*q.v.*).

storey rod Used in staircasing. A length of timber on which are marked the vertical heights of floors and landings; also the positions of the top surfaces of the treads.

stout-heart plywood Plywood having the centre layer thicker than those at the outside to equalise

STOUTHEART PLYWOOD

strength in both directions. That at (A) is 3-ply, and (B) 5-ply.

straddling chair (see *reading chair*).

straight-edge A strip of wood planed dead true at one edge, used for testing the straightness of work. It is usually made from a piece of well-seasoned, reliable hardwood. The edge is trued with a trying or jointing plane, and the usual workshop method of testing giving reasonable working accuracy is to make a pair of straight-edges using the same plane for both, and try the two together in both directions. The only really reliable test is to make three, any of them fitting closely to either of the others in both directions. This however is usually regarded as being unnecessary for general workshop use. Steel straight-edges are also made, but are generally not so suitable for woodwork as the wood type, as they can mark or bruise the wood if used carelessly.

straight from the saw Applied to joints such as mitres, butt joints which have been cut with the saw but not trimmed with the plane. Also to timber generally which has been converted on the saw but not planed.

straight grain Applied to the grain of timber which runs parallel to the length. The grain shows as a series of more or less parallel lines.

straight-line production Factory operation in which the manufacturing processes proceed in a steady sequence.

straight lock One which has only to be screwed to the wood without being let in.

strainer, web For pulling webbing taut. With the lever type (A) the loose end of the webbing is passed through the lever and allowed to hang down. The

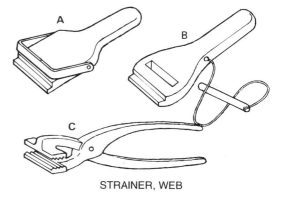

STRAINER, WEB

rebated foot of the strainer is placed on the webbing and the handle levered over.

In the bat type (B) the looped web is inserted in the slot and the peg passed into the loop. At (C) is shown the pincers type which is useful when short ends of webbing are used.

strap and jewel Form of carved decoration popular in the seventeenth century, and consisting of a strapwork (q.v.) and raised bosses and small roundels which might be carved in the solid but sometimes applied. In some cases they took the form of ivory inlay.

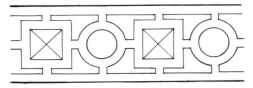

STRAP AND JEWEL

strap hinges For furniture these are usually made from brass or mild steel. Heavy types range in size from 1¾ in (45 mm) to 4½ in (115 mm). Lighter types are 1¾ in (45 mm) to 2¾ in (70 mm). Such hinges are shown at (A). (B) is a baby chair type with skew knuckle to suit the angle of the chair leg. (C) is a chest or box type 6 in (153 mm) to 12 in (305 mm) long, plain or cranked. For carpentry really heavy hinges are also made for screwing or bolting to large doors and gates. These are usually in galvanised iron.

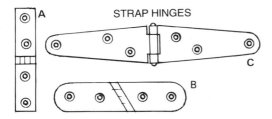

STRAP HINGES

strapwork Form of low-relief carving made up of interlacing bands, but may also refer to marquetry or inlaid work of a similar type.

strawboard An insulating board made chiefly of straw. Used mainly in carpentry work.

straw-work A technique for decorating small objects such as mirrors and small boxes. It involved gluing bleached or coloured lengths of straw into geometrical patterns; French prisoners-of-war in England during the early nineteenth century became proficient in the craft.

streak Marking on timber indicating incipient decay.

stretcher This is usually a rail stretching from leg to leg in cabinets, tables, chairs, etc., to give strength to the legs and also to take away an appearance of bareness. In some cases side stretcher rails are necessary for supporting undershelves.

Stretchers may be in various arrangements, and in some William and Mary furniture may lie flat and be veneered. In chairs there was a tendency to omit stretchers from the beginning of the eighteenth century.

stretch-out Device used in setting out staircases, especially for geometrical work at the well string. The rise remains constant, but the going is dependent upon the radius of the well.

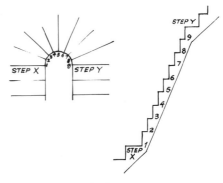

STRETCH-OUT

striking button The rounded boxwood knob let into the top of a wood plane near the front to take the hammer blows when removing the wedge or lessening the cutter projection.

striking knife Alternative name for a marking knife (q.v.).

striking plate The metal plate fixed to the door frame with which the bolt and latch engage. Also used with a ball catch.

strings (1) In cabinet work this refers to narrow inlay strips in boxwood, ebony, or other decorative hardwoods. They vary from about ¹⁄₃₂ in (1.5 mm) square to about ³⁄₁₆ in (5 mm).

strings (2) A second meaning is the inclined sides of a staircase carrying the steps. Closed or housed strings have straight edges reaching above and below the steps and enclosing their ends. Cut or open strings are cut to fit beneath the steps. Cut and mitred strings are mitred to fit the risers, and when ornamental frets or brackets are added the strings are known as bracketed strings. A wreathed string is one having a plan shape which is part of a circle or ellipse, and is used in a geometrical staircase. Wall strings are those adjacent to a wall. An outside string is that away from the wall.

strings (3)   Apart from stair construction, the term is also applied to the sloping members carrying the treads in common household steps.

string piece   The straight horizontal member of a bow-string truss. (See *Belfast truss*.)

stringy-bark (*eucalyptus acmeniodes*)   New South Wales timber of 46lb (737kg). Used locally for general purposes. Somewhat like ash but colour tones to that of oak. Takes a good finish. A good bending wood, and suitable for wood paving, piles, sleepers, etc.

strip heating   This is low-voltage heating (6 to 12 volts) applied by means of an electrically heated bare metal strip to the glue line. As examples, for gluing wood veneers the temperature should be about 94 degrees C and for plastic laminates 70 degrees C; setting times should be approximately 25 seconds and 2 or 3 minutes respectively. Special adhesives are required, and custom-built jigs are need to apply pressure and the metal strips can be shaped to conform to the joints. The method is normally confined to industry.

strip hinge   Long hinge used primarily for a piano fall, but also found in some bureau and secretaire falls. (See *piano hinge*.)

STRIP HINGE

striping   A term for the process of painting lines on to a contrasting background. It was frequently used, both in Britain and the USA, on late eighteenth and early nineteenth century furniture. The brush used is called a 'striper' and has comparatively few, but very long, bristles.

stripper   For removing paint, polish, etc. Nowadays proprietary strippers are generally used, some of which are of a non-caustic type and thus have no tendency to darken the wood. The following strippers are often used.

1. Caustic potash in water. Apply with a grass brush, leaving surface coated. Wash with clear water, and go over surface afterwards with clear water.

2. Household soda in hot water and used strong. Will remove French polish.

3. 880 ammonia will strip old polish and varnish. Wear stout gloves as otherwise it can be painful, and turn the fingers yellow.

All traces of alkaline strippers must be removed after treatment as otherwise any subsequent finish may be attacked.

stripy figure   The appearance of woods having fairly narrow light and dark streaks mostly parallel with the grain. A notable example is that of some grades of sapele.

stroking   A process used for producing the effect (in paint) of a striated grain. A 2in (50mm) brush is lightly loaded with paint and then stroked out on a newspaper until a striated effect is achieved; it is then lightly stroked on to the wood.

strop   Used to finish off edge tools and get rid of the burr after honing. Consists of a piece of pliable leather dressed with an abrasive such as fine emery powder, carborundum powder, or crocus powder in the case of carving tools. The abrasive is mixed with oil, Vaseline, or tallow. For flat tools such as plane irons and chisels, and for the outside bevel of carving gouges the strop is placed flat on the bench, but for the inside bevel of gouges it is folded up into a crease of suitable size and rubbed inside the gouge.

structure adhesive   An adhesive which can withstand heavy loads and continuous stress without deterioration.

strut   Any short structural member intended to resist compression.

stub   The stump of a felled tree. Also applied to the truncated end of any piece of wood; for example, stub (or short) tenon, stub-dowel, etc.

stub-tenon   One which does not pass right through the member with the mortise. It is used mostly in furniture making.

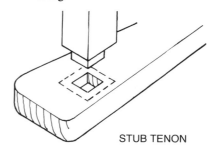
STUB TENON

stucco   (see *compo*).

stuck   The working of a moulding in the solid, that is, in the substance of the item itself, rather than being worked separately and applied.

stud wall   Better called a 'timber stud partition' (*q.v.*).

stuff   A workshop colloquialism for converted wood of any kind. In certain localities the equally homely word 'sticks' is used.

stuff-over   Applied to a chair or settee in which the upholstery covering is taken right over the seat rails. Compare with loose seat (*q.v.*) in which the seat rails are visible.

stump   Trade term for the front arm support of a chair.

stump bedstead   Also called a 'stumpend'. Of eighteenth century origin, this was a wooden bed frame on four short turned or square legs and it was fitted with a headboard. It survived through most of the nineteenth century and, when fitted with a metal spring base, it became the simple wooden bedstead of the 1920's and 30's.

stump foot   Low turned or square-cut foot fitted beneath a piece of furniture.

stump foot   (USA) A plain turned foot used on the back legs of American Queen Anne and Chippendale chairs, the front legs usually being cabriole.

stump tenon   One made thicker near the shoulders to provide extra strength, particularly when the thinner tenon can be used to keep the shoulder tight, the thicker part of stump taking the cross strain.

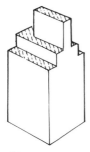

STUMP TENON

sub-plinth   An additional lower plinth to a pedestal or similar item.

substrate   Any surface to which a finish is applied. It is also used as an alternative term to 'groundwork' (*q.v.*), meaning the ground to which a veneer or a plastic laminate is applied.

Suffolk chair   (see *Mendlesham chair*).

Suffolk dresser   Similar in design to the South Wales dresser (*q.v.*) but with cabriole legs and straight shelf uprights.

Suffolk latch   (see *Norfolk latch*).

sugar pine (*pinus lambertiana*)   From Oregon and California. Yellowish white, of good quality, and available in large sizes, free from defects. Widely used in organ building.

sulphate of copper   Blue copperas (see *copperas*).

sulphate of iron   Green copperas (see *copperas*).

sulphate of zinc   White copperas (see *copperas*).

sulphuric acid   Used in the acid finish in french polishing. Both poisonous and harmful to touch. The acid should always be added (slowly) to water. Never add water to the acid as it is dangerous and highly corrosive.

summer wood   (see *springwood*).

sumpter chest   A coffer (chest) with handles and either a domed or gabled lid, and no feet; it was carried on the back of a horse. Used in medieval times. Also called a 'trussing coffer'.

sunburst   A decorative motif representing a sun with its rays; favoured by Louis XIV, the 'Sun King'. (See also *rising sun*.)

sunflower   (USA) The conventionalised motif of a sunflower was often used as a decorative feature on Connecticut case furniture.

sunk   Term applied to any detail which lies below the general surface. (For example see *bead (D), sunk*.)

sunk panel   A panelled recess sunk in the solid material, familiar in pilasters, newel posts, and similar work. Refers generally, however, to any panel below the level of the framework. (See also *recessed panel*.)

sun plane   One which is curved in plan and used by coopers for trimming and stave ends of a barrel. No back iron is necessary as it is used on end grain only. Cutter is set askew. Rarely used today.

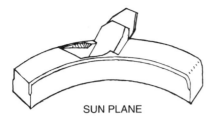

SUN PLANE

super Abbreviation of superficial. (See *superficial measure*.)

superficial measure The square measure of the surface of wood taking no account of the thickness. It is calculated by multiplying the length by the width, in the same units. It is sometimes called 'surface measure'.

'Super' hardboard Another name for tempered hardboard *(q.v.)*.

supper table A pillar and claw table *(q.v.)* with a top which was recessed out to hold cups or plates, and in use in the mid eighteenth century.

surbase Moulding surmounting the base of a pedestal.

surface check A check *(q.v.)* of slight depth only.

surfaced Wood planed on one side or both. Also referred to as dressed.

surface drying A condition where the top skin of a paint or varnish film sets and dries before the underlying material has fully dried; the latter remains more or less permanently soft.

surfacer Machine planer intended to finish one surface only as distinct from a thicknesser *(q.v.)* which also brings wood to even thickness.

surface measure Super or area measurement of wood, irrespective of thickness. (See *superficial measure*.)

surfacing Operation of the machine planer in which one surface of the wood is passed across the planer to true it.

surface planer Also called the 'overhand' planer. It is used to plane wood flat, straight, and smooth. Essentially it consists of two long, flat, metal tables placed end-to-end with a rotating circular cutter block mounted between them. One table is the 'in-

feed' (where the work is introduced) and the other (from which the work is taken off) is called the 'out-feed'; both tables can be raised or lowered. The height of the in-feed table controls the cutting depth, and the out-feed controls the setting. Additionally, there is a vertical fence on the in-feed table which is parallel to it, and this fence can be canted to any angle up to 45 degrees, thus allowing bevelled edges to be machined.

By law, hand-feed machines may only be fitted with circular cutter blocks, and most have two cutters, but a few have three or even four. There are various methods of holding the cutters in the block, the most common being the wedge bar, although the slab or cap method is employed on smaller machines. There is invariably a small flute machined across the full width of the block immediately in front of each cutter tip and this acts as a chip breaker *(q.v.)*.

suspended ceiling One in which separate joists hang from girders or from floor joists.

Sussex chair A chair designed by William Morris about 1865 and based on one seen by him in the country. It has a rush seat and was usually made in birch, painted black.

Sutherland table A table named after the Duchess of Sutherland (a Mistress of the Robes to Queen Victoria). It was a small table and could be called a hybrid of a gate-leg table and a Pembroke; however, its outstanding features were the deep leaves and the narrow bed. Circa 1855.

swag (see *festoon*).

swage saw Circular saw used for cutting thin boards. It is ground thinner at the edge than at the centre so that waste in saw dust is lessened, and less energy is required. The thin stuff curls away from the saw so that there is no binding. Drawing shows section with difference exaggerated.

SWAGE SAW

swage setting Method of setting in which the teeth of a saw are squeezed out and made wider than the rest of the blade so giving clearance. Each tooth cuts to the full width.

swan neck An S-shaped bend used in some handrails combining a ramp and knee to give a quick rise.

swan-neck chisel A curved chisel used in chopping the recess for a mortise lock, enabling the core to be removed easily. (See also *mortise chisels*.)

SWAN-NECK CHISEL

swan-neck pediment Pediment widely used on bookcases and other cabinets in the eighteenth century and later. It often occurs also on longcase clocks. Each half of the pediment has an applied moulding and terminates in a scroll usually with carved patera. The centre is broken and is shaped, often with carved or turned centre ornament.

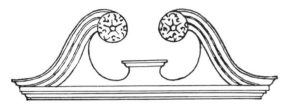

SWAN-NECK PEDIMENT

sweating A fault occurring onaa french polished surface, taking the form of fine cracks. It is caused by imprisoned oil breaking through to the surface. It may be due to the use of too much oil during polishing, failure to work out the oil, or the use of a greasy filler. The latter fault is aggravated when the grain is large and open. It may occur specially in conditions of extreme cold, and usually persists for some time. Usual treatment is to wipe over the surface with a damp, soft cloth and use a reviver *(q.v.)*. If this fails wash with warm water and soap with a little fine pumice powder. The surface will become white when dry, but, after wiping over with a dry cloth, the whiteness can be removed by applying a mixture of spirit, vinegar, and linseed oil. It is advisable to leave until sweating has continued for some time.

sweep A freehand curve of flowing form free from kinks.

sweep of brace The diameter of the circle made by the handle of the brace when revolving.

sweet oil Sometimes used on chamois leather to remove finger marks from varnished work. Old-fashioned name for olive oil.

swelling The opposite of shrinkage, and caused by the absorption of dampness by timber.

swept front Cabinet or similar item having a rounded front rather flatter than a bow front.

swept leg (see *sabre leg*).

swing chisel (see *alternax, Maka*).

swing door A door hung without a stop at the shutting side so that it may open both ways. It is fitted with special hinges. (See *spring hinge.*)

swing-leg table A table with a hinged flap or leaf which is supported when open, by a swinging leg rather than a gate-leg.

swing sash One which is pivoted rather than hinged or sliding.

swing saw (see *pendulum saw*).

swiss-style Windsor chair A Windsor chair in which the laths of the back and arms are replaced by twisted cane; sometimes the upper ends of the backstands protruded through the top rail or the comb. The style was most popular in the middle of the nineteenth century.

swivel-head lathe One in which the complete head with motor and attachments can be turned through 90 degrees. It enables large items to be turned on the face plate, or permits long work to be passed over a circular saw or planer attachment in line with the machine, an advantage in a narrow workshop.

sycamore *(acer pseudoplatanus)* A white or cream-coloured hardwood turning light brown on exposure. From the British Isles and Europe generally. Weight 38–39 lb (609-625 kg). Used in cabinet work, domestic goods, bread boards, textile trade work, etc. When converted on the quarter it discloses a small but pretty figure, and sometimes has a rippled mottle. Sometimes dyed grey when it becomes harewood *(q.v.)*.

synthetic resins These comprise solids, semi-solids, or liquids which are produced by the polymerisation of molecules of compounds such as phenol and formaldehyde. However, some chemically treated natural resins are also referred to as synthetic resins. (See *resin glue, synthetic.*)

T

tabby A silk taffeta with a shot surface.

table brace plate A KD fitting (*q.v.*) for reinforcing the corners of tables and chairs.

table catch, spring Fitting used chiefly on a small table of the tripod type with circular hinged top. By undoing the catch the table top can be tipped up, so taking up less space. Both types are of cast brass.

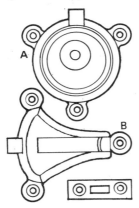

TABLE CATCH, SPRING

table-chair Dual-purpose item often made in the seventeenth century. The table top was made to slide backwards and pivot up, forming a chair back. (See also *monk's bench.*)

table dormant A table used in the fifteenth to seventeenth centuries, consisting of a detachable top which rested on trestles; the latter were joined together with a long stretcher which was often tusk-tenoned through the trestle uprights. They were invariably heavily built and varied from 6 ft (1.830 m) to over 20 ft (approx. 6 m), and were frequently dismantled and removed after the meal.

table, extension One which may be made longer by pulling out leaves or inserting loose ones. An early form was the draw-leaf (A) in which the leaves are beneath the main top and are provided with tapered bearers. When pulled out the leaf rises to the level of the main top, raising the latter as it passes outwards.

The telescopic type (B) was specially popular in the nineteenth century and could be fitted with several loose leaves. Slides of teak or birch with side engagement tongues working in corresponding grooves were fitted, and were cambered about $\frac{3}{8}$ in

(9 mm) over the length to allow for sagging. The whole was fitted with a metal screw for opening or closing. The type is obsolete today.

Another sliding type is that at (C) in which the main top is divided into two, these pulling out on rebated slides engaging with bearers and enabling a loose leaf to be inserted.

The type at (D) is similar except that the centre leaf is not loose but is hinged in two and can be opened out flat as it is pivoted up. (See also *gate-leg table, loose-leaf table.*)

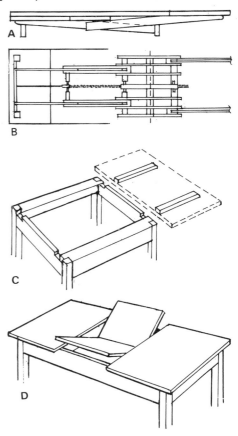

TABLE EXTENSIONS

table flap (see *flap*).

table flap brackets Steel hinged brackets made in pairs. They require a table top projection of 1 in (25 mm) so that the flap clears them when hanging down, and are made R and L hand. They are cheaper to fit than wood brackets with the knuckle joint (*q.v.*). In the case of a narrow flap a single bracket usually suffices.

table haunch   A sloping or secret haunch. (See also *haunch (D)*.)

table joint   Scarf joint cut parallel with the length of the wood, and usually held together with keys or wedges. There are several types.

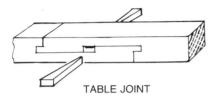

TABLE JOINT

table piano   A type of flat or square piano in the form of a table, popular in the mid nineteenth century in the USA. Presumably it was intended to serve as a table, but the depth of the case made it unsuitable, and the appearance was not attractive.

tablet   Small panel of wood on which an inscription, crest, etc., is carved or inlaid.

tablet-back Windsor chair   A Windsor chair having its top back rail mounted on the upper ends of the backstand; the rail is carved and overhangs the width of the back on each side. Usually the design has diagonally-crossed back stays.

table top hinge   Made specially for the hinged leaf of a table pivoted when the rule joint (*q.v.*). Two essentail features are that the countersinking is on the reverse side from the knuckle, and one flap is made wider than the other to enable it to bridge across the hollow member of the moulding.

TABLE-TOP HINGE

table vice   Small all-metal vice of the type used by engineers. It is provided with a thumbscrew which enables it to be fixed to a table or bench. Often used by woodworkers for filing metal fittings, drilling holes, and so on.

The term also refers to a light form of woodworker's vice, consisting of a pair of beech jaws plate with two screws, usually of hornbeam. Intended to be fitted to the edge of a table.

tabouret   Small footstool, French in its origin, but made in England in the eighteenth century.

tack   The degree of cohesion between paint or varnish and the surfaces to which they are applied.

tacker   Workshop term for an automatic stapling gun; the staples replace tacks in upholstery work. Also workshop slang for an upholsterer.

tack hammer   Small hammer usually of the Warrington type (see *hammer*), generally with rounded, bulbous handle.

tack lifter   Forked and tapered tool that can be forced beneath a tack head and levered, so raising the tack.

tack-rag   A specially prepared rag for dusting off varnished surfaces before papering down or applying another coat. It consists of a piece of lint-free rag dipped in diluted varnish and wrung out.

tacks   Used chiefly for upholstery. Sizes of cut tacks (A) range from ¼ in (6mm) to 1¼ in (32mm) and they are made in various finishes; blued, black, iron tinned, galvanised, copper. Improved tacks are as above but with larger heads. Covered tacks (B) have their heads covered with leather or leather cloth. Wire tacks (C) are round in section instead of being faceted, and are used for fixing webbing, etc. Sizes range from ½in (12mm) to 1in (25mm).

TACKS

tacky   Term used particularly in connection with oil gilding in which the gold size is allowed to half-dry so that it is sticky and so holds the gold leaf. It is also used in connection with any polish, varnish, or adhesive which is half-dry.

taffeta   Also called 'taffety'. A plain woven silk.

tail   The back end of a tool, appliance, or other item.

tail piece   Piece of dense hardwood to which the strings of a musical instrument are fixed.

tail stock   The movable stock of a lathe which can be shifted along the bed to suit various lengths of work. (See *lathe, turning*.)

tail vice   One fixed at the end of a bench. A stop is housed in it and there are stop holes at intervals along the bench top near the edge. Thus wood can be gripped in any convenient position whilst being worked.

taking off Measuring and noting the details of a drawing to enable a cutting list to be prepared, and an estimate made of the time and materials needed for a job.

taking-off table The table on a machine (e.g. a planer) from which work is taken off after having been processed; more commonly called an 'outfeed' table.

tall-back chair Type which became popular for a time in the late seventeenth century. Also called a high-back chair.

tallboy Form of double chest of drawers, one part standing on the other. It became popular in the late seventeenth century when it was invariably veneered with walnut on an oak or pine groundwork. It persisted throughout the eighteenth and nineteenth centuries, and from about 1730 was made chiefly in mahogany, though examples in oak are sometimes seen.

tallow wood (*eucalyptus microcorys*) Timber from Tasmania and Victoria of 45 lb (721 kg) weight. Also known as myrtle beech or Tasmanian beech. Straight-grained wood of fine, even texture with rather featureless pinkish-brown heartwood and narrow sapwood separated from the heartwood by a zone of intermediate colour. Used for cabinet work, flooring, and turnery.

tambour A form of sliding door, shutter, or lid composed of narrow strips of wood assembled side by side and glued to a backing of plastic fabric, linen, or canvas so that the whole assembly is flexible and can be bent round a curve. The strips may be moulded or plain; preferably they should be rebated on the back edges so that they overlap and hide the fabric. When moulded they can have beaded profiles, and narrow

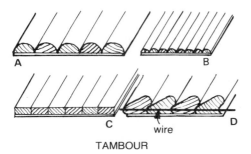

TAMBOUR

designs can be worked in pairs. Plain strips can be of different colours to create an attractive appearance. Heavier tambours may be wired together rather than mounted on a fabric backing (D). In all cases, the tambour runs in grooves at top or bottom, or at the sides, according to purpose; when the tambour is one which slides up and down it is usual to counterweight it to prevent it slamming down. A recent development has been the introduction of plastic strips which interlock to form a tambour.

tang Pointed end of a tool such as a chisel, bradawl, screwdriver, etc., which fits into the handle. In most cases there is a shoulder to prevent its being forced in too far, but some carving tools are made shoulderless.

tang chisel or gouge One having a tang fixing to the handle as compared with a socket fixing.

tangential cutting Method of converting timber in which the cut forms a tangent to one of the annual rings (A). Compare with radial cutting (B). (See also *flat sawn, through and through*.)

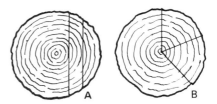

TANGENTIAL CUTTING

tangential section Surface of the wood revealed when a log is cut tangentially to the annual rings. (See *tangential cutting*.)

tanned oak Popular finish for some oak furniture. The wood may be given a weak coat of walnut stain or left bare. It is then finished with garnet French polish.

tannic acid Yellowish powder dissolved in water sometimes used before ammonia when fuming. It gives a somewhat different shade and evens the tone. (See also *pyrogallic acid*.)

tap Used to cut a thread in a hole, and made in pair with a screw box (*q.v.*). Also used in metalwork in conjunction with a die for cutting screw threads.

taped seat (USA) A chair seat closely woven with intersecting strips of scraps of fabric; particularly favoured by the Shakers, an American religious sect.

tape, gummed Strip of brown paper gummed on one side and used chiefly to hold veneer together when jointing.

tape, linen Used chiefly by the upholsterer in measuring for covers, etc.

tapeless jointer Machine for jointing veneer. The edges of the veneer are pressed against a glue-moistening disc, and a series of wheels set at a slight angle press the veneers together. Electrical heating causes the glue to set.

taper bit Used in finishing a hole to a tapered shape after boring with the centre, shell, or other bit. Used chiefly in cask making to receive the spigot or bung.

TAPER BIT

taper centre Used on the tail stock of a lathe. The cone shape is at 60 deg.

TAPER CENTRE

tapered slip joint (USA) A useful corner joint for frames; the tapered cheek of the tenon (and the slot) reduces the risk of telegraphing (*q.v.*) when veneer is laid over the joint.

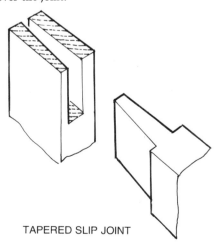

TAPERED SLIP JOINT

tapered splay-leg plate A fitting which is screwed to the underside of a table top: the central hole is tapped to accept a metal pin which is inserted in the end of the leg.

tape, spring measuring Flexible metal rule contained in a circular case and actuated by a spring.

taper haunch (see *haunch (D)*.)

taping Use of gummed tape when making joints in veneer, cross bandings, inlay, etc., to prevent their opening as the glue dries out.

taper jig Appliance used on the circular saw for cutting tapers. It may be merely a tapered or stepped piece of wood, or it may be adjustable. After the first side of the wood has been taper-sawn the jig is opened to double the amount to enable the second side to be sawn.

taper saw Also known as a splitting saw. It is a circular saw ground off on both sides from a centre to a thin periphery. Used with the minimum projection of the blade above the table so that the thick part of the saw is never in contact with the wood. Suitable for cutting thin-section stuff.

TAPER SAW

tar oil Used as a wood preservative. (See *creosote*.)

tarpaulian hessian Heaviest weight of hessian (*q.v.*) used in best quality work. Also known as spring canvas.

tarsia Another name for intarsia (*q.v.*).

Tasmanian beech (see *Tasmanian myrtle*).

Tasmanian myrtle (*nothofagus cunninghamii*). Also known as myrtle beech and Tasmanian beech. From Tasmania and Victoria. Used for cabinet work, flooring, etc. Straight-grained, fine, and even texture.

Tasmanian oak (*eucalyptus gigantea, eucalyptus regnans,* and other *Eucalyptus* species). Timber from Australia and Tasmania of 46-48 lb (737-769 kg) Used for furniture, tool handles, oars, etc.

tavern clocks Large-dialled clocks used in taverns and inns. (See *'Act of Parliament' clocks*.) Also called 'stage-coach clocks'.

tavern table A small, sturdy, rectangular table to seat four persons. Invariably they had four tapered or turned legs united by an underframing; sometimes they contained a drawer under the table top. Used in inns throughout the 18th and 19th centuries.

tawa (*Beilschmiedia tawa*). New Zealand timber of 40lb (641kg) used for furniture, general woodware, and musical instruments. Liable to dull saw teeth in conversion.

TCT Abbreviation for tungsten-carbide-tipped. (See *tungsten carbide, high speed steel, HSS.*)

T.D.A. roof truss Type of truss for house construction developed by the Timber Development Association now known as Timber Research and Development Association (T.R.A.D.A.). It is a relatively light yet really strong structure held together with bolts and toothed timber connectors.

tea caddies The word caddy derives from the Oriental kati which is a weight of slightly more than 1lb (0.45kg); the word first came into use about 1762 as the term 'tea chest' was in use until then. They were divided internally into compartments for different kinds of tea and sometimes a mixing bowl; they were always fitted with locks as tea was a valuable commodity.

teak (*tectona grandis*). Hardwood from India and Burma. Rivalled only by oak as a constructional timber. Used in shipbuilding, railway work, joinery, garden furniture, and in recent years for indoor furniture. It is of yellowish-brown colour, tending to darken on exposure. Somewhat coarse and open in the grain, and noticeably greasy to the touch, for which reason it is not a good glueing wood. Resists damp, is of good fire-resisting quality, and largely immune from attack by the white ant. Trees are girdled about two years before felling, that is, an incision is made around the base of the trunk, so preventing the upward flow of life juices and killing growth. This reduces weight so that the logs can be floated to the mill. An ungirdled log would sink.

teapoy Small table with box-like top standing on a centre pillar. Made in the late 18th and throughout the 19th centuries, the top being fitted up as a tea caddy and often with a compartment for sugar.

tear-drop handle A pear-shaped drop handle (*q.v.*).

tears in wood Pronounced 'tares', the result of planing against the grain. The wood is torn out ahead of the cutting edge. Some woods are specially difficult owing to the changing direction of the grain in parts, or streaks of grain running in opposite directions. It can be minimised by setting the plane fine and having the back iron (*q.v.*) close to the cutting edge. A fine mouth also helps.

tease-tenon Sometimes used where rails meet a post at right-angles at the same level. One tenon is cut away to half the width at the top, and the other correspondingly cut at the bottom so that each can be passed right through the posts and be wedged at the outside if necessary.

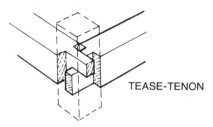

TEASE-TENON

tea trolley Light serving trolley usually with top and one shelf, and sometimes two shelves. Fitted with large castors to enable it to pass easily over carpets, etc.

technical school plane This, when of wood, is similar to an ordinary jack plane but is cut away at the back so that the handle is lower, giving better control. The metal plane has a detachable side handle, convenient when the plane is used on the shooting board. It is rarely seen today.

Tectool Tool for cutting grooves and rebates. Its chief value is for working around curved edges for which a plough or rebate plane could not be used, though it can also be used for straight work.

tee-bar cramp A cramp having a bar or T-section. (See *T-section cramp.*)

tee nuts A KD fitting, it is a socket with an internal thread. The socket is mounted on either (a) a screw-on plate or (b) a pronged plate which can be driven into the wood. The fitting enables metal rods or studding to be fixed at right angles to a wooden surface.

TEE NUT

teeth, saw There are many varieties according to the type and purpose of the saw; the illustrations show the main shapes but there are many others. Size of teeth is measured in 'points per inch' (25mm) or 'teeth per inch' (25mm) and this is sometimes abbreviated to TPI (*q.v.*). (See also *'points'*.) The measurement must include the teeth at both ends. Saws intended for cutting with the grain are filed square straight across, whereas those for cross-cutting are bevel-filed so that the teeth present a series of knife-like points which cut the sides of the kerf. Most teeth have 'set', that is, they are given a slight lateral projection so that the kerf is wider than the saw plate and so has clearance. For cutting green wood the set is increased. An exception is the circular planer saw which is hollow-ground to give clearance. Those shown are:

Handsaws
A. rip; B. crosscut; C. lightning crosscut.

Two-man crosscut
D. peg; E. lightning.

Bandsaws
F. standard; G. Argentine.

Circular
H. hardwood rip; I. softwood rip; J. crosscut; K. radial crosscut; L. peg; M. combination; N. firewood; O. tipped.

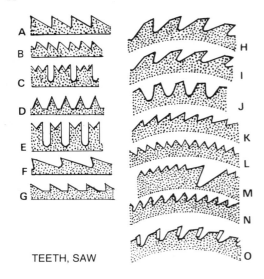

TEETH, SAW

telegraphing   This is the term applied to the effect whereby the core strips of a blockboard impart a ripple to the appearance of veneers laid on it; the effect does not show up until the veneers have been polished or finished.

telescopic table   Extending dining table in which the movement is operated by a metal screw. The slides or runners move one within the other. (See *table, extension.*)

tempera   (see *pastiglia*).

tempered hardboard   Oil-tempered hardboard (also called 'super' boards) which contain additives to make them weather and water resistant; suitable for exterior use when the edges are properly protected.

tempering   Treatment of steel to make it hard enough to do its work without being brittle. It is first made dead hard by heating to a cherry red and quenching in water and sometimes oil. In this state the steel is brittle and needs to be let down. This is done by heating and noting the colour the steel assumes and plunging into water when the required colour is reached. For wood chisels and plane irons the required colour is gold with a touch of brown. For knives the colour reaches purple, and for a screwdriver, blue. In the case of a tool in which only the tip needs to be brought to the required hardness as in a screwdriver, the stem is heated away from the tip and the progress of the colours towards the tip noted. As soon as the colour reaches the tip the tool is quenched. In this way the stem or body of the tool is less hard and able better to resist the twisting strain. Chisels and plane irons which need to be of the required hardness throughout are reheated on a hot metal plate and quenched when the required colour is reached. Rubbing the tool with emery paper after hardening enables the colour to be observed more easily.

template   Corruption of 'templets' (*q.v.*).

templets, Maco   (see *Maco templet.*)

templets (1)   Appliance used in marking or cutting mitres, square cuts, or stopped chamfers. That at (A) is for mitreing the stuck mouldings of a framework, the chisel lying flat on the sloping surface. At (B) the square end enables a squared line to be transferred to

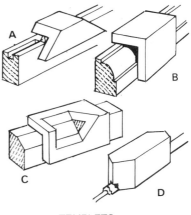

TEMPLETS

the adjoining surfaces across the intervening moulding. For cutting a stopped chamfer, either square or at 45 deg, the templet at (C) is used. That at (D) is for mitreing the moulding of a barred door. The angles may have to vary to suit the mitres of mouldings meeting at different angles. Note that as most of the mouldings are grooved at the underside to fit over the bars, a small fillet of wood is glued to a flat board to support the underside of the groove which would otherwise split out under the action of the chisel. This fillet is gradually nibbled away as further cuts are made.

2. The term also applies to a pattern cut in thin material — plywood, hardboard, metal, card, etc., and used for making out shapes or for testing. (See also *Maco templet and mitre templet.*)

tenon The projecting end of a member which fits into a corresponding recess, the mortise (See *mortise and tenon*). There are many varieties. (See under *box, chased, double, draw-bored, forked, foxtail, wedged, franked, haunched, long-and-short shoulder, notched, oblique, open, plug, stub, stump, tease, triple, tusk, twin, wedged.*)

tenon, dovetailed Joint sometimes used in carpentry when two rails meet in the same plane meet at a post. The mortise in the latter is cut extra long, its end sloping, so that after the two rails have been entered a wedge can be driven in, so locking the whole together.

tenoned brace One used in a ledged-and-framed door, having stub-tenons at the ends. The tenons are invariably barefaced to enable the boarding to be fixed.

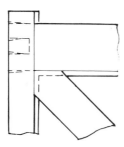

TENONED BRACE

tenoners There are four types - the single-end; the double-end; the rounded-end; and the double-ender and profiler. The single-end consists of a basic casting on which are mounted a rolling work-table and a vertical arm which carries the two tenoning cutter blocks (always called 'heads'), plus a cut-off saw

which determines the length of the tenon, and one or two scribing heads which control the shape of the shoulders. Thus, if a rail is tenoned into a circular leg, the scribing heads can shape the shoulders to fit round the curve.

double-ender Basically, this machine incorporates two machine heads, one sliding and one fixed so that the first can be moved to or away from, the other. Two feed chains run from front to back between these machine heads, and the chains are fitted with pressure pads mounted on other chains to hold the work steady. Each machine head carries a cutting head unit which consists of cut-off saws, tenoning heads, and scribers. The machine works on the same principle as the single-end tenoner.

rounded-end This is essentially either a single-end or double-ended tenoner which has the added facility of imparting rounded sides to the tenon so that it will fit into the round-ended mortise produced by an oscillating bit mortiser.

double-ender and profiler This is a double-end tenoner to which additional cutter heads may be fitted to do such additional work as panel sizing, rail haunching, panel edge moulding, panel edge shaping, panel tongueing and grooving, panel tongue haunching, panel end stopped grooving, housings, corner locking, mitre sawing, and drilling.

tenon, loose Often used in furniture repair work when an existing tenon has crumbled or broken away.

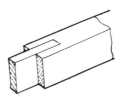

TENON, LOOSE

tenon saw A saw with brass or iron back to its blade, fitted with a closed handle as at (A). The blade is 12 in (305 mm) to 16 in (406 mm) long with teeth 12 to 14 points per inch (25 mm). When intended solely for cutting tenons the teeth are filed straight across as in a rip saw, since it is cutting with the grain. Most woodworkers need it for general benchwork, however, which includes cutting across the grain, and in this case the teeth are bevel-filed at an angle as in a crosscut saw. A small edition of the tenon saw is the dovetail saw (B). Both are also known as backsaws (*q.v.*).

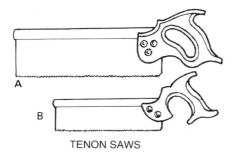

TENON SAWS

tension Term used in connection with handsaws and back saws in which, by a hammering process, the blade is stiffened. Without it the blade would be floppy, difficult to control, and insufficiently rigid for its work. The same applies to a circular saw which is tensioned by hammering. In a bandsaw tension refers to the degree of tautness given to the blade by pushing the upper wheel upwards. The bearing of this latter is usually spring-loaded to enable the degree of tautness to be varied.

The term also refers to a stretching force acting on a constructional member.

tension sleeve Tube-like fitting having a right-hand thread at one end, and left-hand at the other. Used to give tension as in some bowsaws and framesaws, tie rods, etc.

tension spring Used chiefly to support loose cushions on upholstered furniture. They consist of tightly wound spring wire in the form of cables and are usually covered with plastic sleeves to avoid marking the upholstery. They are fixed by engaging hooks or links at their ends into holes drilled in a metal strip screwed to the side seat rails, the tension being $1\frac{1}{2}$ in to 2 in (38 mm to 51 mm) over an 18 in (457 mm) span, or its equivalent for other spans.

tension wood Timber cut from the convex side of a curved tree or leaning tree, resulting in its having elongated and thin-walled cells.

tent bed One having a shaped canopy in which the supporting framework is concealed by the fabric. Used in the second half of the 18th century and onwards.

tenterhook Hooked-shaped nail pointed at both ends. The French polisher uses them to hold down loose parts whilst polishing the surface, driving the long end into the bench so that the cranked end bears on the wood.

terebine A light yellow liquid (poisonous) used as a drier when oil polishing (*q.v.*) and in making some revivers (*q.v.*).

term A pedestal tapering towards the foot, and used to hold a bust or carved figure.

terminal A turned or square-cut ornamental finish to a staircase newel or standard. Also sometimes fitted to the apex of a greenhouse or shed roof. Also known as a finial (*q.v.*).

tern foot Of French origin, having a three-scroll arrangement. Used originally in Louis XV work and in this country by Chippendale. Similar to a Braganza foot (*q.v.*).

tessellated Inlaid work of checkered formation consisting of small squares or oblongs assembled as a mosaic.

tester In furniture this is the flat framework over a four-poster bed. A half tester covers the head of the bed only. The term is also applied to the canopy or sounding board over a pulpit.

tête-à-tête A two-seat sofa or ottoman.

tetrahedron A regular solid with four equilateral triangles forming the sides.

texture Applied to the distribution, arrangement, and fineness or coarseness of the fibres and other woody elements in timber. (See also *grain*.)

thermoplastic resins A synthetic resin which melts or softens on heating and re-hardens on cooling without chemical change.

thermosetting resin A synthetic resin which undergoes irreversible chemical and physical changes on curing. They are widely used in adhesives.

thicknesser A machine which planes wood to an even thickness; it is also called a 'panel planer'; as a general rule thicknessers have square cutter blocks, while those of a panel planer are circular. The wood must have one face planed true, and this must be on the side opposite to the face being thicknessed. The machine has a cutter block mounted above the material to be planed, with a rise-and-fall table immediately beneath. This houses two free-running rollers which help to carry the wood through and these are set slightly above the level of the table surface to break any frictional resistance between the wood and the table. Above, and in line with, these rollers are the feed rollers, which are power-driven and feed the wood past the cutter block; the first of these rollers (called the 'in-feed roller') has a fluted or ridged surface to grip the wood and is spring-loaded to counter any small imperfections in the wood. Between the in-feed roller and the cutter block is a 'chip breaker' which both holds down the wood and provides an edge on which the chips can break. On the 'out-feed' side of the cutter block is the pressure bar which bears down on the wood to prevent it falling under its own weight; this is followed by another power-driven spring-loaded roller, which pulls the wood through.

Larger industrial machines employ the same principles but often incorporate cutting blocks above and below the work, and additional cutters which shape the edges at the same time.

thicknessing (1) Bringing wood to an even thickness after planing one side true. In hand work a gauge line is marked on the edges and the surplus planed away. In machine work a thicknesser (*q.v.*) automatically reduces the wood to even thickness.

thicknessing (2) The glueing on of a narrow strip to the underside of a top or to the side of a cabinet end to give the appearance of greater thickness. Its purpose may be to reduce cost or to save weight. It is important that the grain is the same throughout so that the whole shrinks evenly, otherwise there is risk of splitting in the event of shrinkage.

thicknessing attachment An attachment added to a surface plane or edger enabling it to bring wood to an even thickness.

T. hinge (see *cross-garnet*).

thinners Liquid used in bringing polish, paint, lacquer, to a less thick consistency. In the case of French polish this is methylated spirit, but for paints and lacquers the thinner made or recommended by the manufacturer should be used.

thitka (*Pentace burmanica*) From Burma of 40 lb (641 kg) weight. Used for furniture, panelling, etc. Grain tends to be interlocked.

thread hole The hole in which the thread of a screw bites into the wood as distinct from the clearance hole through which the shank passes. In

THREAD-HOLE

diameter is should equal or be a trifle bigger than that of the screw stem at the root of the thread.

three-centred arch Pointed arch struck from three centres. Another form is rounded, but the shape

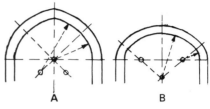

THREE-CENTRED ARCH

is not so pleasing as the elliptical arch (*q.v.*) struck by the trammel or string method.

three-in-one plane Name sometimes applied to a shoulder plane (q.v.) with interchangeable parts, enabling it to be used as a shoulder plane, bullnose plane, and chisel plane.

three-jaw chuck Self-centreing chuck for a lathe in which the jaws are operated by a scroll or side-threaded ring which moves all the jaws simultaneously. Used to grip circular or hexagonal work.

three-ply Term used for a panel made up of three layers glued together, the grain of the inner layer or core at right-angles with those at the outside. More usually known today as plywood (*q.v.*). (See also *multiply* and *stoutheart plywood*.)

three-way joint Needed where three members meet at the same point. Its form varies according to the purpose of the item and the section of the parts. It sometimes occurs in the stretchers of a table, but its

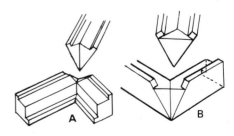

THREE-WAY JOINT

commonest application is in the corners of a showcase where the rails are rebated at both sides. In the simplest way plain mitred joints are used as at (A) and strips of canvas glued in the internal angles. A stronger method, however, is that at (B) in which the members are part mitred and part butted. Sometimes two small dowels are added at the butted part, but in all these showcases the main strength is in the plate glass panels, these being bedded in mastic which binds the whole together.

three-way miter (USA) A joint where three members meet. The end of one member has two adjoining faces mitred off and mortised; the ends of the other two members are tenoned to fit.

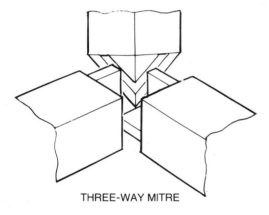

THREE-WAY MITRE

three-way strap Metal plate used in roof work to fix together the principal rafters to the king post. (See *king post roof.*)

three-winged slotting bit Used in slot mortising. It is fed a short way into the wood, the latter is then shifted to complete the mortise length and the operation repeated until the complete depth is reached. The ends of the mortise are round and need to be finished square unless the sides of the tenon can be rounded.

THREE-WING SLOTTING BIT

throat Term applied to an opening or channel in a tool or machine through which chips or shavings can pass. May also be known as the escapement (*q.v.*).

throating Groove cut beneath a window cill or other projecting member to prevent water from creeping back and running down a wall or other part.

Also used beneath a casement window to prevent capillarity or the capacity of water to climb above its own level in a confined space. Also known as a 'capillary' groove.

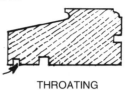

THROATING

throne chair A large and imposing chair, with arms and a tall back, designed to give prominence to the occupant.

through dovetail Joint in which both dovetails and pins pass right through the entire thickness of the wood. The joint is therefore exposed on both sides of the corner.

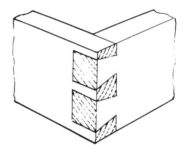

THROUGH DOVETAIL

through and through Method of converting a log with a series of parallel cuts straight through. Also known as tangential cutting (*q.v.*).

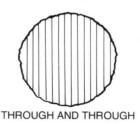

THROUGH AND THROUGH

throwing An old term for turning (*q.v.*), now obsolete.

thrown chair One made entirely of turned members, or nearly so. Popular in the first half of the seventeenth century or a little earlier. The type was made in oak or ash and probably originated in Scandinavia.

thrust wheel Small flat wheel or disc fitted to the rear of a bandsaw blade to prevent its being pushed off its wheels when sawing. It sometimes takes the form of a roller rather than a wheel. It should be free to revolve when the back of the saw touches it, but should not be in contact with it when the saw is running free.

thumb catch Catch recessed into the sides of a secretaire. It holds the fall in the 'up' position. Thumb pressure releases the fall.

thumb latch (see *Norfolk latch*).

thumb moulding Small rounded moulding, usually elliptical but may be circular, worked at the edge of wood, generally with a fillet.

THUMB MOULDING

thumb plane A miniature plane about 3½in long (89mm) made of wood, with either flat or curved sole, held by the thumb and fingers, and used for rabbeting or moulding, etc. They are used today by musical instrument makers. (See *finger, palm, planes.*)

thumb screw Small cramp similar to the G cramp (*q.v.*) but smaller and lighter. Usual kind is made of metal strip bent to shape with the screw passing through one end. Its weakness is at the corners, and the best cramps have specially strengthened corners which are not liable to flatten out under strain. Also known as a fret cramp.

thunder shake An upset across the grain of wood, especially African mahogany, generally considered to be caused during felling by impact across an obstruction such as another log, or by severe bending during high winds. Extremely difficult to detect until after the wood is worked. The timber may fracture completely even under light stress.

thurming Method of forming square balusters rather than the normal turned type. The work is done on a special form of lathe which has extra depth of clearance above the bed. The squares to be thurmed are fixed around a form of drum, and the latter revolved. After the shape has been cut on one side, each square is revolved through 90 degrees and the same section cut in, and so on until all four sides have

been completed. The resulting surfaces are slightly rounded, the degree of curvature depending upon the diameter of the drum on which they are mounted.

thuya (*tetraclinis articulata*) From Algeria and Morocco, somewhat like amboyna in figuring and reddish brown in colour but with lighter yellowish patches. Used for small decorative items.

ticketer Tool used for turning the edge of a cabinet scraper, turning scraper tool, or the cutter for a French spindle. Also known as a scraper sharpener. It is a hard steel rod with smooth surface. By pressing back the edge of the scraper it gives a small hook to the tool which cuts without tearing out the grain. (See also *burnisher.*)

ticking Material used for the case of a mattress, etc. It can be cotton, damask, or linen.

tie A cross-member of a frame or other structure such as a roof truss. The rails between chair or small table legs are sometimes referred to as tie rails. In general it is any member (usually horizontal) which serves to prevent two other members from spreading.

tie rail Any rail built into a carcase which has the effect of holding together two ends or other members.

tie rod Iron rod used in place of a tie beam. (See under *tie.*)

Tiffany finish (USA) A blended multicolour paint finish which can have either a smooth or a textured finish.

tiger's eye A type of quartz which is fibrous with long silky filaments and iridescent markings resembling a tiger's eye. Imitated as a paint decoration on table tops, etc.

tight cooperage (see *wet cooperage*).

tight face The side of veneer farthest from the log as it is sliced. When practicable this should be uppermost when the veneer is laid because the under or convex side may have small cracks or splits.

tight knot (see *knot, live*).

tiling battens Battens nailed to the rafters or roofing boards to hold the tiles. They range from ¾ in to 1¼ in (19-32mm) thick by 1½ in to 3½ in (38-89mm) wide. The tiles hook over them.

till Archaic term for a small drawer or small box fitted into a chest or cabinet, and not necessarily associated with money.

till drawer block Wood block with hollowed-out circular depression to facilitate the removal of coins. Usually elm and with various sizes of depressions.

till lock Alternative name for a drawer lock.

tilt arbor A device which allows the motor of a circular saw, with its spindle and blade, to tilt and so produce sawcuts at an angle.

tilting fillet A triangular strip of wood used in roof work at the eaves to support the lower end of the bottom tiles. (See also *sprocket piece*.)

tilting table The table of a circular saw, bandsaws, or jigsaw that can be tilted laterally to enable wood to be sawn at an angle.

timber Wood cut from trees and used for building and for the manufacture of furniture and domestic items of every description. In this handbook no attempt is made to describe the thousands of timbers of commerce, but many of them are listed under their own names.

timber abbreviations The following are abbreviations applied to timber: a.d. = air dried; bd. = board; hdwd. = hardwood; k.d. = kiln dried; m.c. = moisture content; p.a.r. = planed all round; p.e. = plain edged; p.t. and g. = planed, tongued and grooved; S1E = surfaced one edge; S2E = surfaced two edges; S1S = surfaced one side; S2S = surfaced two sides; S1S1E = surfaced one side and one edge; S1S2E = surfaced one side and two edges; S2S1E = surfaced two sides and one edge; s.e. square-edged; t & g = tongued and grooved; t.g.b. = tongued, grooved and beaded; t.g.v. = tongued, grooved, and V-jointed; u.s. = unsorted.

timber brick Wood block built into a wall to give a fixing for joinery.

timber connectors (see *bulldog; shear plate; spike grid; split-ring, toothed,* and *toothed-ring connectors*).

timbers, densities and weights of Timbers vary greatly in density and consequently in weight; density = weight divided by volume. In this dictionary, the densities of the timbers are given per cubic foot (and kilogrammes per cubic metre in brackets). Figures can only be approximate, however, owing to variations in moisture content. It is generally reckoned that the stated weight of a timber is when it is in 'air-dry' condition; that is, when the moisture content approaches equilibrium with the surrounding atmosphere.

Among the lightest woods are:- balsa 9-10 lb (144-160 kg); Western red cedar 22 lb (352 kg); by contrast, African blackwood, cocobolo, and lignum vitae reach 88 or 89 lb (1410 or 1426 kg). Great weight does not necessarily imply great strength or durability.

timber terms (see under *batten, baulk, board, deal, flitch, half-timber, plank, quartering, scantling, square, slab, strip, waney-edged*).

timber stud partition A comparatively thin non-loadbearing wall composed of a timber framing clad with wallboards (often insulation boards). The top horizontal member is called the 'headpiece', and the bottom horizontal member is the soleplate or sill. Vertical posts called 'studs' are fixed equidistantly between them, and shorter horizontal rails called 'noggings' are fixed between the studs.

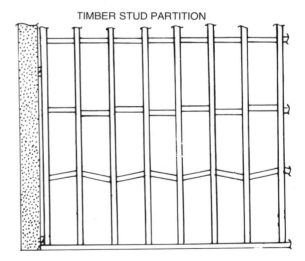

TIMBER STUD PARTITION

tip, gilder's (see *gilder's tip*).

tipped saw Circular saw having teeth of tungsten-carbide. It is specially useful for cutting timbers of an abrasive type, and made-up panels assembled with resin glue. The tipped teeth ensure a much longer working sharpness than the ordinary saw.

TIPPED SAW

tip speed (see *peripheral speed*).

toad's back Handrail having its top surface worked to a flattish curve.

toad back moulding Double ogee moulding, sometimes with centre bead. Used in furniture legs in the second half of the eighteenth century.

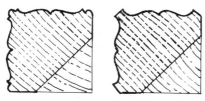

TOAD-BACK MOULDING

toat Handle of bench plane.

toe The front or lower end of an item such as a strut. Also used in connection with a plane as distinct from the heel which is the back, or a handsaw, the toe being the narrow end of the blade, and the heel nearest the handle.

In furniture it refers also to any small member on which a box, footstool, or small cabinet may rest. Also frequently applied to the bottom end of a chair, table, or stand leg. In joinery it refers to the bottom of the shutting edge of a door.

toilet glass Small mirror, rectangular, elliptical, or shield shape pivoted on posts, the last-named forming part of a stand, or rising from a box with drawers. Popular during the eighteenth and nineteenth centuries. Generally the mirror frame was cross-banded.

toilet table Alternative name for a dressing table (*q.v.*).

tommy bar Metal rod used to loosen the centres of a lathe when removal is necessary. It is passed through a hole in the side of the centre and used as a lever. The term is also applied to any metal rod used for similar purposes.

tongue Projecting member at the edge of wood fitting into a corresponding groove cut in the joining (A). A barefaced tongue (B) is flush at one side with only one shoulder. A double tongue is given at (C), and corner twin tongue at (D). (See also *loose tongue*.) The term also refers to the shorter arm of a steel (roofing) square. The longer arm is the blade.

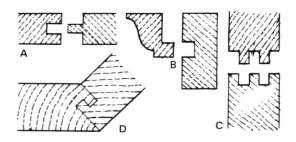

TONGUES

tongued-and-grooved boards These cover a large class of milled timber. The commonest variations are: (A) tongued and grooved (T.G.); (B) tongued, grooved, and beaded (T.G.B.); (C) tongued, grooved, and V jointed (T.G.V.J.). Type (A) is used chiefly for floor boards and sometimes for sheds; (B) and (C) are usually for indoor partitions, etc. (See *flooring* and *match boarding*.) In the case of (B) the bead may be on one or both sides. The V may also be on both sides in (C). These prepared boards are also known as matching or match boarding. They are normally available in widths of 4 to 6 in (102 to 152 mm) and in thicknesses of ½ in to 1 in (12 to 25 mm). Sizes are nominal, however, the machined material finishing less. (See also *floor boards* and *weather boards*.)

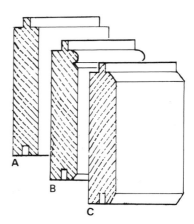

T & G BOARDS

tongue and rabbet joint (USA) A tongued and grooved joint for use where strength is not the consideration; the disadvantage is that end-grain on one or other of the pieces has to be glued to long grain on the other. Also called a 'tongue and dado' joint.

Tonk's strip. (see *shelf supports*).

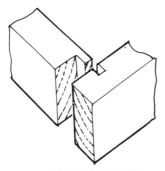

TONGUE & REBATE JOINT

tool marks   In normal woodwork these are a defect pointing to skimped or poor work. In carving however they are intentionally left as they give character to the work.

tool, pad   Handled tool with a chuck in which various tools, chisel, screw driver, saw, awl, etc., can be fitted.

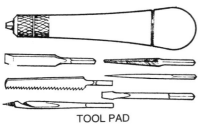

TOOL PAD

tool post   Socketed casting fitted to the lathe bed in which the tool rest is fixed.

tool roll   Holder for brace bits, carving tools, etc. with pockets in which the tools fit. For carving tools the roll is often made double, tools pointing towards each other, but in this case the pockets should be staggered so that one row of tools clears the other. Made in convas, baize, etc.

tooling wheel   Used for embossing a leather table top. The wheel is heated over a gas ring, wiped clean and applied to the leather with fair pressure. Gold leaf, obtainable in tape form, can be used on the embossing.

toon (*cedrela toona*)   From India and Burma of 30 to 40 lb (481 to 641 kg). Mild red timber used or cigar boxes and domestic purposes. Also known as Moulmein cedar and Burma cedar.

tooth Alternative name for a spur *(q.v.)* or nicker of a metal fillister plane.

toothed chain   Used in the chain mortiser. Chains up to $\frac{1}{2}$ in (12 mm) wide have two outer and one inner link. Wider ones have two outer and three inner links.

toothed connector   A circular steel plate with prong-toothed edges, either single or double-sided. The single-sided connectors can be used back-to-back for demountable structures, or can be employed for wood-to-metal fastenings.

toothed-ring connector   A ring made of corrugated steel, each corrugation projecting to form a pronged tooth. Pressure is exerted by a through bolt which embeds the ring into the adjoining faces of the timber parts.

toothing plane   Tool used for scoring the surface of the groundwork before veneering to give a better key for the glue. It also serves to take out any inequalities left by the ordinary bench plane. It is worked in all directions. The cutter is set vertically in the plane stock or nearly so, and its back has a series of grooves in it so that when sharpened it presents a saw-like edge. Cutters are made with coarse, medium, and fine serrations. It is sharpened similarly to an ordinary plane cutter except that the back is not rubbed on the stone to turn back the burr. Wide joints in laminated work are usually toothed, again to improve the glueing grip and to smooth out plane marks.

TOOTHING PLANE

top sawyer   The sawyer who stood on the log when wood was cut in the saw-pit. (See *pit-saw.*)

topping   The operation of levelling the teeth of a saw which have become uneven. A flat file is run back and forth along the tops of the teeth with light but firm pressure. To prevent the file from slipping and injuring the hands it should be fitted into a slot in a piece of wood. The wood thus acts as a fence.

topping plane   (see *sun plane*).

229

toppings   The clear liquid suspended above the stock solution of French polish. It is strained off the polish and sometimes used as a finishing glaze.

topping up   The process of filing the backs or tops of circular saw teeth, neglecting the gullets. It should not be repeated too often as the depth of the gullets (spaces between the teeth) are important to the efficient action of the saw.

tops   The upper length of a felled tree which is not classed as commercial timber.

torchère   Stand primarily to hold a candle or lantern, usually in the form of a column, often with tripod feet. Sometimes used to display a bust or other decorative item.

torch wood   (see *amyris*).

tortoiseshell   Used in some period furniture and particularly in clock cases. The most widely-used shell was that of the hawksbill tortoise *(caretta imbricata)*. Real tortoiseshell is difficult to stick down, especially on curved surfaces, since it is liable to crack unless softened in hot water or by steaming, or by moistening in warm vinegar. Veneering with imitation shell is easier and moreover it is available in larger sizes. It is also fairly pliable and glue or adhesive cement has a better grip. Real tortoiseshell was used extensively as a decoration for clock cases, hand mirrors, etc. in the eighteenth century. Being semi-transparent, it must not be roughened too heavily to provide a key for the glue. Abrasive paper is better than a file. It needs to be held down with a caul or sandbag until the adhesive sets. This also applies to imitation shell. Although fresh skin glue may be used, a synthetic resin glue is advised. The adhesive is usually coloured and rouge powder is often used for the purpose. Gold leaf is also used as it gives a brilliant effect through the transparent material. (See *'faux'*.)

torus   One of the classical basic moulding sections from ancient Greece or Rome. It is a bold rounded section, either part of a circle (A) or an ellipse (B).

TORUS

totara *(podocarpus totara)*   New Zealand softwood, reddish in colour.

tourniquet   Made from cord or several strands of good quality string and used to tighten the arms of a bow saw or chairmaker's saw *(q.v.)*, or sometimes as a form of cramp, particularly in repair work. Sometimes called a 'Spanish Windlass'.

toy furniture   (see *baby furniture*).

TCT   An abbreviation for Tungsten-Carbide-Tipped. (See *tungsten carbide*.)

T. gauge   (see *grasshopper gauge*).

T. halving   (see *halving joint*).

TPI   The abbreviation for 'teeth per inch' (25 mm) on a saw blade; the measure must include the teeth at both ends. (See *teeth, saw*.)

tracery   Ornamental geometrical pattern found in Gothic carving. Sometimes the curves are set out geometrically with instruments, but many carvers prefer to sketch in the shapes freehand, using instruments only when their use seem obvious as in circles, etc. The feature originated in the treatment of windows, but was also used extensively in carving flat panels which might be pierced or merely recessed in the wood when it was known as 'blind tracery'.

The idea was also used in Chippendale Gothic designs for barred doors, for bookcases, china cabinets, etc. Tracery was also used as decoration in the 19th century during the Gothic revival.

tracheids   The tubular cells of soft woods. Thin-walled cells are produced in the spring, and thick-walled cells in summer and autumn.

tracker   (see *jointer*).

tracking   The operation of adjusting the top wheel of a bandsaw so that the saw tends to keep in position centrally on the tyre. Refers to a similar operation on a belt sander so that the sanding belt does not run off the drums.

track, sliding door   (see *sliding door runners and track*).

Trafalgar furniture   A term applied to furniture of various kinds which were produced just after the death of Nelson in 1805. They can be identified by the inclusion of such nautical motifs as anchors, ship's ropes, etc., and by the use of black lines as mourning motifs.

transfer gold   Used in gilding, especially oil gilding. Each leaf is held to tissue paper by a film of wax, enabling it to be handled more easily, especially in outdoor work. It is put up in books of 25 leaves, each 3¼ in (83 mm) square. (See also *loose leaf gold.*)

trail (USA) An undulating or serpentine pattern including stylised berry, leaf, or floral motifs.

transmission belts (see *belt; also pulley*).

transom A lintel or horizontal member between main window (or French doors) and upper light. Also the cross beam between a door and fanlight.

transom window A window above the transom of a door.

transparent polish French polish made from bleached and dewaxed shellac. Almost water-clear, but with slight yellowish tint.

transverse section The section of an item at right angles to its length, and usually therefore at right angles with the grain direction.

transverse shake (see *thunder shake*).

trap door A hinged door fitted horizontally in a floor or ceiling.

trapezium Quadrilateral figure with no sides parallel.

trapezoid Quadrilateral figure with two sides only parallel.

traveller's pieces Miniature replicas of furniture produced by the traveller's firm to be shown to prospective customers.

traverse A partition of wood placed as a screen across a room; can also be in the form of curtains.

traversing Planing wood across the grain, generally at an angle between 45 and 90 deg, when it is necessary to reduce the thickness of a wide board. It reduces the wood quickly to approximate flatness before finishing in the grain direction. Traversing requires less effort than planing with the grain.

trays These are defined by Sheraton as 'boards with rims round them, on which to place glasses, plates and a tea equipage'. There are but a few examples which pre-date 1750; after that date they were made in a multiplicity of designs, the most favoured shapes being oblong or oval. (See also *voyders.*)

tray stand A stand or table for supporting trays; used in a dining room in the 18th century.

tray-top table Small table with raised edging around the top to prevent items from falling off. The edging in old tables was usually fretted or made with small turned posts supporting a rail.

treacle moulding A form of drip moulding. It is often used as a drawer pull moulding with a projecting nose and deep hollow on the underside. Used also as an outside nosing to carry off water.

TREACLE MOULDING

treads The horizontal members of a staircase as distinct from the risers *(q.v.)*.

T rebate plane Wood rebate plane with sole wider than the body of the plane. Made with both straight and curved sole, the latter for shaped work. Used mainly by coach builders, but practically obsolete today.

treen A comprehensive term which includes miscellaneous articles made in wood; generally one would expect them to be made in some other material such as porcelain, bronze, or metal. Typical examples are small carved human or animal figures, tableware such as spoons, snuff boxes, trinket boxes, etc.

trefoil Detail found in Gothic tracery in which three small circles are placed in a large one.

trellis Open work in the form of a fence or division consisting of laths crossing each other at right angles or sloping. The term is also sometimes applied to the criss-cross arrangement of the members of Chinese Chippendale chairs and cabinets.

trenail Peg of hardwood used chiefly by shipwrights to fix wood parts together. It is usually of cleft oak. It is pronounced 'trunnel'.

trench A groove, generally referring to one across the grain.

trencher (1) Originally (15th century) a thick slice of bread on which meat was placed; after the meat was eaten the trencher was given to the poor. Later (16th century onwards) it came to mean a wooden dish.

trencher (2) Alternative name for a dado head *(q.v.)*.

trenching plane Alternative name for a dado plane *(q.v.)*.

trespolo A small table intended to stand against a wall and to carry a vase, ornament, or candlestick. The top was supported on a sinuous-shaped carved column which terminated in a tripod. Popular in the 18th century, particularly in Italy.

trestle A stout batten or bearer supported by four splayed and sometimes braced legs. Used for sawing and for generally carpentry purposes. Often a V notch is cut at one end of the bearer to enable cuts to be made in short pieces without the latter overhanging.

trestle table One which has its top supported by end trestles. Quite often in early tables the top was loose, and the trestle held together with rails, the tenons of which passed right through and held with wedges at the outside, enabling the whole to be dismantled when necessary. The type can be traced back to the 14th century though few specimens as early as this have survived.

tridarn Properly a 'cwpwrdd tridarn'. A form of high cupboard or 'cwpwrdd deuddarn' *(q.v.)* which had an additional shelf added to the top for displaying china, pewter, etc. First introduced in the middle of the 17th century.

triglyph An ornament on a Doric frieze consisting of a tablet with three vertical grooves.

1

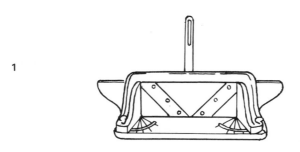

2

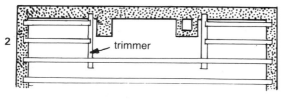

TRIMMER

trimming Applied to the squaring, or levelling of the end of a board, joint, or moulding.

trimmer (1) Hand-powered machine for cutting the ends of rails or squares at right angles or at any other angle. (See also *mitre trimmer.*)

trimmer (2) Member used in floor work in fitting joists around a fireplace or staircase, or between joists or rafters.

trimmer (3) Form of guillotine for cutting veneers to size and trimming away faulty parts.

trimmer (4) A small hand-held tool for trimming the edges of plastic laminate. (See also *edge trimmer.*)

trio tables A nest of three tables following the same style as quartetto tables *(q.v.)*.

triple tenon Strong joint sometimes used for a heavy framework. The outer tenons are usually a form of bridle joint.

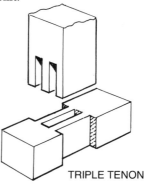

TRIPLE TENON

tripod stool One with three legs. The type is usually associated with kitchen or farm use, in which case it is usually a quite crude item with roughly shaped legs passing into and usually through a top rounded in shape.

tripod table One with three legs jointed to a centre spindle or column and with circular top. Often the latter has a piecrust edging *(q.v.)*. The type became popular in the mid 18th century. In many cases the top was made to revolve, and was pivoted to enable it to fold flat when not in use.

Tripoli powder Fine mineral powder, also called rottenstone, sometimes used in finishing a French polished surface. It is lightly dusted across the hard polish, leaving a finely scratched appearance and taking off the extreme brilliance.

polish, leaving a finely scratched appearance and taking off the extreme brilliance.

triptych An altar piece made in three parts; namely a central panel and two side panels folding over it.

trochilus Scotia moulding (*q.v.*).

trompe l'oeil A French term describing the technique of employing painted or inlaid decoration, or marquetry, to deceive the eye. Thus, a secretaire could have the fall inlaid with writing accessories; but probably the widest use was in large houses where large panels would be so rendered as to deceive the onlooker into thinking there were more rooms than there actually were. It was a 17th and 18th century device, although it is still popular.

truckle bed Also called a 'trundle bed' or a wheeled bed. A plain low bed on wheels for servants; when not in use it was wheeled under the main bed. 14th to 19th centuries.

true shape section Transverse section of a raking moulding, or the radial section of a circular moulding.

truing up Making a surface or edge true and straight in both directions and free of winding. Compare with cleaning up.

truncated An object with its upper part cut off. Thus a truncated cone is the part of a cone left when the vertex has been cut off.

trunk The tree stem.

trunnel (see *trenail*).

truss (1) Timbers fastened together, usually in triangular form to support a roof. Hence the term roof truss.

truss (2) A shaped pilaster with decorative head.

truss (3) A console, or shaped bracket.

trussing bed A medieval bed which could be dismantled and packed up for travelling.

trussing coffer Alternative name for a 'sumpter chest' (*q.v.*).

try or trying plane Wood plane 20 to 24 in (508 to 609 mm) long fitted with a cutter 2¼ to 2½ in (58 to 63 mm) wide. It is similar to jack plane but with closed handle. It is used mainly for truing the edges of wood

as when jointing. The term does not appear to be used for metal planes, those of similar length being known as jointing planes (*q.v.*).

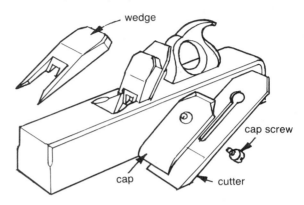

TRY PLANE

try square Tool used for marking and testing wood. Usual wood-worker's pattern has a brass-faced stock and steel blade. Usual sizes range from 6 in to 12 in (152 to 305 mm). (See also *square*.)

T section cramp Form of sash cramp (*q.v.*) but of extra heavy T bar section. The lower edge of the bar usually has a projecting flange to enable it to stand upright on floor or bench, the work being laid across it. Made in lengths of 3 ft (914 mm) to 7 ft (2.13 m) (cramping capacity about 6 in (152 mm) less), with lengthening bars from 3 ft to 6 ft (914 to 1828 mm). Generally made in two sections, normal and extra heavy. Used for large, heavy framings.

tuart (*eucalyptus gomphocephela*) Wood of 58 lb (929 kg) from New South Wales, of reddish brown colour. Used in marine and structural work generally. Somewhat difficult to work as it has a marked dulling effect on tools.

tub chair Upholstered easy chair with sides and back in one continuous curve, roughly forming a semicircle in plan. Top of arms and back are also in a continuous sweep, the back only slightly higher than the arms.

tubular mortise lock (see *mortise lock*).

tuckaway table (USA) A gate-leg table with a hinged leaf and an X-shaped leg frame which folds.

Tudor rose Conventional treatment of a rose consisting of five petals with various treatments at centre and with darts between the petals. Found in carved work of the Tudor period.

tuft Small items of wool or cotton passed beneath the twine when making a mattress. The twine passes right through the mattress and serves to keep the stuffing in place. The tufts prevent the twine from pulling right through the covering.

tulip foot Another name for an onion foot (*q.v.*).

twisted-scroll Windsor A scroll-back Windsor chair having a back stay which is carved into a twist, barley-sugar pattern.

tulip oak (*argyodendron perastal*) Queensland timber of 45 to 58 lb (721 to 929 kg), pink to light red colour. Used for veneers, bentwood furniture, etc.

tulip tree (see *Canary whitewood*).

tulip wood (*dalbergia oliveri*) Timber from Burma of 66 lb (1057 kg). Has many shades of red and is used chiefly for inlay; also for xylophone keys. It has no connection with the tulip tree (*canary whitewood*).

tumbled joints Joints in which the shoulders, etc. have to be specially cut to align with variations in the timber. They may be needed to suit warped wood, but more particularly they are used in timber buildings in which the members retain the natural curves of the wood.

tumbler Form of movable lever in a lock which prevents the bolt from being withdrawn until raised by a correctly shaped key.

tumbling box Box in which small items are placed with an abrasive or polishing compound. The whole is revolved so that the contents tumble against each other and become polished.

Tunbridge ware Small wooden articles such as trinket boxes, snuff boxes, picture frames, trays, etc. which were decorated with intricate mosaic patterns of differently coloured woods. The mosaics were produced from solid blocks composed of thin rods (often the same thickness as a match-stick) glued together; the rods being of various colours. A thin slice was cut off the block and applied as a veneer. In true Tunbridge ware the colours must be the natural hues of the woods and no dyeing is permitted. First started in the middle of the 17th century; it became really popular in Victorian times.

tung oil An oil extracted from the nuts borne by the Chinese tung tree; it is used in paint manufacture and also as a hand-finishing oil, when it is transparent and highly resistant to water and alcohol.

tungsten carbide Cutters tipped with this material are used for manufactured boards bonded with any adhesive which has a pronounced abrasive nature. Generally they do not cut so sweetly as cutters of high speed steel, but they are better able to withstand abrasion. Owing to their long life they are widely used in woodworking machines in general. The abbreviation is TCT. (See *tipped saw.*)

tupelo (*nyssa aquatica*) From southern USA of 45 lb (721 kg). Straight grained wood used for picture mouldings. Greyish white colour.

Turkey oilstone Natural grey-coloured, fine-cutting stone, originally popular but seldom available today. Being hard with fine grain, cutting is slow but a superior cutting edge is obtained. Excellent for carving tools and for finishing off edges already sharpened on a coarser stone.

Turkey-work A knotted wool pile on a canvas base, similar to embroidery and used to upholster chairs in the 16th and 17th centuries.

turnbuckle Small metal catch to hold a cabinet door in the closed position and operated by turning an outer knob or handle. Also an alternative name for a tension sleeve (*q.v.*).

turned chair One made entirely of turned spindles, except for the seat. Such chairs were fairly common in the first half of the 17th century. (See *thrown chair.*)

turning box Long, open-topped box used to hold turnings and tapered legs while inlaying or moulding. The item is held in position either by a screw or with wedges, and a scratch-stock worked along the box side. Thus the scratchstock could be worked in line with the axis of the turning, or, by shifting one end, it could be parallel with the taper or radiate between taper and axis. A series of radiating flutes could thus be worked on a tapered leg.

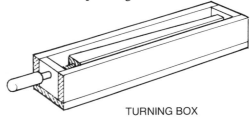

TURNING BOX

turning chisel Taged chisel with long handle, ground both sides, and either square (A) or long-cornered (C). Available from ¼ in wide to 2 in (6 to 51 mm). Also made long and strong (L&S) for heavy work in hardwood.

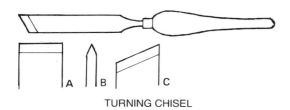

TURNING CHISEL

turning gouge Tanged gouges with long handles and ground either to a nose (A) or square (B). Made half-round section (C) and deep (D); also shallow. Turning gouges are made normal weight or long and strong (L&S) for heavy work. Made in widths from ¼ in up to 2 in (6 to 51 mm).

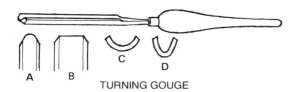

TURNING GOUGE

turning piece Solid piece of wood curved at the top to the curvature of an arch, and used to support the brickwork. It is adjusted with folding wedges.

turning plane Used in rounding long rod-like handles for agricultural implements. There is a centre hole with cutter set at an angle to it.

turning saw (see *compass saw*).

turning, wood The process of rounding and shaping a work-piece on a lathe *(q.v.)* by shaping it with chisels, gouges, or scrapers as it revolves between the headstock and tailstock *(q.q.v.)*. This is called 'between centres' or 'spindle' turning. The term also includes face-plate turning where the work-piece (such as a bowl, platter, or small table top) is held on a metal face-plate which is fixed to the headstock. (See also *centres, face-plate, headstock, tailstock, lathe, mandrel, turning chisels, and gouges.*)

turpentine *(syncarpia laurifolia)* Timber of 58 lb (929 kg) from New South Wales used in general structural and marine work. Reddish-brown colour and rather featureless. Tends to blunt tools rapidly.

turpentine An oleoresin exuding naturally, or from incisions in the bark, of several conifer trees, notably the terebinth tree. Used as a vehicle or as thinners in paints and varnishes.

turpentine substitute Also called 'white spirit'; in the USA 'mineral spirits'. A spirit which is distilled from petroleum and used as thinners for paints and some lacquers.

turpentine, Venice Sometimes added to freshly made animal glue for sticking metal inlay to wood.

turnscrew (see *screwdriver*).

turnscrew bit (see *screwdriver bit*).

turtle back (USA) A type of cabochon *(q.v.)* shaped like a turtle's back.

Tuscan One of the five architectural orders; it is a variation of the Doric order.

tusk tenon Joint used chiefly for flooring timbers, particularly in jointing a trimmer *(q.v.)* to a joist. The main stress is taken by the lower shoulder, the wedged tenon serving to force and hold the parts together. The illustration shows a single tusk tenon, but sometimes there are two steps when it is known as a double tusk tenon.

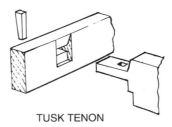

TUSK TENON

Tutch-latch Proprietary name for a catch which avoids the need for knobs and handles on doors. It is secured automatically when closed and needs only a light push to open it.

twin tenon (see *double tenon*).

twine Used in upholstery. For springwork a heavy twine is needed, and a finer yet strong one for the general stitching of rolls, running through, etc. A heavier twine is known as laid cord and is used to lash together the tops of spiral springs. Twines are made from Dutch, Flemish, Irish and Russian flax, and Italian and other hemp. Quality depends upon both the yarn and the method of manufacture. A cheap twine may weigh heavier and thus give less yardage to the ball.

twist bit　Spiral form of bit used in boring deep holes as when dowelling. It seems to have been invented in the early years of the 19th century but was not generally used until later. It usually has a screw point for drawing it into the wood. Made in several patterns. (See under *Gedge, Irwin, Jennings, Russell-Jennings, Scotch nose,* and *solid nose.*)

twist drills　(see under *drill bits*).

twist turning　Decorative form of turning applied mostly to furniture legs, staircase spindles, rails, etc. It is not the product of pure turning. A main cylinder is turned to the over-all diameter with hollow or round members at the ends as may be needed. The spiral is marked out with a strip of card wrapped spiral-wise around the cylinder, and the hollow spiral cut with gouges and chisels, and finished off with rasps, files, scrapers, and lastly abrasive paper. Many patterns are possible; single bine (A), double bine (B), triple bine (C); and the section may take various forms such as the plain rounded section (A), barley sugar (D), and various combinations of them. Nowadays commercially made twists are wholly machined. After the preliminary turning of a cylinder, the work is placed in a form of lathe and moved sideways under the control of a screw which slowly revolves the wood as it is shifted sideways. A revolving cutter is fed into the work and removes the hollow portion of the twist.

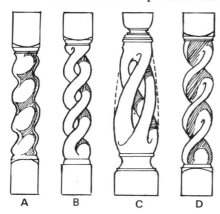

A　　B　　C　　D

TWIST TURNINGS

two-man saw　Long cross-cut saw with handle at both ends. Lengths range from 3 ft to 8 ft (914 mm to 2.44 m) and teeth in a wide range of patterns such as the British Champion, British raker, Fallers King, Great American, Lance Lightning, Tasmanian, and

tenon. Chief patterns are the standard and hollow back felling saw. Good saws are ground thin towards the back to give better clearance, and in the best way are radial ground, the grinding lines parallel with the teeth so that the latter are of even thickness throughout.

two-wing slotting bit　Used for slot mortising, similarly to the three wing bit *(q.v.).*

TWO-WING SLOTTING BIT

two-wing 'throw-away' cutter　(see *spindle moulder*).

TWO-WING THROW-AWAY TIP CUTTER

tyre　The rubber covering of bandsaw wheels.

U

UF adhesives　(see *urea-formaldehyde resin*).

ultimate strength　The point at which timber breaks when under test.

umber　Pigment sometimes used in the French polishing process, either to tint polish or to colour defects. Raw umber is a fairly light brown shade, and burnt umber a darker colour.

umbrella roof　Roof which is supported by central posts. An example is that of a lych gate.

umbrella stand　Usual height is 30 in (762 mm) with the top front rail placed lower down to accommodate ladies' umbrellas. May be square in plan (about 8-9 in) (203-228 mm) or of oblong form. A metal or plastic pan takes drips.

UMF adhesives Urea-melamine-formaldehyde. (See *urea formaldehyde resin*.)

under-bed wardrobe A box about 4 ft (1218 mm) long by 2 ft (609 mm) wide by 1 ft (305 mm) deep with hinged lid and running on small castors. Drawer pulls or handles are fitted at the ends and double handles at the front side so that the wardrobe can be pulled out from beneath a bed. Often made in plywood on a light framework. Handy for holding bed clothes.

undercut Term applied specially to carving in which the edge of the work slopes inwards towards the underside. Also refers to the edge of an item which is planed slightly out of square so that it presents a tight joint at the top. Sometimes the shoulders of a tenon are also slightly undercut for the same reason, though anything more than the slightest amount is regarded as bad practice.

underframing The framed-up structure usually consisting of legs and rails, supporting a table, chair, or cabinet.

unit furniture Items such as cupboards, chests, etc. made to standard sizes which can be added one above or to the side of the other, and which can be given various arrangements.

Universal Combination plane, No. 55 Plane for grooving, moulding, rebating, etc. originally made by Stanley, but no longer available today largely owing to its place being taken by portable electric tools. It differed from the combination or multi-plane which is still on sale in that, whereas the latter can work only those mouldings which are of even depth both sides, it can cut sections which project farther at one side than at the other. It does this by virtue of having a sliding section which is adjustable in height as well as laterally. A useful tool when machinery or power is not available, but of use rather for softwood than hardwood, and of little value for end grain.

universal table A type of Pembroke table *(q.v.)* included by Sheraton in his 'Cabinet Dictionary' (1808).

universal tool Household implement comprising a nail extractor, case opener, hatchet, and hammer. It is of heavy steel, sometimes with wooden handle.

universal woodworker Consists basically of a motor-driven machine such as a lathe or a saw-table to which auxiliary components such as belt sanders, disc sanders, and mortisers, can be connected. More sophisticated designs can have one, two, or three motors driving such machines as saws, spindle moulders, planer/thicknessers, or mortisers; there is also a single-motor type which drives similar auxiliary machines by means of belting.

unsorted Timbers suitable for joinery are graded as unsorted, which means a mixture of grades of seconds, thirds, and fourths, sometimes including firsts. (See *select merchantable*.)

unwrought Timber straight from the saw.

upholder Term used originally for the upholsterer.

upholsterer's chair An alternative name sometimes used for a farthingale chair *(q.v.)*.

upholsterer's hammer (see *hammers*).

upholsterer's ripper (see *ripping chisel*).

upholsterer's webbing stretcher (see *strainer, web*).

upholstery springs (see *springs, upholstery*).

upholstery tacks (see *tacks*).

upholstery webbing (see *webbing, upholstery*).

upset (see *thunder shake*).

urea-formaldehyde (UF) resins Thermo-setting synthetic resins which are created by condensing urea with formaldehyde; the resulting adhesives can be cured very rapidly by heat and pressure and are widely used in plywood and chipboard manufacture. Greater resistance to surface abrasion and to the impact of boiling water can be imparted by including melamine in the composition, when the adhesive is designated as UMF. (See *resin glues, synthetic*.)

urethane lacquer (see *polyurethane lacquer*).

urn Decorative motif in the form of a vase. Used particularly by Adam both in carved and inlaid form. Also refers to the pairs of turned vases which formed either knife-boxes or water urns used on late 18th century sideboards.

utile (*entandrophragma utile*) Hardwood from Ghana and the Ivory coast of 42 lb (673 kg) weight. A reddish-brown timber sometimes slightly purplish. Similar to sapele. Used for furniture and interior joinery.

Utility furniture   During the 1939 to 1945 Second World War a design committee (under the chairmanship of Sir Gordon Russell) was set up to design a range of furniture which was the only one that could be produced. In fact, two ranges were eventually introduced, the first one being the Chiltern, followed by the Cotswold, which was less austere.

V

vacuum bag   Rubber bag in which comparatively small shaped work to be veneered is placed. The air is exhausted by a pump so that atmospheric pressure forces the veneer into close contact with the groundwork.

vacuum press   Press for veneering large work in which atmospheric pressure is used to force down the veneer. Used chiefly for shaped work, especially that with compound curvature. The work with the veneer position is placed beneath a rubber sheet and the air exhausted by an electric pump. The sheet wraps around the work, forcing the veneer into close contact with the groundwork.

valance   A fringe of drapery hanging from a cornice or bed rail.

valley   The intersection of two roof surfaces forming an internal angle. The reverse of a hip. (See *hip rafter*.)

valley rafter   Sloping rafter at the intersection of roof surfaces in a valley. The jack rafters are cut to fit it and are nailed to it.

Vandyke brown   Deep brown pigment which may be in powder form or one of the aniline dyes. Used in staining and water coating.

Vandyke crystals   Old-style basic stain for dark oak. The crystals are dissolved in water and make a rich brown stain which can be varied from light to dark. A little glue size can be added to act as binder, and in this case the stain is applied warm. A little strong ammonia (point eight-eighty) added to the stain helps to drive it into the grain. The crystals are widely used for floors. If used for walnut it is advisable to dilute it considerably. A diluted solution is also sometimes used on mahogany when a cold brown tone is needed. Also known as walnut crystals.

varnishes   There are two principal types of varnish, namely spirit varnish, and oil varnish.

Spirit varnishes are usually made from shellac dissolved in spirit, sometimes with additions such as sandarac or other gums, or naphtha. They include white hard, brown hard, naphtha, and shellac varnishes. They are generally used for interior work only and are not resistant to water, heat, or chemical spillage, but are quick-drying.

Old-style oil varnishes were a solution of natural resins in a drying oil (usually linseed or tung); they are slow-drying as they dry by oxidisation and not by evaporation. They were further divided into hard varnishes for interior work and elastic varnishes for exterior use; the former contained less oil than the latter and were called 'short oil' as opposed to 'long oil'. The two varnishes should never be used in combination as this would lead to cracking owing to the differences in elasticity.

Modern oil varnishes are usually compounded from tung and/or linseed oil, and alkyd or phenolic resins, and are particularly suited to exterior use.

Microporous varnish which often contains a stain is a recent development which, although presenting a conventional varnish appearance, allows the wood to move without affecting the finish in any way.

There are also anti-vandal/anti-thief varnishes which are made to be permanently slippery.

vase, baluster   Turned or square-cut or baluster, similar in general form to an elongated vase.

vaulting   Arched work in roofs and ceilings.

Vauxhall glass   Mirror glass made in the late 17th century and until 1780 at Vauxhall, London. It had a pale bluish tinge.

V belt   Endless transmission belt for machines. The correct size for the pulleys must be used. It should fit so that it is flush with the periphery of the pulley with a gap at the bottom. Size is the internal circumference when the belt is opened as a circle. (See also *pulley*.)

V block   Block having a V-shaped groove along its top edge in which cylindrical work can rest whilst being bored or otherwise worked.

vegetable black   Pigment sometimes used in staining and colouring.

vehicle   The liquid part of a paint or varnish which carries the pigment.

veiner Carving tool which is more than a semi-circle in section. It is made straight, curved, and front-bent. (For details of these shapes see *carvers' gouges*.)

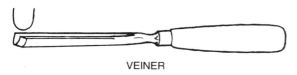

VEINER

velvet Silk fabric having a dense, short pile which can be looped or cut.

veneer The vast majority of veneers today are knife-cut. Originally saw-cut veneers were also obtainable, these being considerably thicker and more expensive because of the great waste in sawdust. Most decorative veneers are flat-sliced, but woods such as bird's eye maple are rotary sliced as also are the plain-grained veneers used for plywood manufacture and for laminated and bent work. The grain of rotary-cut veneers is usually plain and uninteresting. It is always advisable to store veneers between flat boards to prevent buckling. (See also *knife-cut veneer, half-rotary, slicing, half-round slicing, peeler*.)

veneering The covering of a plain-grained, sound wood or built-up panel such as plywood or laminboard with a thin sheet of choice wood. Medium-density fibreboard (or MDF) makes an ideal groundwork. (See *MDF*.) The veneer may be in a single piece or consist of a built-up pattern such as a halved or quartered design. There are three main methods of application; hammer, caul, and press. For the first use animal glue or PVA adhesive, the veneer being pressed down and the surplus glue squeezed out by the zig-zag movement of a veneering hammer. The caul is a flat board or zinc-covered board which is warmed and cramped down over the veneer for the same purpose. A veneer press may be either manually worked by large wing nuts fitted over screws or be hydraulically controlled. The groundwork must be sound and free from defects, and in the best work both sides are veneered to avoid the groundwork being pulled hollow.

veneering hammer Tool used to press veneer into close contact with the groundwork, and to squeeze out surplus glue. It consists of a wood stock with handle let in at right angles, and with brass strip recessed into a groove at one edge. It is worked zig-zag fashion over the veneer, preferably in line with the grain so that the veneer is not stretched with subsequent liability to shrink. The veneer is lightly dampened, and a warm flat iron passed over the surface to liquefy the glue.

An electrical hammer is also available, one side having the thin metal strip for squeezing, and the other an electrically heated block to replace the flat iron.

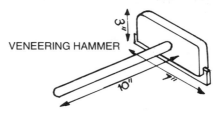

VENEERING HAMMER

veneer jointer (see *jointer, tapeless*).

veneer knife Used for cutting knife-cut veneers to size. For removing blemishes from veneer, and to cut built-up patterns around a zinc templet the specially sharpened point is generally used, as it will negotiate an acute curve.

VENEER KNIFE

veneer-keyed mitre Mitre joint strengthened with pieces of veneer glued into saw kerfs made across the joint. Also called a slipfeather (*q.v.*).

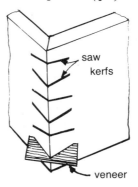

VENEER-KEYED MITRE

veneer matching (see under *matched*).

veneer pin Small gauge wire nail with a small head used to hold veneers temporarily, to hold inlays in position, and for small work generally. Corresponds to 'brad' (USA).

veneer press Various types are made: hand press, in one type of which a large metal screw forces down a caul plate, or a form of bench or table with several cross-bearers which press down over a caul, hinged screws with wing nuts engaging with slots at the ends of the bearers (see *hand press*); or multi-plate hydraulic presses in which there are plates between which the panels are placed. Such presses are invariably thermostatically controlled so that the press can be released quickly for a fresh batch of work (see *hydraulic press*); vacuum presses *(q.v.);* and air pneumatic presses which work by direct pressure rather than by exhausting atmospheric pressure.

veneer punch   (see *veneer punch*).

veneer saw   Saw with curved edge so that it does not dig in, and with flush handle screwed to one side. It is used to cut sawcut veneer. It is sometimes used on the mitre shooting block to cut short return lengths of moulding. The flush handle enables it to lie flat on the block, and there is no danger of scoring the latter since the teeth have no set.

Venetian red   Powder, mainly ferric oxide, used for colouring plaster filling and for colouring generally.

venice turpentine   (see *turpentine, Venice*).

verge board   Alternative name for a barge board *(q.v.)*.

vernis Martin   This was a varnish invented by the brothers Martin to be used either in conjunction with, or as a substitute for, Oriental lacquer. There were four brothers and two of them, Guillaume and Etienne, were granted a monopoly for its manufacture by their patroness, Madame la Marquise de Pompadour (1721 to 1764). Another brother, Robert, developed a variation of the varnish which produced a monochrome colour dusted with gold. The varnishes were widely used in Britain but none reached the excellence of the originals.

vessels   (see *pores*).

vice, bench   Today this is invariably of metal with jaws ranging from 6 in to 10½ in (153 to 267 mm). All types are fitted with steel slides which keep the jaws parallel, and some have a quick-release lever which withdraws the nut engaging with the screw, enabling the front jaw to be slid in and out to any position. Another type is released by a slight backward turn of the handle, enabling the jaw to be immediately adjusted to position, but gripping when the handle is tightened. In all cases the steel jaws need to be wood-lined to avoid marking the work. For those who prefer a wood vice, a steel bench screw 1 in (25 mm) or 1⅛ in (29 mm) dia. is available. This usually needs a small secondary screw with threaded and rotating block, this being used to hold the jaws parallel.

Vienna chalk   Precipitated chalk, being a white, soft variety of slaked lime containing magnesia. It is used with diluted sulphuric acid in the acid finish of french polishing.

vignette   A Gothic detail comprising a running ornament of fine leaves and tendrils.

vinhatico (*plathymenia reticulata*)   Hardwood from eastern Brazil of 38 lb (609 kg) used in furniture making and boat building. Orange-brown shade, often with darker markings. Tones to reddish-brown. Fairly fine texture and seasons well. Hard to saw but stains and polishes satisfactory.

violet wood   (see *kingwood*).

vitrine   A French display cabinet popular in the eighteenth century. The designs were very ornate and included ormolu mounts; the carcase was usually bombé shaped.

vitriol, oil of   Archaic name for Sulphuric acid.

Vitruvian scroll   A decorative feature consisting of scrolls connected with each other, thereby giving the impression of waves. It was commonly used on early eighteenth century furniture, particularly on friezes and tables rails. The term derives from Vitruvius Pollio who was the author of a treatise on Architecture circa 40 BC, but the origins of the ornament pre-date him.

VITRUVIAN SCROLL

Vix bit   (USA) A self-centering bit used to drill holes for screws. The required depth of hole is achieved by loosening the set screw, inserting the drill bit and re-tightening the set screw.

V joint   Chamfers on the edges of some match boarding. (See *tongued-and-grooved boards*.)

volute   A spiral scroll prominent as a feature of column capitals of the Ionic order. Adapted in carved work.

voyders   Archaic name (Middle Ages) for a tray used to remove soiled cutlery, left-over food etc.

V tool   Alternative name for a parting tool *(q.v.)*. The bruzze *(q.v.)* is also sometimes known as a V tool.

wadding Used in upholstery, particularly over hair stuffing, as otherwise the hair is liable to work through the cover. Sold in sheets or packets. Also used in making the rubber for french polishing. (See *cotton wool.*)

wagon castor (see *castor under (F), trolley table*).

wagon chamfering Removal of the edge of a square member, usually at 45 deg., often with decorative stops (see *chamfer*). So-called because it was common practice in wood wagons and carts, partly for its decorative effect, but chiefly to reduce weight without loss of strength.

wainscot Loosely applied to panelling up to dado height, but refers specifically to oak panelling. In Middle Ages it referred to oak imported from the Baltic.

wainscot chair A design of chair which followed on from the 'joyned chair' in the sixteenth century. It was, however, lighter in appearance and the back was often inlaid with patterns of floral sprays, small birds, or plain chequer board (diapered). There was an ornamental crest rail surmounting the back and overhanging it at each side.

wainscot cupboard Alternative name for a press cupboard *(q.v.).*

wainscot oak Oak which is quarter-cut to reveal the figuring of the medullary rays. (See also *quartering.*)

wainscot plank Central plank from a log from which wainscot billets have been sawn. Being radial to the log it is richly figured, and not liable to twist.

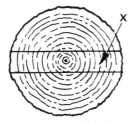

WAINSCOT PLANK

waist Centre part of a longcase (grandfather) clockcase below the hood and above the plinth or base.

walings Horizontal timbers used in the timbering of excavations.

walking line Term used by joiners denoting a line 18 in (457 mm) distant from the centre of the handrail. Used particularly in connection with the winders of a staircase.

wall board Manufactured boards of large dimensions. Made of various substances according to their purposes. They include wood fibre, wood pulp, plaster, and synthetic fire-retardant materials. They are in various grades, and may be heat- or sound-insulating, fire-resistant, damp-repellent, or purely to provide a suitable surface for decorations.

wall chisel Used by carpenters to cut recesses in brickwork, etc. to receive wood plugs.

wall clocks Pendulum-controlled and weight-driven clocks which had the movement (clockwork) contained in a hood so that they resembled the upper parts of longcase clocks; however, the dials were much smaller, averaging 5 to 9 inches diameter (127 to 229 mm). The pendulum, weight-chains, and weights were exposed, and the clock itself either stood on a bracket or was fixed to the wall by means of a spike in the back.

wall furniture Any item of furniture intended to stand against a wall rather than in the middle of the room.

wall plate Timber fixed on the top of a wall to receive and give a fixing to the notched rafters forming the roof. Additionally it serves to distribute the load over the wall.

wall string (see *strings*).

wall table A drop-flap hinged to a bearer on wall and supported by brackets.

walnut bean Alternative name sometimes given to Queensland walnut *(q.v.).*

walnut, Circassian (or Caucasian) Timber producing most attractive veneers, especially from the butts, and often rendering fine curls and burrs. Sometimes known as Black Sea walnut.

walnut crystals (see *Vandyke crystals*).

walnut, European *(juglans regia)* Cabinet hardwood of 40-46 lb (641-737 kg) used for furniture making, panelling, veneers, gun stocks, etc. Fine quality timber, seasons and polishes well, strong and tough yet elastic. When cut at the junction of a branch fine curls *(q.v.)* are produced which are valued for veneers; and the same applies to burrs *(q.v.)*.

American black walnut (juglans nigra) is a hardwood of 37-38 lb (593-609 kg) an excellent timber widely used in cabinetmaking. It is of a rich purple-brown colour, not of the same fine figuring of the European variety, but sound and reliable.

African walnut (lavoa klaineana). Not a true walnut, but a similar colour to the European and American walnuts. Its weight is 31 lb (497 kg) and it has been used widely for furniture making.

Walnut, Japanese (juglans sieboldiana). Straight-grained timber used locally for furniture. Lighter in colour than European walnut.

walnut oil   Ideal as a finish for wooden salad bowls or any other wooden artefact used for eating. The oil is best applied very hot as it dries much quicker and several applications will be needed.

walnut, satin   (see *satin walnut*).

wandering heart   Log in which the heart or pith takes a crooked path so that when converted the saw cuts across it in places. The resulting timber has short grain and is lacking in strength, apart from being difficult to work.

wandoo *(Eucalyptus redunca)*   Timber from Western Australia of 70 lb (1121 kg) used for sleepers, wharf, and bridge work. Hard and heavy, reddish brown in colour.

wandoo *(eucalyptus redunca)*   Timber from Western Australia of 70 lb (1121 kg) used for sleepers, wharf, and bridge work. Hard and heavy, reddish brown in colour.

warding file   A thin file used mainly in key-cutting. Usual length minus the tang is 3-6 in (76-152 mm).

wardrobe   Made in all sizes and styles, and, as some are constructed in two or more carcases, there can be no standard dimensions. A height of 6 ft (1828 mm) is generally regarded as usual. The front-to-back inside carcase depth should not be less than 19 in (482 mm) to allow comfortable inside clearance for coat hangers. A long mirror is usually fitted to the inner face of the door. Lighter wardrobes are often made as narrow as 3 ft (914 mm) or even 2 ft 6 in (762 mm) and the so-termed tall-boy wardrobe is kept down to about 5 ft (1524 mm) in height.

wardrobes, development of   Wardrobes evolved from the cupboards and presses of the sixteenth and seventeenth centuries. André Boulle (1642 to 1732) made several for the French court, when they were called 'armoires' and consisted of a straight upright cupboard enclosed by two doors and with one or two interior shelves. The term 'wardrobe' was not used until the late 18th century.

wardrobe hooks   These may be of brass, copper-bronze, or chromium-plated. (A) is a single type. It is screwed to the back or sides. Double types are available. (B) is a hook for sliding on a horizontal brass rod. (C) is revolving hook to be screwed beneath a shelf.

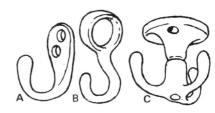

WARDROBE HOOKS

wardrobe lock   Many patterns are available, but all have self-latching spring bolt actuated by either a handle or push button, and also a locking device operated by a key.

wardrobe rail   A hanging rail fixed from side to side of a wardrobe, usually consisting of a 1 in (25 mm) dia chromium plated steel, or brass, tube. An alternative design is fixed from front to back and extends forward.

wardrobe stay   (see *stays*).

warping   The twisting or casting of wood so that its surface is no longer in a plane surface. It is frequently

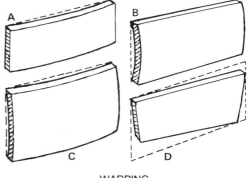

WARPING

caused by faulty seasoning, though some timbers are much worse in this connection than others. Damp conditions may also cause it, or it may be the result of the wood being veneered on one side only. The illustration shows the chief ways in which wood warps.

Warrington hammer   (see *hammers*).

wash coat   A thin sealing of protective film of any finishing material.

washiba *(tecoma)*   Hardwood from tropical South America of 56-60lb (897-961kg). Used for fishing rods, bows, etc. Good bending properties, and somewhat like greenheart in appearance.

washing stand   These began to appear in the middle of the eighteenth century. Generally, there were two main types; one which was a three- or four-legged stand with a circular hole cut in the top to hold the basin, and a central shelf or drawer under which there was provision for the water-jug; the other was a more solid design consisting of a cabinet with a compartment at the top to hold the basin, and drawers for toilet articles. Sheraton, who delighted in mechanical novelties, designed several which had built-in water cisterns and basins for the waste. Until comparatively recent times soap was made in the shape of a ball and some washing stands have metal globes for holding soap balls.

Washita oilstone   A natural oilstone quarried in America, cutting at a medium rate and giving a fine edge. There is some element of luck in its choice as some stones are liable to become hard and fail to cut properly. Made in various sizes, the 8in by 2in by 1in (203 by 51 by 25mm) being a popular one for woodwork. A variety of slips is available. (See *oilstones*.)

waste   The oddments of timber cut away in forming joints, etc. Also the unusable stuff cut away from the log in conversion.

water coating   Used at one time on the back of unimportant furniture. Consisted of powder colour mixed with water with size added as a binder. It was painted over the work as a sort of distemper, and, being opaque, hid all blemishes.

water, distilled   Sometimes used in the acid finish of French polishing. The acid is added drop by drop to the distilled water. (See *acid finish.*)

water gilding   The laying of gold leaf on a wood item, the surface of which has been given several coats of gesso *(q.v.)* followed by Armenian bole. The gold leaf is applied over this, the surface to be covered being moistened with water or thin size. Finally the work is burnished with an agate burnisher. (See also *gilding* and *oil gilding..*)

water leaf   An ornamental detail resembling an elongated laurel leaf often used in Hepplewhite and Sheraton work.

Waterloo leg   (see *sabre leg*).

watermarks   These are sometimes found on a French polished surface. They can often be removed by rubbing with a hot rag several times, or with equal quantities of linseed oil and turps. Alternatively camphorated oil followed by vinegar may be effective. may be effective.

water-resistant glue   Today the resin glues are invariably used. There are several proprietary makes. Some are completely waterproof, but most are highly water-resistant, and can be used successfully for outdoor work particularly if protected with paint. (See *PF, RF,* and *UF adhesives.*)

water seasoning   An old-fashioned method of partially seasoning timber by leaving it in running water for several months so that the sap is washed out. The timber is then air-dried in the usual way.

water stain   (see *staining*).

water varnish   Gum arabic or isinglass dissolved in water, used sometimes to protect paper.

water-white   A term used to describe any liquid which is transparent, like water.

wave moulding   One of undulating surface (A) formed by movement towards and away from the machine cutter produced by an eccentric. Also a Gothic moulding of serpentine section (B).

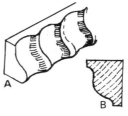

WAVE MOULDING

waves Undulations of a surface caused in planing or by casting. They become obvious if the hand is passed lightly over the surface. On the groundwork for veneering they are got rid of by using a toothing plane in all directions.

wavy grain Undulating grain resulting in light and dark streaks across the grain owing to the saw cutting straight through the undulations. (See *fiddle-back figure.*)

wax (see *beeswax* and *carnauba wax*).

wax inlaying Wax of the required colour and rosin are melted in a tin and flowed into the prepared grooves cut in the surface of the wood. When set the wax is levelled with the surface of the wood with a chisel followed by rubbing with coarse, medium, and fine glasspaper. If some of the colour becomes rubbed into the grain a steel scraper will clear most of it away. For some designs the grooves should be cut with veiner.

wax polish One of the simplest of all polishes to apply. It is usually associated with oak. It gives a fine eggshell gloss and can be renewed at any time. A drawback is that it does not keep out dirt well, and for this reason the work is usually bodied up or cellulosed first. If the work is oil stained it should be given two coats of French polish first to fix it, otherwise the turps in the wax polish may lift it in patches. Wax polish is made from beeswax in turps or a combination of waxes in a petroleum spirit base. The latter will absorb the shredded wax, but the process can be hastened by heating the container over a vessel of hot water (do not use a naked flame). Sometimes a little carnauba wax is added to harden the polish, or a little powdered resin for the same purpose. It is applied with a brush of the boot-brush type, and left until the turps has evaporated (no shine can be built up until this has happened). Another brush is used for polishing, and finally a rag free from fluff.

For the general run of polish raw beeswax is used; bleached wax for light woods; and raw wax and turps to which lamp black is added for antique wax. This leaves a dark deposit in the open grain and other recessed parts. White wax for the liming process is made with bleached wax in turps with powdered zinc white added whilst molten. The consistency of wax polish when applied should be about that of semi-melted butter. Many proprietary waxes have various additives to speed up the process and avoid water marking.

wax, staining (see *staining*).

weather-and-boil-proof plywood Classed as WBP, these boards are bonded with phenol-formaldehyde (PF) adhesive and are intended for use in the most adverse conditions.

weather boards Used for outdoor wood structures. Fixed horizontally so that water is thrown off. Types shown are: (A) plain, (B) rebated, (C) ship lap, (D) log siding, (E) moulded.

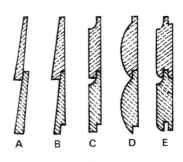

WEATHERBOARDS

weather check (see *throating*).

weathered oak Oak treated with chemicals to turn it a grey shade. Generally, however, it lasts only a few years and the wood gradually reverts to its natural colour. Alternatively, a grey-blue shade is obtained by the use of green copperas (see *copperas*).

weathering Sloping a surface from the horizontal to enable water to drain away outwards.

weather moulding Canted stip of wood fixed to the bottom of an exterior door to keep out driving rain and wind. It is tongued into the door and is throated at the underside.

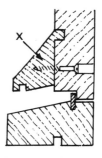

WEATHER MOULDING

web foot (see *drake foot*).

webbing Used on chairs, settees, divan beds, etc., as a basis for springing or stuffing. Best grade is a black and white twill weave of pure flax. Cheaper grade of black and white web are made from a mixture of jute and cotton or hemp, sometimes with linen threads in the selvedges. Generally 2 in (51 mm) wide, but may be 2⅛ in (53 mm) or 2¼ in (55 mm) wide in some qualities. All black and white webs are known as English. Brown or striped brown webbings are jute and are cheaper. They may vary from 1½ in (38 mm) to 3 in (76 mm). (See also *rubber webbing*.)

webbing strainer (see *strainer, web*).

wedge, handle Metal 3-pronged wedge made specially for driving into the end of a hammer, axe, or other tool shaft to spread the wood and give a dovetail hold. The centre prong is bevelled on the opposite side to the other two so that they tend to bend in opposite directions and grip securely.

wedging Applied to tenon joints, either to give a dovetail grip, or to lock the parts together. The through tenon of the carpenter is usually wedged at the outside (A), the wedges being glued to the tenon only, whereas the cabinet maker generally makes a saw cut near the edges of the tenon and drives the wedges into the kerfs so spreading the tenon (B). Sometimes, especially for garden furniture, a member is through-tenoned (C), the tenon projecting at the outer side. A hole with sloping side is cut in this tenon to receive a wedge. Note that the inner side of the hole in the tenon must be recessed slightly into the upright so that the wedge bears against the latter. Another

form of wedged tenon is that at (D) the wedge forcing the dovetail shape upwards. (See also *folding wedges* and *fox wedging*.)

wedge, splitting Used in riving timber, notably oak. It is of steel and is driven into the log in line with the medullary rays. Often a wood wedge is used after the preliminary insertion. The advantage of this is that it follows the natural line of cleavage, whereas a steel wedge would tend to cut through the grain.

Wedgwood plaques Sometimes used in Adam furniture for decorative purposes.

weep hole Hole bored in wood, either vertical or sloping, to enable water, particularly condensation, to drain away.

weight of wood (see *timber, densities and weights of*).

well The central space between the outer strings of an open newel *(q.v.)* or geometrical staircase *(q.v.)*.

Welsh dresser Term used in the trade to describe a type rather than to denote place of origin. Many had a shallow upper portion, often with side cupboards. Oak was generally used, though later specimens often had walnut or mahogany (generally in veneer form) used side by side with the oak. Lower carcase was invariably fitted with drawers. (See individual designs.)

Welsh slate oilstone Sometimes used for sharpening tools as it gives a really fine edge. The quality varies widely, however.

Western red cedar *(thuja plicata)* Softwood from British Columbia of 22 lb (352 kg). Used in general building work. Often used for shingles. Resistant to severe weather conditions.

wet-and-dry paper Silicon carbide waterproof abrasive paper. Commonly used for fine flatting-down between coats of finish (for instance, lacquers, but not French polish). Can be bought in grits up to 1400, which is the finest.

wet-cemented Method of assembling the cheaper grades of plywood in which the veneers are not dried before pressing. Such plywood is used for packing cases and similar work only.

wet cooperage Barrels and casks intended to hold liquids as distinct from dry cooperage which is used for dry goods.

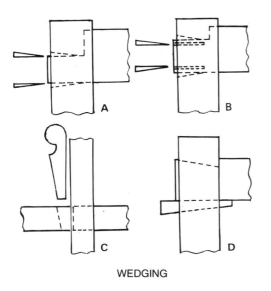

WEDGING

wet grinding   Grinding of tools on a stone kept wet with water. The latter keeps the steel cool and acts as a lubricant; the method is preferable to using a powered grinder. (See *grindstone*.)

wet rot   Timber decay due to exposure to severe weather conditions, resulting in timber remaining permanently wet, or being alternately wet and dry. (See also *dry rot*.)

Weymouth pine   (see *yellow pine*).

what-not   Small piece of furniture consisting of a series of shelves, usually three, supported by turned or shaped uprights. A popular item in the Victorian period intended to hold oddments — books, ornaments, tea cups, etc.

wheat ears   A decorative feature used by Hepplewhite. It was also widely used in the USA by McIntire and by Phyfe.

wheatsheaf back   Chair back with pierced central slat which roughly resembles a sheaf of wheat in shape. There were many variations. Used from about 1760 and onwards.

wheel back chair   Windsor chair with a splat having pierced detail in it in the form of a wheel with spokes. The term is also applied to some late eighteenth century chairs in which the entire back takes the general form of a wheel with radiating spokes, though in fact the overall shape is generally oval rather than round.

wheel burnisher   (USA) A hand-held device for applying the burr on a cabinet scraper. It is a block of wood about 6 in (152 mm) long which is rebated along one side. This rebate is lined with a metal milled guide and this, in combination with a hardened steel wheel which is let into the wood at right angles to the guide, applies the burr.

wheel dresser   Used to dress a glazed grinding wheel. It is fitted with plain discs alternating with pointed wheels, all free to revolve. It is held on the rest of the machine, and, when offered to the grinding wheel, the pointed wheels pick out the glaze, metal particles, and dulled grit.

wheele bed   (see *truckle bed*).

whet-stone   (see *oilstone*).

whipping   The tendency of a long, thin rod or spindle to rotate unevenly when being turned on a lathe; there are special 'steadies' to prevent this occurring although an expert wood turner can control it by hand.

whips   Marks or ridges in French polishing due to the use of too wet a rubber. The marks follow the path of the rubber, and need to be flattened out by further working before they harden. Failing this a grinder *(q.v.)* will have to be used.

whiskers   Fibres left attached to the underside of wood when being cross-cut on the circular saw or bandsaw. On the circular saw they can be minimised by giving the saw the minimum projection above the top of the wood. Keeping the saw sharp also helps to avoid them.

white Bombay   *(Terminalia procera)*   Timber from the Andaman Islands of 40 lb (641 kg). Used for furniture and indoor fitments. Light in colour when newly felled, but turning to a light brown on exposure. Straight-grained and rather coarse. Sometimes known as badam.

white-chuglam   (see *silver greywood*).

white flock   Also known as cotton linters *(q.v.)*, a waste product from cotton.

Whitehill cutter block   A steel disc with a central hole for fixing to a spindle moulder *(q.v.)*; cutters may be bolted or otherwise fixed into slots located in the periphery. Whitehill is the name of the manufacturer; they are made by several manufacturers and therefore bear different names, but the working principle is the same, the difference being in the method of fastening the cutter heads.

WHITEHILL CUTTER BLOCK

white mineral oil   Light liquid paraffin, sometimes used to lubricate the rubber when French polishing.

white olivier   (see *nargusta*).

white pine   (see *yellow pine*).

white polish   A French polish made by dissolving 6 oz (17 grams) of bleached shellac in 1 pint (0.56 litre) of methylated spirit. White wax polish may be prepared by from bleached wax dissolved in American pure turps. Alternatively paraffin wax can be used. To leave a white deposit in the grain as when liming, add zinc white powder to white wax polish until the whole becomes white.

white shellac   Used to make white French polish (see *white polish*). It is in stick or cake form and should be stored in damp sawdust or under water as it quickly becomes denatured if exposed to the air and in that state cannot be dissolved. It is dried before being added to methylated spirit.

white spirit   Turpentine substitute. Corresponds to US 'mineral spirits' *(q.v.)*.

white spruce   *(picea glauca)*   Softwood from Canada, USA, and Europe of 28 lb (449 kg). Used for floor boards, building work, and packing cases.

white wax polish   (see under *wax polish*).

whitewood, American canary *(liriodendron tulipifera)*   Hardwood from USA and Canada of 28-29 lb (449-465 kg) and of canary colour varying from light to deep shade. The latter is the best. Used for interior work, veneer groundwork, piano parts, etc.

whiting   A white powder (calcium carbonate) used to make geso for the gilding process. Sometimes added to French polish to make stopping in French polished work. For the latter it is essential to paint the depression with polish first.

whittle   To carve or fashion with a knife.

whorl foot   Scrolled foot, usually known as the French scrolled foot (see *scroll, B*).

wicker chairs   These are of great antiquity and 'beehive' designs of such chairs were exported from Britain to Rome during the Roman Occupation. Cheap chairs made of osiers and twigs were produced in the sixteenth and seventeenth centuries; one design which incorporated the hood and sides associated with the beehive chair *(q.v.)* was then called a 'Child-bed' chair as it was used in confinements.

wicket   Small door contained within a large one, or the lower half of a stable door.

Wigan chair   A ladder-back chair with a solid seat, and a crest rail surmounting the ladder-back and overhanging the back feet at each side. Many thousands were produced for use in Non-Comformist chapels.

willow *(salix alba* or *salix viridis)* or black willow *(Salix nigra)*   From Europe, except black willow from USA 24 lb (384 kg). Used chiefly for cricket bats.

winder   Step of tapered shape used in a staircase at a change of direction. (See *geometrical stairs*.)

winding   Term applied to a framework, carcase or other structure which is twisted, that is, surfaces which should be in the same plane are out of alignment. It also refers to boards which have become twisted. A carcase or board which is true is often referred to as 'free of wind'. Pronounce to rhyme with 'kind'.

winding strips   (see *parallel strips*).

wind shake   A cup *(q.v.)* or ring shake.

Windsor chairs   All kinds of Windsor chairs have two distinguishing characteristics, namely a solid (unupholstered) seat, and a back framing which is entirely separate from, but jointed to, the legs and underframing. There are many different patterns and they are included under their individual names.

wine cisterns   Although most of these were made of brass or marble, some were made of wood. They were bowl-shaped, either oval or circular, and contained ice or water in which bottles of wine, and the wine glasses, were kept cool. They were, of course, lined with lead.

wine cooler   Usually made of mahogany with coopered sides and lead lining.

wine waiter   These resembled a stool on the top of which was a tray with partitions for wine bottles; castors were fitted to the feet so that it could be pushed around the dining room.

wing chair   An upholstered chair which originated in the late seventeenth century. The back, which was high, had projecting return side pieces to protect the user from draughts.

wing furniture   Large item, such as bookcase or wardrobe with deep centre portion and shallower flanking or wing portions. (See *break front*.)

wire cramp   Length of strong wire with four metal corner pieces, one of which is fitted with a screw which enables the whole to be tightened, so drawing the corner joints together. Used for such work as large mitred frames, and for repair work on such items as chairs which can only be partly dismembered.

wire edge   (see *burr*).

wire nails   General term applied to nails which are of circular section and made from wire, but more particularly referring to French nails *(q.v.)*.

wobble saw   (see *drunken saw*).

wood bed lathe   Preferred by many turners as it makes a springy bed. Two pieces of B.C. pine are generally used with spacing pieces between.

wood alcohol   (USA) Alcohol which is obtained from the destructive distillation of wood. Also called 'methanol' or 'methyl alcohol'.

wood blocks   Used for flooring, as a rule over concrete. A dovetail shape is worked at the edges and the whole set in hot mastic.

wood boring insects   Three of the most destructive timber boring pests are: death-watch beetle, furniture beetle, and powder post beetle. (See under individual entries.) Frequently they are referred to as 'worm'. The storing of old furniture is a fruitful cause of the invasion of boring insects, and when firmly established the pest is difficult to evict. There are several proprietary insecticides.

wood craft   Knowledge of forestry and woodland life.

wood cramp   Originally widely used in general woodwork, but now almost obsolete, being replaced by the metal sash cramp. Usually made of beech with hornbeam screw. The end of the screw has a centre projecting point which bites into the wood and prevents it from shifting when pressure is applied. A softening block made from waste is necessary to prevent damage to the work.

wood cut   An engraving cut in wood for printing. At a period when printing blocks, etc., were largely wood cuts the blocks were usually the end grain of boxwood.

wood filler   (see *filler*).

wood flour   Finely powdered wood waste used in the manufacture of some wall boards, and in making some forms of stopping.

wood screws   (see *screws*).

wood-turning tools   (see *turning chisels and turning gouges*).

wood-ware   Wooden utensils for domestic purpose such as kitchen and dairy items, pastry boards, wash boards, pails, bread platters, ladles, spoons, etc. In former days there was a far greater demand and variety.

wood wool   Long, narrow shavings used for packing, and for insulating roof panels. Made by machine. Cotton wood and bass are frequently used but almost any cheap wood which is straight-grained, odourless, and free from resin can be used. Sometimes used as a filling in upholstery. It can be stitched to a good edge but makes for hard upholstery.

wool, linsey   (see *linsey wool*).

working drawing   A full-sized representation of an object with elevations, plans, and sections. Complicated parts are shown (usually) full size or to a large scale.

worm holes   (see under *death watch beetle, furniture beetle*, and *powder post beetle*. Also *flight hole*.)

woven board   Form of fencing in which thin slats are interwoven.

wreath   Part of a continuous stair hand rail which is curved in plan.

wreathed string   The curved part of a geometrical staircase string beneath the wreath.

wriggle nails   (see *corrugated joint fasteners*).

writing cabinets   Early form of secretaire used in Italy and Spain in the late sixteenth century. It consisted of a cabinet with a vertical fall-front; the interior was fitted with small drawers and shelves; sometimes the cabinet was mounted on a stand but other designs were intended to stand on a convenient table.

writing chairs   Once literacy had spread among the upper classes, these chairs appeared (circa 1720). The characteristic feature of a writing chair is that the arms should not extend forwards to the full depth of the seat but only partway so that the chair can be drawn close to a table. There were two principal types, namely the spoon-back *(q.v.)* and the corner chair *(q.v.)*.

writing tables These began to appear about the end of the seventeenth century and were often fitted with gate-legs so that they could also be used as card or side tables. During the eighteenth century the massive knee-hole writing tables became popular and were also known as 'library tables'. At the end of the eighteenth and during the early nineteeth centuries, lighter and more delicate designs were made and the ladies' 'cheveret' table, and the 'Carlton House' table (*q.q.v.*) are good examples.

wrought timber Planed timber as distinct from stuff from the saw.

X

X chair Type of chair that became popular in this country during the early seventeenth century. It is of X form, hence the name, and was usually entirely covered with material and with a loose cushion. (See *Glastonbury* and *Savanorola chairs*.)

X stretcher One which connects diagonally the legs of a stand, chair, or other piece of furniture. Often the members are of a serpentine shape. (See *saltire*.)

Y

Yale night latch Cylinder lock (*q.v.*). The plate projection is sunk flush with the edge of the door stile, and this must be allowed for when boring the hole to receive the lock.

Yankee ratchet screwdriver (see *spiral ratchet screwdriver*).

Yarwood guard A guard used on a spindle moulder (*q.v.*).

yellow clay An earth mixed with equal parts of pipe clay and water, and used in the gilding process.

yellow ochre A yellow powder pigment used for colouring wood filler and in water coating.

yellow pine (*pinus strobus*) Also known as white pine, a fine-grade softwood from Canada and north-eastern USA of 26lb (417kg). Difficult to obtain nowadays owing to the heavy inroads made on it and its consequent high cost. Takes a satin-like finish, is easy to work, and is reliable. Often used as a goundwork for veneer, and has many uses in pattern-making. Best grades are often knot-free.

yew (*taxus baccata*) Softwood from British Isles and Europe of 48-50lb (768-801kg). Used for making bows, chairs, and sometimes table tops. It is capable of a fine natural polish, and has both strength and elasticity. Is difficult to obtain in wide boards free from shakes.

Y lever Term given to the metal lever in an adjustable metal plane. It controls the projection of the cutter. So called because its Y form engages with the grooved sides of the screw control.

yoke Pieces of timber bolted together in the form of a rectangle, and used to hold the formwork used in making concrete pillars and other similar items. Their purpose is to prevent the formwork from spreading under the weight of the concrete.

Yoke rail An alternative name for the back stay rail of a chair.

York pitch The angle of 50deg at which some plane cutters are set. The normal pitch of a bench plane is 45deg, and York pitch is used for some smoothing planes which are needed for difficult timbers. The higher pitch gives the plane more of a scraping action which is less liable to tear out the grain. Such planes offer greater resistance in use. (See also *pitch*.)

Yorkshire chair Popular type in the mid-seventeenth century, square in plan with slightly recessed wood seat and arcaded back rails.

Yorkshire dresser Form of dresser with low back, usually in oak or pine.

Z

Zambesi redwood (*baikiaea plurijana*) Hardwood of 57lb (913kg) also known as Rhodesian teak. A dark reddish-brown colour, often with darker streaks. Fine, even texture and stable when dry. It is resistant to wood-rotting fungi.

zebra wood   (see *marble wood*).

Zebrano   A West African timber which is light gold in colour with narrow streaks of brown or black. The texture of the timber is coarse and it often contains resin pockets; it is usually converted into veneer and is particularly favoured for crossbandings.

zig-zag moulding   (see *chevron moulding*).

zig-zag spring   (see *springs, upholstery*).

zinc caul   Used in veneering. It is a sheet of zinc which is heated and cramped down over veneer, with a wood backing. It retains its heat longer than a caul made solely of wood.

zinc slate nails   Cut from solid zinc, not merely coated. Usually $1\frac{1}{4}$ in (32 mm) long, square-tapering, with flat head.

zinc white   A white powder sometimes added to Scotch glue to lighten its colour when used on light woods. Also used in some liming processes, being added to wax to form a white deposit in the open grain of oak.

Zyliss vice   The proprietary name of a special vice which allows wood of any length to be worked as well as performing all the functions of a normal vice. It is portable and can be fixed to any suitable piece of timber.

British and USA Designers and Craftsmen

Adam, Robert (1728 to 1792) Son of William Adam of Kirkcaldy, Fife, who was a well-known architect in the area. Robert Adam made the 'Grand Tour' and returned from Italy in 1758 when he set up an architectural practice in association with his younger brothers James and William and later, two sisters. In 1773 he and his brother James began publishing *Works in Architecture.*

While in Italy, Robert Adam absorbed both ancient Greek and Roman architectural styles and was particularly interested in the Palladian movement *(q.v.).* In his furniture he employed motifs from them all and in his own words explains his aims in designing: 'The massive entablature, the ponderous compartment ceiling, almost the only species of ornament formerly known in this country, are now universally exploded and in their place we have adopted a beautiful variety of light mouldings, gracefully formed, delicately enriched, and arranged with propriety and skill . . . (we) have added grace and beauty to the whole by a mixture of grotesque stucco, and painted ornament.'

Affleck, Thomas (USA) Born in Scotland, he was appointed by John Penn as resident cabinet-maker in Philadelphia, where he died in 1795. He achieved fame for his individual interpretation of Chippendale's designs which became known as 'Philadelphian Chippendale'.

Barnsley, Ernest (1863 to 1926) One of the fore-runners of the Arts & Crafts Movement *(q.v.).* In 1886 he was an architectural student and met Ernest Gimson *(q.v.)* who worked in the same office. In 1887 he set up his own architectural practice in Birmingham but in 1893 he was persuaded to join his brother Sidney *(q.v.)* and Gimson in a furniture-making venture in the Cotswolds. In 1901 he entered a partnership with Gimson to have furniture made to their own designs by skilled cabinet-makers, but in 1905 he left the partnership to return to his architectural practice.

Barnsley, Sidney (1865 to 1926) Younger brother of Ernest Barnsley *(q.v.).* He was a close friend of Ernest Gimson *(q.v.)* and became one of the members of the Arts & Crafts Movement *(q.v.),* and was instrumental in setting up Kenton & Co. *(q.v.).* During 1889 and 1890 he travelled widely in Europe and in 1893 he left London to accompany Gimson and Ernest Barnsley to the Cotswolds. In 1894 he married Lucy Morley and shortly afterwards went to

work on his own at Sapperton, near Cirencester, Gloucestershire. He was one of the few craftsmen who both designed and made his own furniture; he was fond of working in oak and believed in simple, honest designs which displayed their construction as a means of decoration. There is a permanent exhibition of his work at Cheltenham Museum, Gloucestershire.

Chapin, Eliphalet USA (1741 to 1807) He was a member of a well-known family of Connecticut cabinet-makers, but worked for a time in Philadelphia. He was instrumental in adapting Chippendale's designs by incorporating handsome pediments, pierced scrolls, and elegant finials; his pieces were usually made in native cherrywood rather than mahogany.

Chippendale, Thomas, Senior (1718 to 1779) Opinion is divided as to whether he was born in Otley, Yorkshire or London; in any case, his father was a joiner on a country estate.

Little is known of him until 1748 when he married Catherine Redshaw in London; he also opened a workshop at St. Martin's Lane, London, at about the same time. He was first of all in partnership with James Rannie, who died in 1766; he then took Thomas Haig as partner in 1771; Haig had probably been bookkeeper to Rannie and outlived Chippendale to continue the partnership with Chippendale junior *(q.v.)* until 1796.

Chippendale senior's book *The Gentleman and Cabinet-maker's Director* was first published in 1754, with a second edition in 1755 and an enlarged edition in 1762, and although not the first book ever to have dealt with the subject, it was certainly the most comprehensive.

His designs fall into three main categories — Rococo, Gothic and Chinoiserie *(q.q.v.)*. The rococo style derived from the French and was superseded about the middle of the 18th century by the Gothic revival. The craze for Oriental designs (known as 'Chinoiserie') was the result of the opening-up of trade markets in the East and the fashion persisted from the beginning until almost the end of the 18th century. By the early 1760's a classical revival had begun and was fostered by Robert Adam *(q.v.),* for whom Chippendale produced many of his finest pieces.

Chippendale, Thomas, Junior (1749 to 1822) He was the eldest of eleven children and carried on the family business after his father's death in 1779. His partner was Thomas Haig and the firm traded under the style of Haig and Chippendale. Haig retired in 1796 and died in 1803. In 1804 the firm became bankrupt and a large quantity of stock was sold, but Chippendale managed to restore its fortunes.

His designs are characterised by a restrained Regency influence with overtones of the Palladian style which had been popular a few years before; the country house of Stourhead in Wiltshire contains a large number of his pieces. His only publication was a small book in 1779 entitled *Sketches for Ornament.*

Eames, Charles (USA) An architect who was one of the fore-runners in exploiting new modern methods and the anthropometric approach to design. His first design for a chair in moulded plywood and aluminium appeared in 1940, but more significant was his DAR chair (1949) with a moulded glassfibre seat which was the first of its kind in a new medium. He was particularly fond of bent laminated rosewood frames for his chairs, often combined with metal fittings.

Eastlake, Charles Locke An eminent Victorian designer who wrote several books, the most widely read being *Hints on Household Taste* which was published in 1868. He advocated a return to simple methods of construction using joints without glue or any other fastening (apart from pegs), and with a plain oiled or waxed finish. He particularly disliked faked antiques and considered that the ordinary masses of people should be taught to appreciate honestly-made furniture in good taste. His ideas and books were very popular in the USA.

Gibbons, Grinling (1648 to 1721) Born in Rotterdam, he emigrated to England and was found by the diarist, John Evelyn, carving a representation of Tintoretto's *Crucifixion* — a work so magnificent that it is now housed in the Victoria and Albert Museum, London. Some of his best work is at Petworth House, Sussex and he was responsible for much of the carving in Wren's churches when they were rebuilt after the Great Fire of London (1666).

Gibbs, James (1682 to 1754) A successful architect who also designed furniture which was mainly in the Baroque style but without any individual touches. At Blenheim Palace, Oxfordshire, there are a State Bed and two mirrors from his designs. In 1728 he published a *Book of Architecture.*

Gillows, The firm of Established about 1731; about 1815 (after the death of Richard Gillow) there were no further members of the family in the firm although it continued under their name. They produced all kinds of furniture consistent with the prevailing taste and demand but two designs in particular are associated with them. One was their clothes press which was known as a 'Gentleman's Wardrobe' which had sliding trays in the upper cupboard section and a chest of drawers in the lower portion. The other was the 'Davenport' small writing desk, presumably named after a Captain Davenport who first ordered one. It has been suggested that Gillows originated some of the designs which Hepplewhite included in his *Guide*, notably the shield-back chair — some authorities claim that Hepplewhite was at one time apprenticed to Gillows. They were the only English firm to adopt the admirable habit of marking or stamping their products, which is, of course, a boon to furniture antiquarians.

Gimson, Ernest (1864 to 1919) Inspired by William Morris (*q.v.*), Gimson became one of the founder members of the Arts & Crafts Movement (*q.v.*), together with Ernest and Sidney Barnsley. After travelling widely in Europe during 1889/90 he began designing for chairmaking and plasterwork, but soon joined four young architects (William Lethaby, Sidney Barnsley, Mervyn Macartney and Reginald Bloomfield) in setting up a firm called Kenton & Co. to produce good quality furniture.

In 1893 he left London in company with Sidney Barnsley (*q.v.*) and moved to Pinbury Park, Gloucestershire. In 1901 he went into partnership with Ernest Barnsley (*q.v.*) to employ craftsmen to make fine furniture; in 1903 he entered another partnership with Edward Gardiner to produce chairs. His partnership with Barnsley was dissolved in 1905 and Gimson's firm (now at Daneway, near Sapperton, Gloucestershire) flourished until his death — it was then continued by his foreman, Peter Waals.

Goddard, John USA (1723 to 1785) A first-class cabinet-maker from Rhode Island, who was the originator (jointly with his brother-in-law, John Townsend (*q.v.*) of 'block-front' case furniture and also shell-carved coving.

Halfpenny, W. and J. 18th century architects and furniture designers. From 1750 to 1752, William and his son, John, published *New Designs* in parts — these gave designs for the Chinese furniture which was so popular at the time. They also produced another book (1752) entitled *Royal Architecture in the Chinese Taste.*

Hepplewhite, George (date of birth unknown; died in 1786). A cabinet-maker and designer who was probably apprenticed to the firm of Gillows of Lancaster; he appeared in Cripplegate, London, about 1760.

His book, *Cabinet-maker and Upholsterer's Guide* was published by his widow Alice in 1788 — two years after his death; there were two further editions in 1789 and 1794. There are also ten plates in the *Cabinet-Maker's London Book of Prices* (1788) signed either 'Hepplewhite' or 'Heppelwhite' but they cannot be proved to be authentically his designs.

He was not an innovator and his work owes much to the influence of Robert Adam and to contemporary French fashion; although he did not introduce the heart- and shield- shapes for chair backs *(see Gillow)*, he certainly popularised them.

Holland, Henry (1746 to 1806) An architect who was one of the leaders of the Graeco-Roman Revivalist School; he had a preference for rosewood as the principal wood in his pieces, embellished with gilt ormolu mounts. He was in charge of renovating and redecorating Carlton House for the Prince Regent in 1783.

Hope, Thomas (1769 to 1831) He was a wealthy connoisseur and an amateur archaeologist who visited the sites of the ancient civilisations of Egypt, Greece, Syria and Turkey. In 1807 he published *Household Furniture and Interior Decoration;* the designs were characterised by a skilful adaptation of ancient Egyptian and Greek motifs to furniture. In particular, he originated the 'lion monopodium' table which was widely copied; it was a small table with a circular top supported on three legs, each of which terminated in a curious representation of a lion — although Hope called it a 'chimera', which was a mythical beast. In 1805 he built a house at Deepdene, Surrey (it no longer exists) which was decorated and furnished with his designs.

Ince, William and Mayhew, John Partners in a cabinet-making and upholstery business. Between 1759 and 1762 they published the *Universal System of Household Furniture* and dedicated it to the Duke of Marlborough. It appears to have been largely based on Chippendale's *Director* and some designs are obvious copies — especially the chair backs. In general, the designs are in the rococo style, with the addition of some Gothic and Chinese motifs.

Johnson, Thomas A carver and designer who (like Matthias Lock) pioneered the rococo style in England, notably in his book (1755) entitled *Twelve Girandoles.* His designs were very elaborate and fanciful and some of them were virtually incapable of being made up.

Jones, Inigo (1573 to 1652) He was first apprenticed to a joiner in St. Paul's Churchyard, London, and then became a painter and designer of scenery and effects for court entertainment, which led to his being appointed Surveyor of the King's Works to James I in 1615.

He visited Italy twice and studied both Classical and Renaissance architecture, particularly the Palladian style *(q.v.);* he can be regarded as the most successful exponent of the latter and, although he was not strictly a furniture designer, the furniture chosen for his buildings (notably the Banqueting House in London) incorporated Palladian characteristics.

Jones, William (died 1757) In 1759 he published the *Gentlemen's or Builder's Companion,* which comprised twenty designs of side-tables and pier glasses; no text was included other than the captions for the illustrations. The designs were all Georgian in character and were the usual ones being employed by architects of the time.

Kent, William (1686 to 1748) A coach painter who later became a painter; he was sent to Rome to study painting by a consortium of wealthy patrons. In return he brought works of art and sent them back to his patrons. After his return from Italy he came under the patronage of Richard, third Earl of Burlington. During this period he produced most of his work which was strongly influenced by Palladian styles; probably his greatest achievement was the designing, building, and furnishing of Holkham Hall, Norfolk.

Langley, Batty (1696 to 1751) He was an architect and designer who published (1740) the *City and Country Builder's and Workman's Treasury of Designs* in collaboration with his younger brother, John, who was a draughtsman and engraver. The 25 designs in the book are obviously based on French designs by Jean Berain (senior), Andre-Charles Boulle and Daniel Marot.

Linnell, John (died 1796) A contemporary of Thomas Chippendale senior *(q.v.);* in fact, some furniture attributed to Chippendale has been found to have been produced by Linnell. His designs range from the Rococo, through Chinoiserie, to Neo-classical styles similar to those of Adam *(q.v.).*

Lock, Matthias (Working 1740 to 1769) A carver and designer who was a pioneer of the Rococo style, and later an exponent of the Chinese fashion. In 1740 he published a *New Drawing Book of Ornaments, Shields, Compartments, Masks, etc.* which contained rococo designs, and in 1752 his *New Book of Ornaments* was the first book of Chinoiserie designs to be published.

Mackintosh, Charles Rennie (1868 to 1928) A

leader of the Glasgow School of Design, he appeared to regard furniture as an adjunct to the general decor of a house and that it should therefore conform visually. Some of his designs (particularly chairs) are undeniably elegant but certainly not comfortable. Much of his work is similar to the Continental Art Nouveau *(q.v.)*. He was fond of painting his pieces in soft colours and, indeed, a tightly-furled rose painted in a conventionalised style was his hallmark. Additional motifs were inset panels of stained glass, enamel, or mother-of-pearl.

Macmurdo, Arthur Heygate (1851 to 1942) A leading member of the Century Guild, which was founded in 1882 to promote the brotherhood of craftsmen. He believed that the designer should be inspired by natural forms and that even the most familiar household articles should be ornamental as well as functional. His ideas were consonant with those emerging on the Continent at that time, and his work often shows signs of the ensuing style of Art Nouveau *(q.v.)*.

Marot, Daniel (1663 to 1752) Although born in Paris, he sought refuge from religious persecution and fled to Holland where he undertook commissions for William, Prince of Orange. When William became King of England in 1689, Marot came to England and worked here from 1694 to 1698. His designs can best be described as an elaborate form of Baroque, and a State Bed at Dyrham Park, Gloucestershire, is typical of his style.

Morris, William (1834 to 1896) Morris's aim was to return to a craft-based society as a reaction against the vulgarisation of design by mass-production and the use of machinery, which was already making its presence felt. In 1861 he formed a company called Morris, Marshall, Faulkner and Co (which became Morris & Co in 1865), the object being to design, make and sell good quality furniture, stained glass, embroidery, glass, metal work, wall paper, fabrics, tapestries and similar artifacts.

The style envisaged was a kind of neo-medievalism and one characteristic of their furniture was the inclusion of painted scenic panels. Unfortunately it proved impossible to sell their products at prices which the general public could afford; nevertheless the firm continued to exist until 1939.

Many artists, architects and designers were associated with the firm and among them were: Philip Webb, Charles Lock Eastlake, Ford Madox Brown, J. P. Seddon and also Burne-Jones and Rossetti who supplied painted decoration.

Nicholson, Peter, and Michaelangelo Peter

(1765 to 1844) was the father of Michaelangelo (who died in 1842). Peter was apprenticed to a cabinet-maker and worked in Edinburgh until moving to London in 1788; later he moved to Glasgow where he practised as an architect. His son, Michaelangelo, was an expert draughtsman and illustrated their book, the *Practical Cabinet-maker, Upholsterer, and Complete Decorator* published in 1826/7, with subsequent editions in 1835 and 1843. Their designs were largely based on Regency styles *(q.v.)* with added motifs and ornament taken from classical sources; they also included a few Gothick designs. It could be said that their designs were the last to have pretensions to elegance before the advent of Victorianism at its worst.

Pabst, Daniel USA (1827 to 1910) A German-born craftsman who worked in Philadelphia; his first pieces were in the rococo and Renaissance styles with massive and elaborate carving. About 1876 he adopted a much more severe and rectilinear approach and applied this to pieces based on the Gothic revival in England.

Palladio, Andrea (1508 to 1580) An Italian architect who lived and worked in Vincenza; he was well-known for his designs of country villas and residences.

He was a great admirer of Vitruvius *(q.v.)* and in 1570 he published *I Quattro Libri dell Architettra* (The Four books of Architecture) and these had a significant effect on the designs of English architecture and furniture, notably through the work of Inigo Jones *(q.v.)*.

Phyfe, Duncan USA (1768 to 1854) Scottish by birth, he emigrated to Albany, NY and in 1790 moved to New York City. His furniture was distinctive for its gracefulness and elegance; he used Sheraton and French Empire styles as his inspiration and was especially fond of the 'lyre' motif. He also employed a great deal of carving as well as reeding, veneering, and inlay (often with brass); his elaborate mirrors were also popular as they were produced with matching pier tables. He retired in 1847.

Shearer, Thomas Little is known of him except that he was the principal contributor to the *Cabinet-makers London Book of Prices*, published in 1788; Hepplewhite *(q.v.)* may have been another contributor. No other records of Shearer's work exist, although there is a charming break-front bookcase at Dyrham Park, Gloucestershire, which may be his.

Sheraton, Thomas (1751 to 1806) He was born in Stockton-on-Tees, and was the son of a cabinet-maker. He arrived in London about 1790 and published his first edition of the *Cabinet-maker and Upholsterer's Drawing Book* in 1791 with subsequent editions in 1793, 1794 and 1802. He also published a *Cabinet Dictionary* in 1803, and was working on a *Cabinet-maker, Upholsterer and General Artists' Encyclopaedia* at the time of his death.

No proof exists that he ever made up any of his own designs; in general he adopted features of style and decorative motifs from his predecessors and contemporaries and blended them into a light and elegant style which, in its later manifestations, was strongly influenced by classical Greek and French motifs, including animal figures, heads and feet as decoration. His chair designs, in particular, display a lightness and delicacy which had been sadly lacking up to that time.

He had a liking for mechanical contrivances; the best-known example was probably his 'Harlequin' Pembroke table, but he also invented a cot which was rocked automatically by a clock spring!

Smith, George   A practising cabinet-maker, he published *A Collection of Designs for Household Furniture and Decoration* in 1808; he drew upon the designs of Thomas Hope *(q.v.)* with additional motifs from the Egyptian, Gothic and Chinese styles. His second book (1826) was *The Cabinet-maker and Upholsterer's Guide* which contained designs that were completely different from those in his first book and presaged the type of furniture which was so abhorrent to William Morris and his companions. They included lumpy and bulbous sofas, heavy and ugly sideboards, and spindly chairs — altogether an uninspired and ill conceived mixture.

Talbert, Bruce   Published two books, namely *Gothic Forms applied to Furniture* and *Examples of Ancient and Modern Furniture, Tapestries and Decoration* in 1867 and 1872 respectively. He was

fond of employing ornamental ironwork in his furniture combined with Medieval and Gothic motifs. His pieces were frequently massive, heavy and oversize.

Townsend, John   USA (born 1733) A member of a family of renowned cabinet-makers, he lived at Norwich but later moved to Middletown, Connecticut. He was the co-originator, with his brother-in-law John Goddard *(q.v.),* of 'block-front' case furniture.

Voysey, C. F. A.   (1857 to 1941) A founder member of the Art Workers Guild, and an architect. His furniture was mainly in oak and structurally simple although tending to be massive. He favoured heavy ornamental hinges and overlays in metal. His designs were very popular in the USA.

Webb, Philip   A Victorian designer who was co-founder of the firm of Morris, Marshall, Faulkner & Co *(see under Morris, William)*. He designed much of the furniture first made by the firm and was responsible for the Chaucer Cabinet (painted by Burne-Jones) which was a wedding present for William Morris. He also designed the well-known 'Morris' chair which was rush-seated elbow chair, usually in birch stained black, and with most parts turned — large quantities were produced after 1865. The design was based on one observed by Morris on a trip through Sussex. Another characteristic of his was his liking for a green stain, which he used on many of his oak tables.

Wyatt, James   (1748 to 1813) A celebrated architect who spent six years in Italy and returned to England in 1768. He was a follower of the Gothick (or mock-medieval) style, and one of his greatest projects was to design cabinets to house some of the gems of Catherine the Great.

British and USA Furniture Styles

Amish Furniture (USA) A religious sect (the Mennonites) who came from Germany and settled in Philadelphia and northern Ohio. Their furniture is reminiscent of their German peasant origins, and is characterised by simple turnery (particularly the bulbous 'turnip foot') and was often painted with natural motifs such as birds, flowers and fruit. The best-known craftsman was Henry Lapp (1862 to 1904) who was an itinerant cabinet-maker and designer in Philadelphia.

Arts and Crafts Movement Founded in 1888 by T. J. Cobden-Sanderson, a master-bookbinder, who suggested the formation of an Arts and Crafts Exhibition Society. The term then became synonymous with a philosophy which aimed to produce furniture and other domestic artifacts of simple and honest design with the emphasis on sound construction and fitness for purpose. Characteristics of the furniture were the use of native woods, particularly oak which was often left plain; rush seating for chairs; and ornament which was usually confined to large metal hinges and plaques, such as those used by C. F. A. Voysey *(q.v.)* on his designs.

The Movement was associated with several other groups including The Century Guild founded by A. H. Mackmurdo *(q.v.)* in 1882; C. R. Ashbee's Guild and School of Handicraft (1888); and the Cotswold School of Ernest Gimson and the Barnsley brothers *(q.q.v.)*.

The philosophy also spread to the USA and several communities came into being, including the Rycroft Community begun by Elbert Hubbard at East Aurora in 1895; the Rose Valley Community founded by architect William L. Price in 1901; the Byrdcliffe Colony at Woodstock; and the Elverhoj Community in Washington. Another notable figure was Gustav Stickley who had workshops at Syracuse, NY. Other American designers influenced were Frank Lloyd Wright, Charles Sumner Greene, and Arthur F. Mathews and his wife.

Art Deco (1930's) This style, which began with the Paris International Exhibition of 1925 and lasted until the outbreak of war in 1939, is better described by the term 'Jazz Moderne'. Paradoxically it has come to be applied to anything crudely or vulgarly modern, despite the fact that the Exhibition was quite traditional in its outlook. In its best manifestations, the style is characterised by the use of rare and exotic veneers and woods combined with lacquer, leather, and mounts of precious metals, and by the inclusion of Egyptian, South American, and African motifs. Unfortunately it was debased by mass-production manufacturers who produced ill-conceived and bastardised versions of the real thing.

Some of the designers associated with the style are: Charpentier, Deskey, Follot, Eileen Gray, and Ruhlmann.

Art Nouveau (From about 1889 to 1925) The name derives from a shop opened by Siegfried Bing in Paris in 1985 but the style first appeared at the *EXPOSITION UNIVERSELLE*, 1889, in Paris. The designs are characterised by the use of sinuous plant tendrils, natural plant forms, and inlays of mother-of-pearl or pewter. The pieces were always graceful and slender in their proportions.

Some of the designers associated with the style are: Georges de Feure, Eugene Gaillard, Emile Galle, Louis Majorelle, Eugene Vallin, and Henry van de Velde.

In England a similar style was emerging, led by such designers as C. R. Mackintosh and A. H. Mackmurdo *(q.q.v)*.

Baroque (circa 1620 to 1700) The name derives from an Italian word meaning 'irregular pearl'; and shells, especially oyster shells, were some of the principal motifs of the style. However, the French word *baroque* is applied to anything that is grotesque, irregular, or strange and this is a most expressive description. The designs were many and varied and included such decorative features as sculptured figures and caryatids, complicated mouldings which were faceted to reflect the light, barleysugar twisting, marquetry, reversed-scroll legs, ormolu, and gilding.

Bauhaus School (1919 to the present day) A school of designers founded at Weimar in Germany by the architect Walter Gropius. Essentially, students were taught to ignore the previous history of design and to base their creations on a philosophy which emphasised the need to consider function, form, colour, and constructional techniques and apply them to designs for everyday use — not just for furniture but for saucepans and kettles as well! In addition, students had to attain certain standards in practical workmanship so that they thoroughly understood the material they were working in.

Undoubtedly the Bauhaus produced the first industrial designers and its influence was widespread, not just in Europe but in the USA as well, as many students emigrated there when Hitler came to power in Germany. It would not be pretentious to claim that the Bauhaus School was the origin of a large proportion of modern design.

Designers associated with the style are: Walter Gropius, Marcel Breur, Le Corbusier, Charles Eames, Maxwell Fry, and Mies van der Rohe.

Chinese style   (late 16th century to circa 1670) The style is sometimes referred to as 'Chinoiserie'. The vogue for all things Oriental began with the importation of Chinese works of art by the East India Company, which was founded in 1600. The beauty of the Chinese lacquer was particularly admired but in spite of the efforts of many imitators it was never successfully reproduced. By 1750 the style showed signs of becoming absurd in its extravagances and contemporary writers complained that 'according to the present prevailing whim, everything is Chinese or in the Chinese taste . . . even our most vulgar utensils are all reduced to this new-fangled standard.'

By 1770 the craze had almost spent itself but it was given a short lease of life by the Prince Regent in his Carlton House (1783) and the Brighton Pavilion (1815).

Designers associated with the style were: Thomas Chippendale (senior), *(q.v.),* John Linnell and Matthias Locke.

Empire, American   After the 1812 to 1814 Anglo-American War, the Americans turned to the French Empire style for inspiration. By 1820 many of its characteristics had been adopted, including eagle's heads, caryatids, swags, griffins, sphinxes and the like; also chaises-longues, scroll-ended couches, *klismos* chairs and boat or sleigh-shaped beds had all become fashionable. Pedestals on supports in the form of pineapples, or lyres mounted on four lion's paw feet; Pembroke tables with drop-leaves and serpentine-curved card tables — all become popular, but by 1830 the pendulum had swung back to the classical idiom.

Designers associated with the style were: Joseph B. Barry,. Michel Bouvier, Charles Lannvier, Duncan Phyfe, Anthony G. Quervelle and Charles H. White.

Federal style   (USA) The Federal Constitution was signed in 1787 and Philadelphia became the seat of government while the city of Washington was being built. In 1794/5 a new pattern book was published called the *Philadelphia Journeyman, Cabinet and Chairmaker's Book of Prices* which set standards of quality and prices.

The Federal style was based on strictly classical precepts, but carving on the original models was replaced by inlays and large mouldings and pilasters were transformed into stringing or bandings. Marquetry was also widely employed and chairs were

often painted with panels depicting scenes from American life. At first the style retained motifs from such designers as Hepplewhite but these gradually gave way to a severe classicism, and by about 1812 the style was supplanted by the American Empire *(q.v.)*.

Designers associated with the style were: John Aitken, Samuel McIntire, Duncan Phyfe, John Seymour, and John Shaw.

French Empire Style   *See Neo-Classicism.*

Georgian period   (1714 to 1760) Includes the Palladian Revival, the Baroque, the Gothic, the Rococo, and Chinoiserie *(q.q.v)*.

Gothic   (1740 to 1780) The name has nothing to do with the Goths but is more likely to have come from Giorgio Vasari (1511 to 1574); he was an enthusiastic supporter of the Renaissance and dismissed all previous architecture as 'Gothic' in much the same way as we would use the term 'Vandals'.

The style as we know it imitated some of the principal features of medieval architecture and transferred them to furniture. Examples are: the lancet arch and later, the ogee arch; foliated tracery patterns (trefoil, quatrefoil, etc.); cluster-column legs; blind and pierced trellis tracery and pinnacles. The style was indulged in by most of the 18th century designers and makers; notably, of course, by Thomas Chippendale.

In the middle of the 19th century, the style was revived and was often termed 'Gothick'. No doubt the strong admiration for all things medieval in Sir Walter Scott's novels had much to do with it and the fashion flourished mightily into all the byways of craftsmanship.

The furniture was usually massive and over-ornamented with inapposite carving which the designer fondly imagined was an improvement. Another feature was the inclusion of painted panels which often depicted scenes from medieval life. It was in this period that many of the public buildings in London and the provincial cities were built, a well-known example being the interior woodwork in the Houses of Parliament which was designed by A. W. N. Pugin (1812 to 1852) and started in 1834.

Designers associated with the style were: William Burges, William Morris, J. P. Seddon, and Philip Webb.

Gothick   *See Gothic*

Jacobean Period   (1603 to 1660) The Continental influences which had begun to be felt at the end of the Tudor period *(q.v.)* grew more pervasive and there was a wider use of inlays and carving, especially on chest and drawer fronts. Drawer and table construction became more sophisticated and the first dovetails were introduced; also, the draw-leaf extending table which had originated in the last years of the Tudor period was refined and developed into the system which is still in use today. The form of the chest became more commodious and was often fitted with drawers and cupboards — chairs, too, progressed from being mere back-stools into pieces of furniture in their own right, frequently having both the backs and seats upholstered from about 1645 onwards. Towards the end of the period the universal use of oak was supplanted by walnut.

The time had not yet arrived when the individual designer had begun to make his mark and the only well-known designer of the time was Inigo Jones (1573 to 1651) *(q.v.)*.

Neo-Classicism (1750 to 1830) This was a reaction against the frivolities of rococo ornamentation and its supporters advocated a return to the disciplines of the classical Greek, Roman, and Eutruscan styles. No doubt the feeling was strengthened by the discovery of Roman artifacts revealed by archaeological 'digs' at Herculaneum and Pompeii. So rectilinear outlines replaced the sinuous and restless curves of rococo and symmetry ousted asymmetry, and the bombe front gave way to the 'break-front.' Cabriole legs gradually disappeared and were replaced by square- or round- tapered legs which were decorated in a restrained fashion. Designers associated with the style were: Robert Adam, Jacques-Louis David, George Hepplewhite, Henry Holland, Thomas Hope and J. H. Riesner.

Neo-Classicism developed into the French Empire style following Napoleon's campaigns in Egypt at the beginning of the 19th century, when motifs such as sphinxes, lions' heads and vases were employed. Classical features such as the lyre motif, the *klismos* chair (which had sabre-shaped legs), stools of the *curule* type with X supports, tall slender tripod tables with circular tops, the classical type of couch with scrolled ends, the boat-shaped bed, and the use of marble slabs — all became fashionable. Strangely, these motifs were also taken up in England between the years 1804 to 1810 and applied to the Regency style *(q.v.)*. Designers associated with the French style were: Pierre Fontaine, Charles Percier and David Roentgen.

Palladianism (1715 to 1750) The style was introduced into England by a Scottish architect, Colin Campbell, and it was stimulated by the publication in 1715 of *Vitruvius Britannicus* which was a translation of an architectural treatise written by Vitruvius Pollo, circa BC30. An English edition of Andrea Palladio's

Four Books of Architecture in 1570 gave added impetus, and as might be expected from such an illustrious ancestry, the style was characterised by purely classical features such as pediments, mouldings and columns, all derived from the Classical Orders of Architecture.

Designers associated with the style were: Inigo Jones and William Kent.

Queen Anne (1702 to 1714) During her reign furniture styles became more elegant; in particular such pieces as bureau-bookcases and wardrobes tended to become taller and slimmer. Chairs, too, were designed to be more comfortable and the solid wood shaped splat in chair backs appeared; cabriole legs were introduced from France, and the characteristic carved shell on the knee decoration arrived.

Designers associated with the style were: Colen Campbell, William Kent and Daniel Marot.

Regency (late 1780's to 1837) The actual regency of George, Prince of Wales lasted from 1811 until 1820, but the furniture style covered a longer period (see above).

The inspiration for the style was a close study of Roman designs of architecture and domestic decoration based on the ruins unearthed at Herculaneum and Pompeii. The aim was to adapt the classical motifs to the furniture of the time and this led to the inclusion of such decorative elements as archaic lion masks, the hooked animal leg, caryatids and (borrowed from the French) sphinxes, winged griffins and ancient helmets. The lyre motif was enormously popular and was often employed in the supports for sofa tables; scroll-ended couches, boat beds and tripod tables were fashionable, too. Two specific designs are worthy of mention — the sabre (or scimitar) shaped chair leg based on the Greek *klismos* chair, and the 'lion monopodium' table originated by Thomas Hope.

Designers associated with the style were: Thomas Chippendale (junior), George Hepplewhite, Henry Holland, Thomas Hope and Thomas Sheraton.

Renaissance The term refers to a resurgence of interest in the classical precepts of Ancient Greek and Roman architecture and one of its principal exponents was Petrarch (1803 to 1374). He was a poet who was passionately interested in classical culture and collected early manuscripts and antiquities. From his studies he formulated a philosophy of humanism which included a style of architecture. One of the manuscripts he discovered was *De Architectura*, a treatise written by Vitruvius Pollio, a Roman military engineer. His book was summarised by Leon Battista

Alberti in a book *De Re Aedificatoria* (1485); the author set out mathematical calculations for planning and design and re-stated the ideal proportions for the four Classical Architectural orders.

Three years after its publication some ruins were unearthed in Rome which stimulated sufficient interest for Raphael to exploit the classical motifs which had been discovered in his paintings and for Romano and Udine (two Italian architects) to use them in their architectural designs.

But the most important man of all was probably Andrea Palladio (1518 to 1580) whose designs for villas and country residences inspired such English designers as Colen Campbell, Inigo Jones and William Kent *(q.q.v.)*.

The artistic centre for the Renaissance was undoubtedly Florence in Italy and it took some time for the new ideas to spread to the rest of Europe; probably the break-through came as a result of the unsuccessful invasion of Italy by the French King Charles VIII in 1495, as it led to a steady and sustained Italianisation of French culture.

Restoration (Carolean) period (1660 to 1685) Charles II was restored to the English throne in 1660 after the Commonwealth or Interregnum which lasted from 1649 to 1660. It is surprising that in the mere twenty-five years of his reign the aesthetic appreciation of the applied arts by the public grew into the firm basis for the many and varied styles that were to come in the 18th century.

Charles had spent much of his exile in Holland and consequently encouraged Continental craftsmen to follow him to England — a move which immeasurably added to the quality of the native British craftsmanship. During the period, we see the importation of looking-glasses from Venice and cane from the East (which was used to cane the backs and seats of chairs and day-beds); the imports of Chinoiserie also increased. People began to collect porcelain, china, books and objet's d'art and needed display cabinets and bookcases for them, so techniques of construction improved. Gilding and carving, too, reached heights of accomplishment which have scarcely been surpassed since. Another innovation was the replacement of oak by walnut — a change that took only a few years to come into full effect.

As with the Jacobean Period *(q.v.)* there were few individual designers who can be identified but mention must be made of Grinling Gibbons (1648 to 1721) and the architect Sir Christopher Wren (1632 to 1723).

Rococo (circa 1700 to 1770) The name derives from the French work *rocaille* meaning rock and shellwork

of the type found in grottoes in parks and gardens.

Principal features of the style were C-scrolls, carved rocks, shells, cascading and dripping water, Chinese figures and pagodas and the designs were always assymetrical. There were two innovations during the period, namely the sarcophagus shape and the bombe front, both of which were applied to case furniture. Gilding and lacquer were widely used and many attempts were made (unsuccessfully) to reproduce the true Oriental lacquers.

Designers associated with the style were: Andre-Charles Boulle, Thomas Chippendale (senior), Matthias Lock, Juste—Aurele Meissonier, Nicolas Pineau and Bernard van Risenburgh.

Shaker Furniture (USA) More correctly, 'The United Society of Believers in Christ's Second Appearing' — a religious sect founded by Mother Anne Lee, who emigrated from Manchester, England. The members set up their communities in the states around New York.

Their philosophy regarding work was best summed up by their founder when she said 'Put your hand to work, and your hearts to God ... Do your work as though you had a thousand years to live, and as if you were to die tomorrow.' Their furniture designs were based on fitness for purpose and they believed that if a piece was truly functional it thereby achieved beauty. And it is true to say that although their products were plain and simple they attained an elegance and grace which has never been surpassed.

Stuart period (1603 to 1649) Includes the Jacobean and Renaissance Classical styles *(q.q.v)*.

Tudor period (1500 to 1600) In the early part of the period furniture was basically utilitarian and such decoration as there was, was based on the medieval Gothic style *(q.v.)* found in the churches and monasteries and in England this meant little more than simple chip carving and lancet or rounded arches. By the time Elizabeth I came to the throne (1558) Renaissance influences were being felt and ornamentation such as linenfold carving, Romayne medallions, nulling, acanthus leaf carving and inlays appeared, and furniture in general became more luxurious. Throughout the period oak was the principal timber used.

Victorian period (1837 to 1901) Includes Gothick, Art Nouveau and Arts & Crafts Movements *(q.q.v)*.

William & Mary (1689 to 1702) William was Dutch and married to Mary, daughter of James II and when William came to England he brought many

Dutch craftsmen with him; they were some of the finest craftsmen of the time.

It was during this period that veneering became popular and fancy veneer work such as quartering, crossbanding, herringbone banding and 'oysters' made their appearance. It was soon realised that they could be laid on cheaper woods such as pine and deal rather than expensive hardwoods — a not-too-happy decision which led to troubles with veneered surfaces for later generations. Hand-made metal screws made their appearance and replaced the 'pegs' which had been used previously as fastenings for table tops, etc. Toilet furniture such as toilet mirrors and dressing tables came into wide use, and the habit of tea drinking led to the invention of a variety of small tables on which to drink tea from.

The period also saw the beginning of the flow of design and pattern books which was to be such a feature of the 18th and 19th centuries; the principal designer of the time was French-born Daniel Marot (1663 to 1752) who was employed by Willam as artistic adviser between the years 1694 and 1698.